French
Grammar
and Usage

French Grammar and Usage

ROGER HAWKINS & RICHARD TOWELL

Native Speaker Consultant
Marie-Noëlle Lamy

SECOND EDITION

McGraw-Hill

A Division of The **McGraw·Hill** *Companies*

McGraw-Hill

*A Division of The **McGraw·Hill** Companies*

This edition published in 2001 by The McGraw-Hill Companies

Originally published by Edward Arnold, a member of the Hodder Headline Group.

10 9 8 7 6 5 4

ISBN 0-658-01798-5

Cover design by Jenny Locke

McGraw-Hill books are available at special quantity discounts to use as premiums and sales promotions, or for use in corporate training programs. For more information, please write to the Director of Special Sales, Professional Publishing, McGraw-Hill, Two Penn Plaza, New York, NY 10121-2298. Or contact your local bookstore.

This book is printed on acid-free paper.

Contents

Guide for the user

This reference grammar of French has been written specifically to cater for the needs of English speakers. Such grammars are seldom read like novels. Usually, readers either want information on a specific grammatical point. ('In what order do the pronouns *me* and *le* occur in imperatives?'; 'How do I translate "should" into French?'), or they want information about the behaviour of a class of grammatical phenomena like 'pronouns', or 'modal verbs', or 'negation', and so on.

For this reason, and in common with most other grammars, *French Grammar and Usage* is divided into a number of chapters which deal with broad classes of grammatical phenomena; there are 17 chapters in all. But within each chapter there are two further subdivisions: the first into particular phenomena, and the second into specific grammatical points concerning those phenomena. This gives rise to three kinds of heading in the text. For example:

Chapter 2	Determiners
Chapter 2.6	Omission of the article
Chapter 2.6.6	Omission of the article with nouns in apposition

Chapter 8	Verb constructions
Chapter 8.2	Intransitive constructions
Chapter 8.2.2	Intransitive verbs and auxiliary *être*

The chapters and their major subdivisions are listed in the *Contents* at the beginning of the book. If you want information about a broad class of grammatical phenomena, you will probably find it most quickly by looking here. At the end of the book we have provided a more detailed *Index* where key French and English words and expressions are listed, along with grammatical points. The items listed here will direct you to a specific section of the grammar dealing with the property you want to know about.

If you are not familiar with grammatical terms, try the *Glossary of key grammatical terms*, which comes just after this *Guide for the user*. We briefly define common terms like subject, object, transitive verb, intransitive verb, phrase, clause, and so on, illustrating them from French.

The variety of French described in *French Grammar and Usage*

We have focused on one variety of French: standard European French. This is the variety used by university-educated speakers throughout metropolitan France. Within this variety we have distinguished two media of communication: written French and spoken French. In the normal case, we describe grammatical phenomena which are appropriate both to the spoken and the written forms of standard European French.

But in some cases particular constructions may be appropriate either to one or the other, but not both. For example, the simple past tense form of verbs – *je partis* 'I left', *elle mangea* 'she ate' – is normally restricted to written French. Questions formed by putting a question word at the front of a sentence without subject-verb inversion – *Où il est, le patron?* 'Where's the boss?' – are normally restricted to spoken French. Where there are such restrictions we say so. Where we say nothing, assume that a construction is possible in both written and spoken French.

Register

All languages have constructions and vocabulary which are appropriate to some contexts but not others. For example, in English when people are writing in an academic or literary style (as they do in grammars!), they tend not to use contracted forms. They would write sentence (1) rather than sentence (2):

> (1) Who would have thought that they would not have succeeded?
> (2) Who'd've thought they wouldn't've succeeded?

In spoken English, however, you are much more likely to hear (2) than (1). These context-related differences in the form of a single variety of language are often called 'registers'. A variety of language has a number of different registers appropriate to different contexts.

In *French Grammar and Usage* we have distinguished just two broad registers: **formal French**, which is the kind of French used in contexts where native speakers are careful in what they say and write, where they employ grammatical and stylistic devices which they may have learned at school (like the simple past, the imperfect subjunctive, or the inverted forms of questions). We also refer to **informal French**, which is used when speakers are engaged in relaxed, spontaneous communication and are less attentive to the form of what they are saying.

Where particular grammatical phenomena are typical only of formal French, or of informal French, but not both, we say so. Where we say nothing, assume that a construction is possible both in formal French and informal French.

It is important to be aware that informal French is not the same thing as 'slang' or 'dialect forms'. Informal French is just as much standard French as formal French is – it is the relaxed register used by speakers of standard educated European French. 'Slang' and 'dialect forms' are different, non-standard, varieties. On odd occasions we may signal some usages as being non-standard by using the term **colloquial**.

Prescriptive and descriptive approaches to French grammar

One of the problems facing any writer of a grammar of French is deciding what weight to give to the view of those French grammarians, legislators, educators, newspaper columnists and others who wish to prescribe how French should be written and spoken, within the framework of a description of how French writers and speakers actually use French. We have tried to steer a middle path in this respect. Where a grammatical phenomenon is clearly widespread and normal in the French of educated speakers and writers, but in conflict with prescriptive norms, we have described the usage. An example is the widespread omission of *ne* in *ne...pas* 'not', frowned upon by some, but in widespread use in informal spoken French (see Chapter 16.4).

Where there is variability or hesitation in the use of a grammatical phenomenon by speakers or writers, or where there is a change in progress in the language which has not yet been fully accepted, and there is an established prescriptive norm, we have presented the prescriptive norm. For example, agreement of the past participle with preceding direct objects, as in *La lettre que j'ai écrite* 'The letter I wrote', is subject to considerable variability in some contexts. Some speakers make the agreement, some do not. In this case we have followed the prescriptive norms (see Chapter 9.3).

Conventions

In many places in this grammar, we have presented examples not only of what native speakers do say and write, but also of what they do NOT say and write. Such ungrammatical sentences are preceded by an asterisk *. For example:

> Les cinq personnes (NOT *gens) qui ont mangé avec nous
> *The five people who ate with us* (see Chapter 1.1.2)

Round brackets placed around a French or English word or part of a word in an example mean that it is optional, and its presence or absence has little or no effect on the meaning. For example:

> par instant(s) *at odd moments*
> (You can use either *par instant* or *par instants*)

> par milliers *in (their) thousands*
> (*par milliers* can be translated either by 'in thousands' or 'in their thousands')

Glossary of key grammatical terms

Items in bold in the definitions are also defined in the glossary.

adjective – a class of words which **modify nouns**. Adjectives appear adjacent to nouns or separated from them by verbs like *être, devenir, rester*: e.g. *un PETIT problème* 'a small problem'; *une boîte CARRÉE* 'a square box'; *Cette robe est CHÈRE* 'This dress is expensive'.

adverb – a class of words which **modify** words, **phrases** and sentences: e.g. *Tout est SI clair* 'Everything is so clear'; *Je fume MODÉRÉMENT* 'I smoke moderately'; *JUSTE avant le départ du train* 'Just before the train leaves'; *SOUDAIN, j'ai entendu un bruit* 'Suddenly I heard a noise'.

adverbial – a word or phrase which can function as an adverb, although it also has other functions: e.g. *parler BAS* 'to talk quietly' (*bas* = an **adjective**); *Je lui rends visite DE TEMPS EN TEMPS* 'I visit her from time to time' (*de temps en temps* = a **prepositional phrase**); *Elle travaille LE MATIN* 'She works in the mornings' (*le matin* = a **noun phrase**).

affirmative sentence – a sentence which is not a negative: e.g. *Elle parle* 'She is speaking'; *Parle-t-elle?* 'Is she speaking?'; *Parle!* 'Speak!' (as opposed to the negative sentences: *Elle ne parle pas, Ne parle-t-elle pas? Ne parle pas!*).

agreement – a form the **verb** must take to be compatible with a given **subject**: e.g. *NOUS mangeons* 'We're eating'/*VOUS mangez* 'You're eating'. A form a **determiner** and an **adjective** must take to be compatible with a given **noun**: e.g. *UN BON REPAS* 'A good meal'/*UNE BONNE BIÈRE* 'A good beer'. A form a **past participle** must take to be compatible with a preceding **direct object**: e.g. *le coffre? Je L'AI OUVERT* 'The car boot? I've opened it': *La porte? Je L'ai OUVERTE* 'The door? I've opened it'; and so on.

article – definite article = *le, la, les*; indefinite article = *un, une, des*. The 'partitive' article – *du, de la, des* – indicates that a **noun** refers to something which is part of a larger mass: e.g. *du gâteau* 'some (of the) cake'; *des abeilles* 'some bees'.

auxiliary verb – the verbs *avoir* or *être* which accompany a **past participle** in compound **tenses** or the **passive**: e.g. *Elle A mangé* 'She has eaten'; *Le vélo A ÉTÉ réparé* 'The bike has been repaired'.

cardinal number – a number in the series *un* (1), *deux* (2), *trois* (3), etc.

clause – a string of words which contains just one **verb phrase** and a **subject** (whether overt or implied): e.g. *ELLE PART* 'She's leaving' – one clause; *DEPUIS JANVIER LES PRIX ONT AUGMENTÉ* 'Since January, prices have gone up' – one clause; *IL EST HEUREUX/PARCE QU'IL EST RICHE* 'He is happy because he is rich' – two clauses; *ELLE EST PRÊTE/À PARTIR* 'She is ready to leave' – two clauses (in *à partir* the subject is implied: She is ready, and she will leave); *LES CIR-CONSTANCES AIDANT/LE PARTI GAGNERA CES ÉLECTIONS* 'If the conditions are right, the party will win this election' – two clauses; *IL DIT/QU'ON CROIT/QU'ELLE VA PARTIR* 'He says that they think that she will leave' – three clauses. Also see **coordinate clause, relative clause, subordinate clause**.

comparative – a way of **modifying adjectives** and **adverbs** to draw a comparison between one entity and another: *Il veut acheter une PLUS GRANDE/une MOINS GRANDE/une AUSSI GRANDE voiture* 'He wants to buy a bigger car/a car which is not as big/a car which is just as big'; *Cette voiture-ci roule PLUS VITE/MOINS VITE/AUSSI VITE QUE l'autre* 'This car goes faster/slower/as quickly as the other one'.

complement – any phrase which follows a **noun, verb, adjective, adverb**, to form an expression with a cohesive meaning: e.g. *un appartement À LOUER* 'a flat to let'; *Ils se réunissent LE DIMANCHE AU STADE* 'They meet on Sundays at the stadium'; *Pierre est difficile À VIVRE* 'Pierre is difficult to live with'.

coordinate clause – a **clause** linked to another by *et, ou, mais*: e.g. *Il est riche ET il est heureux* 'He is rich and he is happy'.

declarative sentence – a sentence which makes a statement (as opposed to a **question** or an **imperative**).

demonstrative – demonstrative determiner = *ce, cette, ces*; demonstrative pronoun = *celui, celle, ceux, celles*.

determiner – an **article** *(un, une/le, la, les/des, etc.)*, **demonstrative** determiner *(ce, cette, etc.)* or **possessive** determiner *(mon, ma/ton, ta, etc.)* which **modifies** a **noun**.

direct object – *see* **object**.

directly transitive verb – *see* **transitive verb**.

ditransitive verb – *see* **transitive verb**.

finite verb – a **verb** which is marked for **tense** and **agreement**, as opposed to non-finite forms like the **infinitive, imperative, participles**: e.g. *Je PARLE* 'I'm speaking'; *J'AI PARLÉ* 'I spoke'; *Je SAIS parler français* 'I can speak French'.

formal French – in this grammar 'formal French' refers to a style used by speakers of standard educated French when they are paying particular attention to the form of what they are saying or writing. It is a style usually appropriate when someone is speaking in an official capacity (lectures, sermons, speeches, etc.), or writing in learned, academic or literary style. Features of formal French which are absent from **informal French** include: the use of the simple past tense (*Il SORTIT* 'He went out'), the use of the past anterior tense (Aussitôt qu'il FUT SORTI ... 'As soon as he had gone out ... '), retention of *ne* in *ne . . . pas*.

gender – a division of **nouns** into two classes: masculine and feminine. The distinction shows up mainly in **determiners** (*le* versus *la*, *ce* versus *cette*, *mon* versus *ma*, etc.), in **pronouns** (*il* versus *elle*) and in the **agreement** of adjectives with nouns (*beau* versus *belle*). Gender distinctions are grammatical and need not correspond to sex distinctions in the real world (although they mostly do): e.g. *médecin* 'doctor' is masculine, but can refer to men or women; *personne* 'person' is feminine but can refer to men or women.

gerund – *see* **participle**.

imperative – a form of the **verb** used to give orders, express encouragement or give advice: e.g. *Asseyez-vous!* 'Sit down!'; *Allez!* 'Come on!'; *Fais attention*! 'Watch out!'

impersonal – refers to a **pronoun** (usually a subject pronoun) which does not refer to any person, place, thing, idea etc. *il, ce, cela, ça* can be impersonal pronouns in French: e.g. *Il est temps de partir* 'It's time to leave'; *Ça me fait peur d'y aller la nuit* 'It scares me to go there at night'.

indicative – the set of forms of the verb which are not **subjunctive**, **imperative**, **infinitive** or **participial**.

indirect object – *see* **object**.

indirectly transitive verb – *see* **transitive verb**.

infinitive – a form of the **verb** which ends in *-er, -ir, -re, -oir*, and corresponds to English 'to': *aimer* 'to like', *finir* 'to finish', *vendre* 'to sell', *recevoir* 'to receive'.

informal French – in this grammar 'informal French' refers to a style used by speakers of standard educated French in contexts of relaxed, spontaneous communication when they are interacting with friends, colleagues, family, etc. Features of informal French include: the non-use of the simple past or past anterior tenses, and the regular omission of *ne* from *ne ... pas*.

intransitive verb – a **verb** which has no **direct object**: e.g. *La neige tombait* 'Snow was falling'.

modify, to – to add to the meaning of a **noun**, **verb**, **adjective**, etc. by adding another word or phrase to it: e.g. *manteau, un manteau, un manteau gris; oiseau, un oiseau, un oiseau qui chante; parle, il parle, il parle lentement; grand, si grand, elle est si grande*.

negator – one of the elements *aucun, jamais, ni, nul, pas, personne, plus, rien* which can create negative expressions (see Chapter 16).

noun – a class of words which refers to people, places, things, ideas, and so on; it is usually preceded by a **determiner**: e.g. *un ami; la France; une bière; le bonheur*.

noun phrase – the phrase consisting of a noun alone, or a noun and the elements which modify it. Each of the following is a noun phrase: *Pierre, le soleil, un cher ami* 'a dear friend', *une bière bien froide* 'a really cold beer', *chacun de mes amis les plus chers* 'each of my dearest friends'.

number – a grammatical distinction between **nouns** or **pronouns** which are singular and those which are plural. Number distinctions need not correspond to real singular and plural distinctions in the world, and can differ between English and French (although mostly the grammatical and real-world distinctions coincide): e.g. 'hair' (singular) versus *cheveux* (plural); 'trousers' (plural) versus *pantalon* (singular). See also **cardinal number** and **ordinal number**.

object – a direct object is the **noun phrase** or **pronoun** affected directly by the action described by the verb: e.g. *Il a pris le train* 'He took the train'; *Il l'a pris* 'He took it'. An indirect object is the noun phrase or pronoun affected indirectly by the action described by the verb. In French, indirect object noun phrases are always introduced by *à*: e.g. *Il a envoyé un cadeau à sa mère* 'He sent a present to his mother'. An object of a preposition is any noun phrase which follows a preposition, including indirect objects introduced by *à*: e.g. *dans* LE HALL 'in the hall', *à côté* DU RESTAURANT 'beside the restaurant', *à* SA MÈRE 'to his mother'.

object of a preposition – *see* **object**.

ordinal number – a number in the series *premier* (1er), *deuxième* (2e), *troisième* (3e), etc.

parenthetical expression – an aside made by a speaker to indicate a reservation he/she has about what is being said. It is the equivalent of putting something in brackets ('parentheses'): e.g. *Pierre,* SEMBLE-T-IL, *a gagné le prix* 'Pierre, it seems, won the prize'. Parentheticals are kinds of **adverbial**.

participle – past participles are forms of the verb which occur with avoir or être: e.g. J'ai MANGÉ 'I've eaten'; *Elle est* PARTIE 'She has left'. Present participles end in *-ant* and correspond to English verbs ending in -ing: e.g. *disparaissant* 'disappearing', *attendant* 'waiting'. Gerunds are present participles preceded by *en*: *en disparaissant* 'while disappearing; by disappearing', *en attendant* 'while waiting; by waiting'.

passive – a form of a normally **transitive verb** where the **direct object** becomes the **subject** and the verb is turned into an *être* + **past participle** construction: e.g. *Il a réparé le vélo* 'He repaired the bike'; LE VÉLO A ÉTÉ RÉPARÉ 'The bike has been repaired'.

past participle – *see* **participle**.

person – the three categories into which **noun phrases** or **pronouns** can be divided depending on whether they refer to the person(s) speaking (*je, me, moi, nous* – first person), the person(s) being spoken to (*tu, te, toi, vous* – second person), or the person(s) or thing(s) being talked about (*il, elle, lui, ils,* etc. – third person). **Pronouns** take different forms in the first, second and third person, and **finite verbs** change their form to **agree** with the person of the **subject** (e.g. *je parle, nous parlons, vous parlez,* etc.).

personal pronoun – a first **person**, second person or third person **pronoun** which stands for a **noun phrase** mentioned or implied elsewhere in a text or discourse. Personal pronouns contrast with **impersonal** pronouns which do not refer to other noun phrases. Personal pronouns are pronouns like *je, me, moi, nous; tu, te, toi, vous; il, elle, lui, les* etc. They take their name from the fact that they can be classified as first, second or third person, and do not necessarily refer to people; e.g. *elle* is a personal pronoun, but it refers to the inanimate *émission* in: ELLE *est intéressante, cette émission* 'That programme's interesting'.

phrase – any string of words which gives rise to an expression with a cohesive meaning: e.g. MON ONCLE JACQUES 'my uncle Jacques' (**noun phrase**); *Pierre* MARCHE LENTEMENT 'Pierre walks slowly' (**verb phrase**), etc.

possessive – possessive determiner = *mon, ma, ton, votre,* etc.; possessive pronoun = *le mien, la mienne, le tien, le vôtre,* etc.

preposition – words like *à, de, dans, en, sur,* etc., which are followed by **noun phrases** and indicate the direction, location, orientation, etc., of an entity.

prepositional phrase – a phrase consisting of a **preposition** and its **complement**. The following are all prepositional phrases: À MIDI 'at noon'; À CHAQUE VIRAGE 'at every bend'; AU CHEVET DE MA MÈRE 'at my mother's bedside'.

present participle – *see* **participle**.

pronoun – a form which is used in place of a **noun phrase** when that phrase is already known from the context: e.g. *je, tu, nous, le, la, leur*, etc. Pronouns have different forms depending on whether they are **subjects, direct objects, indirect objects** or **objects of a preposition**.

proper noun – names like *Marie-Paule, le Canada,* are proper nouns.

quantifier – a **determiner**-like expression which measures or quantifies a **noun** or **noun phrase**: e.g. BEAUCOUP D'*argent* 'a lot of money'; LA PLUPART DES *spectateurs* 'most of the spectators'; TOUS *les jours* 'every day'.

question (direct versus **indirect)** – a direct question is addressed directly to the hearer or reader: e.g. VIENS-TU? 'Are you coming?'. An indirect question reports the asking of a question: e.g. *Il a demandé* SI TU VENAIS 'He asked if you were coming').

reciprocal – a type of sentence where either the direct **object**, the indirect object or the object of a preposition refers to the same person, thing, idea, etc., as a plural **subject**, and the sentence is intepreted so that the subjects are doing things to each other: e.g. *Les boxeurs* SE *sont blessés* 'The boxers injured each other'; *Les participants* SE *sont posé des questions* 'The participants asked each other questions'; *Les manifestants ont lutté* LES UNS CONTRE LES AUTRES 'The demonstrators fought with each other'.

reflexive – a type of sentence where either the direct **object**, the indirect object or the object of a preposition refers to the same person, thing, idea, etc., as the **subject**: e.g. *Je* ME *lave* 'I am washing (myself)'; *Elle* SE *cache la vérité* 'She hides the truth from herself'; *Elle parle* CONTRE ELLE-MÊME 'She is speaking against herself'.

relative clause – a **clause** which **modifies** a **noun phrase** or a **pronoun**: e.g. *Il y avait deux hommes* QUI SORTAIENT DU BAR 'There were two men who were coming out of the bar'; *C'est lui* QUI ME L'A DONNÉ 'He is the one who gave it to me'.

subject – the **noun phrase** or **pronoun** in a **clause** about which the **verb** and its **complement** say something. Subjects usually appear in front of the verb: e.g. LE DÎNER *est servi* 'Dinner is served'; SA FEMME *parle lentement* 'His wife speaks slowly'; DELPHINE *a été battue* 'Delphine was beaten'. It can appear after the verb in some constructions. See **subject-verb inversion**.

subject-verb inversion – subjects normally precede finite verbs in French. But in questions, and after certain adverbs, the subject and the finite verb may change places: e.g. AIME-T-IL LE *Roquefort?* 'Does he like Roquefort cheese?; *A peine* S'EST-IL ASSIS *qu'on lui a demandé de se déplacer* 'Hardly had he sat down when someone asked him to move'.

subjunctive – see Chapter 11 for discussion.

subordinate clause – a **clause** which is part of a larger sentence, and whose meaning is secondary to that of the main clause: e.g. PARCE QU'IL EST RICHE, *Pierre est heureux* 'Because he is rich, Pierre is happy' – *parce qu'il est riche* is subordinate to *Pierre est heureux*; *Jean a complètement rénové le grenier* DEPUIS QU'IL EST CHEZ NOUS 'Jean has completely renovated the loft since he has been at our house' – *depuis qu'il est chez nous* is subordinate to *Jean a complètement rénové le grenier*.

superlative – a way of modifying adjectives and adverbs to single out an entity as the best or the worst of its kind: e.g. *C'est la route* LA PLUS DANGEREUSE/*LA MOINS DANGEREUSE de la région* 'It's the most dangerous road/least dangerous road in the region'; *Cette voiture-là est* LA PLUS VITE/LA MOINS VITE 'That car is the fastest/the least fast'.

tense – a form of the **verb** which indicates the time at which an event took place relative to other events being talked about: e.g. *Je* PRENDS [present tense] *la route par où nous* SOMMES VENUS [compound past tense] 'I'm taking the road along which we came'. Tenses have names like present, future, simple past, compound past, etc. – see Chapter 7 for the forms of verbs in different tenses, and Chapter 10 for their uses.

transitive verb – a verb which has a direct **object**: e.g. *Elle mange* UNE POMME 'She is eating an apple'. In this grammar we also distinguish directly transitive verbs, which have direct objects, from indirectly transitive verbs which have prepositional **complements**: e.g. *Il parle* DE SES PARENTS 'He is talking of his parents', and from ditransitive verbs which have complements consisting of a direct object and a prepositional object: e.g. *J'ai envoyé* LA LETTRE À MON FRÈRE 'I sent the letter to my brother'.

verb – a class of words which refers to actions, states, events, accomplishments, and so on, and has different forms to indicate **tense** and **agreement**: e.g. *Elle* PARLE 'She is speaking'; *L'eau* SCINTILLAIT 'The water was sparkling'.

verb phrase – the phrase consisting of a **verb** alone, or a **verb** and the elements which **modify** it (but excluding the **subject**). Each of the following is a verb phrase: *marchait* 'was walking'; *marchait lentement* 'was walking slowly'; *a envoyé un cadeau d'anniversaire à sa tante* 'sent a birthday present to his aunt'.

Acknowledgements

The influence of others is apparent in all forms of writing, but it is particularly pervasive in the writing of a grammar of French. So much has been said and written about French grammar over the centuries. The influence of the work of those who have gone before, the views of our colleagues and contemporaries who teach French or are interested in the structure of French, have shaped the presentation of nearly every item we discuss.

It would therefore be impossible for us to cite all the sources of ideas and examples on which we have drawn in writing *French Grammar and Usage*. Nevertheless, we would like to single out some sources, and some friends and colleagues, for making a direct and significant contribution. A list of the main works referred to is given in the bibliography. The following friends and colleagues have taken time to comment on drafts of various chapters: Marie-Anne Hintze, Tony Lodge, Chris Lyons, Jean-Pierre Mailhac, Annie Rouxeville, Raphael Salkie and Carol Sanders. John Butt, co-author of *A New Reference Grammar of Modern Spanish* (London, Arnold, 1988) provided us with valuable feedback on an early draft, as did several anonymous readers. Elaine Murphy, supported by the secretarial staff in the Department of Modern Languages at the University of Salford, skilfully typed and copied countless drafts of the book. We would like to thank all of these for their interest and their help, and also Lesley Riddle at Arnold for waiting patiently for the final version while we juggled writing with the demands of running large university departments during difficult times.

We have discovered in undertaking this work that there are as many views about how a point of grammar should be presented and exemplified as there are people who are consulted. Those who have given us the benefit of their advice may not agree with the way we have finally decided to present the grammar of French. But we are certain that the end product is far better than it would have been without their advice.

Roger Hawkins and Richard Towell
Colchester and Salford,
January 1996

Acknowledgements for the second edition

This second edition of *French Grammar and Usage* has benefitted considerably from the comments of friends, colleagues and students who used the first edition and found areas where it could be improved. We would particularly like to thank the following for their significant help: Aidan Coveney, Jim Dolamore, Annick Leyssen, Matthew McNamara and Jonathan Mallinson. We alone are responsible for any errors or weaknesses of presentation which remain.

Roger Hawkins and Richard Towell
Colchester and Salford
September 2000

1

Nouns

1.1 Types of noun

1.1.1 Abstract versus concrete nouns

Concrete nouns refer to entities with physical attributes which can be seen, heard, touched, etc. Abstract nouns refer to entities without such physical attributes:

Typical concrete nouns		**Typical abstract nouns**	
bière (f)	*beer*	beauté (f)	*beauty*
bonbon (m)	*sweet*	bonheur (m)	*happiness*
cadeau (m)	*present*	bonté (f)	*goodness*
carte (f)	*card*	patience (f)	*patience*
disque (m)	*record*	mœurs (f pl)	*customs, morals*
église (f)	*church*	savoir (m)	*knowledge*
livre (m)	*book*	silence (m)	*silence*
mannequin (m)	*(fashion) model*	soif (f)	*thirst*

Abstract nouns in French are usually accompanied by a definite article whereas English has no article:

La patience est une qualité qui se fait rare
Patience is a quality which is becoming rare

Je cherche **le** bonheur
I'm looking for happiness

But when abstract nouns refer to a particular example of 'patience', 'happiness', 'knowledge', and so on (for instance, when they are modified by an adjective), they occur with an indefinite article:

Il a fait preuve cette fois d'**une** patience appréciable
The patience he showed on this occasion was appreciated

Il s'est alors produit **un** silence absolu
Absolute silence ensued

Un bonheur en vaut un autre
One kind of happiness is the same as any other

(See Chapter 2 for definite and indefinite articles.)

1.1.2 Mass versus count nouns

Count nouns identify individual entities, and usually have both singular and plural forms. Mass nouns treat the entity or entities they refer to as a single unit, and typically have only a singular form (although some mass nouns only have a plural form):

Typical count nouns		Typical mass nouns	
une bouteille	*a bottle*	de l'air	*air*
des bouteilles	*bottles*	du beurre	*butter*
un chien	*a dog*	de l'eau	*water*
des chiens	*dogs*	du gâteau	*cake*
une personne	*a person*	des gens	*people*
des personnes	*people*	du sable	*sand*

Mass nouns in French are usually accompanied by the partitive article (see Chapter 2.4) – *du, de l', de la* or *des* – in those cases where English has 'some' or no article at all:

> Je voudrais **du** lait, s'il vous plaît
> *I would like some milk, please*

> Il y a **du** vin dans le placard
> *There's wine in the cupboard*

Personnes and *gens*

personnes and *gens*, both of which mean 'people', differ in their uses because *personne* is a count noun and *gens* a mass noun. Only *personne* can be preceded by a number (e.g. *cinq*), or the quantifiers *plusieurs* 'several', *quelques* 'a few', *un certain nombre de* 'a certain number of':

> Les cinq personnes (NOT *gens) qui ont mangé avec nous
> *The five people who ate with us*

> Plusieurs personnes (NOT *gens) sont restées tout l'après-midi
> *Several people stayed for the whole afternoon*

By the same token, *gens* is preferred in contexts where 'people' are treated as a mass:

> Les gens (NOT *personnes) n'aiment pas rester à table trop longtemps
> *People don't like to spend too long over a meal*

NB: *gens* can be preceded by *beaucoup de* 'many', *peu de* 'few', *tous les* 'all the' and *la plupart des* 'most'.

Mass nouns used countably

Some mass nouns can be used countably to refer to specific examples of the substance in question:

les vins de France	*the wines of France*
les Eaux et Forêts	*the French Forestry Commission*
les fromages de Normandie	*the cheeses of Normandy*
un pain	*a loaf of bread*
un petit pain	*a bun*

Some count nouns can also be used as mass nouns:

Prenez du poulet	*Have some chicken*
Il met du citron dans tout	*He puts lemon in everything*

1.1.3 Collective nouns

Collective nouns refer to collections of people or things.

Typical collective nouns

assistance (f)	*audience*
comité (m)	*committee*
équipe (f)	*team*
foule (f)	*crowd*
gouvernement (m)	*government*
linge (m) de maison	*household linen*
main-d'œuvre (f)	*workforce*
peuple (m)	*people*
vaisselle (f)	*dishes, crockery*

When a collective noun is the subject of a clause, the verb is usually singular. This contrasts with English, where the verb can be either singular or plural:

Le gouvernement a (NOT *ont) décidé d'interdire la publicité pour les cigarettes
The government has/have decided to ban cigarette advertizing

L'équipe s'entraîne (NOT *s'entraînent) le jeudi soir
The team trains/train on Thursday evenings

(For more on subject-verb agreement see Chapter 9.1.)

1.1.4 Proper nouns

Proper nouns are names like *Marie-Paule, Paris, Toulouse, Le Havre, La Seine, La France, Le Canada.*

With persons there is usually no article:

Marie-Paule viendra demain
Marie-Paule will come tomorrow

In some cases an article is inserted in informal speech:

Dis donc, elle était pas fière, la Marie-Paule!
So Marie-Paule must have felt a bit of a fool!

T'aurais vu la tête qu'il faisait, le Jérôme!
You should have seen Jérôme's face!

This conveys a familiar, affectionate attitude towards the individual concerned.

When reference is made to a family, as in 'the Jones family', a plural article is used, but the name itself is not pluralized:

J'ai invité les Martin à venir manger dimanche
I have invited the Martins for Sunday lunch

When a person's title is used, it is normally accompanied by the definite article:

Je vous présente **le** Professeur Bodin
May I introduce Professor Bodin

chez **le** Docteur Gleizes
c/o Dr Gleizes (on an envelope or package)

When proper nouns are modified by preceding adjectives, they require a definite article:

le petit Jules	*little Jules*
le gros Henri	*fat Henri*

Unlike in English, regions and countries are normally used with a definite article:

J'ai visité **la** Normandie	*I visited Normandy*
la France d'aujourd'hui	*today's France*
Nous survolons **la** Belgique	*We're flying over Belgium*

(See Chapter 2.2.2 for the use of articles with regions and countries.)

1.1.5 Use of *an/année, jour/journée, matin/matinée, soir/soirée*

English has only one word for each of 'morning', 'evening', 'day' and 'year'. French has two, but each are used under different circumstances. It is often said that the *-ée* forms are used when the activity which takes place during the morning, evening, etc. is highlighted. Compare:

Je travaille chaque **matin/soir/jour**
I work every morning/evening/day
(where the frequency rather than the activity is highlighted)

J'ai travaillé toute la **matinée**/la **soirée**/la **journée**
I worked all morning/evening/day
(where the length of work is highlighted)

But there are other cases where the forms have distinct uses which appear to be the result simply of convention:

au début de la matinée/la soirée/la journée
at the start of the morning/the evening/the day

en fin de matinée/	*at the end of the morning/*
soirée/journée	*the evening/the day*
par une belle matinée	*on a beautiful morning*
tôt le matin	*early in the morning*
Un beau matin il est parti	*One fine morning he up and left*
tous les jours/matins/ans	*every day/morning/year*
l'an 2000	*the year 2000*
le jour de l'an	*New Year's Day*
le nouvel an	*the New Year*
souhaiter la bonne année à qn	*to wish so a Happy New Year*
les années 70	*the 70s*
l'année précédente/suivante	*the previous/following year*

With preceding numbers the forms without *-ée* are normally used:

Il a cinq ans	*He is five*
trois fois par jour	*three times a day*

But if an adjective modifies the noun as well this seems to highlight the activity:

trois bonnes années	*three good years*
six longues journées	*six long days*

1.2 Gender

Nouns in French are either masculine or feminine. Unfortunately there are no simple rules which non-native speakers can use to predict with complete accuracy the gender of a given noun. However, there are some patterns, either in the form or meaning of nouns, which can normally be used to predict the correct gender with greater than chance accuracy. The reader should remember, however, that these patterns are not comprehensive, and that there are exceptions.

1.2.1 Gender signalled by the final letters of the written forms of nouns

Masculine

Many nouns whose singular written form ends in a **consonant** are masculine:

- -c   un franc *a franc* (un lac *a lake*, le public *the public*, etc.)
- -d   le bord *the edge* (le fond *the bottom*, le pied *the foot*, etc.)
- -g   un camping *a camp site* (un parking *a car park*, un shampooing *a shampoo*, etc.)
- -l   un détail *a detail* (le travail *work*, le soleil *the sun*, etc.)
- -r   le fer *iron* (l'hiver *winter*, un couloir *a corridor*, etc.)
- -t   le chocolat *chocolate* (le climat *the climate*, un jouet *a toy*, un poulet *a chicken*, le ciment *cement*, un jugement *a judgement*, etc.)

Exceptions are typically found with nouns which end in *-n*, *-r*, *-s*, *-t*, and *-x*:

une maison	*a house*
une cuiller	*a spoon*
la mer	*the sea*
une tour	*a tower*
une fois	*one time*
une dent	*a tooth*
une nuit	*a night*
une jument	*a mare*
une croix	*a cross*

Nouns ending in *-on* are usually masculine (*un poisson* 'a fish', *un sillon* 'a furrow', etc. Although *une chanson* 'a song' is an exception). But nouns ending in *-aison*, *-(s)sion*, *-tion* or *-xion* are usually feminine:

une comparaison	*a comparison*
une liaison	*a liaison*
une maison	*a house*
une raison	*a reason*
une saison	*a season*
une décision	*a decision*
la tension	*tension, blood pressure*
une vision	*a vision*
une émission	*a broadcast*
une connexion	*a connection*

Exception: un bastion *a bastion*

Nouns ending in *-eur* are usually masculine (*un ordinateur* 'a computer', *le bonheur* 'happiness', etc.), but the following frequently-used nouns are feminine:

la chaleur	*the heat*
une couleur	*a colour*
une erreur	*a mistake*
une fleur	*a flower*
la largeur	*the width*
la longueur	*the length*
la peur	*fear*
la profondeur	*the depth*

Many nouns whose singular written form ends in a vowel (but excluding *-e* without an acute accent) are masculine, although there are a significant number of exceptions:

-ai, -oi

un délai	*a time limit*
un essai	*an attempt (a 'try' in rugby)*
un emploi	*a job*
un roi	*a king*

Exceptions: la foi *faith*, une loi *a law*, une paroi *a wall*

-é

le café	*the café* or *coffee*
un fossé	*a ditch*
le marché	*the market*
le thé	*tea*

Exception: une clé *a key*

-eau

un couteau	*a knife*
un marteau	*a hammer*
le niveau	*the level*
le réseau	*the network*
un tableau	*a picture*

Exceptions: l'eau *water*, la peau *skin*

-i

l'abri	*shelter*
un cri	*a shout*
un pari	*a bet*
un pli	*a fold*
un raccourci	*a short-cut*

-ou

un bijou	*a jewel*
un caillou	*a pebble*
un clou	*a nail*
un genou	*a knee*
le hibou	*the owl*

Feminine

Many nouns whose singular written form ends in *-e* without an acute accent are feminine:

l'audace *daring*, la façade *the front, the outside*, une salade *a salad*
une baie *a bay*, la haie *the hedge*

une douzaine *a dozen*, une fontaine *a fountain*
une ambulance *an ambulance*, une flèche *an arrow*
une thèse *a thesis*, une grève *a strike*, etc.
une araignée *a spider*, une bougie *a candle*, etc.

But there are a large number of exceptions to this rule:

-isme
Nouns ending in *-isme* are masculine: *le romantisme* 'romanticism', *le tourisme* 'tourism', *un idiotisme* 'an idiom (linguistic)', etc.

-ède, -ège, -ème
Nouns with these endings are usually masculine:

un intermède	*an interlude*
un cortège	*a procession*
un piège	*a trap*
un stratège	*a strategist*
un poème	*a poem*
le système	*the system*
le thème	*the theme* or *translation into a foreign language*

la crème 'cream' is an exception (but see 1.2.4).

-age
Nouns ending in *-age* are usually masculine, but there are some notable exceptions:

le courage	*courage*
un garage	*a garage*
un message	*a message*
un stage	*a work placement*
un voyage	*a journey*

Exceptions: une cage *a cage*, une image *a picture*, une page *a page*, une plage *a beach*, la rage *rabies*.

Other common exceptions:

un grade	*a rank*
un stade	*a stadium*
un groupe	*a group*
le monde	*the world*
le capitaine	*the captain*
le domaine	*the area*
le silence	*silence*
un musée	*a museum*
un lycée	*a (sixth-form) college*
un trophée	*a trophy*
un génie	*a genius*
un incendie	*a fire*
un cimetière	*a cemetery*
le derrière	*the backside*
un magazine	*a magazine*
le platine	*platinum*
un pare-brise	*a windscreen*
un intervalle	*an interval*
le rebelle	*the rebel*
le chèvrefeuille	*honeysuckle*

un chêne	*an oak tree*
un hêtre	*a beech tree*
un gorille	*a gorilla*
un portefeuille	*a wallet*
un carosse	*a carriage*
un squelette	*a skeleton*
un renne	*a reindeer*
le mercure	*mercury*
le murmure	*a murmur*
un gramme	*a gram*
un kilogramme	*a kilogram*
un mètre	*a metre*
un kilomètre	*a kilometre*
un litre	*a litre*
un parapluie	*an umbrella*

NB: Most words with the prefix *para-* are masculine: *un parachute* 'a parachute', *un paratonnerre* 'a lightning conductor', *le parapente* 'paragliding', *un paravent* 'wind-shield, screen'.

1.2.2 Nouns which refer both to males and to females
Some nouns can refer either to males or to females simply by changing the determiner from masculine to feminine:

un/une adulte	*an adult*
un/une adversaire	*an adversary*
un/une artiste	*an artist*
un/une bibliothécaire	*a librarian*
un/une camarade	*a comrade*
un/une célibataire	*a bachelor/spinster (an unmarried person)*
un/une chimiste	*a chemist (scientist)*
un/une collègue	*a colleague*
un/une compatriote	*a compatriot*
un/une complice	*an accomplice*
un/une concierge	*a porter*
un/une convive	*a guest*
un/une dentiste	*a dentist*
un/une élève	*a (school) pupil*
un/une enfant	*a child*
un/une esclave	*a slave*
un/une fonctionnaire	*a civil servant*
un/une gosse	*a kid (a word for a child in informal French)*
un/une interprète	*an interpreter*
un/une journaliste	*a journalist*
un/une libraire	*a bookseller*
un/une locataire	*a tenant*
un/une malade	*a person who is ill*
un/une partenaire	*a partner*
un/une patriote	*a patriot*
un/une pensionnaire	*a boarder (as in boarding school)*
un/une philosophe	*a philosopher*
un/une photographe	*a photographer*
un/une pianiste	*a pianist*
un/une pique-assiette	*a sponger*
un/une secrétaire	*a secretary*
un/une touriste	*a tourist*

NB: *pupille* meaning 'pupil of the eye' is feminine only. In set expressions such as *pupille de la Nation, pupille de l'Etat* the noun refers to a child whose education is paid for by the state. With this meaning *pupille* may be masculine or feminine according to the sex of the child.

1.2.3 Nouns which change form when they refer to males or to females

Regular patterns

For words ending in *-i, -é, -u, -l* an *-e* is added in the written form and the pronunciation remains the same:

un ami	une amie	*a friend*
un employé	une employée	*an employee (worker)*
un rival	une rivale	*a rival*

For words ending in *-d, -t, -ois, -ais, -er, -ier* an *-e* is added and the final consonant, previously not pronounced, is pronounced:

un marchand	une marchande	*a trader*
un candidat	une candidate	*a candidate*
un avocat	une avocate	*a lawyer*
un bourgeois	une bourgeoise	*a bourgeois(e)*
un boulanger	une boulangère	*a baker*
un berger	une bergère	*a shepherd*
un fermier	une fermière	*a farmer*
un caissier	une caissière	*a checkout operator*
un romancier	une romancière	*a novelist*

For words ending in *-ien, -on, -an, -in, -ain* in written form *-(n)e* is added and the final vowel, previously pronounced as a nasal vowel, is pronounced as an oral vowel plus *-n*:

un chien	une chienne	*a dog/a bitch*
un lion	une lionne	*a lion/a lioness*
un paysan	une paysanne	*a farmer*
un gitan	une gitane	*a gypsy (pejorative)*
un voisin	une voisine	*a neighbour*
un Africain	une Africaine	*an African*

Some nouns add *-esse*.

un âne	une ânesse	*a donkey*
un chanoine	une chanoinesse	*a canon/canoness (religious)*
un comte	une comtesse	*a count/countess*
un diable	une diablesse	*a devil/she-devil*
un drôle	une drôlesse	*someone a little odd*
un hôte	une hôtesse	*a host/hostess*
un ivrogne	une ivrognesse	*a drunkard*
un maître	une maîtresse	*a master/mistress*
		(in the school context)
un ogre	une ogresse	*an ogre*
un pauvre	une pauvresse	*a poor person*
un prêtre	une prêtresse	*a priest/priestess*
un prince	une princesse	*a prince/princess*
un Suisse	une Suissesse	*a Swiss person*
un tigre	une tigresse	*a tiger/tigress*

Nouns ending in *-eur* which are not derived from a French verb, change *-eur* to *-rice*:

un ambassadeur	une ambassadrice	*an ambassador*
un directeur	une directrice	*a director*
un empereur	une impératrice	*an emperor/empress*

Those ending in *-eur* which are derived from a French verb change to *-euse*:

un chanteur	une chanteuse	*a singer*
un menteur	une menteuse	*a liar*
un voleur	une voleuse	*a thief*

Irregular patterns

In addition to these regular patterns there are a number of masculine/feminine forms where the words are quite different:

un héros	une héroïne	*a hero/heroine*
un époux	une épouse	*a husband/wife*
un neveu	une nièce	*a nephew/niece*
un homme	une femme	*a man/woman*
un fils	une fille	*a son/daughter*
un garçon	une fille	*a boy/girl*

1.2.4 Nouns which change meaning when they change gender

Some nouns have different meanings when they are masculine and when they are feminine:

un aide	*a helper*	l'aide (f)	*help*
un chèvre	*a goat's cheese*	une chèvre	*a goat*
un crème	*a white coffee*	la crème	*cream*
le crêpe	*crêpe (cloth)*	une crêpe	*a pancake*
un critique	*a critic*	une critique	*a criticism*
un espace	*a space*	une espace	*a space (in printing)*
un laque	*artwork*	une laque	*a hair lacquer or gloss paint*
un livre	*a book*	une livre	*a pound (money or weight)*
un manche	*a handle*	une manche	*a sleeve*
		La Manche	*the English Channel*
un manœuvre	*an unskilled worker*	une manœuvre	*a manoeuvre*
un mémoire	*a dissertation*	la mémoire	*memory (faculty of)*
un merci	*a thank you*	la merci	*mercy*
un mode	*a way of . . .*	une mode	*a fashion*
(un mode de vie)	*(a way of life)*		
un moule	*a mould*	une moule	*a mussel*
un pendule	*a pendulum*	une pendule	*a clock*
le physique	*appearance*	la physique	*physics*
un poêle	*a stove*	une poêle	*a frying pan*
un poste	*a job, TV or radio set*	la poste	*the Post Office*
le solde	*balance (in an account)*	la solde	*pay (usually with reference to soldier's pay)*
un somme	*a nap*	une somme	*a sum (of money)*
un tour	*a turn, trick*	une tour	*a tower*

le Tour de France	bicycle race	La Tour Eiffel	the Eiffel Tower
un vase	a vase	la vase	mud
un voile	a veil	une voile	a sail

(a) *chose* is normally feminine when it means 'thing': *la/une chose*. But the expressions *quelque chose* 'something', *autre chose* 'something else', *peu de chose* 'nothing much', *pas grand-chose* 'not a great deal' are masculine:

Quelque chose est **arrivé**   versus   Cette chose est arrivée
Something happened   *This thing happened*

(b) *gens* 'people' requires immediately preceding adjectives or quantifiers to be feminine, but following adjectives/participles or preceding adjectives/quantifiers separated from *gens* to be masculine:

Ces **vieilles** gens sont **heureux**   *Those old people are happy*
certaines gens   *some people*
tous les gens   *everyone*

Rassurés, les gens qui manifestaient se sont dispersés
Having been reassured, those demonstrating dispersed

(c) *amour* 'love' is normally masculine singular. It is sometimes, however, **feminine** plural: *les amours*. When feminine plural it can mean 'amorous adventures' or it can be a more poetic way of referring to love.

1.2.5 Nouns which have the same spoken form but two different written forms, with different genders and different meanings

There are some words which, in spoken French, are pronounced in the same way but which have different meanings and different genders:

un cal	a callus	une cale	a wedge		
un faîte	a summit	une fête	a party		
le foie	the liver	la foi	the faith		
le maire	the mayor	la mer	the sea	une mère	a mother
un pet	a fart	la paie	the pay	la paix	peace
le poids	weight	la poix	pitch	un pois	a pea
un rai	a ray of light	une raie	a parting (in hair) or a skate (fish)		
le sel	salt	une selle	a saddle		
le sol	earth	une sole	a sole (fish)		
un tic	a tic (nervous)	une tique	a tick (insect)		
le vice	vice (crime)	une vis	a screw		

1.2.6 Gender of countries, towns, islands, rivers, regions and states

Countries

Some countries are masculine, some are feminine. The best generalization is that they are masculine unless they end in *-e*, in which case they are feminine:

le Canada	Canada	la Chine	China
le Danemark	Denmark	la Finlande	Finland
le Japon	Japan	la Libye	Libya
le Koweït	Kuwait	la Norvège	Norway
le Liban	Lebanon	la Mauritanie	Mauritania
le Maroc	Morocco	la Roumanie	Romania

le Nigéria	*Nigeria*	la Suisse	*Switzerland*
le Portugal	*Portugal*	la Syrie	*Syria*

NB: Les Etats-Unis (m pl).

Exceptions: *le Cambodge* 'Cambodia', *le Mexique* 'Mexico', *le Mozambique* 'Mozambique', *le Zaïre* 'Zaire', *le Zimbabwe* 'Zimbabwe'.

'To' or 'in' a country is either *en* or *au(x)*. *en* is used with countries of feminine gender, and countries of masculine gender beginning with a vowel. *au* is used with countries of masculine gender beginning with a consonant, and *aux* with those countries whose names are plural, whether masculine or feminine (see Chapter 13.2.3 and 13.26.1):

en Chine	au Canada
en Norvège	au Japon
en Suisse	aux Etats-Unis
en Iran (m)	
en Israël (m)	

Towns

Towns, in normal usage, are masculine. In formal written French they are sometimes feminine, particularly those which end in *-e*:

Cambridge est plein(e) de touristes en été
Cambridge is full of tourists in summer

Where the name of a town includes a definite article, adjectives and participles must agree with the gender of the article:

La Baule est situé**e** sur le littoral atlantique
La Baule is on the Atlantic coast

Le Touquet est désert l'hiver
Le Touquet is deserted in winter

Islands

Islands are usually feminine:

la Sardaigne	*Sardinia*
la Crète	*Crete*
la Nouvelle-Zélande	*New Zealand*

But *le Groënland* 'Greenland' is an exception.

Rivers, regions and states

For rivers, French *départements*, French regions, for states and regions in other countries, the best generalization is that if they end in *-e* they are feminine:

Rivers

le Rhin	*the Rhine*	la Sâone	*the Sâone*
le Tarn	*the Tarn*	la Seine	*the Seine*
le Cher	*the Cher*	la Tamise	*the Thames*

Exception: *le Rhône* 'the Rhône'.

Départements

le Calvados	la Haute-Garonne
le Gers	la Marne
le Jura	la Vendée

Exception: *le Finistère.*

French regions

le Berry	la Normandie
le Limousin	la Bretagne
le Périgord	la Champagne

States and regions in other countries

For example, American states:

le Massachusetts	la Louisiane
le Nevada	la Californie
le Texas	la Floride

Exception: British counties appear mostly to be treated as masculine, even those ending in '-shire':

le Kent
le Perthshire
le Yorkshire

1.2.7 Gender of makes of vehicle and machines

Usually, the gender of makes of vehicle or makes of machines, like cars, lorries, planes, lawnmowers, dishwashers, and so on, is the same as the gender of the general name for the vehicle or machine.

voiture 'car' is feminine, so makes of car are feminine:

une Renault
une Citroën DS
une Nissan Priméra

camion 'lorry' is masculine, so makes of lorry are masculine:

un Berliet
un Foden

avion 'plane' is masculine, so types of plane are masculine:

le Concorde
un Boeing 747

cuisinière 'cooker' is feminine, so makes of cooker are feminine:

une Arthur Martin
une Belling

and so on.

1.2.8 Names of ships and restaurants

The names of ships are usually masculine because *navire* is masculine e.g. *Le Normandie*. However, smaller vessels may be feminine e.g. *La Marie-Joseph* because *la corvette* and *la frégate* are feminine. The names of restaurants also tend to be masculine, because *restaurant* itself is masculine. A restaurant named after a region famed for its excellent produce, such as *la Normandie*, will be called *Le Normandie*.

1.2.9 Nouns which are only masculine or only feminine, but can refer both to men and women

Some nouns which have only one gender refer to jobs or professions undertaken both by men and women. The following are all masculine in gender:

un architecte	*an architect*
un auteur	*an author*
un chef	*a chef*
un compositeur	*a composer*
un forçat	*a convict*
un ingénieur	*an engineer*
un juge	*a judge*
un magistrat	*a magistrate*
un médecin	*a doctor*
un peintre	*a painter*
un professeur	*a teacher*
un sculpteur	*a sculptor*
un témoin	*a witness*
un vampire	*a vampire*

When they refer to women, to make it explicit that the reference is to a woman and not a man, *femme* can be added either before or after the noun:

une femme médecin/**un** médecin femme
une femme ingénieur/**un** ingénieur femme

Alternatively, and more usually, the context can be allowed to determine the sex of the person referred to:

Elle est médecin dans un grand hôpital à Montréal
She is a doctor in a large Montreal hospital

Some titles are also only masculine, for example *le Maire* 'the Mayor', *le Juge* 'the Judge', *le Notaire* 'the Solicitor', etc. A woman playing this role will be addressed as *Madame le Maire, Madame le Juge*, etc.

This is an area which has given rise to considerable controversy. Whereas a few years ago, the above list would have contained *écrivain* and *avocat* as masculine-only terms, it would seem that *écrivaine* and *avocate* may now be passing into current usage. Canadian French has adopted a number of similar feminine forms not adopted in France.

There are a small number of nouns which are only feminine in gender, but which may refer both to men and women:

personne	*person*
recrue	*recruit*
sentinelle	*sentry*
star/vedette	*star* (*in the entertainment business*)
victime	*victim*

personne meaning 'person' is feminine: *la/une personne. personne* in *ne . . . per-sonne* meaning 'nobody' (see Chapter 16.13) is masculine:

Personne n'est **venu**	versus	Cette personne est venu**e**
Nobody came		*That person came*

1.2.10 Nouns with genders which English speakers often get wrong
The following nouns are **masculine**:

le caractère	*character/temperament*	un légume	*a vegetable*
un choix	*a choice*	le manque	*lack, lacuna*
le crime	*crime*	le mérite	*merit*
l'espace	*space*	un parachute	*a parachute*
l'exode	*exodus*	un parapluie	*an umbrella*
un groupe	*a group*	le silence	*silence*

NB: *espace* is feminine when it means 'a space in printing' (see 1.2.4).

The following nouns are **feminine**:

une croix	*a cross*	une forêt	*a forest*
une espèce	*a type, kind*	une noix	*a nut*
la fin	*the end*	une vis	*a screw*

1.2.11 Gender of compound nouns
Compound nouns fall into six main types in French, and it is possible to determine broadly the gender of a compound on the basis of the type it belongs to (although with some exceptions).

Adjective + noun compounds
Adjective + noun compounds normally take their gender from the noun. The noun part of the compound is highlighted in the following examples:

un **arc**-boutant	*a buttress*
un **bas**-côté	*a verge (e.g. of a motorway)*
une basse-**cour**	*a farmyard*
une belle-**fille**	*a daughter-in-law*
un **cerf**-volant	*a kite*
un **coffre**-fort	*a safe*
un grand-**parent**	*a grandparent*
un rond-**point**	*a roundabout*

Exception: *un rouge-gorge* 'a robin'.

Noun + noun compounds
In noun + noun compounds the gender is determined by the more important noun. *un camion-citerne* 'a tanker (lorry)' is a type of *camion* 'lorry', so *camion* is the more important noun, and the compound is masculine. *un homme-grenouille* 'a frogman' is a type of *homme* 'man' (not a type of frog!), so *homme* is the more important noun, and the compound is masculine. The important nouns are highlighted in the following examples:

une auto-**école**	*a driving school*
un **bateau**-mouche	*a Parisian tourist boat*
un **bateau**-citerne	*a tanker (ship)*

un **camion**-citerne	*a tanker (lorry)*
un **chou**-fleur	*a cauliflower*
un **homme**-grenouille	*a frogman*
un **hôtel**-Dieu	*a hospital*
une **idée**-force	*a central idea*
un **mot**-clé	*a keyword*
un **oiseau**-mouche	*a humming-bird*
du **papier**-toilette	*toilet paper*
une **pause**-café	*a coffee break*
une **porte**-fenêtre	*a french window*
un **timbre**-poste	*a stamp*
une **voiture**-restaurant	*a restaurant car*
un **wagon**-lit	*a sleeping car*

Adverb + noun compounds

In adverb + noun compounds, the compound is usually the same gender as the noun, but there are exceptions:

une arrière-**pensée**	*a second thought*
l'arrière-**plan** (m)	*the background*
une contre-**offensive**	*a counter-offensive*
un demi-**tarif**	*a half-price ticket*
une demi-**bouteille**	*a half bottle*
un hors-**bord**	*a speedboat*
une mini-**jupe**	*a miniskirt*
un haut-**parleur**	*a loudspeaker*
un sans-**travail**	*an unemployed person*

Exceptions: *l'après-guerre* (m) 'the post-war period', *un en-tête* 'a letterhead', *le sans-gêne* 'the lack of embarrassment'.

Noun + prepositional phrase compounds

The gender of noun + prepositional phrase compounds is usually that of the first noun:

un **aide**-de-camp	*an aide-de-camp*
un **arc**-en-ciel	*a rainbow*
un **chef** d'œuvre	*a masterpiece*
un **coup** d'œil	*a glance*
un **coup** de pied	*a kick*
un **croc**-en-jambe	*a trip*
une **langue**-de-chat	*a long, flat, finger biscuit*
la **main** d'œuvre	*the workforce*
un **mont**-de-piété	*a pawnshop*
une **pomme** de terre	*a potato*
un **pot**-de-vin	*a bribe*

Exceptions to this generalization are: *un tête-à-queue* 'a spin' (head to tail in a car), *un tête-à-tête* 'a tête à tête conversation'.

Verb + noun compounds

Verb + noun compounds are usually masculine:

un abat-jour	*a lampshade*
un accroche-cœur	*a (kiss) curl*
un appui-tête	*a headrest*
des casse-noisettes	*nutcrackers*

un cache-nez	*a scarf*
un coupe-papier	*a paper-knife*
un couvre-lit	*a bedspread*
un cure-dents	*a toothpick*
un essuie-mains	*a hand towel*
un gratte-ciel	*a skyscraper*
un ouvre-boîtes	*a tin-opener*
un pare-brise	*a windscreen*
un pare-chocs	*a bumper*
un porte-avions	*an aircraft carrier*
un porte-bagages	*a luggage rack*
un porte-monnaie	*a wallet*
un soutien-gorge	*a bra*
un taille-crayons	*a pencil sharpener*
un tire-bouchon	*a corkscrew*
un trompe-l'œil	*a `trompe l'œil' (art)*

Verbal phrase compounds

Compounds constructed from verbal phrases are masculine:

le manque-à-gagner	*lost revenue*
le on-dit	*rumour, gossip*
le ouï-dire	*hearsay*
un m'as-tu-vu	*a show-off*
le qu'en dira-t-on	*the 'what might people say'*
un faire-part	*an announcement card (weddings, births, funerals)*
un laisser-passer	*a pass (document)*
le savoir-faire	*know-how*

1.3 Number

All nouns must be either singular or plural. Although many nouns are marked for plural in written French, few differ in singular and plural form in spoken French. Usually, number is marked in the determiner in spoken French (*le/la* versus *les*, *ce/cette* versus *ces*, *mon/ma* versus *mes*, and so on).

1.3.1 Regular plurals

Regular plurals add -*s*, which is not pronounced, to the singular noun in written French:

une loi	des lois	*law(s)*
un drap	des draps	*sheet(s)*
une voiture	des voitures	*car(s)*
une remarque	des remarques	*remark(s)*
un chat	des chats	*cat(s)*
un enfant	des enfants	*child(ren)*
une maison	des maisons	*house(s)*
un chandail	des chandails	*cardigan(s)*
un éventail	des éventails	*fan(s)*

(For words ending in -*ail* which have an irregular plural see 1.3.6.)

1.3.2 Plurals of nouns ending in -s, -x, -z

With these words there is no change between singular and plural:

un pois	des pois	*spot(s)*
une croix	des croix	*cross(es)*

un nez	des nez	*nose(s)*
un as	des as	*ace(s)*
un prix	des prix	*price(s)*
un corps	des corps	*body(ies)*
un bras	des bras	*arm(s)*

NB:

(a) *un os* 'bone': In the singular the final 's' is pronounced. In the plural it is not pronounced: *des os* 'bones'.

(b) *un as* 'ace': The 's' is pronounced in both the singular and the plural.

1.3.3 Plurals of nouns ending in *-eu, -au, -eau*

These nouns form their plural by adding -*x*:

un cheveu	des cheveux	*hair(s)*
un tuyau	des tuyaux	*pipe(s)*
un manteau	des manteaux	*coat(s)*
l'eau	des eaux	*water(s)*

Exceptions:

un bleu	des bleus	*bruise(s)*
un pneu	des pneus	*tyre(s)*
un landau	des landaus	*pram(s)*

1.3.4 Plurals of nouns ending in *-ou*

Nouns ending in *-ou* form their plural with *-s*:

un fou	des fous	*madman/men or jester(s)*
un trou	des trous	*hole(s)*

But there are seven words which form their plural with -*x*:

un bijou	des bijoux	*jewel(s)*
un caillou	des cailloux	*stone(s)*
un chou	des choux	*cabbage(s)*
un genou	des genoux	*knee(s)*
un hibou	des hiboux	*owl(s)*
un joujou	des joujoux	*toy(s)*
un pou	des poux	*louse(lice)*

1.3.5 Plurals of nouns ending in *-al*

Most nouns ending in *-al* form their plural as *-aux*:

un bocal	des bocaux	*jam jar(s)*
un cheval	des chevaux	*horse(s)*
un idéal	des idéaux	*ideal(s)*
un journal	des journaux	*newspaper(s)*
un mal	des maux	*evil(s)*
un terminal	des terminaux	*terminal(s)*
un val	des vaux	*valley(s)*
	(limited to poetic language)	

There are, however, a number of exceptions which form their plural with -*s*:

un bal	des bals	*dance(s)*
un cal	des cals	*callus(es)*

un carnaval	des carnavals	*carnival(s)*
un cérémonial	des cérémonials	*ceremony(ies)*
un chacal	des chacals	*jackal(s)*
un festival	des festivals	*festival(s)*
un récital	des récitals	*recital(s)*
un régal	des régals	*feast(s)*

1.3.6 Irregular plurals for nouns ending in -*ail*

Many nouns ending in -*ail* have a regular plural, e.g. *des détails, des chandails, des éventails*, as indicated in 1.3.1, but a number of -*ail* nouns also make their plural with -*aux*:

un bail	des baux	*lease(s)*
un corail	des coraux	*coral(s)*
un émail	des émaux	*enamel(s)*
un soupirail	des soupiraux	*window(s)*
le travail	les travaux	*work(s)*
un vitrail	des vitraux	*stained glass window(s)*

1.3.7 Nouns which exist only in plural form

des affres (f)	*agonies*
aux alentours (m)	*around*
des annales (f)	*annals*
des archives (f)	*archives*
des armoiries (f)	*(coat of) arms*
des arrérages (m)	*arrears*
des arrhes (f)	*a deposit*
des bestiaux (m)	*animals*
des condoléances (f)	*condolences*
des ébats (m)	*frolicking*
des entrailles (f)	*entrails*
des environs (m)	*surroundings*
des fiançailles (f)	*engagement*
des fringues (f) (*colloquial*)	*clothes*
des frusques (f) (*colloquial*)	*clothes*
des funérailles (f)	*funeral*
des gens	*people (for gender see 1.2.4)*
des honoraires (m)	*fees*
des intempéries (f)	*bad weather*
des mœurs (f)	*customs*
des obsèques (f)	*funeral*
des vêpres (f)	*vespers*
des victuailles (f)	*victuals*

1.3.8 Nouns with irregular plurals

These are most notably:

un os	des os (pronounced as 'eau')	*bone(s)*
un œil	des yeux	*eye(s)*
un ciel	des cieux	*sky(ies)*
un œuf	des œufs (pronounced as 'œu')	*egg(s)*
un bœuf	des bœufs (pronounced as 'bœu')	*bullock(s)*

1.3.9 The plural of compound nouns

Adjective + noun compounds

In adjective + noun compounds (see 1.2.11), both elements become plural:

un arc-boutant	des arcs-boutants
un bas-côté	des bas-côtés
une basse-cour	des basses-cours
une belle-fille	des belles-filles
un cerf-volant	des cerfs-volants
un coffre-fort	des coffres-forts
un grand-parent	des grands-parents
un rond-point	des ronds-points

NB:	un grand-père	des grands-pères		
	un grand-oncle	des grands-oncles		
	une grand-mère	des grands-mères	or	des grand-mères
	une grand-tante	des grands-tantes	or	des grand-tantes

	un bonhomme	des bonshommes
BUT	un bonjour	des bonjours

Noun + noun compounds

In noun + noun compounds (see 1.2.11) the norm is for both nouns to become plural:

un bateau-citerne	des bateaux-citernes
un bateau-mouche	des bateaux-mouches
un camion-citerne	des camions-citernes
un chou-fleur	des choux-fleurs
un homme-grenouille	des hommes-grenouilles
une idée-force	des idées-forces
un mot-clé	des mots-clés
un oiseau-mouche	des oiseaux-mouches
une pause-café	des pauses-cafés
une porte-fenêtre	des portes-fenêtres
une voiture-restaurant	des voitures-restaurants
un wagon-lit	des wagons-lits

Exceptions:

une auto-école	des auto-écoles
un bain-marie	des bains-marie
un hôtel-Dieu	des hôtels-Dieu
un timbre-poste	des timbres-poste

Adverb + noun compounds

In adverb + noun compounds (see 1.2.11), the noun alone becomes plural, (although some remain invariable):

une arrière-boutique	des arrière-boutiques
une arrière-pensée	des arrière-pensées
un arrière-plan	des arrière-plans
une contre-offensive	des contre-offensives
une contre-offre	des contre-offres
une demi-bouteille	des demi-bouteilles
un demi-tarif	des demi-tarifs

un haut-parleur	des haut-parleurs
un hors-bord	des hors-bords
une mini-jupe	des mini-jupes
un non-lieu	des non-lieux
un non-paiement	des non-paiements

Exception: un sans-travail, des sans-travail

Noun + prepositional phrase compounds

In noun + prepositional phrase compounds (see 1.2.11) only the first noun becomes plural:

un aide-de-camp	des aides-de-camp
un arc-en-ciel	des arcs-en-ciel
un chef d'œuvre	des chefs d'œuvre
un coup d'œil	des coups d'œil
un coup de pied	des coups de pied
un croc-en-jambe	des crocs-en-jambe
une langue-de-chat	des langues-de-chat
la main d'œuvre	des mains d'œuvre
un mont-de-piété	des monts-de-piété
une pomme de terre	des pommes de terre
un pot-de-vin	des pots-de-vin

But not all change:

un pot-au-feu	des pot-au-feu
un tête-à-queue	des tête-à-queue
un tête-à-tête	des tête-à-tête

Verb + noun compounds

In verb + noun compounds (see 1.2.11), there are three possibilities:

(i) The form remains invariable whether its singular form contains a noun in the singular or plural. This is the usual pattern:

des abat-jour
des essuie-mains
des gratte-ciel
des ouvre-boîtes
des porte-monnaie

(ii) The second word becomes plural, normally -*s* or -*x*. This is the case with:

des accroche-cœurs
des tire-bouchons
des couvre-lits

These would appear to have been assimilated to the one-word versions, such as:

| le(s) portemanteau(x) | *coat peg(s)* |
| le(s) portefeuille(s) | *wallet(s)* |

(iii) The first word becomes plural (which is an indication that it is no longer related to any verbal form). This is the case with:

des appuis-tête
des soutiens-gorge

It has to be said that in the area of compound nouns not all 'authorities' agree on the rules and attempts to introduce 'logical' rules appear to have added further confusion to an already confused situation!

Verbal phrase compounds

These do not generally have a different plural form:

> des manque-à-gagner
> des on-dit
> des ouï-dire
> des m'as-tu-vu
> des qu'en dira-t-on
> des laisser-passer
> des savoir-faire

1.3.10 Number differences between French and English nouns

Some nouns which are singular in English are plural in French, and others are plural in English and singular in French. The following are examples which sometimes cause difficulty for English speakers:

English singular	**French plural**
applause	les applaudissements
darkness	les ténèbres
sb's funeral	les funérailles de qn
hair	les cheveux
information	des informations, des renseignements
knowledge	les connaissances
to make progress	faire des progrès
to do research/my research	faire des recherches/mes recherches

English plural	**French singular**
economics	l'économie
grapes	du raisin
(*grape* = un grain de raisin)	
linguistics	la linguistique
physics	la physique
pyjamas	un pyjama
shorts	un short
stairs	l'escalier
tights	un collant
trousers	un pantalon
underpants	un slip

NB: Some mass nouns in French can also be used as count nouns more freely than their English equivalents:

un fruit	*a piece of fruit*
un pain	*a loaf of bread* (NOT *a bread)
un raisin	*a type of grape*

2

Determiners

2.1 Articles

TABLE 2.A *Summary table of articles*

	Definite		Indefinite		Partitive	
masc	le, l′	*the*	un	*a*	du, de l′	*some*/no article
fem	la, l′	*the*	une	*a*	de la, de l′	*some*/no article
plur	les	*the*	des		*some*/no article	

2.1.1 Form of the article with adjectives and nouns beginning with a vowel or an *h*

le and *la* are shortened to *l′*, and *du* and *de la* become *de l′* if they immediately precede an adjective or noun beginning with a vowel:

l'univers (m)	*the universe*
l'électricité (f)	*electricity*
de l'acier (m)	*steel*
de l'eau (f)	*water*
l'ancien régime (m)	*the Ancien Regime*

They also behave in the same way when they immediately precede an adjective or noun beginning with a so-called 'silent h' or *h muet*. This is a written *h* which has no counterpart in the spoken language:

l'hiver (m)	*winter*
l'histoire (f)	*history*
de l'héroïsme (m)	*heroism*
de l'herbe (f)	*grass*
l'horrible silence (m)	*the terrible silence*

There is also another set of adjectives and nouns beginning with a written *h* which do have a counterpart in the spoken language. This is misleadingly called an 'aspirate h' or *h aspiré*. It is misleading because there is no 'h' sound in spoken French. Rather, words which begin with an 'aspirate h' in written French also happen to block reduction of the article to *l′* or *de l′* in spoken French:

le hibou (m)	*the owl*
la haine (f)	*hate*

du hachis (m)	*minced beef*
de la honte	*shame*
la haute montagne	*high up in the mountains*

There is no easy way to distinguish adjectives and nouns which begin with a silent *h* from those which begin with an aspirate *h*. Some cases are idiosyncratic. For example, *héros* 'hero' does not allow contraction of the article: *le héros;* but *héroïne* 'heroine or heroin' and *héroïsme* 'heroism' do: *l'héroïne, l'héroïsme*. Many dictionaries indicate an aspirate *h* by putting ['] at the beginning of the phonetic transcription of the word. For example:

hibou ['ibu] (m)	*owl*
histoire [istwar] (f)	*story, history*

The final consonant of *les* and *des* is pronounced [z] when they immediately precede an adjective or a noun beginning with a vowel or a silent *h*:

les [z] enfants	*children*	BUT	les hérissons	*hedgehogs*
des [z] amis	*friends*	BUT	des haricots	*beans*
des [z] héroïnes	*heroines*	BUT	des héros	*heroes*

The final *n* of *un* is pronounced when *un* immediately precedes an adjective or noun beginning with a vowel or silent *h*, but not otherwise:

un [n] hôtel	*a hotel*	BUT	un homard	*a lobster*
un [n] honnête homme	*a decent man*	BUT	un haut fonctionnaire	*a senior civil servant*

NB: Verbs beginning with an *h* in the written language also divide into those which require contraction of *je, me, le, la, ne*, etc., and those which do not:

J'habite Londres	Je hais Londres
I live in London	*I hate London*
Je l'héberge	Je la heurte dans son orgueil
I am letting him stay with me	*I hurt her pride*

2.2 Typical use of the definite article

(a) One of the uses of the definite article in French is parallel to its use in English: to accompany nouns which are already known from the context:

> Achetez une nouvelle Panthéra GT6. **La** Panthéra GT6 vous va!
> *Buy a new Panthéra GT6. The Panthéra GT6 suits you!*

> Tu as laissé dans le jardin **le** livre que tu as acheté hier
> *You left the book which you bought yesterday in the garden*

A pretty good guide to this usage is: if English uses a definite article, use one in French.

(b) A second use of the definite article in French is to refer to a general class of phenomena, a unique phenomenon or an abstract quality:

Les cochons sont très propres de nature
Pigs are naturally very clean

Les médecins pensent que **la** rougeole réapparaît
Doctors think that measles is coming back

La jungle est un endroit dangereux
The jungle is a dangerous place

La peur de prendre l'avion le retient en Grande Bretagne
Fear of flying keeps him in Britain

This contrasts with English which more often than not uses no article when a general class or an abstract quality are indicated:

Pigs are quite clean by nature

Fear of flying keeps him in Great Britain

The definite article is obligatory in French in these cases.

2.2.1 Fused forms of the definite article

Definite articles fuse with preceding *de* or *à*:

du (= de + le) pain	au (= à + le) cinéma
de l'effort	à l'école
des (= de + les) épices	aux (= à + les) animaux

Such contraction is only possible with articles, however. It is not possible when *le, la, les* are pronouns (see Chapter 3.2): *J'ai essayé de le comprendre* 'I tried to understand it' (NOT **J'ai essayé du comprendre*).

An archaic contraction of *en les* to *ès* is still found in the set phrase: *licencié ès lettres* 'Bachelor of Arts'.

2.2.2 Use of the definite article with names of countries, regions, *départements*

In French the definite article is normally used with the names of countries, regions and *départements*, whereas in English it is not:

La France est un très beau pays
France is a very beautiful country

Progressivement, la Champagne est devenue terre de rencontre et de conflits
Over time, Champagne (a French region) became a land of meetings and confrontations

Ramassage de coquillages interdit dans le Calvados
Shellfish fishing banned in Calvados (a French département)

When *en* 'to/in' or *de* 'from' are used with feminine countries or regions (or with masculine countries beginning with a vowel: *en Irak*), the definite article is omitted:

Nous irons en France l'année prochaine
We shall go to France next year

des pommes de Normandie
apples from Normandy

> des vacances en Ille-et-Vilaine
> *holidays in Ille-et-Vilaine*

But with masculine countries, regions and *départements*, the definite article is retained with *à* 'to/in', *dans* 'in' and *de* 'from':

> Les hôtels au Mexique sont d'un très bon niveau
> *The hotels in Mexico are of a very high standard*

> J'ai acheté une maison dans le Finistère
> *I have bought a house in Finistère*

> des pommes du Calvados
> *apples from Calvados*

(For the gender of countries see Chapter 1.2.6, and for the use of *en, à, dans* see Chapter 13.26.1.)

2.2.3 Use of the definite article with names of languages

The names of languages in English start with a capital letter and have no article. The names of languages in French start with a small letter, normally have a definite article and are masculine in gender:

> Ici les étudiants étudient **le** français, l'allemand et l'italien
> *Here students study French, German and Italian*

> **Le** grec possède un alphabet tout à fait différent du nôtre
> *Greek has an alphabet which is quite different from our own*

In the expressions *parler français, parler allemand*, etc., the name of the language functions more like an adverbial than a noun, so no article is used. But note the following contrast:

> Je parle français/Je parle souvent **le** français/Je parle bien **le** français
> *I speak French/I often speak French/I speak French well*

When adverbs like *souvent, bien* are present, *français* becomes a noun again, requiring the definite article.

2.2.4 Use of the definite article with seasons

Seasons in French are usually accompanied by a definite article, except when they are preceded by *en*:

> **L'**hiver est une saison de repos pour nous
> *Winter is a restful season for us*

> **L'**été nous réserve parfois des surprises mais à l'automne le temps est toujours plus prévisible
> *Summer sometimes has some surprises in store for us, but autumn weather is always more predictable*

> Tout se réveille **au** printemps
> *Everything awakes in spring*

BUT

en hiver	*in winter*
en été	*in summer*
en automne	*in autumn*

(See also Chapter 13.26.1.)

2.2.5 Use of the definite article with titles

Titles in French prefaced by *Monsieur* or *Madame* include the definite article:

Monsieur **le** Maire	*Mr Mayor*
Madame **le** Maire	*Madam Mayor*
Monsieur **le** Président-Directeur-Général	*Mr Chairman*

Such forms of address as: *Monsieur le Directeur des Achats* 'Mr Purchasing Director', *Madame le Directeur du Personnel* 'Madam Personnel Director' are frequent in French in writing (e.g. letters) or in very formal speeches, but almost unheard of in English.

The definite article is similarly present in French in greetings or expressions of encouragement like:

Salut **les** gars!	*Hi, guys!*
Allez **les** bleus!	*Come on, you blues!*
Au lit, **les** enfants!	*Off to bed, kids!*

With kings and queens, however, French leaves out an article with numbers where English puts one in:

François I (François premier)	*François the first*
Henri III (Henri trois)	*Henry the third*
Elizabeth I (Elizabeth première)	*Elizabeth the first*
Elizabeth II (Elizabeth deux)	*Elizabeth the second*

(See also Chapter 6.4.2.)

2.2.6 Use of the definite article with superlatives

In superlatives involving adjectives which follow the noun (see Chapter 4.12.2), it is compulsory to repeat the definite article, which then agrees with the noun:

Le moment **le** plus intense de ma vie
The most exciting moment of my life

Les virages **les** plus dangereux de la région
The most dangerous bends in the region

2.2.7 Use of the definite article with quantities

Where English uses 'so much **a** pound', French refers to *tant* **la** *livre*/**le** *kilo*, etc.:

Les pommes? C'est 4,50 F **le** kilo
Apples? They are 4.50 francs a kilo

Les bonbons sont à 5,40 F **les** 100 grammes
Sweets are 5.40 francs for a 100 grammes

Ces chaises sont vendues à 500 F **la** pièce (or 500 F pièce)
These chairs are sold for 500 francs each

2.2.8 Use of the definite article with parts of the body

(a) In simple descriptions of body parts, French uses a definite article where English uses a possessive determiner (e.g. *his, my, their*):

Il a **les** yeux bleus	*His eyes are blue*
Elle a **les** cheveux coupés court	*She has her hair cut short*

(b) When people activate parts of their own bodies, French also uses a definite article with the body part:

Il a plissé **les** yeux	*He screwed up his eyes*
Elle a agité **le** bras	*She waved*
J'ai baissé **la** tête en y entrant	*I lowered my head as I went in*
Elle a hoché/secoué **la** tête	*She nodded/shook her head*

(c) When people do things which affect their own bodies, or those of others, the usual construction is a definite article in front of the body part, and a reflexive or indirect object pronoun:

Je **me** suis fracturé **la** jambe	*I broke my leg*
Elle **s'**est fait couper **les** cheveux	*She had her hair cut*
Je **lui** serre **la** main	*I shake his hand*
On **lui** a coupé **la** tête	*They cut his head off*
Elle **lui** essuie **les** yeux avec un mouchoir	*She wipes his eyes with a handkerchief*

These constructions are also possible with a possessive determiner, as in English, however:

Je prends **sa** main	*I take her hand*
Elle caresse **mes** cheveux	*She strokes my hair*
J'appuie **mes** deux mains sur sa poitrine	*I press with both my hands on his chest*

(d) When body parts are the subject of a sentence, they usually have a possessive determiner, as in English, rather than a definite article:

Mon coeur s'est arrêté une fraction de seconde	*My heart stopped for an instant*
Ma tête me fait mal	*My head hurts*
Ses paupières se sont abaissées	*His eyelids lowered*
Leurs regards se sont croisés	*Their eyes met*

(e) When descriptions of parts of the body or items of clothing are used adverbially, they are accompanied by the definite article:

l'homme **au** nez retroussé	*the man with the turned-up nose*
le comédien **au** chapeau de paille	*the actor in the straw hat*
Il parlait, **le** sourire aux lèvres	*He spoke, with a smile*
Elle est partie, **les** mains dans **les** poches	*She left with her hands in her pockets*
Il s'est agenouillé, **le** chapeau à **la** main	*He knelt down with his hat in his hands*
Il a avoué son crime, **les** yeux abaissés	*He confessed his crime, looking down*

2.2.9 Singular or plural when a number of individuals have one item each

When reference is made to one body part, one item of clothing, or one more general personal attribute, but two or more people are involved, the entity is usually referred to in the singular:

Nous nous sommes tous **les** deux cassés **le bras**
We both broke our arms
Ils ont levé **la main droite**
They raised their right hands

Les étudiants sont priés d'inscrire **leur nom de famille** à l'endroit prévu
Students are requested to write their surnames in the space provided

Ils ont tous accroché **leur manteau** dans l'entrée
They all hung their coats up in the entrance hall

Les jumeaux ont vécu **leur vie** d'une manière indépendante
The twins lived their lives independently

2.2.10 Use of the definite article to indicate a habitual action

Where English uses 'on + ...day(s)' to indicate a habitual action e.g. 'On Monday(s) I go to the market', French uses the definite article: *Je vais faire mon marché le lundi*:

Nous allons au cinéma **le** vendredi soir
We go to the cinema on Friday evenings

Le cours d'histoire a lieu **le** mercredi
The history lecture is on Wednesdays

Ils viennent ramasser les poubelles **le** lundi et **le** jeudi
They come to empty the dustbins on Mondays and Thursdays

2.2.11 Repetition of the definite article

In French the article usually has to be repeated with each noun, whereas in English one use at the beginning of a 'list' is enough:

Je dois ramener chez moi le fer à repasser, la planche à repasser et la corbeille à papiers
I must take home with me the iron, ironing board and waste-paper basket

2.3 Typical use of the indefinite article

(a) One use of the indefinite article is to introduce a new, countable, concrete noun (*maison, tableau, livre, voiture*, etc.) into the discourse:

Je me suis trouvé **une** belle maison en Ecosse
I have found myself a lovely house in Scotland

Voulez-vous voir **un** Picasso?
Do you want to see a Picasso?

(b) Another is to describe a general class of countable, concrete entities:

Normalement **une** voiture a quatre roues et **une** moto en a deux
Normally a car has four wheels and a motorbike two

Il s'agit là d'une erreur caractéristique d'**un** étudiant de première année
That's an example of a typical error made by a first year student

In this 'generic' use, the indefinite article is usually interchangeable with a plural definite article:

Normalement **les** voitures ont quatre roues et **les** motos en ont deux
Il s'agit là d'une erreur caractéristique **des** étudiants de première année (*de +* definite article *les*)

(c) Abstract nouns (*courage, beauté, réalisme, importance*, etc.) are normally accompanied by the definite article (see Chapter 1.1.1). But when they are modified by an adjective they take an indefinite article. Compare:

Il admire **le** courage
He admires courage

Il a fait preuve d'**un** courage peu ordinaire
He showed extraordinary courage

La beauté du paysage nous étonnait
The beauty of the countryside astonished us

Le paysage était d'**une** beauté étonnante
The countryside was astonishingly beautiful

2.3.1 The plural indefinite article *des*

The plural indefinite article *des* refers to an unspecified quantity of entities described by a plural count noun. In English the article is most frequently omitted:

Je lui ai offert **des** roses
I gave her roses

Les places avaient déjà été réservées par **des** Américains
The seats had already been reserved by Americans

Vous me posez **des** questions impossibles
You ask me impossible questions

NB: An error often made by English speakers is to omit the article; plural indefinite *des* cannot be omitted in French: NOT **Je lui ai offert roses.*

2.3.2 Omission of plural indefinite *des* after the preposition *de*

When the plural indefinite article is preceded by the preposition *de*, it is omitted in French. Compare:

Elle a été accusée **d'un** meurtre particulièrement horrible
She was accused of a particularly nasty murder

Elle a été accusée **de** meurtres particulièrement horribles
(être accusé de + des meurtres horribles)
She was accused of particularly nasty murders

Avec l'aide **d'une** amie, elle a fini son projet
With the help of a friend, she finished her project

Avec l'aide **d'**amies, elle a fini son projet
(avec l'aide de + des amies)
With the help of friends, she finished her project

Omission of plural indefinite article *des* only occurs after the preposition *de*. With other prepositions it is not omitted:

Elle est sortie **avec des** amies
She went out with friends

des attaques violentes **contre des** policiers
violent attacks on policemen

Because plural indefinite *des* is omitted after the preposition *de*, this means that

it is omitted when it is the complement of a number of verbs which are always
followed by the preposition *de* (see Chapter 8.4):

> Il a déjeuné **de** fruits
> *His lunch consisted of fruit*
> (versus Il a mangé **des** fruits)

> Elle parlait **de** choses oubliées depuis longtemps
> *She spoke of things long since forgotten*
> (versus Elle décrivait **des** choses oubliées depuis longtemps)

Plural indefinite *des* is also omitted after many quantifiers (see Chapter 6.9) or
quantifier-like expressions which incorporate the preposition *de*:

> Il y a un bon nombre **de** participants au tournoi
> *There are a good many participants at the tournament*

> Un kilo **de** cerises, s'il vous plaît
> *A kilo of cherries, please*

> Beaucoup **de** personnes ont déjà remarqué ton absence
> *Many people have already noticed your absence*

> J'ai déjà entendu assez **d'**excuses de ta part; je n'en accepterai plus
> *I have heard enough excuses from you; I won't accept any more*

> Où as-tu mis la boîte **de** sardines?
> *Where did you put the tin of sardines?*

Exceptions: *bien des* 'many', *encore des* 'still more':

> Bien **des** personnes ont déjà remarqué ton absence
> *Many people have already noticed your absence*

> J'ai encore **des** questions à vous poser
> *I still have more questions to ask you*

2.3.3 Comparing the use of plural indefinite article *des* with preposition *de* + definite article *les*

Compare the use of the plural indefinite article and the plural definite article
in similar contexts:

> Elle mangeait **des coquillages**
> *She was eating shellfish*

> Elle mangeait **les coquillages qu'elle avait achetés au marché**
> *She was eating the shellfish she had bought in the market*

When the highlighted expressions follow the preposition *de*, *des* is deleted
(2.3.2), but *de* + *les* becomes *des* (2.2.1):

> Elle déjeunait **de** coquillages
> *She dined on shellfish*

> Elle déjeunait **des** coquillages qu'elle avait achetés au marché
> *She dined on the shellfish which she had bought in the market*

Thus *des* can be either a plural indefinite article corresponding to English 'some'
or no article, or a plural definite article fused with the preposition *de*.

Note the following contrasts with quantifiers:

Beaucoup **de** personnes (indefinite) trouvent cela difficile
Many people find that difficult

Beaucoup **des** personnes (definite) à qui nous avons parlé trouvent cela difficile
Many of the people to whom we spoke find that difficult

Un kilo **de** cerises, s'il vous plaît
A kilo of cherries, please

Un kilo **des** cerises espagnoles, s'il vous plaît
A kilo of the Spanish cherries, please

2.3.4 *d'autres* and *des autres*

A contrast which English speakers often find difficult is between *d'autres* and *des autres*. *d'autres* 'other(s)' is an indefinite expression which is not accompanied by the plural indefinite article *des*:

Dans son article, elle a présenté **d'autres** idées (NOT *des autres idées)
In her article, she presented other ideas

D'autres (NOT *des autres) auraient agi différemment
Others would have acted differently

J'en ai vu **d'autres** (NOT *des autres)
I saw others

des autres is only used where *des* is the fused form of preposition *de* and the definite article *les* of *les autres* 'the others':

Elle parlait **des** autres projets qu'elle dirige
She spoke of the other projects she directs

Je ne me rappelle rien **des** autres jours de ce mois
I remember nothing of the other days of that month

NB: This is a case where a change appears to be in progress. In spoken French *des autres* is often generalized to all these contexts.

2.3.5 The use of *de* when an adjective precedes the noun

When an adjective precedes the noun, it is customary, at least in written French, to use *de* and not *des*:

Je lui ai offert de jolies roses
I gave her pretty roses

De gros miroirs comme ça, on n'en voit plus beaucoup
You don't see many large mirrors like that any more

NB: This does not apply when the adjective and the noun are joined in a compound noun or something which is seen as a single unit: *des jeunes gens, des jeunes filles, des petits pois, des petites annonces, des grands magasins, des grands jours.*

2.4 The partitive article: *du, de l', de la, des*

The partitive article *du, de l', de la, des* is used with mass nouns in French where English uses 'some' or no article at all:

Il charriait **du** bois pour son voisin
He carted wood about for his neighbour

Vous auriez dû acheter **du** lait en même temps
You ought to have bought some milk at the same time

Avec **de l'**ail ça aurait encore meilleur goût!
It would taste even better with garlic!

Il me manque **de** l'argent
I'm lacking funds

The partitive article is also used with abstract nouns like *courage, beauté, patience, silence* when these qualities are attributed to people or things:

Il faut avoir **de la** patience avec les enfants
You must be patient with children

Elle a **de** l'intelligence à revendre
She is really intelligent

Vos enfants ont **de la** malice
Your children are mischievous

When a partitive article follows the preposition *de* it is deleted, just as plural indefinite *des* is deleted (see 2.3.2):

beaucoup **de** bois	*a lot of wood*
une bouteille **de** lait	*a bottle of milk*
une tête **d'**ail	*a bulb of garlic*
J'ai besoin **d'**argent	*I need money*

2.4.1 Use of *faire* + partitive: *faire du/de la*

Many constructions exist with *faire* + noun, introduced by the partitive:

Faire du sport	*To take part in sport*
Faire du basket	*To play basketball*
Faire du piano	*To play the piano*
Faire de la politique	*To go in for politics*
Faire du bien (à quelqu'un)	*To do good (to somebody)*
Faire du mal (à quelqu'un)	*To do harm (to somebody)*

2.5 Use of indefinite and partitive articles after the negative forms *ne ... pas, ne ... jamais, ne ... plus, ne ... guère*

After *ne ... pas, ne ... jamais, ne ... plus, ne ... guère,* any indefinite article (*un, une, des*) or partitive article (*du, de l', de la, des*) accompanying a direct object normally becomes *de* :

Elle n'a pas écrit **de** lettre
She didn't write a letter

Nous ne vendons pas **de** chaussettes
We don't sell socks

Elle ne porte jamais **de** casque
She never wears a helmet

Pourquoi ne peut-on jamais acheter **de** vêtements d'hiver au printemps?
Why can you never buy winter clothes in spring?

Je n'ai plus **de** crayon
I don't have a pencil any more

Il n'a plus **de** médicaments
He doesn't have any more medication

Il n'y a guère **de** visiteurs
There are hardly any visitors

There are three cases where this does not apply:

(a) when a contrast is made between a negative and a positive direct object:

Je ne veux pas **des** chaussettes mais **des** chaussures
I don't want socks, but shoes

Je n'ai pas **un** cours de grammaire mais **un** cours d'histoire
I haven't got a grammar class but a history class

(b) after the verb *être*:

Ce n'est pas **un** oiseau   *It isn't a bird*

(c) when the meaning is 'not a (single) one' rather than 'not a':

On n'entendait pas **un** bruit dehors
We couldn't hear a single noise outside

2.6 Omission of the article

There are a number of cases where no article is used in French.

2.6.1 Omission of the article in compound nouns linked by *à*

In compound nouns linked by *à*, there is usually no article in front of the second noun:

une brosse à dents	*a toothbrush*
un couteau à pain	*a bread knife*
une corbeille à papiers	*a waste-paper basket*
une cuiller à café	*a tea (coffee) spoon*
une planche à roulettes	*a skateboard*
une planche à voile	*a sailboard*
une tasse à café	*a coffee cup*
une tasse à thé	*a tea cup*
un verre à vin	*a wine glass*
un verre à pied	*a stemmed glass*

2.6.2 Omission of the article in noun constructions linked by *de*

The article is frequently omitted before the second noun in noun + noun constructions linked by *de*, where the second noun functions like an adjective (and is often translated into English as an adjective):

une ambassade de France	*a French embassy*
une carte de visite	*a visiting card*
une carte de France	*a map of France*
un billet de bus	*a bus ticket*
un arrêt de bus	*a bus stop*
un tableau d'affichage	*a notice board*
une question d'argent	*a question of money*
une affaire de coeur	*a matter of the heart*
un problème de liquidité	*a cash-flow problem*
une salle de classe	*a classroom*

une salle de bains	*a bathroom*
une agence de voyages	*a travel agent/agency*
un verre de vin	*a glass of wine*
une tasse de thé	*a cup of tea*
une tasse de café	*a cup of coffee*

But note that when the second noun is modified (by an adjective or a clause, for example) it becomes definite, and a definite article appears:

une carte **de la** France métropolitaine
a map of mainland France

Il va être question **de l**'argent que je t'ai prêté
There'll be a discussion about the money I lent you

un arrêt **du** bus no 25
a stop for the number 25 bus

2.6.3 Omission of the article in participle + noun constructions linked by *de*

The article is omitted after *de* in participle + noun constructions where the participle functions as an adjective:

couvert de boue	*covered with mud*
rempli de rancune	*filled with rancour*
dépourvu de sens	*lacking any meaning*
comblé de bonheur	*overwhelmed with happiness*
entouré d'imbéciles	*surrounded by idiots*

2.6.4 Omission of the article after *sans, avec, en, sur, sous, par, ni . . . ni*

The article is frequently omitted when a noun alone follows *sans, avec, en, sur, sous, par,* or two nouns alone appear in the expression *ni . . . ni*:

sans arrêt	*continuously*
sans difficulté	*without difficulty*
sans délai	*without delay*
sans sucre	*without sugar*
sans manche	*with no handle*
avec patience	*with patience*
avec difficulté	*with difficulty*
en colère	*angry*
en guerre	*at war*
en réparation	*being repaired*
en théorie	*in theory*
en marbre	*in marble*
sur commande	*by order*
sous verre	*under glass*
sous pression	*under pressure*
deux fois par semaine	*twice a week*
par pitié	*out of pity*
Il ne portait ni chapeau	*He was wearing neither a hat*
ni cravate	*nor a tie*

(For *ne . . . ni . . . ni* see Chapter 16.14.)

But if the noun is modified (for example by an adjective) the article is not omitted:

sans **la** moindre difficulté	*without the least difficulty*
sans même **le** plus petit retard	*without even the slightest delay*
avec **une** patience admirable	*with admirable patience*
sous **la** pression du gouvernement	*under pressure from the government*

NB: *en* cannot normally co-occur with an article. When an article is required, the preposition changes to *dans*:

en théorie	BUT	dans la théorie d'Einstein
in theory		*in Einstein's theory*
en pratique	BUT	dans la pratique
in practice		*in practice*

2.6.5 Omission of the article in set phrases and verbal constructions

avoir besoin (de)	*to need*
avoir envie (de)	*to desire*
avoir peur	*to be afraid*
avoir raison	*to be right*
chercher noise (à)	*to try and pick a quarrel (with)*
demander pardon	*to ask for forgiveness*
donner congé (à)	*to sack*
faire attention	*to pay attention*
garder rancune (à)	*to bear a grudge (against)*
prendre fait et cause (pour)	*to defend*
rendre justice (à)	*to be fair (to)*
rendre service	*to help*
tenir parole	*to keep one's word*

2.6.6 Omission of the article with nouns in apposition

When proper nouns are juxtaposed with common nouns which identify them, the common nouns are said to be in apposition. In such cases the article is usually omitted:

Versailles, palais de Louis XIV et son entourage
Versailles, the palace of Louis XIV and his court

Juliette Lagrange, concierge, cherchait un nouveau poste
Juliette Lagrange, caretaker, was looking for a new job

Chantal, fille de dentiste, a annoncé son mariage avec Jean-Michel, fils de médecin
Chantal, a dentist's daughter, has announced her marriage to Jean-Michel, a doctor's son

Le Bergerac, vin de qualité, est vendu dans toute l'Europe
Bergerac, a quality wine, is sold throughout Europe

But when the common noun is modified, for example by an adjective, the article is not omitted:

Chantal, **la** fille **aînée** du dentiste, . . .
Versailles, **le célèbre** palais de Louis XIV . . .

2.6.7 Omission of the article with nouns following the verbs *être, demeurer, devenir, élire, nommer, rester*

When a noun alone follows the verbs *être* 'be', *demeurer* 'stay', *devenir* 'become', *élire* 'elect', *nommer* 'appoint', *rester* 'stay', the article is omitted:

Sa mère est ingénieur	*Her mother is an engineer*
Il est devenu architecte très tôt	*He became an architect early on*
Elle est restée maire de la commune	*She remained mayor of the village*
On l'a élu président	*He was elected president*
Pierre a été nommé Directeur des Achats	*Pierre was appointed Purchasing Director*

But when the noun is modified, for example by an adjective, the article is not omitted:

Depuis, il est devenu un architecte innovateur
Since then, he has become an innovatory architect

Pierre a été nommé le premier Directeur des Achats
Pierre was appointed as the first Purchasing Director

2.6.8 Omission of the article in lists

In lists of nouns the article is frequently omitted:

Hommes, femmes et enfants sont tous invités à la fête
Men, women and children are all invited to the party

J'ai acheté pommes de terre, tomates, courgettes, prunes et navets chez le même marchand de primeurs
I bought potatoes, tomatoes, courgettes, plums and turnips at the same greengrocer's

NB: Either all the articles are omitted (as in these examples) or they are all included (see 2.2.11).

2.7 Demonstrative determiners

TABLE 2.B *Summary table of demonstrative determiners*

		Proximate	Non-proximate
masc	ce, cet *this, that*	ce, cet ... ci *this ... (here)*	ce, cet ... là *that ... (there)*
fem	cette *this, that*	cette ... ci *this ... (here)*	cette ... là *that ... (there)*
plur	ces *these, those*	ces ... ci *these ... (here)*	ces ... là *those ... (there)*

NB: Masculine *cet* appears only when the demonstrative determiner immediately precedes a noun or adjective beginning with a vowel or a 'silent h' (*h muet*) (see 2.1.1):

cet enfant	*this child*
cet ancien marin	*that ex-sailor*
cet héroïsme	*that heroism*

2.7.1 Typical use of demonstrative determiners

Demonstrative determiners imply a contrast between the entity referred to by the noun they accompany and other entities of a similar type:

> **Cette** voiture a fait le tour du monde
> *This car has been around the world*

(The car referred to is implicitly contrasted with other cars which haven't been around the world.)

> A **cet** instant, la porte s'est brusquement refermée derrière eux
> *At that moment the door suddenly closed behind them*

(The moment referred to is implicitly contrasted with other moments when the door didn't close.)

Note that *ce, cet/cette* translate both 'this' and 'that', *ces* translates both 'these' and 'those'. The form *-ci* can be added to the noun accompanied by *ce*, etc., to stress proximity in space or time. Proximity in English is part of the meaning of 'this', but it can also be emphasized by stressing 'this' or sometimes by adding 'here' after the noun:

> **Cette** voiture-**ci** a fait le tour du monde
> *THIS car/This car here has been around the world*

> **Ce** mois-**ci** je ne peux pas vous payer
> *THIS month I can't pay you*

The form *là* can be added to the noun accompanied by *ce*, etc., to stress non-proximity in space or time. Non-proximity in English is part of the meaning of 'that', but it can also be emphasized by stressing 'that' or sometimes by adding 'there' after the noun:

> Cette année-là nous ne sommes pas allés à la mer
> *THAT year we did not go to the sea*

> Ce matin-là, je m'étais réveillé très tard
> *THAT morning I had woken up very late*

-ci and *-là* are necessary if a comparison is made between 'this X' and 'that X':

> Est-ce que vous préférez **cette** voiture-**ci** ou **cette** voiture-**là**?
> *Do you prefer this car or that car?*

2.8 Possessive determiners

TABLE 2.C *Summary table of possessive determiners*

First person	**masc**	mon	*my*	notre	*our*
	fem	ma	*my*		
	plur	mes	*my*	nos	*our*
Second person	**masc**	ton	*your*	votre	*your*
	fem	ta	*your*		
	plur	tes	*your*	vos	*your*
Third person	**masc**	son	*his, her, its*	leur	*his, her, its*
	fem	sa	*his, her, its*		
	plur	ses	*his, her, its*	leurs	*their*

Possessive determiners agree in gender and number with the nouns they precede:

> Elle a levé **son** verre *She raised her (or his) glass*
> Il a rempli **sa** tasse *He filled his (or her) cup*
> Il a cassé **ses** lunettes *He broke his (or her) glasses*

The feminine singular forms *ma, ta, sa* become *mon, ton, son* when they immediately precede a noun or adjective beginning with a vowel or 'silent h' (*h muet*) (see 2.1.1):

> **ma** classe   *my class*   BUT   **mon** école   *my school*
> **sa** permission   *her permission*   BUT   **son** approbation   *her approval*
> **ta** hardiesse   *your audacity*   BUT   **ton** hésitation   *your hesitation*

The determiners *votre, vos* can both be used to refer to more than one possessor:

> Messieurs et mesdames, **votre** table est prête
> *Ladies and gentlemen, your table is ready*

and as a polite form:

> Suivez-moi, monsieur, **votre** table est prête
> *Follow me, sir, your table is ready*

(For the use of the definite article rather than possessive determiners with parts of the body see 2.2.8.)

(For the use of a singular determiner when a single item is possessed by more than one person see 2.2.9.)

3

Personal and impersonal pronouns

3.1 Subject pronouns

TABLE 3.A *Summary table of subject pronouns*

Person	Singular		Plural	
First person	je	*I*	nous	*we*
Second person	tu	*you*	vous	*you (plural, polite)*

Third person
   masculine
   feminine
   non-specific
	il
	elle
	on
		he, it
		she, it
		one, we, people, they
			ils
			elles
				they
				they

neutral	ce, cela, ça	*it, that*		
impersonal	il, ce, cela, ça	*it, that, there*		

3.1.1 Position of subject pronouns

In declarative sentences, subject pronouns normally appear immediately before the verb which carries the tense:

> **Nous** voulons voir le directeur
> *We want to see the manager*

> **Tu** comprends vite
> *You catch on quick*

> **Elle** a servi le vin chambré
> *She served the wine at room temperature*

They can only be separated from this verb by the *ne* of negation, and by other pre-verbal pronouns:

> Elle **ne** prend pas de café
> *She's not having any coffee*

> Tu **l'**as mangé
> *You ate it*

Vous **ne le** ferez pas
You won't do it

Unlike in English, subject pronouns cannot normally be separated from the verb by adverbials or parenthetical expressions:

NOT *Je souvent dîne avec Laura
I often dine with Laura

NOT *Il, paraît-il, ne prend pas de café
He, it seems, isn't having coffee

versus the grammatical *Je dîne souvent avec Laura, Il ne prend pas de café, paraît-il.*

In direct questions involving inversion (see Chapter 14.2.3), subject pronouns appear immediately after the verb which carries the tense:

Sait-**il** nager?   *Can he swim?*
Est-**elle** arrivée?   *Has she arrived?*
Ont-**ils** mangé?   *Have they eaten?*

(For the formation of direct questions, see Chapter 14.2.)

When subject pronouns follow the verb in this way nothing else can intervene:

Ne le croyez-**vous** pas?   *Don't you believe it?*
Ne le lui avez-**vous** pas donné?   *Didn't you give it to him?*
Dînent-**ils** souvent ensemble?   *Do they often dine together?*

3.1.2 The use of *vous* and *tu*

vous can have two functions: to address more than one person, and as a polite form of address to one person when there is a certain 'social distance' between the speaker and the addressee. *tu* is used only to address one person when there is no social distance between speaker and addressee.

In its plural use, *vous* refers simply to more than one addressee, whether social intimates or not:

Vous voulez aller au match dimanche?
Do you want to go to the match this Sunday?
(e.g. several friends discussing where to go)

Vous allez me refaire ce devoir
You lot are going to have to do this homework again
(e.g. a teacher talking to a class)

When one person is being addressed it is difficult to give hard and fast rules about when to use *tu* and when to use the polite *vous*. Generally, one can say that the non-native speaker would be well advised to use *vous* from the outset, and to allow the native speaker to take the initiative about any change to *tu*. The following table (Table 3.B) illustrates some uses of *tu* and polite *vous*, but it is not possible to give an exhaustive list of such usage. Individual speakers may vary in their own preferences for use of *tu* or polite *vous*, and that usage may vary regionally (for example, it is often said that *tu* is used more readily in the south of France than it is in the north).

TABLE 3.B *Examples of the use of* tu *and polite* vous

Context	Typical usage by two speakers
Adult strangers meeting for the first time in formal contexts: e.g. business meetings, interviews, dealing with state administration and services.	Both use *vous*.
Adults meeting in informal contexts: e.g. neighbours, socializing, shopping.	Initially both use *vous*, but with continued contact it is likely that they will change to *tu*, especially with young adults (under 40).
Professional superior and inferior	Generally both use *vous*, but in some organizations the inferior may use *vous* and the superior *tu*.
Professional equals	Both use *tu*, but older speakers (50-ish or over) may use *vous*.
Immediate family	Both use *tu*.
Distant relatives: e.g. second cousins, great aunts/uncles, etc.	Both use *tu*, but there is a tendency to use *vous* when older family members are involved.
Friends	Typically *tu* but older speakers (50-ish or over) may use *vous*. This does not necessarily indicate less warmth in the friendship.
Adults to young children	Adults use *tu* to young children up to early adolescence. When very young they will respond with *tu*, but as they grow older they are expected to learn when and where *vous* is required of them.
Teachers and pupils	Teachers typically use *tu* to children under 14 and *vous* to older pupils, but some teachers continue to use *tu*, either to express power over their pupils, or solidarity with them. The younger the teacher, the greater the likelihood that *tu* will be used. Pupils typically use *vous* to teachers, occasionally *tu*. Under tens are rarely expected to say *vous* to their teacher.
Students	Both use *tu* from the first meeting.

3.1.3 'Marked' use of *tu*

Certain social sub-groups have their own internal norms for the use of *tu* and polite *vous*. For example, in sports teams, in left-wing political parties, and in trade unions, *tu* is the generalized form of address.

There are also a number of contexts where the expected use of polite *vous* between speakers is not met, and the actual pronoun form used is *tu*. For example, a stranger approaching you in the street and using the *tu* form, where normally *vous* is expected, may create the impression of an unwanted degree of intimacy; or it may indicate arrogance or contempt. Other examples of such 'marked' use are:

> In street altercations, e.g. between motorists. The effect produced is one of insult.

> Police interrogating suspects use the *tu* form, but suspects are expected to reciprocate with the *vous* form. The effect produced is one of domination.

> As a special case of the use of *tu*, Protestants have always addressed God with the *tu* form, but Catholics have only done so since 1967; before that 'He' was addressed with the *vous* form.

3.1.4 Use of *il/ils* and *elle/elles*

The third person pronouns *il/ils* and *elle/elles* normally refer to people and things (both concrete and abstract) and the choice of which one to use is usually determined by the grammatical person, gender and number of the noun referred to:

> Qu'est-ce qu'il fait, le facteur? **Il** est en retard
> *What's the postman up to? He's late*

> **Il** est intéressant, ce livre
> *That book's interesting*

> Où est la directrice? **Elle** est en réunion
> *Where's the headmistress? She's in a meeting*

> **Elle** est intéressante, cette émission
> *That programme's interesting*

> Il n'y a plus d'abricots. **Ils** sont finis
> *There are no more apricots. They're finished*

> **Elles** sont dangereuses, ces falaises
> *These cliffs are dangerous*

3.1.5 Grammatical and real gender

With a handful of nouns, the real gender (sex) of the person referred to may determine the choice of third person pronouns *il/ils* or *elle/elles*. For example, *victime, recrue, sentinelle* are grammatically feminine nouns, but not all 'victims', 'recruits' or 'sentries' are necessarily female: *mannequin, recteur, conseiller municipal* are grammatically masculine nouns, but not all 'models', 'university Vice-Chancellors' or 'town councillors' are necessarily male. In such cases the **real** gender of the person referred to normally determines the choice of *il/ils* or *elle/elles*:

> Nous avons fait une nouvelle recrue. **Il** va se joindre à nous ce soir
> *We have gained a new recruit. He will join us this evening*

C'est une femme qui a été nommée recteur de l'université. **Elle** n'a que 42 ans
A woman has been appointed as Vice-Chancellor of the university. She is only 42

3.1.6 Grammatical and real number

With grammatically singular nouns that refer to more than one person or thing, the choice of pronoun is normally singular *il* or *elle*:

Quant au gouvernement, **il** ne prendra jamais les mesures qui s'imposent
As for the government, they will never take the necessary steps

Le comité va-t-**il** élire un nouveau président?
Will the committee elect a new chairperson?

En ce qui concerne l'équipe française, on peut dire qu'**elle** est en grande forme en ce moment
As for the French team, they are currently on top form

For collective nouns see Chapter 1.1.3.

3.1.7 Pronouns referring to groups of mixed gender

When a group (of people or things) of mixed gender is referred to, *ils* is the pronoun used. Compare:

Le directeur, son frère et son neveu? **Ils** sont tous les trois démissionnaires
The director, his brother and his nephew? All three are resigning

Louise, sa fille et sa petite-fille étaient dans la voiture. **Elles** sont toutes les trois mortes dans l'accident
Louise, her daughter and her granddaughter were in the car. All three died in the accident

with:

Louise, sa fille et son petit-fils étaient dans la voiture. **Ils** sont tous les trois morts dans l'accident
Louise, her daughter and her grandson were in the car. All three died in the accident

3.1.8 *ils* with arbitrary reference

Plural *ils* may be used to refer to an indefinite or arbitrary group of people:

Ils ont encore augmenté le prix de l'essence
They have put the price of petrol up again

Ils disent qu'il va y avoir de l'orage
They say that there will be a storm

Comment votent-**ils** par ici?
How do they vote around here?

3.1.9 Coordination of subject pronouns

When clauses containing unstressed subject pronouns are coordinated by *et, ou* or *ne . . . ni*, the second pronoun may be deleted:

Elle se réveille et (elle) regarde l'horloge
She wakes up and looks at the clock

Je ne lis ni (je) n'écris à présent
I am neither reading nor writing at the moment

When the verb is accompanied by auxiliary *avoir* or *être*, if the subject pronoun is deleted, the auxiliary must be too:

Il a chanté et (il a) dansé
(NOT *Il a chanté et a dansé)
He sang and danced

3.1.10 Use of *on*

on can refer to a person or people whose identity is not really known:

On dit que la première année de mariage est la plus difficile
People say that the first year of marriage is the most difficult

C'est une région où l'**on** continue de mourir davantage de maladies de coeur
que du cancer
It is an area where more people continue to die from heart disease than from cancer

On n'en fabrique plus
They don't make them any more

On m'a volé tout mon argent
Someone stole all my money

3.1.11 *on* as an alternative to the English passive

A construction with *on* can often be used where a passive is used in English:

On croyait la crise du logement définitivement réglée
The housing shortage was definitely thought to be over

On ne soupçonne guère le véritable rôle économique joué par les enfants
The real economic role that children play is thoroughly underestimated

On sait qu'il a eu des démêlés avec la police, mais **on** ne sait pas pourquoi
It is well known that he was once in trouble with the police, but it is not known why

(For the passive see Chapter 8.6.)

3.1.12 *on* as an equivalent for English 'you'

on can sometimes be used where English uses 'you' and French could use *vous*
or *tu*:

Est-il vrai qu'**on** distingue un Américain d'un Français à cent mètres?
Is it true you can tell an American from a Frenchman at a hundred metres?

Avec le moteur devant, **on** est au moins protégé
With the engine at the front you are at least protected

Comment savoir si **on** est doué pour la musique si l'**on** n'a jamais essayé?
How do you know whether you have a talent for music if you've never tried it?

3.1.13 *on* as an equivalent for *nous*

on can often be used as a synonym for *nous*:

On avait d'abord tenté l'opération inverse
We had at first taken the opposite tack

On sait à quelles extrémités peuvent arriver certaines personnes
We know to what extremes some people can go

On s'y est habitué depuis longtemps
We have been used to it for a long time

The use of *on* instead of *nous* is very frequent in informal spoken French:

Pourquoi **on** rentre pas à la maison?
Why don't we go home?

> **On** avait chanté la Marseillaise, tu te souviens pas?
> *We sang the Marseillaise, don't you remember?*

> **On** y va?
> *Shall we go?*

NB: When *on* refers to more than one person, many writers make any adjective or past participle which should indicate agreement show plural agreement. Not all native speakers agree with this. Teachers, for instance, require the masculine singular agreement to be observed.

> On est tous très fatigués
> *We are all very tired*

> Après on est tous allés dans une boîte de nuit
> *Afterwards we all went to a night-club*

3.1.14 Use of *l'on*

l'on is sometimes used in French for *on* when it follows a word ending in a vowel (like *et, ou, qui, que, si,* etc). This is a feature of written, rather than spoken, French:

> Comment savoir si **l'on** ne demande pas?
> *How can you know if you don't ask?*

> Il faut savoir choisir l'homme avec qui **l'on** s'engage pour la vie
> *You have to be careful choosing the man to whom you will commit your life*

The use of *l'* is not obligatory, however.

3.1.15 Use of *ce, cela, ça* as neutral pronouns

When *ce, cela* and *ça* are used as neutral pronouns they normally refer to events, actions, states or general classes of people or things:

> Vous viendrez dîner ce soir. **C'est** prévu.
> *Come to dinner this evening. It's all taken care of*
> (*c'* referring to 'coming to dinner')

> L'élection d'un nouveau président aura lieu en mars. **Ce** sera l'occasion pour le pays de s'exprimer
> *The election of a new president takes place in March. The country will be able to have its say*
> (*ce* referring to 'the election of a president')

> L'extérieur, **ce** n'est rien. Il faudrait voir l'intérieur
> *The outside is nothing. You should see the inside*
> (*ce* referring to the 'state of the outside')

NB: *il* cannot usually be used to refer to events. actions, states or general classes.

While *ce* is normally used with *être* (see also 3.1.23), *cela* and *ça* are used with other verbs:

> Partez à l'étranger. **Cela** vous fera du bien
> *Travel abroad. It will do you good*
> (*cela* referring to 'travelling abroad')

> Ils y sont allés un peu fort. **Cela** risque de faire du bruit
> *They went a bit far. It is likely to cause a stir*
> (*cela* referring to 'having gone a bit far')

J'essayais pas d'être premier. Ça m'intéressait pas.
I wasn't trying to come first. It didn't interest me.
(*ça* referring to coming first)

cela tends to be used in written French, or for emphasizing the subject in spoken French; *ça* is widely used as the unstressed subject in the spoken language.

Written French:

Plus de la moitié de la population adulte d'aujourd'hui a étudié le latin à l'école. **Cela** montre bien le décalage entre les formations scolaires et les activités professionnelles
More than half of today's adults studied Latin at school. This clearly shows the gap that exists between school education and professional activity

3 millions de Français ne savent pas lire. **Cela** incite à poser des questions sur l'efficacité du système éducatif
3 million French people cannot read. This raises questions about the effectiveness of the educational system

Spoken French:

Elle est heureuse. **Ça** se voit
She's happy. You can tell just from looking at her

Ça lui servira de leçon
That'll teach him

3.1.16 Comparing neutral *ce, cela, ça* with personal *il/elle, ils/elles*
il/ils and *elle/elles* refer to people and things (both concrete and abstract). *ce, cela, ça* refer to events, actions, states or general classes of phenomena. Compare:

C'est bon, le vin
Wine is good
(refers to wine in general)

Il est bon, le vin
The wine is good
(refers to a specific example of wine)

C'est lourd, cette valise
This suitcase is heavy
(implies that it is heavy to carry)

Elle est lourde, cette valise
This suitcase is heavy
(refers to the object itself)

J'adore m'occuper des enfants. **C'**est si câlin à cet âge-là
I love looking after children. They're so cuddly when they're that age
(*ce* referring to small children in general)

J'adore m'occuper de tes enfants. **Ils** sont si câlins
I love looking after your children. They're so cuddly
(referring to specific small children)

In informal spoken French many speakers use *ça* where *il/ils, elle/elles* are used in more formal spoken and written French:

J'ai astiqué mes casseroles. Regardez comme **ça** brille!
I gave my pans a scrub. Look how shiny they are!

Les pintades, **ça** couche souvent dehors
Guinea-fowl often sleep outside

Tu sais, ces gens-là, **ça** boit
You know, those people, they like their drink

NB: Because this usage is regarded as a feature of informal spoken French, the foreign learner should avoid using it in the written language.

3.1.17 Use of *il, ce, cela* and *ça* as impersonal pronouns

The clearest use of impersonal subject pronouns is with verbs where *il, ce, cela* and *ça* simply mark the subject position without referring to someone or something elsewhere in the conversation or text:

Il pleut	*It's raining*
Il neige	*It's snowing*
Il fait du vent	*It's windy*

C'est difficile de le joindre au téléphone
It's difficult to reach him by phone

C'est dommage qu'elle ne soit pas venue
It's a pity that she didn't come

Cela inquiète ma mère de les savoir dehors par ce temps
It worries my mother to know that they are out in this weather

Ça m'étonne qu'elle n'ait rien dit
It amazes me that she said nothing

In these cases *il, ce, cela, ça* express very little meaning (indeed, in some languages impersonal constructions are characterized by the absence of a subject, for example Spanish *Llueve* '(it) is raining'). This impersonal use of *il, ce, cela, ça* in French corresponds to the impersonal use of 'it', and sometimes `there' in English.

3.1.18 Impersonal subject restricted to *il*

Some impersonal verbs and verbal expressions always take impersonal subject *il* (and NOT *ce, cela* or *ça*):

Expressions of clock time do:

Quelle heure est-**il**?	**Il** est 6 heures
What time is it?	*It's 6 o'clock*
Il est midi	
It's noon	

As do the related time expressions:

Il est temps de, que ...	*It's time to, that ...*
Il est tard	*It's late*

Certain frequently occurring constructions also take impersonal *il*:

- **Il** y a (quelqu'un, deux hommes à la porte)
  There is/are (somebody, two men at the door)

Il est question de (lui interdire l'accès aux enfants)
There's talk of (stopping her seeing the children)

Il s'agit de (refaire les fondations)
It's a question of (rebuilding the foundations)

Il faut (se lever tôt le matin)
You've got to (get up early in the morning)

Il reste (des phénomènes qu'il est difficile de catégoriser)
There remain (phenomena which it is difficult to classify)

Il convient (de faire le point)
It is advisable (to take stock)

Il vaut mieux (rester chez vous)
It's better (for you to stay at home)

NB: *Il s'agit de* is a frequently-used impersonal construction which learners often misuse because one way of translating it into English can be as 'X is about Y', e.g. *Il s'agit dans ce roman d'une jeune fille* 'This novel is about a girl'. *Il s'agit de* can never have a personal subject, however:

NOT *Ce roman s'agit d'une jeune fille*

By contrast, the verb *agir* 'to act' must have a personal subject:

Pierre agit de façon bizarre
Pierre is acting in a strange way

Il agit en ami
He is acting as a friend

(For impersonal verbs see also Chapter 8.8.)

3.1.19 *il* or *ça* with impersonal verbs

Some impersonal verbs and verbal expressions have *il* as subject in written French, but *il* or *ça* may occur in spoken French; *ça* is used in informal styles.

Some weather verbs behave in this way:

Il pleut, ça pleut	*It's raining*
Il neige, ça neige	*It's snowing*
Il gèle, ça gèle	*It's freezing*
Il bruine, ça bruine	*It's drizzling*

Constructions not listed under 3.1.18 also behave in this way:

Il/ça se peut que la carte soit démagnétisée
Perhaps the card has lost its magnetism

Il/ça n'empêche pas qu'elle ait raison
That doesn't stop her from being right

Il/ça suffit de voir ce qui se passe
You only have to see what's happening

3.1.20 *il/ça* alternating with clauses or infinitives as subjects

Some impersonal verbs allow both *il* (or *ça* in informal spoken French) and a clause or infinitive as a subject:

Il convient à ma mère que les Durand habitent à côté *or*
Que les Durand habitent à côté convient à ma mère
It suits my mother to have the Durands living next door

Ça me fait peur d'y aller la nuit *or*
D'y aller la nuit me fait peur
I am afraid to go there at night

Others:

Il/ça déplaît à Olivier de/que . . .
It displeases Oliver to/that . . .

Il/ça fait mal à Arnaud de/que . . .
It hurts Arnaud to/that . . .

Il/ça fait plaisir à Céline de/que . . .
It gives Céline pleasure to/that . . .

Il/ça va à Romain de/que . . .
It suits Romain to/that . . .

Il/ça arrive à Béatrice de/que . . .
It sometimes happens to Béatrice that . . .

Verbs of this type which have **direct objects,** as opposed to indirect objects
introduced by *à*, always take the impersonal subject *cela* (or *ça* in informal
spoken French) and NOT *il:*

Cela/ça amuse Pierre qu'elle fasse de la planche à voile *or*
Qu'elle fasse de la planche à voile amuse Pierre
It amuses Pierre that she goes wind-surfing

Cela/ça ennuie Georges de devoir recommencer *or*
De devoir recommencer ennuie Georges
George finds it annoying to have to start again

Cela/ça attriste Antoine de/que ...	... *saddens* ...
Cela/ça effraye Véronique de/que ...	... *frightens* ...
Cela/ça énerve Joël de/que ...	... *annoys* ...
Cela/ça épuise Fabien de/que ...	... *exhausts* ...
Cela/ça étonne Jérôme de/que ...	... *astonishes* ...
Cela/ça fatigue Charlotte de/que ...	... *tires* ...
Cela/ça gêne Violette de/que ...	... *embarrasses* ...
Cela/ça inquiète Maud de/que ...	... *worries* ...
Cela/ça intéresse Rachel de/que ...	... *interests* ...
Cela/ça irrite Sophie de/que ...	... *irritates* ...

3.1.21 *il/ça* alternating with noun phrase subjects

A handful of common verbs alternate between an impersonal construction with
il (or *ça* in informal spoken French) and a personal construction with a noun
phrase subject:

Il semble que Pierre soit passé lundi *or*
Pierre semble être passé lundi
It seems that Pierre came round on Monday

Il apparaît que vous êtes le dindon de la farce *or*
Vous apparaissez comme étant le dindon de la farce
It seems that you have been made a fool of

Il s'est avéré que Sophie était consciencieuse *or*
Sophie s'est avérée consciencieuse
It turned out that Sophie was conscientious

3.1.22 Choosing between *il est* and *c'est*

il est versus *c'est* with reference to professions, nationality or social status

There are two ways of indicating a person's profession, nationality or social status: *il/ils* and *elle/elles* are used with the verbs *être, devenir, rester* and a noun **without** an article:

Il est médecin	*He is a doctor*
Elle est devenue professeur	*She became a teacher*
Elles sont avocates	*They are lawyers*
Elle est toujours restée femme au foyer	*She always was a housewife*
Ils restent hollandais, bien qu'ils aient quitté les Pays-Bas il y a 20 ans	
They remain Dutch, although they left the Netherlands 20 years ago	

ce is used when the noun is preceded by a determiner (*un, une, le, la*, etc.):

C'est un Russe	*He's a Russian*
C'est un avocat	*He's a lawyer*

When the noun is modified, a determiner is required and therefore *ce* (not *il/elle*) must be used:

C'est un médecin connu	*He's a famous doctor*
C'est un boxeur professionnel	*He's a professional boxer*
C'est une avocate qui connaît le droit anglais	*She's a lawyer who knows English law*
C'est un professeur de Toulouse	*He's a teacher from Toulouse*

il est versus *c'est* in more general contexts

When *être* is followed by anything other than an adjective, *ce* is the pronoun to use, NOT *il*:

C'est un plaisir	(NOT *il est un plaisir)
It's a pleasure	
C'est Marie	(NOT *il, *elle est Marie)
It's Marie	
C'était en été	(NOT *il était en été)
It was in summer	
Ce sera pour elle	
It'll be for her	

il est versus *c'est* when *être* is followed by an adjective alone

When *être* is followed by an adjective alone, both *il* and *ce* are possible but there is a difference in meaning. In these examples, *il* is personal but *ce* is impersonal or neutral:

Il est stupide	will normally mean	*He is stupid*
C'est stupide	will normally mean	*That's silly*
Il est curieux	will normally mean	*He's inquisitive*
C'est curieux	will normally mean	*That's odd*

Il est incroyable   will normally mean   *He's amazing*
C'est incroyable   will normally mean   *That's unbelievable*

il est versus *c'est* when *être* is followed by adjective + clause or infinitive

But when *être* is followed by an adjective which is itself followed by a clause or infinitive, both *il* and *ce* are possible and both are then used in an impersonal sense:

Il/c'est difficile de formuler une politique
It's difficult to formulate a policy

Il/c'est intéressant d'observer les passants
It's interesting to watch the passers-by

Il/c'est impossible d'ouvrir ces huîtres
It's impossible to open these oysters

Some grammars will sometimes claim that *il est* is the only form to use in these constructions, but *c'est* is widely used in all spoken styles of French, and is often also found in these constructions in the written language.

Other common adjectives which behave in this way are:

agréable	*fun*	intéressant	*interesting*
bon	*good*	inutile	*useless*
commode	*convenient*	mauvais	*bad*
dangereux	*dangerous*	nécessaire	*necessary*
difficile	*difficult*	pénible	*tiresome*
étrange	*odd*	périlleux	*perilous*
évident	*obvious*	possible	*possible*
facile	*easy*	peu probable	*unlikely*
important	*important*	utile	*useful*
impossible	*impossible*	vrai	*true*
insupportable	*intolerable*		

NB: In the impersonal constructions illustrated above, the preposition which links the adjective to the following infinitive is always *de*.

(For discussion of adjective + infinitive constructions see Chapter 12.7.)

il versus *ce* used with *être* + adjective + *à*

In the examples immediately above, *il* and *ce* are impersonal. They are used like 'it' and 'there' in English without reference to anything else in the conversation or text: in these cases the adjective is linked to the infinitive by the preposition *de*. But *il* can also be used as a personal pronoun, and *ce* as a neutral pronoun in similar constructions when the preposition linking the adjective and the infinitive is *à*:

Leur politique est difficile **à** accepter
(Leur politique), elle est difficile **à** accepter
(Leur politique), c'est difficile **à** accepter

Ce document est intéressant **à** analyser
(Ce document), il est intéressant **à** analyser
(Ce document), c'est intéressant **à** analyser

Here *il, elle* and *ce* refer to something mentioned elsewhere in the conversation or text (in this case to *leur politique, ce document*).

(For more on these constructions see Chapter 12.7.)

3.1.23 ce, and compound forms of être

ce can be used with various compound forms of *être*, like *ce doit être, ce peut être, ç'a été*:

> Ce pourrait être un facteur important
> *It could be an important factor*

> Ce doit être Marianne
> *It must be Marianne*

> Ç'aurait été trop
> *It would have been too much*

When the phrase following *être* in this construction is plural, some grammars suggest that the verb should be in the third person plural form:

> Ce sont mes amis
> *It's my friends*

> Ce devraient être eux/elles
> *It should be them*

But many speakers use *c'est* etc. in these cases:

> C'est mes amis
> Ce doit être eux/elles

When first or second person plural pronouns *nous* or *vous* follow *être* in these constructions, the verb is always singular:

> C'est vous, c'est nous
> *It's you, it's us*

3.2 Object pronouns

Correctly identifying the direct and indirect objects in English and French

Many of the problems which learners have with pronouns are not caused by a failure to know what the pronouns are, but by a failure to recognize which pronoun French requires in a particular structure. This is especially true of indirect object pronouns. The structure of English and French verbs, even when they have similar meanings, is not necessarily the same: in a given sentence it is **essential** to know whether the object is direct or indirect in relation to the **French** verb and NOT the English verb.

Thus, in the English sentence 'They advised Stéphane to leave', 'Stéphane' is the **direct object** of 'advised', and with a pronoun the sentence becomes 'They advised **him** to leave'. But in the French equivalent – *Ils ont conseillé à Stéphane de partir* – Stéphane is the **indirect object** of *conseiller*. With a pronoun the French sentence becomes:

> Ils **lui** ont conseillé de partir

For a full list of verbs which behave differently with respect to objects in English and French see Chapter 8.

TABLE 3.C *Summary table of object pronouns*

Person	Singular		Plural	
First person Direct and indirect	me	*(to) me*	nous	*(to) us*
Second person Direct and indirect	te	*(to) you*	vous	*(to) you* plural or polite
Third person Direct 　masculine 　feminine	le la	*him, it* *her, it*	les les	*them* *them*
neutral	le	*it*	——	
Indirect 　masculine 　feminine	lui lui	*to him, to it* *to her, to it*	leur leur	*to them* *to them*
Direct and indirect 　reflexive, 　reciprocal, 　benefactive	se	*(to) oneself*	se	*(to) themselves*

TABLE 3.D y *and* en

Pronoun	Stands in the place of
y	a phrase introduced by *à, en, dans, sur* e.g. *à Paris, en ville, dans sa chambre*
en	a phrase which begins with *de* e.g. *de son idée*

3.2.1 Direct object and indirect object pronouns: differences between English and French

The following common French verbs take **indirect object pronouns**; learners often treat them as if they required direct object pronouns, perhaps because their English equivalents take direct objects:

> Sa sœur **lui** a appris à parler espagnol
> *His sister taught him to speak Spanish*
> (apprendre **à** qn à faire qc)

> Luc **leur** a conseillé de se taire
> *Luc advised them to be quiet*
> (conseiller **à** qn de faire qc)

Sa mère **lui** défendait de fumer à la maison
Her mother used to forbid her to smoke at home
(défendre **à** qn de faire qc)

Le film **lui** a (dé)plu
He (dis)liked the film
((dé)plaire **à** qn)

Elle **lui** manque
He misses her
(manquer **à** qn)

There are several verb constructions which tend to give rise to this problem, each slightly different.

Verbs followed by: ... *à quelqu'un*:

... lui a téléphoné	*... phoned him*
... lui a survécu	*... outlived her*
... lui a (dés)obéi	*... (dis)obeyed her*
... lui a nui	*... disadvantaged him*
... lui ressemble	*... looks like him*

Verbs followed by: ... *quelque chose à quelqu'un*:

... lui a passé le sel	*... passed her the salt*
... lui a permis du repos	*... allowed him some rest*
... lui a promis une lettre	*... promised her a letter*
... lui a reproché son attitude	*... criticized her attitude*
... lui a enseigné le chant	*... taught him to sing*
... lui a donné un cadeau	*... gave her a present*
... lui a envoyé un colis	*... sent her a package*
... lui a offert un whisky	*... offered her a whisky*

Verbs followed by: ... *à quelqu'un de faire quelque chose*:

... lui a ordonné de signer	*... ordered him to sign*
... lui a dit de se taire	*... told him to shut up*
... lui a demandé de partir	*... asked him to leave*
... lui a permis de l'acheter	*... allowed her to buy it*

The following common French verbs take **direct objects**; learners often treat them as if they required indirect objects, perhaps because of a confusion over the status of *à* (or sometimes *de*) which these verbs require when they are followed by an infinitive:

Je **l'**ai aidé à changer la roue
I helped him to change the wheel

Le professeur **l'**avait encouragé à participer
The teacher had encouraged him to take part

Je **les** ai persuadés de venir
I persuaded them to come

Others:

... l'a contraint à rester	*... forced him to stay*
... l'a dissuadée	*... dissuaded her*
... l'a empêché de courir	*... stopped him from running*
... l'a forcée à rester	*... forced her to stay*

... l'a invité à dîner	*... invited him to dinner*
... l'a menacée	*... threatened her*
... l'a obligé à parler	*... forced him to talk*
... l'a remerciée	*... thanked her*

3.2.2 Position of direct and indirect object pronouns

Direct and indirect object pronouns are closely linked with the verb to which they are most closely related in declarative, negative and interrogative sentences.

When the verb is a **main verb** they appear immediately before it:

L'Etat **me** paie	*The state pays me*
Les gens ne **me** remarquent pas	*People don't notice me*
Elle **le** croit	*She believes it*
A son âge, vous ne **la** referez pas	*You won't change her, at her age*
Il **lui** a soufflé quelques mots	*He whispered a few words to her*
Tu **me** donnes une idée	*You've given me an idea*
Ça **leur** apprendra à mentir	*That will teach them to lie*

When the verb is accompanied by the **auxiliary** verbs *avoir* or *être*, direct and indirect object pronouns appear immediately before the auxiliary:

Il **m'**a vu	*He saw me*
M'a-t-il vu?	*Did he see me?*
Vous ne **les** avez pas goûtés?	*Didn't you taste them?*
Il **lui** avait proposé un voyage	*He had suggested a trip to her*
Je **vous** suis très reconnaissant	*I am very grateful to you*

Il **leur** a raconté beaucoup d'histoires passionnantes
He told them a lot of fascinating stories

Nous **l'**avons déjà traduite, cette lettre
We have already translated this letter

NB: The past participle agrees with a preceding direct object in these cases, but not with the indirect object.

(For the agreement of the past participle: see Chapter 9.2 and 9.3.)

Note also that pronouns ending in *-e* (*me, te, se, le*) and *-a* (*la*) are shortened to the consonant alone before verbs beginning with a vowel: *elle m'aide, je t'ai déjà remercié, je te l'ai dit*, etc.

3.2.3 Position of object pronouns with infinitives

When the verb governing a direct or indirect object pronoun is an infinitive (including a compound infinitive made up of an auxiliary verb and a past participle), direct and indirect objects usually come in front of the infinitive:

On peut toujours **lui** téléphoner
He can always be reached by phone

Il pourra **te** voir demain
He will be able to see you tomorrow

Nous irons **leur** raconter l'histoire demain
We will go and tell them what happened tomorrow

Il pourrait bien **l'**avoir dit
He may well have said that

NB: When *à* or *de* followed by *le* or *les* come before the infinitive, these forms do NOT combine to form *au, du, aux, des*: *Je suis obligé **de les** aider.*

3.2.4 Position of object pronouns with *faire, laisser, envoyer* or verbs of perception + infinitive

Where the infinitive has *faire, laisser, envoyer* or perception verbs like *voir, regarder, entendre, sentir* in front of it, direct and indirect object pronouns appear before this other verb if they are understood as the **subject** of the infinitive:

Je **la** voyais venir
(who is coming? 'she' is, therefore *la* is the understood subject of *venir*)
I saw her coming

Sa mère **lui** a fait manger du potage
(who ate the soup? 'she' did, therefore *lui* is the understood subject of *manger*)
Her mother made her eat some soup

Elle **m'**a laissé pleurer
(who cried? 'I' did, therefore *me* is the understood subject of *pleurer*)
She let me cry

Note that the understood subject of the infinitive is realized as an indirect object if the infinitive has a direct object, but as a direct object if it does not. Compare:

Sa mère **lui** a fait manger du potage/Sa mère **le lui** a fait manger
(*du potage* is the direct object of *manger*)
Her mother made her eat some soup/Her mother made her eat it

Sa mère **l'**a fait manger
(*manger* has no direct object)
Her mother made her eat

If the direct or indirect object is understood as the **object** of the infinitive, it normally also comes before the other verb (although some native speakers may allow it to be placed directly in front of the infinitive):

Je **l'**ai envoyé chercher (*le* is the understood object of *chercher*)
I sent (someone) to look for him

Je **l'**ai entendu dire (*le* is the understood object of *dire*)
I have heard it said

Elle **le** fit remplacer (*le* is the understood object of *remplacer*)
She had it replaced

For the ordering of more than one pronoun with these constructions, see 3.2.32.

3.2.5 Position of object pronouns with imperatives

In affirmative imperatives direct and indirect object pronouns come immediately after the verb which governs them, and the pronouns *me, te* become the stressed forms *moi, toi*:

Prends-**les**!	*Take them!*
Suivez-**nous**!	*Follow us!*
Arrêtez-**les**!	*Stop them!*

> Ecoutez-**moi**! *Listen to me!*
> Tais-**toi**! *Shut up!*

BUT in negative imperatives direct and indirect object pronouns precede the verb:

> Ne **les** suivez pas! *Don't follow them!*
> Ne **la** mange pas! *Don't eat it!*
> Ne **me** fais pas rire! *Don't make me laugh!*

(See also Chapter 11.5 on imperatives.)

3.2.6 Position of object pronouns with *voici* and *voilà*

Direct object pronouns may appear before *voici* and *voilà*:

> **Nous** voici *Here we are*
> **Les** voilà *There they are*

3.2.7 Ambiguity of reference of *lui* and *leur*

Because the indirect object pronouns *lui*, *leur* can refer both to masculine and to feminine nouns they are inherently ambiguous:

> Je **lui** ai indiqué le chemin
> *I showed him* or *her the way*
>
> Pierre **leur** a parlé
> *Pierre spoke to them* (either male or female or mixed)

This ambiguity can be resolved if one wishes, however, by copying the pronoun with a stressed pronoun and a preposition:

> Je lui ai indiqué le chemin à **elle**/Je lui ai indiqué le chemin à **lui**
> Pierre leur a parlé à **elles**/Pierre leur a parlé à **eux**

3.2.8 Use of the neutral pronoun *le*

le, in addition to its function as a third person singular pronoun referring to masculine nouns, may also have a 'neutral' function when it refers to states, general ideas or whole propositions:

> Pour que nous vous remboursions vos frais de déplacement, il faut présenter des justificatifs, si vous **le** pouvez (*le* refers to 'justifying the expenditure')
> *For us to be able to pay your travelling expenses, you must prove you have spent the money, if you can*
>
> Vous n'êtes plus président, je **le** sais (*le* refers to 'no longer being the president')
> *You are no longer the president, I know*
>
> Je **le** répète: tu ne travailles pas assez (*le* refers to 'you're not doing enough work')
> *I'll say it again: you're not doing enough work*

In this usage neutral *le* is the object counterpart of the neutral subjects *ce, cela, ça* (see 3.1.15).

3.2.9 Use of neutral *le* where no equivalent exists in English

Sometimes neutral *le* is required in French where English normally has no object pronoun at all, typically where the verb *être* + adjective/identifying expression are involved:

N'ayez pas peur! J'étais en colère, mais je ne **le** suis plus
(*le* refers to 'being angry')
Don't be frightened! I was angry, but I'm not any more

Est-ce qu'elle est prête? Elle **le** sera dans un instant
(*le* refers to 'being ready')
Is she ready? She will be in a moment

Moi, je n'étais pas étonné, mais Myriam **l**'a été
(*le* refers to 'being surprised')
I wasn't surprised, but Myriam was

3.2.10 Wrong use of neutral *le* in phrases where 'it' occurs in English

The English constructions 'find it difficult to', 'consider it easy to', 'reckon it possible that', and similar cases, have French counterparts in which *le* must not appear. The verbs usually involved are *croire, penser, trouver, juger, estimer, considérer*:

Je trouve difficile de me faire des amis
I find it difficult to make friends

NOT *Je le trouve difficile de me faire des amis

Il considère important que tous ses amis soient prévenus
He considers it important that all his friends be notified

NOT *Il le considère important que tous ses amis soient prévenus

The *le* is absent in these cases because the construction is impersonal, and, while English requires 'it', French requires an absence of pronoun. Where the construction is personal (that is, where a person or thing is referred to), *le*, *la*, or *les* are required:

Je trouve ce livre difficile à comprendre
I find this book difficult to understand

Je le trouve difficile à comprendre
(*le* refers to 'the book')

J'ai trouvé le soliste impossible à écouter
I found I couldn't bear to listen to the soloist

Je l'ai trouvé impossible à écouter
(*le* refers to 'the soloist')

(For more on this construction see Chapter 12.7.)

3.2.11 Optional use of neutral *le*

Neutral *le* is optional in the following environments:
(a) With the verbs *croire, penser, dire, vouloir, savoir* when these are used as stock conversational responses to questions or statements by other people:

Ils sont heureux? Oui, je (**le**) pense
Are they happy? Yes, I think so

Est-ce que vous viendrez ce soir? Non, je ne (**le**) crois pas
Will you come this evening? No, I don't think so

Elle revient directement de Londres. Oui, je (**le**) sais
She has come straight back from London. Yes, I know

(b) In the second clause of a comparison (where the particle *ne* is also optional). Both are typical of formal written French:

> Il est autre que je **(ne)** **(le)** croyais
> *He is different from what I expected*

> Un abonnement est moins cher que vous **(ne)** **(le)** pensez
> *A subscription costs less than you think*

> A son âge, il faut admettre que Maurice est plus naïf qu'il **(ne)** devrait **(l')**être
> *When you realize how old he is, you have to admit that Maurice is more naïve than he should be*

3.2.12 Reflexive use of *me, te, se, nous, vous*

Where *me, te, se, nous, vous* refer to the subject of the verb to which they are attached, they are being used reflexively. This use can correspond to English 'my-, your-, him-, her-, it-, oneself; our-, your-, themselves':

> Michel adore **se** regarder dans les vitrines
> *Michel loves looking at himself in shop windows*

> Je **me** connais
> *I know myself*

> Vous **vous** critiquez trop
> *You are too critical of yourselves*

(See also Chapter 8.7.1.)

3.2.13 Reciprocal *se* and cases of potential ambiguity

When the subject is third person plural, *se* may also be interpreted as a 'reciprocal' pronoun, corresponding to English 'each other'. In some cases *se* is therefore ambiguous, having a 'reflexive' or 'reciprocal' interpretation, and the meaning may depend on the context:

> Les deux écrivains **s'**admirent depuis 20 ans

is most likely to be:

> *The two writers have admired each other for 20 years*

but could possibly be:

> *The two writers have (each) admired themselves for 20 years*

> Les deux amis **se** connaissent bien
> *The two friends know themselves* or *each other well*

(See also Chapter 8.7.5.)

3.2.14 Benefactive *me, te, se, nous, vous*

me, te, se, nous, vous may also be used to indicate that the subject 'benefits' from some action. This use, known as the 'benefactive', can often be paraphrased in English by 'for him-, her-, it-, oneself/themselves, etc.':

> Josée **s'**est acheté un nouvel ordinateur
> *Josée bought herself a new computer*

Jacques **s'**est commandé une bière
Jacques ordered himself a beer

J'ai hâte de rentrer et de **me** verser un Martini
I can't wait to get home and pour myself a Martini

Etienne et Madeleine **se** sont offert un baptême de l'air
Etienne and Madeleine treated themselves to a first flight

3.2.15 *se* as an alternative to an English passive
se may be used with a verb as an alternative to an English passive:

Un collant **se** lave en deux minutes
A pair of tights can be washed in two minutes

Le Gamay **se** boit frais
Gamay (light red wine) is best drunk chilled

L'uni **se** vend bien cet hiver
Plain colours are selling well this winter

This usage is restricted to special circumstances. The sentence must describe a state of affairs and not an action and the verb must not suggest through its tense that the action takes place in a limited time span.

(See also Chapter 8.7.6.)

3.2.16 *me, te, se, nous, vous* as part of certain verbs but with no specific meaning
me, te, se, nous, vous also normally accompany some verbs without any detectable reflexive, reciprocal or benefactive meaning:

Robert **s'**est évanoui
Robert fainted

Elle **se** souvient de son arrière-grand-père
She remembers her great-grandfather

La foule **s'**est éloignée
The crowd moved away

(For a list of common pronominal verbs in which *se* has no detectable reflexive, reciprocal or benefactive meaning, see Chapter 8.7.3.)

3.2.17 Emphasizing *me, te, se, nous, vous* by adding a pronoun + *même*
The reflexive and benefactive interpretations of *me, te, se, nous, vous* can be emphasized by the addition of one of the expressions *moi-même, toi-même, lui-même, elle-même, soi-même, eux-mêmes, elles-mêmes*, etc.:

Connais-**toi, toi-même**
Know thyself

Elle est grande maintenant: elle **s'**habille **elle-même**
She's a big girl now, she dresses herself

Puisque personne d'autre ne le fait, Suzette **s'**admire **elle-même**!
Since no-one else does so, Suzette admires herself!

De nos jours, malheureusement, il faut **se** soigner **soi-même**
Nowadays, unfortunately, you have to be your own doctor

3.2.18 Emphasizing the reciprocal use of *se* by adding *l'un l'autre*

The reciprocal interpretation of *se* can be made explicit by the addition of one of the phrases *l'un(e) l'autre*, *l'un(e) à l'autre*, *les un(e)s les autres*, *les un(e)s aux autres*, all with the meaning 'each other', 'one another'.

l'un(e) l'autre or *l'un(e) à l'autre* are used when the subject refers to just two people or things:

> Les deux boxeurs se regardaient fixement **l'un l'autre**
> *The two boxers were staring at each other*

> Mes deux sœurs se copient **l'une l'autre**
> *My two sisters copy one another*

les un(e)s les autres and *les un(e)s aux autres* are used when the subject refers to more than two people or things:

> Les équipiers se connaissent depuis longtemps **les uns les autres**
> *The team members have known each other for a long time*

> Les enfants se sont donné des petits cadeaux **les uns aux autres**
> *The children gave each other small presents*

3.2.19 Constructions which do not allow indirect object pronouns

A small set of verbs and adjectives in French look as if they take indirect objects because they are followed by the preposition *à*, but in fact they do not allow preceding *me*, *te*, *se*, *nous*, *vous*, *lui*, *leur*, and require stressed pronouns to follow *à*:

Il pense **à** Jean	Il pense **à lui** (NOT *Il lui pense)
He is thinking of John	*He is thinking of him*
Il fait allusion **à** Marie	Il fait allusion **à elle** (NOT *Il lui fait allusion)
He is referring to Marie	*He is referring to her*
Elle aura affaire **à** Henri	Elle aura affaire **à lui** (NOT *Elle lui aura affaire)
She will have to deal with Henri	*She will have to deal with him*
Ce sac est **à** Julien	Ce sac est **à lui** (NOT *Ce sac lui est)
This bag is Julien's	*This bag is his*

The explanation for this behaviour seems to be that *à* can have two functions: to introduce indirect objects, and as an ordinary preposition. In the above examples, *à* is a preposition. Since *lui, leur* can only correspond to indirect objects *lui, leur* are not possible in these cases – only stressed pronouns can be used (see 3.3).

Other common verbs followed by *à* which behave similarly are:

en appeler à	*appeal to*
faire appel à	*appeal to*
avoir recours à	*have recourse to*
recourir à	*have recourse to*
faire attention à	*pay attention to*
faire allusion à	*allude to*
s'habituer à	*get used to*
revenir à	*come back to*

rêver à	*dream of*
songer à	*think of*
tenir à	*be fond of*
venir à	*come to*

The set of verbs which behave in this way is quite small. We have listed most of them here.

When the phrase introduced by *à* in these cases refers to things, rather than people, pre-verbal *y* may replace it. (See 3.2.21 and 3.2.23.)

Verbs like these can be made reflexive or reciprocal by adding the appropriate forms *lui(-même)*, *elle(-même)*, etc., or *l'un l'autre*, etc.:

Il pense à lui(-même)
He is thinking of himself

Elles auront affaire les unes aux autres
They will have to deal with each other

3.2.20 Indirect object pronouns used in possessive constructions with body parts

The indirect object pronouns are used in a possessive construction in French with 'body parts' where English would use possessive determiners (like 'my', 'your', 'his', 'her', etc.):

On **lui** a cassé **le** bras
They broke his arm

Elle **s'**était coupé **le** doigt
She had cut her finger

La sueur **me** coulait dans **le** dos
Sweat was running down my back

However, the indirect object construction is not possible with verbs which do not describe actions:

Elle **lui** lave le visage
She is washing his face

BUT NOT: RATHER:

*Elle **lui** aime le visage   Elle aime *son* visage
She likes his face

This construction is also normally impossible with non-body-parts. However, it can be found in some regional varieties of French:

Elle **lui** a cassé le magnétoscope
She broke his video recorder

(See also Chapter 2.2.8 and 8.7.2.)

3.2.21 Use of y

y usually plays the same role in sentences as phrases which follow the verb and are introduced by prepositions like *à, en, dans, sur, sous*, etc.:

Je vais à Paris demain	J'**y** vais demain
I am going to Paris tomorrow	*I'm going there tomorrow*
Elle vit dans une grande maison	Elle **y** vit
She lives in a large house	*She lives there*
Il a écrit son nom sur le cahier	Il **y** a écrit son nom
He wrote his name on the book	*He wrote his name there*

Although *y* can generally replace any phrase of this type, both concrete and abstract (as in the examples below), it is usually restricted to non-animate entities:

Je pense souvent à la retraite
I often think about retirement
J'**y** pense souvent

Elle est fidèle à ses principes
She is faithful to her principles
Elle **y** est fidèle

Nous sommes entrés dans le débat
We joined in the debate
Nous **y** sommes entrés

3.2.22 Non-specific use of y

In a number of common constructions, *y* is used without a very specific meaning being attached to it:

Pensez-**y**!	*Think about it!*
Je n'**y** suis pour rien	*It's nothing to do with me*
J'**y** suis, j'**y** reste	*Here I am and here I stay*
Il **y** a ...	*There is ... there are ...*

3.2.23 Use of y in constructions where à does not introduce an indirect object

y is normally used to refer to non-human objects which occur with verbs like *penser à* where *à* does not introduce an indirect object (see 3.2.19):

Je pense à la guerre	*I'm thinking of the war*
With a pronoun:	
J'**y** pense	*I'm thinking of it*
Je tiens à mes idées	*I'm sticking to my ideas*
J'**y** tiens	*I'm sticking to them*
Je ferai très attention à vos affaires	*I'll look after your belongings very carefully*
J'**y** ferai très attention	*I'll look after them carefully*

y can also be found on rare occasions referring to people with such verbs: *J'y pense* 'I'm thinking of him'.

3.2.24 Use of en

en is the pronoun used to replace phrases introduced by *de* which follow the verb. Where these include a noun, *en* can refer to both human and non-human nouns:

Il a déjà parlé de son idée	Il **en** a déjà parlé
He has already spoken about his idea	*He has already spoken about it*
Il a empêché Jean-Pierre de travailler	Il l'**en** a empêché
He stopped Jean-Pierre working	*He stopped him doing it*
Mémère s'occupe des enfants	Mémère s'**en** occupe
Grandma is looking after the children	*Grandma is looking after them*
Christine est fière de son frère	Christine **en** est fière
Christine is proud of her brother	*Christine is proud of him*

In spoken French, where people are referred to, it is quite likely that a stressed pronoun following *de* will be used instead (see 3.3.3):

> Mémère s'occupe d'eux
> Christine est fière de lui

NB: An exception to the generalization that *en* can replace phrases introduced by *de* is those verbs, such as *permettre*, *défendre* and *interdire*, with a construction using . . . *à quelqu'un de faire quelque chose*. The infinitive clause is treated as a direct object:

> Elle a permis à Jean-Marie d'emprunter sa voiture
> *She allowed Jean-Marie to borrow her car*
>
> Elle **le** lui a permis (*le* means 'to borrow the car')
> *She allowed him to do it*
>
> Il a défendu à Suzanne de sortir ce soir
> *He forbade Suzanne to go out this evening*
>
> Il **le** lui a défendu (*le* means 'to go out this evening')
> *He forbade her to do it*

3.2.25 Use of *en* with numerals and quantifiers

It is important to use *en* when numerals (*deux, trois, une dizaine, une douzaine*, etc.) and quantifiers (*beaucoup, trop, la plupart*, etc.) are on their own after a verb. In English a pronoun is normally absent in these cases, but in French *en* is obligatory:

J'ai acheté une douzaine de roses	J'**en** ai acheté une douzaine
I bought a dozen roses	*I bought a dozen*
Il a commandé une douzaine d'huîtres	Il **en** a commandé une douzaine
He ordered a dozen oysters	*He ordered a dozen*
Elle produit beaucoup de documents	Elle **en** produit beaucoup
She produces a lot of papers	*She produces a lot*
J'ai acheté dix roses	J'**en** ai acheté dix
I bought ten roses	*I bought ten*
Elle a cueilli plusieurs tomates	Elle **en** a cueilli plusieurs
She picked several tomatoes	*She picked several*
Le comité avait demandé certains manuscrits	*The committee had asked for selected manuscripts*
Le comité **en** avait demandé certains	*The committee had asked for selected ones*

Note that *quelques* 'some, a few' belongs to this group, but when *en* is present *quelques* becomes *quelques-un(e)s*:

> On voyait quelques voiles au loin
> *We could see some sails in the distance*
> On **en** voyait quelques-unes au loin

(See also Chapter 6.9.2.)

3.2.26 y and *en* as an integral part of the verb structure

There is a small set of verbs in French which involve *y* or *en* as an integral part of their structure without any detectable specific meaning. Common examples are:

il **y** a . . .	*there is/are . . .*	Il **y** avait trois hommes
s'**en** aller	*go away*	Yvette s'**en** va
en imposer	*impress*	Elle **en** impose
s'**en** prendre à	*lay into*	Il s'**en** est pris à Jacques
en revenir	*get over*	Je n'**en** reviens pas
s'**en** tenir à	*stick to*	Tenez-vous-**en** aux faits
en vouloir à	*hold a grudge*	Je lui **en** veux
en voilà un	*there's someone*	**En** voilà un qui m'énerve
c'**en** est fait	*that's the end of*	C'**en** est fait de nos espoirs
en découdre	*to get into a fight*	Il est toujours prêt à en découdre
Où **en** sommes-nous?	*Where did we get to?*	

3.2.27 Position of y and *en* with negative infinitives

When *y* and *en* appear with negative infinitives, they normally appear directly adjacent to the infinitive, just as all other object pronouns do, but in formal written French they can split the negative:

Most frequent:

> Il vaudrait mieux ne pas **en** parler
> *It would be better not to speak of it*

Formal written French:

> Il vaudrait mieux n'**en** pas parler

Most frequent:

> Elle avait décidé de ne plus **y** penser
> *She had decided not to think about it any more*

Formal written French:

> Elle avait décidé de n'**y** plus penser

3.2.28 y and *en* in French where the English translation has no preposition

The foreign learner of French should remember that the use of *y* and *en* is determined by the presence of *à* or *de* in the **French** verb phrase, and should not be misled by an English equivalent which does not have a preposition, e.g.:

> *to use something* BUT se servir **de** qch
> *I often use it* = Je m'**en** sers souvent

to need something BUT avoir besoin **de** qch
I need it = J'**en** ai besoin

to give something up BUT renoncer **à** qch
I will give it up = J'**y** renoncerai

to enter/join BUT entrer **dans** qch
I joined the firm when I was twenty
Je suis entré **dans** l'entreprise quand j'avais vingt ans
J'**y** suis entré quand j'avais vingt ans

to doubt something BUT douter **de** qch
I doubt it = J'**en** doute

But see the note to 3.2.24.

3.2.29 Order of unstressed object pronouns when more than one is present

When two (and more rarely three) unstressed object pronouns appear before a verb, their order usually follows the pattern indicated in Table 3.E (known by generations of British schoolchildren as the 'soccer team' of pronouns with a ball (*en*), a goalkeeper (*y*), two full-backs (*lui*, *leur*), three midfield players (*le*, *la*, *les*) and five strikers (*me*, *te*, *se*, *nous*, *vous*):

TABLE 3.E *The order of unstressed object pronouns*

POSITION				
First	**Second**	**Third**	**Fourth**	**Fifth**
me te se nous vous	le la les	lui leur	y	en

Examples:

Il **me l'**a dit
He told me about it

Elle **le lui** a dit
She told him about it

Elle **nous les** a donnés
She gave them to us

Nous **le leur** avons dit
We told them about it

Susanne **m'en** a parlé
Susanne spoke to me about it

Nous **nous y** sommes beaucoup attachés
We have become very fond of it

Nous **y en** avons beaucoup trouvé
We found a lot of it there

Elle **les y** a souvent vus
She has often seen them there

Nous **leur en** avons promis beaucoup
We have promised a lot of those to them

Ne **me le** donne pas
Don't give it to me

Lui en auras-tu parlé avant demain?
Will you have spoken to him about it before tomorrow?

En voudriez-vous s'il **y en** avait?
Would you want some if there were any?

M'y accompagnerez-vous?
Will you come there with me?

Il **y en** a beaucoup
There are a lot of them

Nous **y en** avons trouvé plusieurs
We found several of them there

More rarely three pronouns may occur in combination where the first is a bene-factive (i.e. indicates that the action described by the verb is 'for the benefit' of the person in question), although this benefactive use is regarded as colloquial:

Tu vas **me le lui** écrire, et plus vite que ça!
You will write it to her for me, and be quick about it!

In formal French the benefactive interpretation would be expressed through other means:

Tu vas me le lui écrire = Tu vas me faire le plaisir de le lui écrire

3.2.30 Restrictions on possible combinations
Although Table 3.E describes in general the possible sequences of unstressed object pronouns, there are some restrictions on possible combinations. No pronoun from the first column (*me, te, se, nous, vous*) can normally appear in combination with a pronoun from the third column (*lui, leur*):

Whilst:	Je vous présenterai Eve-Marie *I will introduce Eve-Marie to you*
can, with two pronouns, become:	Je vous la présenterai *I will introduce her to you*
the sentence	Je vous présenterai à Eve-Marie *I will introduce you to Eve-Marie*
cannot become	*Je vous lui présenterai *I will introduce you to her*
Instead, you would use:	Je vous présenterai à **elle**
Whilst:	Je vous recommande Jean-Paul *I recommend Jean-Paul to you*

can, with two pronouns, become:	Je vous le recommande *I recommend him to you*
the sentence	Je vous recommande à Jean-Paul *I recommend you to Jean-Paul*
cannot become	*Je vous lui recommande *I will recommend you to him*
Instead, you would use:	Je vous recommande à **lui**

Nor can any pronouns from within the same column appear together:

Richard s'est joint à notre petit groupe
Richard joined our little group

cannot become:

*Il se nous est joint
NOR   *Il nous s'est joint

BUT ONLY:

Richard s'est joint à **nous**
Richard joined us

3.2.31 Order of multiple pronouns with imperatives

When two pronouns follow the verb in affirmative imperatives the ordering of pronouns is slightly different in that pronouns from the first column (*me, te, se, nous, vous*) follow pronouns from the second column (*le, la, les*). The other orders remain the same. Pronouns after imperatives are linked to the verb that governs them by hyphens:

Donne-le-moi *Give it to me*	(NOT *Donne-moi-le)
Passez-les-nous *Pass them over to us*	(NOT *Passez-nous-les)
Nettoyez-la-moi *Clean it for me*	(NOT *Nettoyez-moi-la)

NB: *Donne-moi-le, Passez-nous-les*, etc., are often heard in informal spoken French. The foreign learner should avoid them, however.

BUT:

Donne-le-lui
Give it to him

Passez-les-leur
Pass them over to them

Parlez-lui-en
Talk to him about it

The pronouns *me, te* become *moi, toi* in affirmative imperatives when they are the last pronoun in the sequence, but become *m'*, *t'* before *y* or *en*:

Donne-le-moi	*Give it to me*
Donne-m'en	*Give me some*

In these cases in informal spoken French it is not unusual to hear *moi, toi* retained with a linking *-z-*, but the learner should avoid this usage:

Parlez-moi-z-en	*Talk to me about it*
Accroche-toi-z-y	*Hang on to it*

In negative imperatives pronouns precede the verb, and the order of multiple pronouns is as indicated in the table:

Ne me le donne pas	*Don't give it to me*
Ne me les nettoyez jamais!	*Don't you ever clean them for me!* (i.e. I forbid you to …)

3.2.32 Position of more than one object pronoun with *faire* etc. + infinitive

When the verbs *faire, laisser, envoyer,* and perception verbs like *voir, entendre, regarder, sentir* are followed by an infinitive, there are different ways of placing two pronouns depending on which verb is being used.

If the verb is *faire*, both the pronouns come before *faire* (or *avoir* if *faire* is in a compound tense):

Je **les lui** ferai manger	Je **les lui** ai fait manger
I shall make him eat them	*I made him eat them*

If the verb is *laisser, envoyer* or one of the perception verbs, there are the two possibilities illustrated below:

Tu **les lui** laisses lire?	Tu **la** laisses **les** lire?
Will you let her read them?	*Will you let her read them?*
Je **le leur** ai entendu dire	Je **les** ai entendus **le** dire
I heard them say so	*I heard them say so*
Elle **me** l'envoya chercher	Elle **m'**envoya **le** chercher
She sent me to fetch it or	*She sent me to fetch it*
She had it fetched for me	

(For the structure of sentences involving *faire, laisser, envoyer* and perception verbs, see Chapter 12.3.8 and 12.3.9.)

3.2.33 Position of object pronouns with *devoir, pouvoir* + infinitives

After *devoir, pouvoir* (modal verbs) followed by an infinitive, object pronouns come before the infinitive:

Je dois **vous** l'avouer tout de suite
I must admit it to you immediately

Ils peuvent **nous** le signaler dès son arrivée
They can tell us about it as soon as he arrives

3.2.34 Object pronouns in coordinated clauses

When clauses containing unstressed object pronouns are coordinated by *et* or *ou*, it is normally necessary to repeat the pronoun in the second clause:

Cela **m'**agace et **m'**ennuie
That irritates and bores me

Je **les** ai préconisés et **les** ai proposés
I advocated and proposed them

Elle **l'**a aidé et **lui** a donné de l'argent
She helped him and gave him money

However, where the two pronouns are identical in form and attached to an auxiliary (*avoir* or *être*), the second pronoun and auxiliary may be deleted together:

Je les ai préconisés et proposés

The pronouns must be identical, however, and both the pronoun and the auxiliary must be deleted together. Hence the following are impossible:

NOT   *Je les ai préconisés et ai proposés
NOT   *Cela m'agace et ennuie
NOT   *Elle l'a aidé et donné de l'argent

In this last example it is not so much that the pronouns have different functions (*le* being a direct object and *lui* an indirect object), as that they differ in their surface forms. In the following example the first *me* is a direct object and the second *me* an indirect object, but the second *me* can be deleted with the auxiliary because the two *me*'s are identical in surface form:

Elle **m'**a aidé et **m'**a donné de l'argent
Elle m'a aidé et donné de l'argent

3.3 Stressed pronouns

TABLE 3.F *Summary table of stressed pronouns*

Person	Singular		Plural	
First person	moi	*me*	nous	*us*
Second person	toi	*you*	vous	*you* (plural or polite)
Third person masculine feminine neutral non-specific	 lui elle cela, ça soi	 *him* *her* *that* *oneself*	 eux elles	 *them* *them*

3.3.1 Use of stressed pronouns for emphasis

To highlight or emphasize a pronoun a common strategy is to 'double up' by the addition of a stressed pronoun. This can be done with:

Subject pronouns

Toi, tu le crois peut-être mais **lui, il** ne le croit pas
YOU might believe that, but HE doesn't

Moi, je veux travailler ce soir, mais lui pas
I want to work this evening, but HE doesn't

The stressed subject pronoun copy may equally appear at the end of the clause with the same effect:

Tu le crois peut-être, **toi**, mais **il** ne le croit pas, **lui**
Je veux travailler ce soir, **moi**, mais pas lui

When third person subject pronouns are highlighted or emphasized, the stressed pronoun alone may, on occasions, be used:

Lui pourrait le faire
HE could do it

Eux sauraient quoi dire
THEY would know what to say

This is not possible with first and second person pronouns:

NOT *Moi pourrais le faire (but Moi, je pourrais le faire)
NOT *Toi saurais quoi dire (but Toi, tu saurais quoi dire)

Only stressed pronouns and not unstressed subject pronouns can be separated from the tense-marked verb by adverbs or parenthetical expressions:

Lui, souvent, critique son professeur
(NOT *Il souvent critique son professeur)
He often criticizes his professor

Eux, par exemple, connaissent l'italien
(NOT *Ils, par exemple, connaissent l'italien)
They, for example, know Italian

(For stressed pronouns introduced by *c'est/ce sont*, sometimes followed by relative clauses, see Chapter 9.1.6.)

Object pronouns

A common strategy is to add a second, stressed pronoun at either the beginning or the end of the clause:

Lui, on **le** sait innocent
HE is known to be innocent

Elle se tient à l'écart, **elle**
SHE is keeping well out of it

Il **me** parle à **moi** (et pas à toi)
He confides in ME (and not in you)

Eux, on va **leur** demander de participer aux frais
We'll be asking THEM for a financial contribution

When the unstressed pronoun is an **indirect object,** the stressed pronoun being used to highlight it is preceded by *à* only when it is at the end of the clause:

Nous, elle nous a souvent écrit *or*
Elle nous a souvent écrit, **à nous**
She has often written to US

Moi, cela me ferait plaisir *or*
Cela me ferait plaisir, **à moi**
That would give ME pleasure

This 'doubling' of an unstressed pronoun by a stressed pronoun is also used to disambiguate ambiguous pronouns. In the following sentence *leur* is ambiguous between a masculine and a feminine interpretation:

Simon **leur** a dit de partir
Simon told them to leave

But it can be disambiguated by the addition of stressed pronouns:

Jean leur a dit à **eux** de partir
Jean leur a dit à **elles** de partir

3.3.2 Stressed pronouns standing alone

Stressed pronouns are normally used where the pronoun stands alone, or is in a phrase without a verb:

Qui est là?   **Moi** (NOT *je)
Qui tu as vu?   **Lui** (NOT *il)
C'est elle qui t'aidera, pas **moi** (NOT *pas je)

3.3.3 Stressed pronouns used as the object of a preposition

Stressed pronouns are the forms to use after all prepositions other than *à* (but see 3.2.19):

Je suis venu malgré **lui**	*I came in spite of him*
J'ai agi comme **elle**	*I acted as she did*
Ne le dites pas devant **eux**	*Don't say it in front of them*
Elle s'est assise à côté de **moi**	*She sat down next to me*
Je n'ai rien contre **elles**	*I have nothing against them*

Phrases introduced by *de* are normally pronominalized using *en*, but, when humans are referred to, *de* followed by a stressed pronoun is more usual:

Ma mère avait parlé de **lui**
My mother had spoken of him

3.3.4 Stressed pronouns with *même, aussi, seul, autres, tous* and numerals

Stressed pronouns are used in conjunction with the forms: *même, aussi, seul, autres, tous* and numerals (*deux, trois*, etc.):

Les enfants avaient préparé la salade **eux-mêmes**
The children had prepared the salad themselves

Lui aussi aura des problèmes
He too will have problems

Eux seuls pourraient la convaincre
They alone could persuade her

Nous autres Européens, on se comprend
We Europeans understand one another

> **Vous tous** irez prendre une douche
> *You will all go and have a shower*

NB: Some adjectives, like *fier* 'proud', *fidèle* 'faithful', *sûr* 'sure' are followed by a stressed pronoun alone, and not by *moi-même, lui-même, elles-mêmes*, etc., when used reflexively:

> Elle est très fière d'**elle**
> *She is very proud of herself*

> Je ne suis plus sûr de **moi**
> *I am not sure of myself any more*

3.3.5 Coordination of stressed pronouns

Only stressed pronouns can be coordinated with each other or with other nouns by *et, ou*:

> Marianne et **moi** (NOT *je) en avons discuté à fond
> *Marianne and I have discussed it in depth*

> **Lui** (NOT *il) et vous devrez vous mettre d'accord
> *You and he ought to come to an agreement*

> J'ai dit la même chose à vous et à **lui** (NOT *il)
> *I said the same thing to you and him*

NB: The form the verb takes with coordinated subjects involving stressed pronouns is determined in the following way:

(a) If one of the pronouns is first person, the verb will be first person:

> Lui et moi connaissons la famille
> *He and I know the family*

> Vous et moi connaissons la famille
> *You and I know the family*

(b) In the absence of a first person pronoun, if one of the pronouns is second person, the verb will be second person:

> Vous et lui connaissez la famille
> *You and he know the family*

(See also Chapter 9.1.1.)

A frequent way of expressing the notion 'somebody and I did X' is:

> Avec quelqu'un nous avons fait X

> Avec Christine nous avons ouvert les colis
> *Christine and I opened the parcels*

3.3.6 Stressed pronouns with *ne ... que* and *ni ... ni ... ne*

Stressed pronouns are used with the expressions *ne ... que*, and *ni ... ni ... ne*:

> Ce n'est que **lui**
> *It's only him*

> Francine ne connaît qu'**eux**
> *Francine only knows them*

Pour moi, il n'y a qu'**elle** qui compte
For me, she's the only one who matters

Ni **moi** ni **lui** ne saurons quoi faire
Neither I nor he will know what to do

3.3.7 Use of *soi*

soi is a non-specific stressed pronoun which is normally used either when it refers to non-specific persons or things, or indefinite phrases like *on, chacun, nul, aucun, personne, tout le monde*. It tends to be used after prepositions, with *-même*, and after *ne ... que*:

On pense à soi
People think of themselves

Pour une fois, personne ne songeait à soi
For once, no-one was thinking of themselves

On doit prendre la décision soi-même
One must take the decision oneself

3.4 Demonstrative pronouns

TABLE 3.G *Summary table of demonstrative pronouns*

		Proximate	**Non-proximate**
masc sing	celui *the one*	celui-ci *this one; the latter*	celui-là *that one; the former*
fem sing	celle *the one*	celle-ci *this one; the latter*	celle-là *that one; the former*
masc plur	ceux *the ones*	ceux-ci *these ones; the latter*	ceux-là *those ones; the former*
fem plur	celles *the ones*	celles-ci *these ones; the latter*	celles-là *those ones; the former*

Demonstrative pronouns are used where English uses 'the one'. They agree in gender with the noun they refer to:

Sur ce mur nous voyons deux **portraits. Celui** qui est à droite représente le premier propriétaire de la maison
On this wall we see two portraits. The one on the right is of the first owner of the house

Nous avons acheté trois **propriétés** en Dordogne. **Celle** qui est près de Bergerac sera revendue la première
We have bought three properties in the Dordogne. The one near Bergerac will be resold first

Demonstrative pronouns are used particularly frequently to 'head' relative clauses (see Chapter 15.1):

Ceux qui m'écoutent ce soir sauront que je n'ai rien à cacher
Those who are listening to me tonight will know that I have nothing to hide

Je ne peux rien faire pour vous: il faut vous adresser à **celui** qui est responsable de l'administration
I can do nothing for you: you must talk to the person who is responsible for administration

(For *ce qui, ce que, ce dont*, etc., see Chapter 15.9.)

3.4.1 Demonstrative pronouns with *-ci* and *-là*

The forms *celui-ci/celle-ci/ceux-ci/celles-ci* and *celui-là/celle-là/ceux-là/celles-là* translate English 'this one/these ones' and 'that one/those ones' respectively. These distinctions are mainly used in formal French:

Des deux tissus qui sont sur le comptoir, là-bas, il est évident que **celui-ci** est plus cher que **celui-là**
Of the two pieces of material on the counter over there, it's obvious that this one is dearer than that one

Pour moi tous les diamants se ressemblent. Mais **ceux-ci** coûtent deux fois plus cher que **ceux-là**
To me diamonds all look the same. But these ones here cost twice as much as those over there

NB: The pronouns with *-ci* can also mean 'the latter', and those with *-là* 'the former':

J'ai rencontré Pierre et Jean-Marie au café. **Celui-là** arrivait à l'instant d'un entretien avec le percepteur
I met Pierre and Jean-Marie at the café. The former had just come from a meeting with the tax inspector

Est-ce que vous désirez le flan ou la tarte aux pommes? **Celle-ci** sort directement du four
Do you want the custard pie or the apple tart? The latter has just come out of the oven

3.5 Possessive pronouns

TABLE 3.H *Summary table of possessive pronouns*

First person	msg	le mien	*mine*	le nôtre	*ours*
	fsg	la mienne		la nôtre	
	mpl	les miens		les nôtres	
	fpl	les miennes			
Second person	msg	le tien	*yours*	le vôtre	*yours*
	fsg	la tienne		la vôtre	
	mpl	les tiens		les vôtres	
	fpl	les tiennes			
Third person	msg	le sien	*his hers*	le leur	*theirs*
	fsg	la sienne		la leur	
	mpl	les siens			
	fpl	les siennes		les leurs	

Possessive pronouns agree in gender and number with a noun mentioned or implied elsewhere in the discourse:

Voici ta clef. Rends-moi **la mienne**
Here is your key. Give me back mine

Il portait un chapeau qui n'était pas **le sien**
He was wearing a hat which wasn't his

Ils ont emporté mes notes, mais j'ai gardé **les leurs**
They took away my notes, but I kept theirs

Tu ne peux pas prendre ceux-là, ils ne sont pas à nous. Ce sont **les leurs**
You can't take those, they don't belong to us. They are theirs.

Vos idées ne sont pas toujours **les nôtres**
Your ideas aren't always the same as ours

les siens also has the special meaning of 'one's family': *On travaille pour les siens* 'People work for their families', and *les nôtres* can mean 'with us', as in: *Elle n'était pas des nôtres* 'She wasn't with us'.

4

Adjectives

4.1 Adjectives modifying the noun

Most French adjectives follow the noun. But there is a small set which normally precede, and another set which regularly appear before and after the noun, often with a change of meaning.

4.1.1 Adjectives which normally follow the noun

Since the majority of French adjectives normally follow the noun, English speakers really only need to learn those which can precede. However, here are some typical classes of adjectives which almost always follow the noun:

Colour adjectives

bleu, gris, vert, blanc, noir, violet, etc.:

un manteau gris	une souris grise
a grey coat	*a grey mouse*
un gazon vert	une veste verte
a green lawn	*a green jacket*
un nuage noir	une robe noire
a black cloud	*a black dress*

Adjectives of nationality

français 'French', *britannique* 'British', *américain* 'American', *grec* 'Greek', *tunisien* 'Tunisian', etc.:

un livre français	de la bière française
a French book	*French beer*
du vin algérien	une ville algérienne
Algerian wine	*an Algerian town*
du fromage grec	une antiquité grecque
Greek cheese	*a Greek antique*

NB: Adjectives of nationality in French begin with a small letter, unlike English. When *français, britannique*, etc., are used as nouns, however, they begin with a capital letter. Compare: *Elle est française* 'She is French' with *C'est une Française* 'She is a Frenchwoman'. (See also 4.5 and Chapter 3.1.22.)

Adjectives of shape or form:

rond 'round', *carré* 'square', *rectangulaire* 'rectangular', *oval* 'oval', etc.:

un bureau carré	une boîte carrée
a square desk	*a square box*
un plateau rond	une table ronde
a round tray	*a round table*
un cadre rectangulaire	une cour rectangulaire
a rectangular frame	*a rectangular courtyard*

Adjectives describing religious affiliation

anglican 'Anglican', *catholique* 'Catholic', *musulman* 'Muslim', *protestant* 'Protestant', *orthodoxe* 'Orthodox', *juif* 'Jewish', etc.:

un prêtre catholique	une jeune fille catholique
a Catholic priest	*a Catholic girl*
un père juif	une mère juive
a Jewish father	*a Jewish mother*
un garçon musulman	une jeune fille musulmane
a Muslim boy	*a Muslim girl*

Adjectives which relate to a time or place of origin

une église médiévale	*a medieval church*
une ambiance citadine	*an urban atmosphere*
un paysage rural	*a rural landscape*
un accent campagnard	*a rustic accent*

Past and present participles

un mariage forcé	une grille rouillée
a forced marriage	*a rusty gate*
un élève brillant	une étoile brillante
a brilliant pupil	*a brilliant star*
un voyage fatigant	une voiture puissante
a tiring journey	*a powerful car*

NB: Present participles, which are formed by adding -*ant* to the first person plural stem of a verb (e.g. *amus-ons/amus**ant**, ralentiss-ons/ralentiss**ant**, dev-ons/dev**ant**,* etc.), can function both as a verb in a subordinate clause, and as an adjective. As verbs in subordinate clauses present participles are invariable (see Chapter 17.9.2):

En **enfilant** son manteau, elle a dit au revoir
Putting her coat on, she said goodbye

J'ai rencontré des touristes **prenant** l'air sur l'esplanade
I met some tourists taking a stroll along the promenade

As adjectives they agree in gender and number with the noun they modify, as in the examples above: *une étoile brillante,* (see Chapter 17.9.1).

A number of present participles are also spelled differently when they function as verbs in subordinate clauses, and when they are adjectives. Some common cases are:

Verb in subordinate clause		Adjective	
convainquant	*convincing*	convaincant	*convincing*
différant	*differing*	différent	*different*
équivalant	*being equivalent to*	équivalent	*equivalent*
fatiguant	*tiring*	fatigant	*tiring*
négligeant	*neglecting*	négligent	*negligent*
précédant	*preceding*	précédent	*previous*

4.1.2 Adjectives which normally occur before the noun

autre	une autre histoire	*another story*
beau/bel/belle	un bel homme	*a good-looking man*
bon/bonne	un bon professeur	*a good teacher*
bref/brève	un bref épisode	*a brief episode*
double	un double whisky	*a double whisky*
haut/e	de hautes montagnes	*high mountains*
joli/e	une jolie femme	*a pretty woman*
mauvais/e	une mauvaise odeur	*a bad smell*
nouveau/nouvel/nouvelle	une nouvelle maison	*a new house*
petit/e	un petit problème	*a small problem*
vaste	une vaste enceinte	*a vast arena*
vieux/vieil/vieille	un vieux château	*an old castle*

4.1.3 Adjectives which regularly occur before and after the noun, but with a change of meaning

The meaning given to a certain number of adjectives when they occur after a noun and when they occur after the verb *être* is the same:

> Cette maison est ancienne   *It's an old house*

But when these adjectives occur before the noun the meaning is different. Compare:

> La rue est bordée de maisons anciennes
> *The street is lined with old(-style) houses*

> Son ancienne maison a été détruite
> *His former house was destroyed*

When adjectives occur before the noun they tend to contribute to the meaning of the noun itself. So, *un ancien soldat* is someone who is 'old in the profession of soldiering', i.e. 'an old (ex-)soldier'. *Un gros fumeur* is not 'a fat smoker', but 'a heavy smoker' (*un fumeur gros* is 'a fat smoker').

Common adjectives which have different meanings when they precede or follow nouns are:

ancien	un ancien élève	*an old boy/girl i.e. (ex-)pupil*
	une maison ancienne	*an old house*
brave	un brave type	*a nice guy*
	un homme brave	*a courageous man*
certain	d'un certain âge	*middle-aged*
	une vérité certaine	*a certain truth*
cher	mon cher ami	*my dear friend*
	une robe chère	*an expensive dress*

chic	un chic type	*a nice guy*
	une robe chic	*a smart dress*
curieux	une curieuse histoire	*an odd story*
	une personne curieuse	*an inquisitive person*
dernier	son dernier livre	*his last book (latest)*
	la semaine dernière	*last week*
drôle	une drôle d'histoire	*an odd story*
	une histoire drôle	*a funny story*
fameux	ton fameux problème	*the problem you keep on going on about*
	un vin fameux	*a delicious wine*
franc	une franche idiote	*a real idiot*
	une personne franche	*a frank person*
grand	un grand homme	*a great man*
	un homme grand	*a tall man*
gros	un gros effort	*a big effort*
	un homme gros	*a fat man*
jeune	une jeune femme	*a young woman*
	une femme jeune	*a woman who is not old*
méchant	une méchante histoire	*a nasty business*
	une fille méchante	*an unpleasant girl*
même	toujours les mêmes histoires	*always the same stories/problems*
	le jour même	*that very day*
pauvre	un pauvre homme	*a man you feel sorry for*
	un homme pauvre	*a man who isn't rich*
propre	ma propre chambre	*my own bedroom*
	une serviette propre	*a clean towel*
pure	une pure illusion	*a complete illusion*
	de race pure	*pure bred*
rare	un rare moment de paix	*a precious moment of peace*
	un moment rare de l'histoire	*an exceptional moment in history*
sale	une sale histoire	*a nasty business*
	une nappe sale	*a dirty tablecloth*
seul	le seul inconvénient ...	*the only disadvantage ...*
	un homme seul	*a lonely man*
simple	une simple question de ...	*simply a matter of ...*
	une question simple	*an easy question*
triste	une triste histoire	*a sorry story*
	une histoire triste	*a sad story*
véritable	un véritable problème	*a real problem (serious)*
	un problème véritable	*a genuine problem (not invented)*
vert	une verte réprimande	*a real dressing-down*
	une voiture verte	*a green car*
vilain	une vilaine action	*a bad deed*
	un enfant vilain	*an ugly (or naughty) child*

NB: *neuf* and *nouveau*. *Ma voiture neuve* is likely to be 'my brand new car' (not second-hand), while *ma nouvelle voiture* is a car which is different from the one I had before (it may or may not be 'brand new'). *feu* 'late, deceased' can be used in two ways: *feu la reine/la feue reine*. Both mean 'the late queen', but note that in the first case *feu* does not agree with *reine*. Usually limited to legal papers.

4.1.4 Adjectives which normally follow the noun but can also precede, without significant changes in meaning

Most adjectives which normally follow the noun can occur before it as well, without a significant change in the meaning of the adjective. Such pre-positioning is usually for stylistic effect: to vary sentence structure or avoid having two or more adjectives following the same noun. The position before the noun is favoured where the adjective in some way measures or quantifies the meaning of the noun:

un léger rhume	*a slight cold*
une charmante soirée	*a delightful evening*
une forte odeur	*a strong smell*
un misérable repas	*a measly meal*
une importante augmentation	*a large increase*

4.1.5 Combinations of adjectives

Multiple adjectives before the noun

Cardinal numbers are usually the first in any combination of adjectives preceding a noun, but after that the order of adjectives is the same as it is in English:

les **deux** premières semaines	*the first two weeks*
les **quatre** dernières jolies phrases	*the last four pretty sentences*
au bon vieux temps	*in the good old days*
une autre nouvelle maison	*another new house*
un vrai beau grand château	*a really beautiful large castle*
ce pauvre cher homme	*that poor dear man*

The exception to cardinal numbers occurring first is when a complex number is involved:

Il m'a versé les derniers **sept cents** francs qu'il me devait
He paid me the last seven hundred francs he owed me

To avoid having a long string of adjectives before the noun, one or more may be combined with *et*, and/or moved after the noun. To illustrate, 'a young pretty little cat' could be:

un jeune et joli petit chat *or*
un petit chat jeune et joli

Multiple adjectives after the noun

The order of adjectives after the noun is the mirror image of English. For example, 'the Spanish Civil War' becomes 'the War Civil Spanish':

la guerre civile espagnole

Similarly (these examples are from Waugh, 1977):

des lignes parallèles invisibles	*invisible parallel lines*

des milieux politiques américains	*American political circles*
des feuilles mortes humides	*damp dead leaves*
un agent commercial français	*a French business agent*

4.1.6 Adjectives modified by adverbs and prepositional phrases

When adjectives which normally precede the noun are modified by adverbs or prepositional phrases, they may appear after the noun. The longer the modifying expression, the more likely this is:

un bel homme	*a handsome man*
un très bel homme	*a very handsome man*
un homme vraiment beau	*a really handsome man*
un gros effort	*a great effort*
un effort démesurément gros	*an inordinately large effort*
une jolie figure	*a pretty face*
une figure un peu trop jolie	*a face which is a bit too pretty*
un grand jardin	*a large garden*
un jardin grand comme un mouchoir de poche	*a garden the size of your hand*

This also applies to superlatives (see 4.12.2):

un bref aperçu	*a brief outline*
le plus bref aperçu	*the briefest outline*
un aperçu des plus brefs	*the briefest of outlines*

4.1.7 Adjectives preceded by *de*

When nouns are quantified by numbers, following adjectives may directly follow the noun or they may be preceded by *de*. The use with *de* is found in informal French. For a number of speakers there is a difference in meaning between the two. When *de* is present, the implication is that there were more of the things described by the noun than the number indicates:

Il y avait dix voyageurs de blessés
There were ten travellers injured
(implies that there were more than ten involved, but the rest weren't injured)

Il y avait dix voyageurs blessés
There were ten injured travellers
(has no implication about whether there were other, non-injured travellers)

J'ai une heure de libre aujourd'hui
I have an hour free today (implies that all the other hours in my day are busy)

J'ai une heure libre aujourd'hui
I have a free hour today (has no implication about whether my other hours are busy or not)

Note that the contrast in English is captured by whether the adjective precedes or follows the noun.

4.2 Adjectives which follow verbs or verbal expressions

Some verbs and verbal expressions can be followed by adjectives. With the following verbs/verbal expressions, adjectives must agree in number and gender with the subject:

avoir l'air	*to seem, appear*
être	*to be*
être considéré comme	*to be thought of as*
devenir	*to become*
se montrer	*to show oneself to be*
paraître	*to appear*
passer pour	*to be considered to be*
sembler	*to seem*

Elle est aussi **belle** que sa sœur
She is as pretty as her sister

Les enfants semblent **énervés** par ce temps
The children seem over-excited by this weather

Tous les membres de la famille passent pour **pauvres**
All the members of the family are thought to be poor

With the following verbs, mainly those which express an opinion, adjectives must agree in number and gender with the direct object:

croire	*to believe*	traiter qn de	*to call sb sth*
considérer	*to consider*	trouver	*to find*
deviner	*to guess*	voir	*to see*
imaginer	*to imagine*	se voir	*to see oneself*
s'imaginer	*to imagine oneself*		

Je croyais la bataille **perdue** d'avance
I thought the battle was already lost

Je les devine un peu **fâchés** par cette histoire
I guess they are a little bit annoyed by this affair

Vous les voyez toujours **petits**; mais ils ont grandi
You see them as if they were still little; but they've grown up

Les enfants traitaient les petits voisins de **lâches**
The children were calling the little neighbours cowards

4.3 Adjectives with complements

Some adjectives can be followed by nouns, pronouns or infinitives, with a linking *de* or *à*:

Ils étaient **blancs de** colère
They were white with anger

Ces jeunes femmes sont très **sûres d'**elles
These young women are very self-confident

Je suis très **heureux de** faire votre connaissance
I am very pleased to meet you

Ce problème est **facile à** résoudre
This problem is easy to solve

(For the use of *de* with adjectives followed by nouns see Chapter 13.15.2; and followed by infinitives see Chapter 12.7.)

4.4 Indefinite and negative noun phrases with adjective complements

Indefinite noun phrases like *quelque chose* 'something', *quelqu'un* 'someone', *ceci* 'this', *cela* 'that', *quoi?* 'what?', and negative expressions like *rien* 'nothing', *personne* 'no-one', can be followed by adjectives linked by *de*. The adjective is invariable in this construction:

quelque chose de **bon**	*something good*
quelqu'un d'**intéressant**	*someone interesting*
rien de plus **facile**	*nothing easier*
Quoi de **neuf**?	*What's new?*

4.5 Adjectives used as nouns

In French it is almost always possible to convert an adjective into a noun simply by placing an article in front of it:

Je ne veux que **les mûrs**	*I only want the ripe ones*
Nous prendrons **les grands**	*We'll take the big ones*
Les petits sont déjà partis	*The small ones have already gone*
Les gentils gagnent à la fin	*The goodies win in the end*
Les méchants sont punis	*The baddies are punished*
J'adore **le rustique**	*I love rural styles*
Elle aurait préféré **du moderne**	*She would have preferred something up-to-date*
Le plus énervant, c'est sa voix	*It's her voice that is the most annoying thing*
Le rouge te va bien	*Red suits you*
L'important c'est de partir tôt	*The important thing is to leave early*

As can be seen, because English does not permit the creation of nouns with such freedom, translations either have to use vague terms like 'ones', 'thing(s)' or it is necessary to rephrase the sentence.

NB: Compare the post-verbal use of adjectives as nouns with the post-verbal use of numbers and quantifiers as nouns:

Nous prendrons **les grands**	*We'll take the big ones*
Nous **en** prendrons deux	*We'll take two*
Nous avons acheté **des ovales**	*We bought some oval ones*
Nous **en** avons acheté plusieurs	*We bought several*

With numbers and quantifiers *en* must be inserted in front of the verb (see Chapter 3.2.25 and Chapter 6.1.7).

Adjectives of nationality and nouns of nationality are usually identical in form when used as adjectives or nouns EXCEPT that the nouns are written with capital letters:

Elle est **a**méricaine	C'est une **A**méricaine
She is American	*She is an American*
Tout **F**rançais qui se respecte aime le fromage	*Every true French person loves cheese*
Elle est de nationalité **f**rançaise	*She is of French nationality*

4.6 Adjectives used as adverbs

A limited number of adjectives can also be used as adverbs. In this case they are invariable (see also Chapter 5.3):

bas	Ils parlent bas	*They're talking very quietly*
bon	Le café sent bon	*The coffee smells good*
cher	Cela coûte trop cher	*That's too expensive*
clair	Je n'arrive pas à y voir clair dans son raisonnement	*I can't make much sense of his argument*
droit	Ils marchent droit	*They are walking straight*
dur	Ils travaillent dur	*They work hard*
faux	Elles chantent faux	*They sing out of tune*
fin	Il faut couper le jambon très fin	*You must slice the ham very thinly*
fort	Ils parlent trop fort	*They're talking too loudly*
grand	Ils ont vu trop grand	*They attempted too much*
jeune	Ils s'habillent jeune	*They dress in a youthful manner*
juste	Tu as vu juste dès le début	*You understood from the beginning*
lourd	Cet acte pèse lourd sur ma conscience	*That act weighs heavily on my conscience*
menu	de la viande hachée menu	*meat cut up finely*
vieux	Ils font vieux	*They look old*

4.7 Masculine and feminine forms of adjectives

The general rule is that an -*e* is added to the masculine form of adjectives to produce the feminine form.

4.7.1 A change in written, but not spoken, French

In cases where the masculine form ends in one of the following vowels or consonants, there is a change in the written form but not in the spoken form:

	Masculine	Feminine	
-u	absolu	absolue	*absolute*
	aigu	aiguë	*high (sound)*
	ambigu	ambiguë	*ambiguous*
	contigu	contiguë	*contiguous*

NB: In the case of *aigu, ambigu, contigu*, a diaresis (ë) is added to the feminine -*e* in written French to indicate that the -*u* sound is maintained in spoken French (*aigue* would be pronounced rather like English 'egg' otherwise; compare *long/longue*).

-é	fermé	fermée	*closed*
-er	fier	fière	*proud*
	cher	chère	*expensive*
	amer	amère	*bitter*

NB: In these cases, where the final *r* is pronounced in the masculine, a grave accent is added to the first written *e*.

-i	hardi	hardie	*bold*
NB: Exception:	favori	favorite	*favourite*
-c	public	publique	*public*
	turc	turque	*Turkish*
NB: *c* is maintained in:	grec	grecque	*Greek*
-ct	direct	directe	*direct*
-r	sûr	sûre	*certain*
	pur	pure	*pure*
-al	national	nationale	*national*
	général	générale	*general*
	hivernal	hivernale	*winter*
	final	finale	*final*
-el	personnel	personnelle	*personal*
	professionnel	professionnelle	*professional*
	passionnel	passionnelle	*emotive*
	cruel	cruelle	*cruel*
-ul	nul	nulle	*no-good*

NB: In these cases, it is -*le* which is added and not just -*e*.

-ol	espagnol	espagnole	*Spanish*
-il	puéril	puérile	*childish*
	civil	civile	*civil*

NB: In these cases the *l* is pronounced in the masculine.

By contrast in the following adjectives the final -*il* is pronounced as indicated:

gentil [-i]	gentille [-ij]	*kind*
pareil [-ej]	pareille [-ej]	*similar*
vermeil [-ej]	vermeille [-ej]	*bright red*

4.7.2 A change in written and spoken French

In the following cases, addition of feminine -*e* to the written masculine form also corresponds to the pronunciation of a final consonant in spoken French:

Addition of -*e* without further changes:

-t	petit	petite	*small*
	cuit	cuite	*cooked*
-s	gris	grise	*grey*
	mauvais	mauvaise	*bad*

Addition of -*e* and doubling of the final consonant

-as	bas	basse	*low*
	gras	grasse	*fatty*
	épais	épaisse	*thick*
	las	lasse	*tired*
-et	muet	muette	*mute*
	coquet	coquette	*cute*
-ot	sot	sotte	*stupid*

Addition of -e and a grave accent

-et	complet	complète	*complete*
	inquiet	inquiète	*worried*
	secret	secrète	*secret*
	discret	discrète	*discreet*
	concret	concrète	*concrete*
	replet	replète	*plump*

4.7.3 A change from a nasal vowel to an oral vowel

In the following cases, addition of -e, and sometimes the doubling of the final consonant, corresponds to a change from a nasal vowel to an oral vowel + consonant in spoken French:

grand	grande	*big*
paysan	paysanne	*peasant*
partisan	partisane	*biased*
ancien	ancienne	*old*
enfantin	enfantine	*childlike*
européen	européenne	*European*
féminin	féminine	*feminine*
fin	fine	*fine*
mignon	mignonne	*pretty*
bon	bonne	*good*
brun	brune	*brown*
opportun	opportune	*opportune*

NB: In some cases -ne is added and not just -e.

4.7.4 A change in the final consonant or syllable

In the following cases, addition of final -e is accompanied by a change in the final consonant or the whole of the final syllable:

-ais/aîche	frais	fraîche	*fresh*
-aux/ausse	faux	fausse	*false*
-er/ère	premier	première	*first*
	dernier	dernière	*last*
	étranger	étrangère	*foreign*
-eux/euse	heureux	heureuse	*happy*
	amoureux	amoureuse	*in love*
	nerveux	nerveuse	*nervous*
	affreux	affreuse	*frightful*
	peureux	peureuse	*frightened*
-eux/-eille	vieux	vieille	*old*
-eur/euse	voleur	voleuse	*dishonest*
	flatteur	flatteuse	*flattering*
	trompeur	trompeuse	*misleading*
	moqueur	moqueuse	*likes to make fun of others*
	joueur	joueuse	*playful*
-eur/eresse	vengeur	vengeresse	*vengeful*

-eur/rice	consolateur	consolatrice	*consoling*
	observateur	observatrice	*observant*
	créateur	créatrice	*creative*
	conservateur	conservatrice	*conservative*
-eau/elle	nouveau	nouvelle	*new*
	beau	belle	*beautiful*
	jumeau	jumelle	*twin*
-c/che	sec	sèche	*dry*
	blanc	blanche	*white*
	franc	franche	*frank*
-f/ve	neuf	neuve	*new*
	actif	active	*active*
	bref	brève	*brief*
	créatif	créative	*creative*
	vif	vive	*lively*
-in/igne	bénin	bénigne	*benign*
	malin	maligne	*sharp, clever*
-ong/ongue	long	longue	*long*
-ou/olle	mou	molle	*soft*
	fou	folle	*mad*
-oux/ouce/ousse	doux	douce	*gentle*
	roux	rousse	*red-haired*

NB: *beau, fou, mou, nouveau, vieux* also have a special masculine form – *bel, fol, mol, nouvel, vieil* – which appears when a following noun begins with a vowel or a so-called 'silent h':

un bel effet	*a fine effect*
un fol espoir	*a vain hope*
un nouvel homme	*a new, a changed man*
un mol effort	*a weak effort*
un vieil hélicoptère	*an old helicopter*

4.7.5 No change in written or spoken French
In cases where the adjective already ends in -*e*, there is no change:

manifeste	masculine and feminine	*obvious*
sale	masculine and feminine	*dirty*
tranquille	masculine and feminine	*calm*
utile	masculine and feminine	*useful*

4.8 Plural forms of adjectives

4.8.1 The normal case
In most cases -*s* is added to the singular form of the adjective and there is no change in the pronunciation:

Elle est contente	Elles sont contente**s**
She is happy	*They (f) are happy*
Il est content	Ils sont contents
He is happy	*They (m) are happy*

La veste est rouge
The jacket is red

Les vestes sont rouges
The jackets are red

Le sac est rouge
The bag is red

Les sacs sont rouges
The bags are red

If the word ends in *-s* or *-x*, it will be invariable:

Notre fils est heureux
Our son is happy

Nos fils sont heureux
Our sons are happy

Le cahier est gris
The exercise book is grey

Les cahiers sont gris
The exercise books are grey

4.8.2 Adjectives which end in *-eau* add *x* rather than *s*

Un nouveau magnétoscope
A new video-tape recorder

De nouveaux magnétoscopes
New video-tape recorders

Un beau cadre
A beautiful setting

De beaux cadres
Beautiful settings

4.8.3 Adjectives which end in *-al* generally change to *-aux*

Le chanteur principal
The principal singer

Des chanteurs principaux
Principal singers

Le principe général
The general principle

Des principes généraux
General principles

Un homme marginal
A man on the margins (of society)

Des hommes marginaux
Men on the margins (of society)

Un point de vue normal
A normal point of view

Des points de vue normaux
Normal points of view

Exceptions: *banal, bancal, fatal, glacial, naval, natal*

Un discours banal
A banal speech

Des discours banals
Banal speeches

Un buffet bancal
A sideboard with a damaged leg

Des buffet bancals
Sideboards with damaged legs

Un revirement fatal
A fatal change of heart

Des revirements fatals
Fatal changes of heart

Un vent glacial
A very cold wind

Des vent glacials
Very cold winds

Un chantier naval
A naval dockyard

Des chantiers navals
Naval dockyards

Mon pays natal
My home country

Des pays natals
Home countries

Adjectives which alternate:

idéal	idéals *and* idéaux	*ideal*
matinal	matinals *and* matinaux	*early morning*
pascal	pascals *and* pascaux	*related to Easter*
astral	astrals *and* astraux	*related to stars*

4.9 Adjective agreement with nouns

4.9.1 Adjectives agreeing with just one noun

Adjectives agree in gender and number with the noun whose meaning they modify. This is usually straightforward when there is just one noun:

d'une voix hésitante	*in a faltering voice*
ce fameux dimanche	*that famous Sunday*
L'eau était froide	*The water was cold*
Il lançait aux passants des regards rapides et insistants	*He shot rapid and insistent glances at the passers-by*

NB: A plural noun might be modified by a string of singular adjectives, depending on the meaning: *Les économies* **russe**, **bulgare** *et* **roumaine** *rencontrent de graves difficultés* 'The Russian, Bulgarian and Romanian economies are (each) encountering serious difficulties'.

4.9.2 An adjective agreeing with nouns linked by et, ou or ni

The adjective may agree with the closest noun only:

une table et une chaise bleue	*a table and a blue chair*

The adjective may agree with all the nouns, in which case it will be plural, and will be feminine only if all the nouns are feminine. Otherwise it will be masculine:

une table et une chaise bleues	*a blue table and chair*
Il ne portait ni de veste ni de pantalon bleus	*He was wearing neither a blue jacket nor a blue pair of trousers*
un stylo ou un cahier bleus	*a blue pen or exercise book*

4.9.3 An adjective agreeing with nouns linked by de

The adjective may agree with the first or the second noun, depending on the meaning:

un groupe de **chanteuses** talentueuses	*a group of talented female singers*
une **bande** de voyous agressive	*an aggressive gang of layabouts*
des **bains** de mer fréquents	*frequent dips in the sea*
un geste de **générosité** déplacée	*an act of misplaced generosity*

NB: *un/une drôle de* can be used adjectivally meaning 'weird', 'strange'. Its gender is determined by the following noun: *une drôle d'*idée 'a strange idea', *un drôle de* **type** 'a weird bloke'.

4.10 Invariable adjectives

A number of adjectives do not change either in relation to gender or to number. It is sometimes argued that these are nouns being used adjectivally.

un pull **marron**	une jupe **marron**	des chaussures **marron**
a brown pullover	*a brown skirt*	*brown shoes*
un carton **orange**	une voiture **orange**	des rideaux **orange**
an orange box	*an orange car*	*orange curtains*

un chemisier **crème**	une jupe **crème**	des sous-vêtements **crème**
a cream blouse	*a cream skirt*	*cream underwear*

un lecteur de cassettes **bon marché**	*a cheap cassette player*
une planche à roulettes **bon marché**	*a cheap skateboard*
des fruits **bon marché**	*cheap fruit*

un pull **cerise**	*a cherry pullover*
une tapisserie **cerise**	*cherry-coloured wallpaper*
des uniformes **cerise**	*cherry-coloured uniforms*

Other invariable adjectives:

angora	*angora*
baba	*flabbergasted*
bath	*great*
cucu	*twee*
gaga	*nuts*
gnagnan	*childish, immature*
kaki	*khaki*
pop	*pop*
porno	*pornographic*
riquiqui	*inadequate (too small, too poor etc. depending on context)*
rococo	*rococo*
snob	*snobbish*
sympa	*friendly*

NB: *chic* is invariable for gender but agrees for number:

un tailleur **chic**	une robe **chic**	des vêtements **chics**
a smart suit	*a smart dress*	*smart clothes*

4.11 Compound adjectives

Like compound nouns (see Chapter 1.2.11) compound adjectives can be made up in a variety of ways. Their internal structure determines the way in which they agree with the noun they modify.

4.11.1 Adjective–adjective compounds

Where adjectives are coordinated, both agree with the noun:

sourd-muet	Les enfants sour**ds**-mue**ts** ont fait des progrès exceptionnels
deaf-mute	*The deaf-mute children have made exceptional progress*
aigre-doux	J'adore les sauces aigre**s**-douce**s**
sweet and sour	*I adore sweet and sour sauces*
nouveau-né	Les bébés nouveau**x**-né**s** sont très fatigants pour leurs parents
new-born	*New-born babies are very exhausting for their parents*
dernier-né	Les filles dernière**s**-né**es** profitent de la présence de leurs frères et sœurs
last-born	*Last-born girls take advantage of the presence of their brothers and sisters*
grand-ouvert	Ils dorment la bouche grand**e**-ouvert**e**
wide open	*They sleep with their mouths wide open*

Exception: where the first adjective ends in *-i, -o*, only the second part agrees:

tragi-comique	Toutes ses pièces étaient tragi-comique**s**
tragi-comedy	*All her plays were tragi-comedies*

franco-allemand	Dans le cadre de l'union européenne, les accords franco-allemands ont duré plus de trente ans
Franco-German	*Within the European framework, the Franco-German agreements have lasted for more than thirty years*

4.11.2 Adverb–adjective compounds

Where an adverb and an adjective are combined, the adverb (always the first element) remains invariable and the adjective agrees:

haut placé	Je connais des fonctionnaires haut placés qui pourraient nous aider
highly placed	*I know some highly placed civil servants who could help us*
bien intentionné	Ce sont toujours les personnes bien intentionnées qui créent le plus de problèmes
well-intentioned	*It's always the well-intentioned people who cause the most problems*
avant-coureur	Voilà les signes avant-coureurs d'une maladie grave
early warning	*There are the early-warning signs of a serious illness*

4.11.3 Colour adjective compounds

Combinations of colour adjectives remain invariable:

des cheveux **châtain clair**	*light-brown hair*
une veste **bleu foncé**	*a dark-blue jacket*
une mer **vert-bouteille**	*a bottle-green sea*
une couverture **gris-rouge**	*a red-grey cover*

4.11.4 Compounds involving *demi-*, *nu-* and *mi-*

In combinations involving *demi-*, *nu-* and *mi-*, *demi-* and *nu-* are invariable before the noun, but agree when they follow it:

une **demi**-heure	but	une heure et **demie**
a half-hour		*an hour and a half*
une **demi**-page		une page et **demie**
a half-page		*a page and a half*
nu-tête		sortir tête **nue**
bareheaded		*to go out without a hat*
nu-pieds		sortir pieds **nus**
barefoot		*to go out bare footed*

mi- can only occur before the noun and is invariable:

à **mi**-temps	*part-time (e.g. work)*
la **mi**-juin	*halfway through June*
la **mi**-saison	*middle season (Spring, Autumn)*
la **mi**-journée	*the middle of the day*
mi-américain	*half-American*
mi-clos	*half-open, half-closed*

4.12 Comparative and superlative forms of adjectives

4.12.1 Comparatives

In English, adjectives can be used to compare one entity with another by adding -*er*, or putting 'more' or 'less' in front: 'bigger', 'lighter', 'more dangerous', 'less interesting'. In French, the comparative forms of adjectives are created by putting *plus* 'more' or *moins* 'less' in front of them. The adjective stays in the position it would normally occupy, before or after the noun, and agrees with the noun as usual (see 4.9):

> Il désire avoir une **plus grande** voiture
> *He wants to have a bigger car*

> Je n'ai jamais fait de traversée **plus dangereuse**
> *I have never made a more dangerous crossing*

> Ce film est **moins intéressant** pour les enfants
> *This film is less interesting for children*

> Elle semble **moins malade** aujourd'hui
> *She seems less ill today*

plus and *moins* make unequal comparisons between entities. A related construction is *aussi* 'as' (which often changes to *si* after a negation), which makes a comparison of equality between entities:

> Il désire avoir une **aussi grande** voiture
> *He wants to have as big a car*

> Le courant n'est pas **si dangereux** par ici
> *The current isn't as dangerous here*

NB: Adding *aussi* to a preceding adjective does not alter its position. This contrasts with English. Compare: *une* **aussi grande** *voiture* with '**as big** a car'.

In clauses dependent on nouns modified by comparative adjectives with *plus* and *moins*, writers often insert *ne*, *le* or *ne le* in formal written French:

> Ces virages sont plus dangereux qu'on **(ne) (le)** pense
> *These bends are more dangerous than one thinks*

> Le film est moins intéressant qu'on **(ne) (l')**espérait
> *The film is less interesting than we hoped*

In clauses dependent on nouns modified by comparative adjectives with *aussi*, only *le* may be inserted in formal written French:

> La charge de travail est aussi lourde que je le croyais
> *The workload is as demanding as I thought*

There are two irregular comparative forms of adjectives which are used productively in French:

> meilleur/-e   *better* (comparative of *bon* 'good')
> pire   *worse* (comparative of *mauvais* 'bad')

meilleur is used everywhere that *bon* could be, and agrees with the noun it modifies:

> Il désire avoir une **meilleure** place
> *He wants to have a better seat*

> Ces marchandises sont **meilleures**
> *These goods are better*

Le texte est **meilleur** maintenant que tu l'as raccourci
The text is better now you have shortened it

plus bon 'more good' is only possible where English can use 'more good', but, again as in English, the form is rather unusual:

Il est **plus bon** qu'intelligent
He is more good than intelligent

(For the distinction between *meilleur* and *mieux* see Chapter 5.6.6.)

pire and *plus mauvais* both exist. *plus mauvais* is the most commonly used form, but *pire* will be used where the comparison is between two things which are already both bad:

Le remède est **pire** que le mal
The cure is worse than the illness

or to refer to abstract nouns:

La vérité est pénible, mais le mensonge est **pire**
Truth hurts, but lying is worse

4.12.2 Superlatives
In English, adjectives can be used to describe the best or worst of something by adding '-est' or putting 'most' or 'least' in front of them: 'biggest', 'lightest', 'most dangerous', 'least interesting'. These are superlative forms of adjectives.

In French the superlative forms of adjectives are created by putting the definite article – *le, la, les* – in front of the comparative forms: *la plus grande voiture* 'the biggest car', *la plus forte odeur* 'the strongest smell'. When adjectives follow the noun, this means that there are two definite articles, one before the noun and one before the comparative form of the adjective: **la** *voiture* **la** *plus puissante* 'the most powerful car', **les** *virages* **les** *plus dangereux* 'the most dangerous bends'. Note that the article agrees in gender and number with the noun:

C'était **le plus grand** joueur de tous
He was the greatest player of all

Elle est **la moins ambitieuse** de sa famille
She is the least ambitious in her family

C'est la route **la plus dangereuse** de la région
It's the most dangerous road in the region

NB: 'in' after superlative adjectives is usually *de*: *la route la plus dangereuse **de** la région, la moins malade **de** sa famille.* (See Chapter 13.15.3.)

There are three irregular superlative forms of adjectives which are used productively in French:

le/la/les meilleur(e)(s)	*the best* (superlative of *bon* 'good')
le/la/les pire(s)	*the worst* (superlative of *mauvais* 'bad')
le/la/les moindre(s)	*the least* (superlative of *petit* 'small')

The conditions under which *meilleur* and *pire* are used are the same as those described in 4.12.1:

> Notre chef de cuisine est **le meilleur** de la ville
> *Our chef is the best in town*

> Elle porte **les meilleurs** vêtements
> *She wears the best clothes*

> Cette solution est **la pire** des trois proposées
> *This solution is the worst of the three proposed*

> **Le pire**, c'était qu'elle voulait revenir
> *The worst thing was that she wanted to come back*

le/la/les moindre(s) is used in semi-fixed expressions, and with abstract nouns:

> le principe du moindre effort
> *the principle of least effort*

> Ils ont essayé de suivre la politique du moindre mal
> *They tried to follow the policy which would do the least harm*

Where concrete nouns are involved, however, *le/la/les plus petit(e)(s)* is used:

> Il a choisi **le plus petit** diamant
> *He chose the smallest diamond*

When adjectives which normally precede nouns are used in a superlative form, they may follow the noun they modify on the grounds that they are 'too long' to appear in front of the noun (see 4.1.6):

un bref aperçu	**le plus bref** aperçu *or* l'aperçu **le plus bref**
a brief outline	*the briefest outline*
un jeune homme	**le plus jeune** homme *or* l'homme **le plus jeune**
a young man	*the youngest man*

4.13 Subjunctive versus indicative in clauses dependent on a superlative adjective

Clauses dependent on nouns modified by a superlative adjective have a verb in the subjunctive if the construction claims a unique status for the noun. For example:

> Ils ont acheté le plus grand sapin de Noël qu'ils **aient** pu trouver
> *They bought the biggest Christmas tree that they could find*
> (They couldn't find a bigger tree, so it is unique)

But where the construction does not claim a unique status for the noun, the verb in the dependent clause is in the indicative:

> Ils ont acheté le plus grand sapin de Noël qu'ils **ont** pu transporter dans leur voiture
> *They bought the biggest Christmas tree that they could take in their car*
> (there is no claim that it is the biggest Christmas tree available)

(For more on this construction see Chapters 11.1.8 and 15.11.3.)

4.14 Absolute use of the superlative

One way of translating into French expressions like 'the simplest of all', 'the most interesting imaginable' (known as 'absolute superlatives') is to put the expression *des plus* in front of the adjective: *des plus simple(s), des plus intéressant(s)*. In this construction the adjective must agree in gender with the noun it modifies, but if the noun is singular the adjective may be either singular or plural:

> C'était une journée **des plus intéressante(s)**
> *It was the most interesting of days*

> C'était un voyage **des plus intéressant(s)**
> *It was the most interesting trip imaginable*

In modern French the plural form is probably the more frequent of the two.

Other ways of expressing an absolute superlative are:

> Ce raisonnement est **tout ce qu'il y a de plus simple**
> *This line of argument is of the simplest kind*

> Un raisonnement **on ne peut plus simple**
> *The simplest line of argument of all*

> Il préfère des solutions **les plus simples possible** (*possible* is invariable in this construction)
> *He prefers the simplest possible solutions*

5

Adverbs

5.1 Function of adverbs

Adverbs are words or phrases of invariable form which modify the meaning of words, phrases or whole sentences:

Il est entré dans un monde **étrangement** silencieux   *He entered a strangely silent world*
(*étrangement* modifies just *silencieux*; it is the silence which is strange, not the person or the world he enters)

J'ai entendu un bruit **dehors**   *I heard a noise outside*
(*dehors* modifies just *entendre un bruit*; it indicates where the noise was, not where the person hearing it was)

Soudain j'ai entendu un bruit   *Suddenly I heard a noise*
(*soudain* modifies the sentence and expresses the suddenness of the whole event)

5.2 Formation of adverbs with the ending *-ment*

5.2.1 Adverbs ending in *-ment* derived from the feminine form of an adjective

Most adverbs ending in *-ment* are formed from the **feminine** form of a corresponding adjective:

Adjective		Feminine		Adverb	
affreux	*awful*	affreuse	*awful*	affreusement	*awfully*
clair	*clear*	claire	*clear*	clairement	*clearly*
distinct	*distinct*	distincte	*distinct*	distinctement	*distinctly*
doux	*gentle*	douce	*gentle*	doucement	*gently*
mou	*soft*	molle	*soft*	mollement	*softly*
naturel	*natural*	naturelle	*natural*	naturellement	*naturally*
public	*public*	publique	*public*	publiquement	*publicly*
professionnel	*professional*	professionnelle	*professional*	professionnellement	*professionally*
sec	*dry*	sèche	*dry*	sèchement	*drily*
sûr	*sure*	sûre	*sure*	sûrement	*surely*
vif	*alive*	vive	*alive*	vivement	*lively*

Exception:

gentil	*kind*	gentille	*kind*	gentiment	*kindly*

Although *-ment* corresponds broadly to English *-ly,* French is much less productive than English. Often English *-ly* adverbs must be translated by phrases (see 5.5).

5.2.2 Adverbs ending in *-ment* derived from the masculine form of an adjective

Where an adjective ends in *-i* (not *-oi*), *-é*, or *-u* (not *-eau* or *-ou*), the adverb is formed from the masculine form:

Adjective		Feminine		Adverb	
absolu	*absolute*	absolue	*absolute*	absolument	*absolutely*
ambigu	*ambiguous*	ambiguë	*ambiguous*	ambigument	*ambiguously*
aisé	*easy*	aisée	*easy*	aisément	*easily*
joli	*pretty*	jolie	*pretty*	joliment	*prettily*
vrai	*true*	vraie	*true*	vraiment	*truly*

Exception:

gai	*cheerful*	gaie	*cheerful*	gaiement	*cheerfully*

Seven adjectives which end in *-u* but add a circumflex accent in the adverbial form are:

assidu	*assiduous*	assidue	*assiduous*	assidûment	*assiduously*
continu	*continuous*	continue	*continuous*	continûment	*continuously*
cru	*crude*	crue	*crude*	crûment	*crudely*
dû	*owed*	due	*owed*	dûment	*duly*
goulu	*greedy*	goulue	*greedy*	goulûment	*greedily*
incongru	*incongruous*	incongrue	*incongruous*	incongrûment	*incongruously*
indu	*inappropriate*	indue	*inappropriate*	indûment	*inappropriately*

5.2.3 Adverbs ending in *-amment* and *-emment* derived from adjectives ending in *-ant* or *-ent*

Adjectives ending in *-ant* and *-ent* form the adverb with *-amment* and *-emment*, respectively:

Adjective		Adverb	
abondant	*abundant*	abondamment	*abundantly*
apparent	*apparent*	apparemment	*apparently*
brillant	*brilliant*	brillamment	*brilliantly*
constant	*constant*	constamment	*constantly*
courant	*current*	courammènt	*fluently*
précédent	*preceding*	précédemment	*beforehand*
prudent	*prudent*	prudemment	*prudently*
violent	*violent*	violemment	*violently*
vaillant	*valorous*	vaillamment	*with valour*

There are three forms which do not follow this pattern exactly:

lent	*slow*	lentement	*slowly*
présent	*present*	présentement	*presently*
véhément	*vehement*	véhémentement	*vehemently*

NB: *véhémentement* is quite rare, and *avec véhémence* is usually preferred.

Three forms follow the pattern, but the present participles from which they derive no longer exist in modern French:

précipiter *to precipitate*	précipitamment
(précipitant – old French)	*precipitately*

noter *to note*   notamment
(notant – old French)   *notably*

(scire – old French/Latin)   sciemment
                                                  knowingly

5.2.4 Adverbs ending in -(é)ment derived from past participles

Adverbs can also be formed in a similar way from the masculine form of past participles:

Verb		Past participle	Adverb	
aveugler	*to blind*	aveuglé	aveuglément	*blindly*
conformer	*to conform*	conformé	conformément	*in order*
forcer	*to force*	forcé	forcément	*necessarily*
préciser	*to make precise*	précisé	précisément	*precisely*

In a similar, but irregular, vein we find:

impuni   *unpunished*   impunément   *with impunity*

5.2.5 Adverbs ending in -ément derived from adjectives ending in -e

A small number of adverbs ending in *-ément* have been created from adjectives ending in *-e*: some always end in *-e*, others are the feminine form of adjectives:

Adjectives which always end in -e

Adjective		Adverb	
énorme	*enormous*	énormément	*enormously*
immense	*immense*	immensément	*immensely*
intense	*intense*	intensément	*intensely*
uniforme	*uniform*	uniformément	*uniformly*
commode	*useful*	commodément	*usefully*

Exceptions

probable	*probable*	probablement	*probably*
véritable	*real*	véritablement	*really*

Feminine forms

Adjective		Feminine	Adverb	
commun	*common*	commune	communément	*commonly*
confus	*embarrassed*	confuse	confusément	*embarrassedly*
importun	*disagreeable*	importune	importunément	*disagreeably*
obscur	*obscure*	obscure	obscurément	*obscurely*
opportun	*appropriate*	opportune	opportunément	*appropriately*
profond	*deep*	profonde	profondément	*deeply*
profus	*profuse*	profuse	profusément	*profusely* (literary)

5.2.6 Adverbs ending in -ment derived from words no longer in the language

Some adverbs ending in *-ment* are derived from words which no longer exist in the language:

Adjective	Feminine	Adverb	
bref *brief*	brève	brièvement	*briefly*
(brief – old French)			

grave *serious* (grief – old French)	grave	grièvement	*seriously*
traître *treacherous* (traîtreux – old French)	traîtresse	traîtreusement	*treacherously*
(journel – old French)		journellement	*daily*
(nuitantre – old French)		nuitamment	*nightly*

NB: *grief* is still used in certain set expressions: *faire grief à quelqu'un de quelque chose* 'to hold something against somebody', *formuler des griefs* 'to express grievances'.

5.2.7 Adverbs ending in *-ment* derived from nouns

There are a few adverbs ending in *-ment* which are derived from nouns and function like degree adverbs (see 5.6.2). These would be used only in spoken French: *vachement* in particular is used in very informal spoken French:

bougrement	C'est **bougrement** difficile	*It's bloody difficult*
diablement	Cette voiture est **diablement** lourde	*This car is hellishly heavy*
vachement	Elle est **vachement** jolie	*She's bloody good-looking*

5.3 Adjectives used as adverbs without addition of *-ment*

Not all adverbs derived from adjectives end in *-ment*. The masculine forms of several adjectives can be used as adverbs in combination with a particular set of verbs. They do not change in gender or in number when used in this way:

Adjective	Used in expressions such as	
bas	parler bas	*to talk quietly*
	voler bas	*to fly low*
bon	sentir bon	*to smell nice*
	tenir bon	*to hold on*
chaud	servir chaud	*to serve hot*
cher	coûter cher	*to cost a lot*
	payer cher	*to pay a lot (for sth)*
clair	voir clair	*to see clearly*
court	tourner court	*to come to an abrupt end*
	couper court à qch	*to cut sth short*
	s'habiller court	*to wear one's skirts/dresses short*
creux	sonner creux	*to ring hollow*
doux	filer doux	*to keep a low profile*
droit	aller droit	*to go straight on*
dru	tomber dru	*to fall in stair-rods (rain)*
dur	travailler dur	*to work hard*
faux	chanter faux	*to sing out of tune*
ferme	tenir ferme	*to hold out*
fort	parler fort	*to talk loudly*
frais	servir frais	*to serve cool*
franc	parler franc	*to say what you think*
gras	manger gras	*to eat rich food*
gros	parier gros	*to bet heavily*
	risquer gros	*to take big risks*
haut	être haut placé	*to be in a position of authority*
juste	viser juste	*to aim correctly*
	deviner juste	*to guess right*

lourd	peser lourd	*to weigh heavily*
mauvais	sentir mauvais	*to smell bad*
net	s'arrêter net	*to stop dead*
	casser net	*to make a clean break*
pareil	penser pareil (informal)	*to think the same*
profond	creuser profond	*to dig deep*
serré	jouer serré	*to play a close game*

The fact that some of these adjectives are used as adverbs has allowed the creation of related forms ending in *-ment* with different meanings:

bon: bonnement

bonnement is used almost always with *tout* to give *tout bonnement*: 'quite simply'

cher: chèrement

chèrement is used with the verb *vendre* in the set phrase: *vendre chèrement sa vie*: 'to sell one's life dearly'.

bas: bassement

bassement has taken the meaning: 'in a mean or despicable way' and is used in the set phrase *agir bassement*: 'to act in a mean or despicable way'.

5.4 Phrases used as adverbs

A number of adverbs are composed of invariable phrases. The following are a sample:

au maximum	*to the utmost*
à bon escient	*advisedly*
au fur et à mesure	*as we go along*
à brûle-pourpoint	*point blank*
à côté	*beside*
à l'heure	*on time*
à tire-larigot (informal)	*non-stop*
à tue-tête	*at the top of one's voice*
à plat ventre	*on one's belly*
à qui mieux mieux	*each one more than the next*
à peu près	*nearly*
à la fois	*at the same time*
à part	*separately*
d'ores et déjà	*from this time onwards*
d'habitude	*usually*
d'emblée	*straightaway*
de plus belle	*with renewed vigour*
d'arrache-pied	*flat out (to work)*
de bonne heure	*early*
de temps en temps	*from time to time*
en haut	*up(stairs)*
en bas	*down(stairs)*

en arrière	*behind*
en avant	*in front*
en retard	*late*
en avance	*early*
en amont	*upstream*
en aval	*downstream*
en dehors	*outside*
en vain	*in vain*
en catimini	*in secret*
en général	*in general*
en particulier	*in particular*
en définitive	*finally*
n'importe où	*anywhere*
n'importe quand	*anytime*
n'importe qui	*anybody*
par hasard	*by chance*
par monts et par vaux	*over hill and dale*
par ailleurs	*in addition*
par devant	*in the front*
par dessus	*over and above*
par contre	*on the other hand*
dans la suite	*in what followed*
et ainsi de suite	*and so on*
de suite	*immediately*
par la suite	*in what followed*
sans cesse	*continuously*
sans détour	*straight, to the point*
sur ces entrefaites	*and with that*
tout à fait	*completely*
tout de suite	*immediately*
tout à l'heure	*in a moment, later*
tout d'un coup	*suddenly*
tout de go	*straight out*
côte à côte	*side by side*
ça et là	*here and there*
petit à petit	*little by little*
sur-le-champ	*immediately*
vaille que vaille	*somehow or other*

Borrowings from Latin, frequently heard, are:

grosso modo	*more or less*
a fortiori	*even more so*
a priori	*a priori*
a posteriori	*a posteriori*
vice versa	*vice versa*
in extremis	*at the last moment*

5.5 English and French adverb formation

-ly is a more productive form in English than *-ment* is in French. Therefore, not every English form in *-ly* will find a ready translation in *-ment* in French. The most frequent solution is an adverbial phrase introduced by a preposition such as *avec, d'une manière. . ., d'une façon. . ., sur un ton . . .*:

avec colère, sur le ton de la colère	*angrily*
d'une manière concise, avec concision	*concisely*
avec charme, d'une manière charmante	*charmingly*
avec beaucoup de talent/d'imagination	*creatively*
sur le ton de la plaisanterie	*jokingly*
de façon possessive	*possessively*
de façon réfléchie	*reflectively*
avec tristesse	*sadly*
avec entêtement	*stubbornly*
de façon surprenante, à ma/ta grande surprise	*surprisingly*
sur un ton vengeur	*vengefully*

When colours are used as adverbs they are preceded by *en*:

le colorier en bleu	*to colour it blue*
le peindre en rouge	*to paint it red*

When shapes are used as adverbs, they have to be turned into an expression involving a noun in French:

lui donner une forme ronde	*to make it round*
le couper au carré	*to cut it square*

5.6 Types of adverbs

There are five main types of adverbs: manner adverbs, degree adverbs, time adverbs, place adverbs and sentence-modifying adverbs. Some forms fall into more than one of these categories. Typical examples of each are given in Tables 5.A, 5.B, 5.C, 5.D and 5.E (but the lists are not exhaustive).

5.6.1 Manner adverbs

Adverbs which describe the manner in which something is done are manner adverbs:

Je dors **bien**	*I sleep well*
Les choses tournent **mal**	*Things are turning out badly*

TABLE 5.A *Typical manner adverbs*

Typical manner adverbs	Ending in *-ment*
ainsi *like this/that, so, thus* (can also be a sentence-modifying adverb – see 5.6.17)	affectueusement *affectionately*
bien *well* (can also be a degree adverb – see 5.6.2)	autrement *differently* (can also be a degree adverb – see 5.6.2)
debout *standing*	clairement *clearly*
ensemble *together*	confusément *in a confused manner*
exprès *purposely, on purpose*	correctement *correctly*
mal *badly*	facilement *easily*
mieux *better* (for a comparison with *meilleur* see 5.6.6)	lentement *slowly*
vite *quickly*	précautionneuse- ment *cautiously*
	soigneusement *carefully*
	vaguement *vaguely*
	Invariable phrases
	à dessein *purposely* à genoux *on one's knees* à pied *on foot* à la fois *at the same time* à tort *wrongly* de travers *crookedly*

Representative examples:

Il s'est toujours comporté **ainsi**   *He always behaved like that*
Tu chantes **bien**   *You sing well*
Mets-toi **debout**   *Stand up*
Il a **mal** lu l'étiquette   *He misread the label*

Hier soir ça n'allait guère **mieux**
It was hardly any better yesterday evening

Je l'oublierai très **facilement**
I'll forget it very easily

Elle étendait **soigneusement** son tailleur
She carefully laid out her suit

5.6.2 Degree adverbs

Adverbs which indicate the extent to which something is the case are degree adverbs. As a class they can modify every kind of sentence element: verbs, adjectives, nouns, prepositions and other adverbs. But individually some of them may be restricted to modifying particular categories of item (e.g. *très* can modify adjectives, prepositions and adverbs – *très heureux* 'very happy', *très à la mode* 'very fashionable', *très bien* 'very well' – but not verbs **Je fume très* 'I smoke very'):

Je fume **modérément**
I smoke moderately

Tout est **si** clair maintenant
Everything is so clear

Ce ne sera pas **tout à fait** la vérité
That won't be entirely the truth

Je tends ma main jusqu'à **presque** toucher son visage
I stretch out my hand almost to touch his face

Elle a dressé **trop** brusquement la tête
She lifted her head up too quickly

TABLE 5.B *Typical degree adverbs*

Typical degree adverbs	Ending in *-ment*
assez *sufficiently*	autrement *much more* (can also be a manner adverb – see 5.6.1)
aussi *as* (modifies adjectives and adverbs; *autant* modifies verb – can also be a sentence-modifying adverb – see 5.6.17)	complètement *completely*
autant *as much* (modifies verbs)	démesurément *inordinately*
beaucoup *much*	modérément *moderately*
bien *really* (can also be a manner adverb – see 5.6.1)	particulièrement *particularly*
davantage *more* (can only modify verbs)	tellement *so; so much*
encore *again; still; another*	terriblement *terribly*
juste *just*	vraiment *truly*
même *even* (when it follows a noun it may correspond to English *very*)	
moins *less* (see 5.6.5)	**Invariable phrases**
peu *little*	au moins *at least* (expresses a concrete estimate of a quantity: *au moins dix personnes blessées; du moins* expresses the speaker's view of an event: *du moins, il n'est pas blessé* – see 5.6.17)

TABLE 5.B *(continued)*

Typical degree adverbs		Invariable phrases	
plus (can modify verbs, adjectives, adverbs and prepositions – see 5.6.5)	*more*	à peine	*hardly*
plutôt	*rather*	à peu près	*nearly*
presque (does NOT contract to **presqu'* in front of a vowel: *presque à la fin)*	*almost*	de loin	*by far*
si	*so*	par trop	*by far*
tant	*so much*	tout à fait	*completely*
tout	*completely; quite* (see 5.6.7)	un peu	*a little*
très	*very*		
trop	*too*		

Representative examples

C'est un acteur **assez** connu	*He is quite a well-known actor*
La route tue **autant** que la guerre	*Road accidents are the cause of* *as many deaths as war*
Elle est **autrement** intelligente que sa soeur	*She is much more intelligent* *than her sister*
Ils ont **beaucoup** discuté pendant le weekend	*They spent a lot of time* *discussing over the weekend*
C'est **bien** bête	*That's really stupid*
Il y en a **davantage** qu'on ne le pense	*There are more than you think*
Elle a acheté un billet **juste** avant de prendre le train	*She bought a ticket just before* *catching the train*
On ramène **même** des souvenirs	*They even bring back souvenirs*
Voici le vélo **même** dont il s'est servi	*This is the very bike he used*
un monde **si** étrangement silencieux	*such a strangely silent world*
Elle est **tellement** plus sympathique	*She is so much nicer*
J'ai répondu **tout** de travers	*I replied in a quite confused way*
Je suis ici depuis **très** longtemps	*I have been here for a very long time*
Elle parle **trop**	*She talks too much*

A number of degree adverbs also function as quantifiers modifying nouns (see Chapter 6.9):

assez d'excuses	*enough excuses*
autant d'argent	*as much money*
beaucoup de clients	*many customers*

bien des problèmes	*many problems*
tellement de travail	*so much work*

5.6.3 Comparative and superlative forms of adverbs

In English, the majority of adverbs can be made into comparative forms by putting 'more', 'less' or 'as' in front of them, and into superlative forms by putting 'the most' or 'the least' in front of them:

These days I can remember it

- easily
- more easily (than I used to)
- less easily (than I used to)
- as easily (as I used to)

This window opens

- the most easily (of all of them)
- the least easily (of all of them)

A small set of English adverbs, however, have special comparative and superlative forms:

She finishes

- fast
- faster
- the fastest

She sings

- well
- better
- the best

He behaves

- badly
- worse
- the worst

A similar pattern exists in French where the majority of adverbs can be made into comparative forms by putting the degree adverbs *plus, moins* or *aussi* in front of the adverb, and into superlative forms by putting *le plus* or *le moins* in front of the adverb. In the latter case *le plus* and *le moins* do not change in gender and number:

De nos jours je m'en souviens

- facilement
- plus facilement (qu'auparavant)
- moins facilement (qu'auparavant)
- aussi facilement (qu'auparavant)

Cette fenêtre-ci ouvre

- le plus facilement (de toutes)
- le moins facilement (de toutes)

5.6.4 *bien* 'well', *mieux* 'better', *mal* 'badly', *pis* 'worse'

One adverb in French has special comparative and superlative forms:

bien *well*	mieux *better*	le mieux *the best*
	moins bien *less well*	le moins bien *the least well*

| Elle chante | bien
mieux
moins bien
le mieux
le moins bien | *She sings* | *well*
better
less well
the best
the least well |

The adverb *mal* 'badly' has two sets of comparative and superlative forms, one regular and one irregular:

Regular		
mal *badly*	plus mal *worse*	le plus mal *the worst*
	moins mal *less badly*	le moins mal *the least badly*
Irregular		
pis *worse*		le pis *the worst*

pis and *le pis* only occur these days in fixed expressions like:

tant pis	*too bad*
Les choses vont de mal en pis	*Things are going from bad to worse*
(*or* de pis en pis)	
qui pis est, . . .	*what's worse, . . .*
au pis aller	*if the worse comes to the worst*
en mettant tout au pis, . . .	*at the worst, . . .*

5.6.5 *beaucoup* 'much', *plus* 'more', *peu* 'little', *moins* 'less'

The comparative and superlative forms of the degree adverb *beaucoup* are *plus* and *le plus* (the final *s* is pronounced except in front of words beginning with a consonant); the comparative and superlative forms of the degree adverb *peu* are *moins* and *le moins*:

| Elle mange | beaucoup
plus [s]
le plus [s] (de toutes)
autant (que moi) | *She eats* | *a lot*
more
the most (of all)
as much (as me) |

| Elle mange | peu
moins
le moins (de toutes)
aussi peu (que moi) | *She eats* | *little*
less
the least (of all)
as little (as me) |

plus and *moins* are also used in expressions like:

De plus en plus de femmes enceintes veulent connaître le sexe de leur bébé
More and more pregnant women want to know what sex their baby is

De moins en moins de femmes enceintes fument
Fewer and fewer pregnant women smoke

Plus on est âgé **plus** on a de difficultés à s'adapter au changement
The older one is, the more difficulty one has adapting to change

Moins on a de revenus **moins** on a de choix dans la vie
The less wealthy one is, the fewer choices one has in life

Elle est **encore plus** talentueuse que je n'avais pensé
She is even more talented than I had thought

Ce roman est **encore moins** lisible que je ne croyais
This novel is even less readable than I had thought

5.6.6 Difference between *meilleur(e)(s)* and *mieux*, and *le/la/les meilleur(e)(s)* and *le mieux*

meilleur(e)(s) and *le/la/les meilleur(e)(s)* are the comparative and superlative forms respectively of the adjective *bon* 'good'. *mieux* and *le mieux* are the comparative and superlative forms respectively of the adverb *bien* 'well':

Adjective	bon	*good*	meilleur(s) meilleure(s)	*better*	le meilleur la meilleure les meilleur(e)s	*the best*
Adverb	bien	*well*	mieux	*better*	le mieux	*the best*

Il désire avoir une **meilleure** place   *He wants to have a better seat*
Ces marchandises sont **meilleures**   *These goods are better*
Elle s'habille **mieux** que les autres   *She dresses better than the others*
Elle s'habille **le mieux** de toutes   *She dresses the best of all*

Since the adverb *bien* 'well' can also sometimes function as an adjective close in meaning to *bon*, particularly with *être*, there are contexts where *meilleur* and *mieux* are both possible:

Tout est **bien**/Tout est **mieux**
Everything is fine/Everything is better

Tout est **bon**/Tout est **meilleur**
Everything is good/Everything is better

Elle est **bien** comme directeur/Elle est **mieux** comme directeur
She is fine as a director/She is better as a director

Elle est **bonne** comme directeur/Elle est **meilleure** comme directeur
She is good as a director/She is better as a director

On est **bien** ici/On est **mieux** ici
We're fine here/We're better here

C'est **bon** ici/C'est **meilleur** ici
It's good here/It's better here

5.6.7 Form and uses of *tout*

tout can function as a determiner, a quantifier, a pronoun and an adverb. It behaves differently with respect to agreement in each of these roles, so it is important to distinguish them.

tout as a determiner

tout is a determiner in constructions like the following. Here there is no article and *tout* agrees with the noun which it determines:

Tout parent veut le bien de son enfant
Every parent wants what is best for his or her child

Toutes taxes comprises
All taxes included

Les repas sont servis à **toute** heure
Meals are served at any time

Ils sont venus à **toute** vitesse
They came as quickly as they could

Un tel costume convient à **toute** occasion
Such a suit can be worn on any occasion

tout as a quantifier

tout is a quantifier (see Chapter 6.9) in the following examples. Its translation equivalent in English is usually 'all'. It agrees with the noun which it modifies:

Tous les garçons sont arrivés
All the boys have arrived

Toutes les chansons qu'ils passent sur cette chaîne sont dépassées
All the songs they play on that station are out of date

Il s'en est plaint **toute** la journée
He complained about it all day

tout as a pronoun

tout is a pronoun when it is used as a subject, direct object, indirect object or follows a preposition.

When it has the indefinite meaning 'everything, all' it is invariable:

Tout bien considéré, j'ai décidé de ne pas le faire
All things considered, I've decided not to do it

Tu m'avais dit que **tout** serait réglé avant ce soir
You told me that everything would be sorted out by this evening

When it refers to people or things mentioned or implied elsewhere in the discourse, it agrees in gender and number with those entities, and takes one of the forms *tout, toute, tous, toutes*. In this use the final *-s* of *tous* is pronounced:

Nous sommes infiniment redevables à **tous** (final *-s* pronounced)
We are eternally grateful to everyone

Nous allons chanter **tous** ensemble (final *-s* pronounced)
We'll all sing together

Je n'aime plus ces chansons. **Toutes** sont dépassées
I don't like these songs anymore. They are all out of date

tout as an adverb

tout is an adverb when it modifies another adverb, a preposition or an adjective. It has the meaning of 'completely, very'.

In front of an adverb or preposition it is invariable:

> Elle chante **tout** bas
> *She is singing very quietly*

> Son succès était **tout** bonnement la meilleure surprise de l'année
> *His success was quite simply the best surprise of the year*

> Tu fais **tout** de travers
> *You do everything the wrong way round*

In front of an adjective it agrees if the adjective is feminine and begins with a consonant:

> Les petites filles étaient **toutes** désemparées par l'annonce de la directrice
> *The little girls were completely taken aback by the headmistress's announcement*

> Tes sœurs sont **toutes** prêtes à venir te rejoindre
> *Your sisters are quite ready to come out and join you*

Agreement is optional in front of adjectives which are feminine and begin with a vowel or a silent *h*:

> Tu sais bien que ta sœur serait **tout** (or **toute**) heureuse de te revoir
> *You know full well that your sister would be delighted to see you again*

> Les petites chattes étaient **tout** (or **toutes**) excitées par les mouvement de la bobine de fil
> *The little kittens were thoroughly excited by the movements of the cotton reel*

5.6.8 Time adverbs

Adverbs which indicate the time at which something takes place, or the duration or frequency of an event, are time adverbs (as shown in Table 5.C):

> L'image est nette **à présent**
> *The picture is clear now*

> Il y est **toujours**
> *He is still there*

> **Soudain** il y a eu comme un déplacement d'air
> *Suddenly there was a kind of movement of air*

TABLE 5.C *Typical time adverbs*

Typical time adverbs			
alors　　　　*then, at that time* (can also be a sentence-modifying adverb – see 5.6.17)		soudain	*suddenly*
aujourd'hui	*today*	souvent	*often*
auparavant	*beforehand*	tantôt tantôt . . . tantôt	*this afternoon* *one minute . . . the* *next . . .*
aussitôt	*immediately*	tard	*late*
autrefois	*in the past*	tôt	*early*
bientôt	*soon*	toujours	*always; still*
déjà	*already*		
demain	*tomorrow*	**Ending in *-ment***	
depuis	*since then*	actuellement	*currently*
désormais	*henceforth*	dernièrement	*recently*
dorénavant	*henceforth*	fréquemment	*frequently*
encore　　　　*again; still; yet* (can also be a sentence-modifying adverb – see 5.6.17)		précédémment	*previously*
enfin	*finally*	prochainement	*soon*
ensuite	*afterwards*	récemment	*recently*
entre-temps	*meanwhile*		
hier	*yesterday*	**Invariable phrases**	
		à présent	*at present*
jadis　　　　*in the (distant) past* (the final -s is always pronounced)		dès lors	*from then on*
jamais	*ever*	d'un instant à l'autre	*at any moment*
longtemps	*a long time*	en ce moment	*at the moment*
maintenant	*now*	par la suite	*subsequently*
naguère	*in the recent past*	tout à coup	*suddenly*
parfois	*sometimes*	tout à l'heure	*just now; presently*
quelquefois	*sometimes*	tout de suite	*immediately*

Representative examples:

Actuellement il sort avec ma sœur	*Currently, he's going out with my sister*
Il l'avait rencontrée deux ans **auparavant**	*He had met her two years before*
Dès lors il voulait passer sa vie avec elle	*From then on he wanted to spend his life with her*
Elle s'en est rendu compte **aussitôt**	*She realized immediately*
Ensuite il ne s'est rien passé	*Afterwards nothing happened*
Entre-temps elle avait rencontré quelqu'un d'autre	*Meanwhile she had met someone else*
Son sourire n'a plus été le même **par la suite**	*His smile was never the same afterwards*
Nous avons parlé **longtemps**	*We spoke for a long time*
Le bureau occupe deux étages, **naguère** habités	*The office occupies two floors, formerly living accommodation*
Quelquefois on me conduisait à Roubaix	*Sometimes they took me to Roubaix*
J'ai **souvent** voulu le faire	*I've often wanted to do it*
Sors **tout de suite**	*Get out of here immediately*

5.6.9 *alors*

alors has two distinct adverbial uses. One as a time adverb meaning 'then, at that time':

Il était **alors** directeur d'une petite agence immobilière en province
At that time he was the manager of an estate agency in a small town

In this use it can appear in the middle of a clause, as in the above example (for the position of adverbs see 5.7).

Its other use is as a sentence-modifying adverb meaning 'so', which occurs at the beginning of a clause. This use is as frequent in spoken French as 'so' is in spoken English:

Alors, quoi de neuf?	*So, what's new?*
Alors, qu'est-ce que tu en penses?	*So, what do you think about it?*

5.6.10 *encore* and *toujours*

encore and *toujours* have several meanings, and overlap in one of those meanings, which makes them difficult for the learner. Both *encore* and *toujours* can mean 'still' in clauses which express an ongoing state of affairs:

Est-il **encore/toujours** là?   *Is he still here?*
(His being here is an ongoing state of affairs)

Elle se plaint **encore/toujours**   *She is still complaining*
(Her complaining is an ongoing state of affairs)

In clauses which describe a completed action, or the potential for the completion of an action, however, *encore* means 'again':

Il a **encore** perdu sa clef   *He has lost his key again*
(His losing of the key is a completed action)

J'ai peur de m'évanouir **encore**   *I am afraid of fainting again*
(Although I haven't done so yet, fainting has the potential for being a completed action)

Note that if *encore* modifies the first clause, which expresses a state of affairs, it could mean either 'still' or 'again': *J'ai **encore** peur de m'évanouir* 'I'm still afraid of fainting' or 'Once again I am afraid of fainting'.

Where *encore* modifies noun phrases or other adverbs it means 'still more, further':

Encore du pain, s'il vous plaît   *More bread, please*
Ils ont roulé **encore** dix ou vingt kilomètres
They travelled a further ten or twenty kilometres

Elle est **encore** plus douée que sa sœur
She is even more gifted than her sister

J'aime **encore** mieux votre idée que la mienne
I like your idea even more than mine

toujours, in addition to meaning 'still', can also mean 'always':

Elles ont **toujours** refusé de me parler
They have always refused to talk to me

On s'efforçait depuis **toujours** de me le cacher
They had always tried to hide it from me

In sentences negated by *pas*, if *toujours* precedes the *pas* it means 'still', if it follows it means 'always':

Il n'est **toujours** pas arrivé   *He still hasn't arrived*
Il n'est pas **toujours** arrivé   *He didn't always arrive/turn up*

encore can only follow *pas* and means 'yet':

Il n'est pas **encore** arrivé   *He hasn't yet arrived*

5.6.11 *ensuite* and *puis*

ensuite and *puis* both mean 'afterwards, then', but *ensuite* is a time adverb which can occur in the middle of a clause (for the position of adverbs see 5.7), while *puis* is a coordinating conjunction which can occur only at the beginning of a clause (see Chapter 17.2):

Il a payé l'addition, et il est **ensuite** parti
He paid the bill, and afterwards left

Il a payé l'addition, **puis** il est parti
He paid the bill, then he left

5.6.12 *jamais*

jamais is mostly used with *ne* to mean 'never' (see Chapter 16.9). It can, however, also mean 'ever' in questions, in *si*- clauses or when it is a complement to *sans*:

As-tu **jamais** vu une chose pareille?
Have you ever seen anything like it?

Si **jamais** tu rencontres Jules, tu lui diras bonjour de ma part
If you ever meet Jules, say hello to him from me

Il a fait cet exercice cent fois sans **jamais** se tromper
He's done that exercise a hundred times without ever making a mistake

5.6.13 *tard versus en retard*

Both of these terms translate as 'late' into English. However, *en retard* is restricted in meaning to the idea of 'not on time':

Tu es de nouveau **en retard**. Tu resteras après l'école
You are late again. You'll stay behind after school

tard has a wider range of meaning:

Il est déjà **tard**, nous devons rentrer
It's already late, we must go home

Pour toi, il est trop **tard**. Tu aurais dû le faire il y a plusieurs années
For you it's too late. You should have done it several years ago

Il n'est jamais trop **tard**
It's never too late

5.6.14 *tout à l'heure*

The meaning of *tout à l'heure* is determined by the tense of the verb in the clause which contains it. If the verb is in a past tense it means 'just now'; if the verb is in a present or future tense it means 'presently':

Je suis arrivé **tout à l'heure**
I arrived just now

Elle va arriver **tout à l'heure**
She will arrive presently

5.6.15 Choice of some time adverbs relative to the moment of speaking

The meaning of some time adverbs is determined by their relation to the time of speaking. If someone says:

Je suis arrivé **hier**
I arrived yesterday

hier refers to the day before the day on which the person is speaking. Similarly, if someone says:

J'arriverai **demain**
I'll arrive tomorrow

demain refers to the day after the day on which the person is speaking. By contrast, if someone says:

Je suis arrivé **la veille**
I arrived the day before

they are referring to a day before some point prior to the time when they are speaking. Similarly in:

> Je suis arrivé **le lendemain**
> *I arrived the day after*

le lendemain refers to the day after some point prior to the moment of speaking.

Different series of adverbs must be used depending on whether they refer to before or after the actual moment of speaking, or whether they refer to before or after some point prior to the moment of speaking. Examples are presented in Tables 5.D and 5.E.

TABLE 5.D *Adverbs and time reference 1*

More distant past	Recent past	Concurrent with the time of speaking	Near future	More distant future
avant-hier *the day before yesterday*	hier *yesterday*	aujourd'hui *today*	demain *tomorrow*	après-demain *the day after tomorrow*
	alors *then*	maintenant *now*	bientôt *soon*	
	hier matin hier midi hier après-midi hier soir *yesterday morning, midday, etc.*	ce matin ce midi cet après-midi/ tantôt ce soir *this morning, midday, this afternoon, this evening*	demain matin demain midi demain après-midi demain soir *tomorrow morning, midday, etc.*	
autrefois jadis (literary) *formerly*	tout à l'heure *just now* récemment dernièrement naguère *recently*	actuellement *currently*	tout à l'heure ('tantôt' in parts of France, in Belgium and Quebec) *presently*	à l'avenir *in the future*

TABLE 5.E *Adverbs and time reference 2*

More distant past	Recent past	Prior to the time of speaking	Near future	More distant future
l'avant-veille *the day before the day before*	la veille *the day before*	ce jour-là *that day*	le lendemain *the day after*	le surlendemain *the day after the day after*
	la veille au matin *the morning of the day before*	ce matin-là *that morning*	le lendemain matin *the morning of the day after*	
	la veille à midi *midday of the day before*	ce midi-là *that midday*	le lendemain midi *midday of the day after*	
	dans l'après-midi de la veille *the afternoon of the day before*	cet après-midi-là *that afternoon*	dans l'après-midi du lendemain *the afternoon of the day after*	
	la veille au soir *the evening of the day before*	ce soir-là *that evening*	le lendemain soir *the evening of the day after*	

5.6.16 Place adverbs
Adverbs which describe the place where an event occurs are place adverbs:

> J'entends des pas précipités **dehors**
> *I hear hurried steps outside*

> On m'a tiré **en arrière**
> *I was pulled backwards*

Representative examples:

Nous voulons habiter **ailleurs**	*We want to live elsewhere*
Vous entrez **dedans**	*You go inside*
Quelqu'un, **dehors**, s'est inquiété	*Someone, outside, got nervous*
Derrière il y a un champ de betteraves	*Behind there is a beet field*
Vous trouverez l'étiquette **dessous**	*You'll find the label on the bottom*
L'adresse est marquée **dessus**	*The address is written on the top*
bras **dessus** bras **dessous**	*arm in arm*
On a laissé des papiers un peu **partout**	*Papers were left almost everywhere*

TABLE 5.F *Typical place adverbs*

Typical place adverbs			
ailleurs	*elsewhere*	en amont en aval	*upstream* *downstream*
dedans en dedans au-dedans là-dedans	*inside* *inwardly; facing inwards* *on the inside* *in there*	en avant en arrière	*in/at the front* *in/at the back*
dehors en dehors au-dehors	*outside* *outwardly; facing outwards* *on the outside*	ici	*here*
derrière par derrière	*behind* *from behind*	là	*there* (used a lot to mean here: *'I'm here'* Je suis là)
dessous en dessous au-dessous par-dessous	*underneath, on the bottom* *underneath, on the back* *below* *underneath* (implying motion: *passer par-dessous* 'to go underneath')	loin	*far away*
dessus en dessus au-dessus par-dessus	*over, on the top* *on the top, on the front* *above* *across* (sauter par-dessus 'to jump across')	partout	*everywhere*
ci-contre ci-dessous	*opposite* (on a page) *below* (in a piece of writing: *voir ci-dessous* 'see below')	près	*nearby*
ci-dessus ci-après ci-devant	*above* (voir ci-dessus 'see above') *later* *earlier*		
en bas en haut	*(down) below* *(up) above*		

5.6.17 Sentence-modifying adverbs

Sentence-modifying adverbs fall into two types. Those which establish a link between what has been said already and what is being said now:

> La porte de la pièce est fermée. Je l'ai **pourtant** laissée ouverte derrière moi
> *The door to the room is closed. Yet I left it open behind me*
> (*pourtant* highlights the contrast between a previous state of affairs and the current state of affairs)

> Les arguments en faveur de cette ligne politique sont clairs. Nous devons **donc** la suivre de près
> *The arguments in favour of this policy are clear. Therefore we should follow it closely*
> (*donc* signals a causal link between the first sentence and the second)

The second group of sentence-modifying adverbs express the speaker's assessment of the probability or desirability of the event described by the sentence being true:

> Elle était pauvre, **probablement**   *She was probably poor*
> (*probablement* is the speaker's judgement of the likelihood of her being poor)

> Je n'ai **malheureusement** pas pu venir   *Unfortunately I wasn't able to come*
> (*malheureusement* is an expression of the speaker's regret at not being able to come)

See table 5.G for typical cases.

Representative examples:

> J'ai beaucoup travaillé pour terminer à temps. **Cependant**, ils n'ont pas voulu me payer mon treizième mois
> *I worked very hard to finish in time. Yet they refused to pay me my bonus*

> M Bergamote a expliqué la situation très clairement. **En effet**, nous devrons prendre une décision aujourd'hui même
> *Mr Bergamote explained the situation very clearly. Indeed, we must take a decision this very day*

> Jouer en Bourse est une bonne occupation pour ceux qui s'y connaissent. **En revanche**, cela peut être une catastrophe pour ceux qui n'y connaissent rien
> *Playing the Stock Exchange is a sensible activity for those who know what they're doing. On the other hand, it can be a catastrophe for those who don't*

> Le bateau a coulé au mois de juin. **Néanmoins**, la compagnie d'assurance établissait toujours les faits au mois de décembre
> *The boat sank in June. Nonetheless, the insurance company was still trying to establish the facts in December*

> Mon fils ne m'écrit jamais. Sa sœur, **par contre**, me tient au courant de tout ce qu'elle fait
> *My son never writes to me. His sister, on the other hand, keeps me informed of everything she is doing*

Alors, que préférait-elle?
So, what did she prefer?

Ils me répondraient, **bien sûr**, que j'aurais pu le faire depuis longtemps
They would reply, of course, that I could have done it long before

TABLE 5.G *Typical sentence-linking and speaker-oriented adverbs*

Typical sentence-linking adverbs	Typical speaker-oriented adverbs
ainsi *so, in the same way* (can also be a manner adverb – see 5.6.1)	alors *so* (can also be a time adverb – see 5.6.8)
au contraire *conversely*	assurément *surely*
aussi *so, thus* (can also be a degree adverb – see 5.6.2)	bien sûr *of course*
cependant *yet*	certainement *certainly*
d'ailleurs *moreover, what's more*	certes *certainly*
encore *for all that* (can also be a time adverb – see 5.6.8)	du moins *at least* (expresses the speaker's reservation – *au moins* is a degree adverb (see 5.6.2) used when 'at least' is concrete: *au* *moins dix fois* 'at least ten times')
en effet *indeed*	en général *in general*
en revanche *on the contrary*	évidemment *evidently*
en somme *in sum, briefly*	heureusement *fortunately*
néanmoins *nonetheless*	peut-être *perhaps*
par conséquent *consequently* en conséquence	probablement *probably*
par contre *on the other hand*	sans doute *doubtlessly*
plutôt *rather*	seulement *only*
pourtant *yet*	soit *so be it*
quand même *all the same*	sûrement *surely*
toutefois *nevertheless*	vraisemblablement *in all likelihood*

Je n'aurais **certainement** pas pu le comprendre
I certainly couldn't have understood it

Elle ne s'en doutait **certes** pas
She certainly didn't suspect it

Le prof a **du moins** cette qualité qu'il articule bien
The teacher has at least this quality, that he speaks very clearly

C'est **sans doute** un ami
He's probably a friend

Il a entrepris cette démarche avec de très bonnes intentions. **Seulement**, il ne
possédait pas les connaissances requises
*He took these steps with the very best of intentions. Only he didn't have the knowledge
required*

5.7 Location of adverbs

5.7.1 Location of adverbs modifying adjectives, prepositions, noun phrases and other adverbs

Adverbs which modify adjectives, prepositions, noun phrases, and other
adverbs appear immediately in front of those items:

Je ne suis pas **vraiment** mauvais   (modifying an adjective)
I'm not really bad

Nous irons **loin** au-delà de la frontière   (modifying a preposition)
We'll go far beyond the frontier

Il y a **au moins** dix ans   (modifying a noun phrase)
At least ten years ago

Je suis ici depuis **très** longtemps   (modifying an adverb)
I have been here for a very long time

5.7.2 Location of adverbs modifying verb phrases

Adverbs which modify the verb phrase (manner, degree, some time and place
adverbs) and adverbs which modify the sentence may have several possible
locations.

Manner, degree and time adverbs which consist of just one word usually immediately follow the tense-marked verb:

Elle a **soigneusement** étendu son tailleur sur le lit
She carefully laid out her suit on the bed

On ramène **parfois** des souvenirs
We sometimes bring back souvenirs

J'ai **souvent** voulu le faire
I have often wanted to do it

Ils ont **beaucoup** discuté pendant le weekend
They discussed a lot during the weekend

Il a **mal** lu l'étiquette
He misread the label

Elles ont **toujours** refusé de me parler
They have always refused to talk to me

NB: With verbs in simple tenses it is normal in French for these adverbs to occur between the verb and its complement, but not between the subject and the verb: the reverse is the case in English:

On ramène **parfois** des souvenirs	NOT	*On parfois ramène des souvenirs
Je veux **souvent** le faire	NOT	*Je souvent veux le faire
Elles refusent **toujours** de me parler	NOT	*Elles toujours refusent de me parler

Usually manner, degree and time adverbs consisting of just one word and modifying the verb phrase can also appear at the end of the clause:

Elle a étendu son tailleur **soigneusement**
On ramène des souvenirs **parfois**

But some appear most naturally in a clause-internal position after the verb. This tends to be the case for short monosyllabic adverbs: *bien, mal, vite, trop, tant*. An exception, though, is time adverbs which designate specific moments in the past or future: *hier* 'yesterday', *demain* 'tomorrow', *la veille* 'the day before', and so on. These usually appear at the beginning or the end of a clause, not in the middle:

J'ai ramassé les clefs **hier**   OR   **Hier** j'ai ramassé les clefs
I picked up the keys yesterday

La veille elle avait vendu sa maison   OR   Elle avait vendu sa maison **la veille**
She had sold her house the day before

Adverbs of manner, degree and time which consist of more than a single word, together with place adverbs as a class, usually come at the beginning or end of a clause, not in the middle:

Il a emporté le dossier **à dessin**	*He took the file away on purpose*
Ici tout le monde fait la vaisselle	*Everybody does the washing-up here*
Nous voulons habiter **ailleurs**	*We want to live elsewhere*
Derrière il y a un champ de betteraves	*Behind there is a beet field*
Vous trouverez l'étiquette **dessous**	*You'll find the label on the bottom*
On a laissé des papiers un peu **partout**	*Papers were left almost everywhere*

It is always possible, however, for such adverbs to occur clause-internally with heavy pausing on either side (indicated by commas in written French). This has the effect of stressing the adverb:

J'ai ramassé, **hier**, les clefs
Quelqu'un, **dehors**, s'est inquiété
Il y a, **derrière**, un champ de betteraves

5.7.3 Location of adverbs modifying sentences

Sentence-modifying adverbs can usually appear at the beginning, in the middle or at the end of clauses:

La porte de la pièce est fermée. Je l'ai **pourtant** laissée ouverte derrière moi/**Pourtant** je l'ai laissée ouverte derrière moi/Je l'ai laissée ouverte derrière moi **pourtant**
The door to the room is closed. Yet I left it open behind me

Il s'ensuit **donc** que nous devons la suivre de près/**Donc** il s'ensuit que nous devons la suivre de près/Il s'ensuit que nous devons la suivre de près **donc**
It follows, therefore, that we should follow it closely

Malheureusement, je n'ai pas pu venir/Je n'ai **malheureusement** pas pu venir/Je n'ai pas pu venir **malheureusement**
Unfortunately, I wasn't able to come

There is a tendency in French not to put short constituents at the end of a sentence where a long constituent precedes. This can sometimes determine a preferred location for adverbs. For example, it is less natural to say:

Il s'ensuit que nous devons la suivre de près **donc**

where the short *donc* is in sentence-final position and is preceded by the long constituent *que nous devons la suivre de près*, than:

Il s'ensuit **donc** que nous devons la suivre de près

In a sentence like:

On a laissé des papiers **partout**

the place adverb *partout* would normally appear at the end of the clause, rather than in the middle. But if the direct object is made longer, it becomes more natural to put it at the end, leaving *partout* in the middle:

On a laissé **partout** des papiers couverts de gribouillis
They left papers covered in doodles lying about everywhere

5.7.4 Inversion of subject and verb after some sentence-initial adverbs
In formal written French, a small set of adverbs (drawn from several of the classes described in this chapter) may provoke subject-verb inversion when they occur in sentence-initial position. Inversion is likely with the following adverbs:

A peine Pierre s'est-il assis qu'on lui a demandé de se déplacer
Hardly had Pierre sat down when he was asked to move

Peut-être Alice arrivera-t-elle demain
Perhaps Alice will arrive tomorrow

Sans doute vous a-t-elle écrit
Doubtless she has written to you

Toujours est-il que je ne peux pas vous payer
The fact remains that I cannot pay you

(For the properties of subject-verb inversion see Chapter 14.2.3.)

An alternative in the case of *peut-être* and *sans doute* is the use of a following *que* without inversion:

> **Peut-être qu**'Alice arrivera demain
> **Sans doute** qu'elle vous a écrit

In spoken French *peut-être que* and *sans doute que* are frequent, but inversion is not, speakers locating the adverbs in a different position, or simply not inverting after the adverb.

Other adverbs after which inversion is possible (but less likely) in formal written French are:

> **Ainsi** a-t-elle gagné le prix
> *In that way she won the prize*

> Il n'a plus d'argent; **aussi** doit-il rentrer
> *He has no more money; so he must go home*

> **Du moins** ont-ils gardé leur calme
> *At least they kept their cool*

> **Encore** ne suis-je là que pour prendre des notes
> *For all that, I'm here just to take notes*

> **En vain** a-t-il cherché
> *In vain he searched*

> **Rarement** trouve-t-on une affaire pareille
> *Rarely does one find such a bargain*

6

Numbers, measurements, time and quantifiers

6.1 Cardinal numbers

Numbers like *un, deux, trois*, etc., are called cardinal numbers:

0	zéro	
1	un	*un* (masculine) is used in contexts like the following: *il porte le numéro 'un'*, 'He is wearing the number "one"'; *à la page un*, 'on page one'; *la partie un*, 'part one'. It is also used as a masculine pronoun: *As-tu un stylo? Pierre en a **un*** 'Have you got a pen? Pierre has one'. *une* (feminine) is used as a feminine pronoun: *Il ne m'en reste qu'**une** (carte postale)*, 'I've only got one left (postcard)'. NB: *à la une* 'on the front page'.
2	deux	
3	trois	
4	quatre	*quatre* is invariable and never takes a plural *-s*: *les quatre chats* 'the four cats'.
5	cinq	The final *q* of *cinq* is always pronounced [k], except when it precedes *cent*, where it is not pronounced: *cinq cents*.
6	six	*six* is pronounced with a final [s] when it is at the end of a phrase: *j'en ai vu six* 'I saw six'; it is pronounced with a final [z] when it precedes a noun beginning with a vowel: *six hommes* 'six men'. When it precedes a noun beginning with a consonant the *x* is not pronounced: *six joueurs* 'six players'.
7	sept	
8	huit	*huit* is pronounced with a final [t] when it is at the end of a phrase: *j'en ai vu huit* 'I saw eight', and when it precedes a noun beginning with a vowel: *huit entreprises ont fermé* 'eight firms have closed'. When it precedes a noun beginning with a consonant the *t* is not pronounced: *huit semaines plus tard* 'eight weeks later'.

9	neuf	The final *f* of *neuf* is always pronounced [f], except in *neuf ans* 'nine years' and *neuf heures* 'nine hours, nine o'clock' where it is pronounced [v].
10	dix	The pronunciation of *dix* is the same as for *six*.
11	onze	
12	douze	*douze* is invariable, and never takes a plural *-s*: *douze hommes* 'twelve men'.
13	treize	
14	quatorze	
15	quinze	
16	seize	
17	dix-sept	
18	dix-huit	The pronunciation of *dix-huit* is the same as for *huit*.
19	dix-neuf	The pronunciation of *dix-neuf* is the same as for *neuf*.
20	vingt	*vingt* is pronounced like *vin*, with the following exceptions: it is pronounced with a final [t] when it precedes a noun beginning with a vowel: *vingt exercices* 'twenty exercises', and also in the numbers *21–29* inclusive.
21	vingt et un	*vingt et un(e), trente et un(e), quarante et un(e)*, etc. are used under the same conditions described for *un(e)*.
22	vingt-deux	
23 ...	vingt-trois	
29	vingt-neuf	
30	trente	
31	trente et un	
32 ...	trente-deux	
39	trente-neuf	
40	quarante	
41	quarante et un	
42 ...	quarante-deux	
49	quarante-neuf	
50	cinquante	

51	cinquante et un	
52	cinquante-deux	
...		
59	cinquante-neuf	
60	soixante	
61	soixante et un	
62	soixante deux	
...		
69	soixante-neuf	
70	soixante-dix	In Belgian and Swiss French the word *septante* is used instead of *soixante-dix: septante et un, septante-deux,* etc.
71	soixante et onze	
72	soixante-douze	
73	soixante-treize	
...		
79	soixante-dix-neuf	
80	quatre-vingts	
81	quatre-vingt-un	
82	quatre-vingt-deux	
...		
89	quatre-vingt-neuf	
90	quatre-vingt-dix	In Belgian and Swiss French the word *nonante* is used instead of *quatre-vingt-dix: nonante-un, nonante-deux,* etc.
91	quatre-vingt-onze	
92	quatre-vingt-douze	
93	quatre-vingt-treize	
...		
99	quatre-vingt-dix-neuf	
100	cent	'one hundred, a hundred' is simply *cent*: 'a hundred times' *cent fois*
101	cent un	*cent une réponses* 'a hundred and one answers'

102	cent deux	
...		
111	cent onze	The [t] of *cent* is NOT pronounced in *cent un, cent huit, cent onze*, but it is pronounced when followed by a non-numeral noun beginning with a vowel: *cent ans* 'a hundred years'.
200	deux cents	
201	deux cent un	
202	deux cent deux	
...		
1 000	mille	'one thousand, a thousand' is simply *mille*: 'a thousand times' *mille fois*
1 001	mille un	
...		
1 100	onze cents *or* mille cent	There are two ways of describing numbers between 1100 and 1999: *onze cents* or *mille cent* (1100); *dix-huit cent soixante* or *mille huit cent soixante* (1860); *dix-neuf cent quatre-vingt-dix-neuf* or *mille neuf cent quatre-vingt-dix-neuf* (1999), etc.
1 101	onze cent un OR mille cent un	
...		
1 200	douze cents OR mille deux cents	
1 201	douze cent un OR mille deux cent un	
...		
1 500	quinze cents OR mille cinq cents	
...		
2 000	deux mille	
2 001	deux mille un	
2 101	deux mille cent un	
1 000 000	un million	
1 201 101	un million deux cent mille cent un	
1 000 000 000	un milliard	

6.1.1 et in cardinal numbers

et is used for cardinal numbers ending in -1 between 21 and 71 inclusive (note the absence of hyphens):

21	vingt et un
31	trente et un

41	quarante et un
51	cinquante et un
61	soixante et un
71	soixante et onze

et is NOT used in numbers ending in -1 between 81 and 101 inclusive (note the use of hyphens in the case of 81 and 91), nor in 1 001, 1 000 001 and 1 000 000 001:

81	quatre-vingt-un
91	quatre-vingt-onze
101	cent un
1 001	mille un
1 000 001	un million un
1 000 000 001	un milliard un

6.1.2 Hyphens in written cardinal numbers

Compound cardinal numbers less than 100 are linked by hyphen (other than those ending in -1 between 21 and 71 inclusive):

17	dix-sept	32	trente-deux
18	dix-huit	33	trente-trois
19	dix-neuf	...	
22	vingt-deux	72	soixante-douze
23	vingt-trois	80	quatre-vingts
...		81	quatre-vingt-un

But cardinal numbers of 100 and above are not linked to other numbers by hyphen, in compound numbers:

101	cent un	520	cinq cent vingt
102	cent deux	...	
...		522	cinq cent vingt-deux
192	cent quatre-vingt-douze	...	
...			
10 340	dix mille trois cent quarante		
...			

6.1.3 Plurals in cardinal numbers

The numbers *quatre-vingts* and *deux cents, trois cents, quatre cents*, etc., take a plural -s in the written language when they are used in isolation or phrase-final position:

J'en ai vu **quatre-vingts**	*I saw eighty*
La capacité de la salle est de **huit cents**	*The room can hold eight hundred*

and when they precede non-numeral nouns:

trois cents visiteurs	*three hundred visitors*
quatre-vingts candidats	*eighty applicants*

However, when these numbers precede other numerals, there is generally no plural -s:

quatre-vingt-deux
quatre-vingt-trois
...

> deux cent deux
> deux cent trois
> trois cent mille
> ...

unless those numerals are *millions* or *milliards*:

deux cents millions d'habitants	*two hundred million inhabitants*
cinq cents milliards de francs	*five hundred billion francs*

mille never takes a plural *-s:*

mille personnes	*a thousand people*
dix mille gagnants	*ten thousand winners*
deux mille vingt lecteurs	*two thousand and twenty readers*

6.1.4 When to use figures and when to use words

Numbers are usually written in words, except in the following cases:

> in scientific or academic texts
> in dates: *Elle arrive le **25** mars **1996*** 'She's arriving on the 25th of March 1996'
> in prices: *Cela coûte **32** francs* 'That costs 32 francs'
> in weights and measures: *Il mesure **1** mètre **50*** 'He is 1 metre 50 tall'
> describing kings and queens: *Henri **IV*** 'Henry the Fourth'
> in percentages: ***12** pour cent* '12 per cent'

6.1.5 Conventions for writing cardinal numbers in figures

Where English uses a comma to separate hundreds from thousands, and thousands from millions, French normally uses spaces; and where English uses a full stop to separate whole numbers from decimals, French normally uses a comma:

English	French
1,200	1 200
63,321	63 321
412,633,221	412 633 221
4.25	4,25
.25	0,25
£4.50	4,50FF/4F50 (the latter is more frequent. FF tends to be restricted to banks)

(For money, see 6.8.)

6.1.6 *nombre, chiffre* and *numéro*

nombre refers to a number as a concept:

Pensez à un **nombre**	*Think of a number*
nombres entiers	*whole numbers*
un **nombre** cardinal	*a cardinal number*

> Le **nombre** de femmes qui fument a augmenté
> *The number of women who smoke has increased*

chiffre refers to the figures or digits which make up a number; it can also be used to mean 'statistics':

Ecrire un nombre en **chiffres** et en lettres
To write a number in figures and words

Ces **chiffres** ne reflètent pas la situation exacte
These figures do not reflect the real situation

numéro refers to a numbered entity:

un **numéro** de téléphone	*a telephone number*
le **numéro** d'une maison	*a house number*
Il porte le **numéro** un	*He's wearing the number one*
un **numéro** d'immatriculation	*a car number plate*

6.1.7 Necessity to use *en* when numbers are direct objects

The pronoun *en* must be inserted before the verb when a number on its own (or followed by an adjective, e.g. *deux grands*) is a direct object:

J'**en** prends **deux (grands)**, s'il vous plaît
I'll take two (big ones), please

Elle lui **en** a offert **une douzaine**
She offered him a dozen

This is not the case, however, when a number alone (or followed by an adjective) is a subject:

Deux (grands) ont disparu	*Two (big ones) have disappeared*
Une douzaine me suffira	*A dozen will be enough for me*

en must be similarly inserted before the verb when quantifiers like *quelques-uns*, *plusieurs* and *certains* stand alone as direct objects:

J'**en** ai encore **quelques-uns**	*I still have a few*
J'**en** ai encore **plusieurs**	*I still have several*
J'**en** ai encore **certains**	*I still have some*

(For quantifiers, see 6.9.2.)

6.1.8 Non-agreement of direct object numerals with *coûter, peser, mesurer*

Although past participles normally agree with preceding direct objects (see Chapter 9.3.1), including direct objects involving numerals:

Les cinq cents francs que j'ai **gagnés**
The five hundred francs I won

with the verbs *coûter* 'cost', *peser* 'weigh', *mesurer* 'measure', and other measure verbs, numerals are normally adverbs rather than direct objects, so there is no agreement when the numeral precedes the past participle:

Les cinq cents francs que cela m'a **coûté**
The five hundred francs which that cost me

(See Chapter 9.3.5.)

6.1.9 Simple arithmetic (*le calcul*)

trois et quatre font sept	$3 + 4 = 7$
(trois plus quatre égale sept)	

trois moins un égale deux	$3 - 1 = 2$
(trois ôtez un reste deux)	
deux fois cinq font dix	$2 \times 5 = 10$
(cinq multiplié par deux égale dix)	
dix divisé par deux égale cinq	$10 \div 2 = 5$

NB: As in English, the verbs can vary between singular and plural: *trois et quatre fait/font sept* 'three plus four makes/make seven'.

6.2 Ordinal numbers

Numbers like *premier, deuxième, troisième,* etc., are called ordinal numbers:

English	French	
1st	1$^{er/ère}$	premier, première
2nd	2e	deuxième *or* second, seconde. (*deuxième* and *second* are interchangeable except in *en seconde* 'in second class'; 'in the fifth form')
3rd	3e	troisième
4th	4e	quatrième
5th	5e	cinquième
6th	6e	sixième
7th	7c	septième
8th	8e	huitième
9th	9e	neuvième
10th	10e	dixième
11th	11e	onzième
12th	12e	douzième
13th	13e	treizième
14th	14e	quatorzième
15th	15e	quinzième
16th	16e	seizième
17th	17e	dix-septième
18th	18e	dix-huitième
19th	19e	dix-neuvième
20th	20e	vingtième
21st	21e	vingt et unième
22nd	22e	vingt-deuxième
...		
40th	40e	quarantième
41st	41e	quarante et unième
...		
70th	70e	soixante-dixième
71st	71e	soixante et onzième
...		
80th	80e	quatre-vingtième
81st	81e	quatre-vingt-unième
...		
90th	90e	quatre-vingt-dixième
91th	91e	quatre-vingt-onzième
...		
100th	100e	centième
...		
1000th	1000e	millième

6.3 Fractions

6.3.1 Ordinal numbers as fractions

The majority of fractions can be constructed from the ordinal numbers, and are masculine in gender. They are usually introduced by the definite article (as opposed to the indefinite article or absence of article in English):

> **Le cinquième** des élèves ont été recalés
> *A fifth of the pupils have failed*

> **Les sept dixièmes** de la population du monde sont pauvres
> *Seven-tenths of the world's population are poor*

6.3.2 'half', 'third', 'quarter'

'Half', 'third', 'quarter' have their own names. 'Half' is translated by *la moitié (de)* when it is a noun (i.e. is followed by *de* or stands alone):

> **La moitié des** conducteurs ont dépassé la limite de vitesse
> *Half of all drivers have broken the speed limit*

> **La moitié** seront recyclés
> *Half will be retrained*

However, 'half' is translated by *demi* when it is part of a compound noun (and is invariable):

> un **demi-verre** de cognac   *a half-glass of brandy*
> une **demi-heure**   *a half an hour*
> la **demi-finale**   *the semi-final*

It is also translated by *demi* in compounds involving *et*, but here it agrees with the preceding noun in gender:

> deux heures et **demie**   *two and a half hours*
> un litre et **demi**   *one and a half litres*
> deux kilos et **demi**   *two and a half kilos*

Some compounds are constructed with invariable *mi-*:

> la **mi-trimestre**   *half-term*
> à **mi-chemin**   *half-way*
> **mi-clos**   *half-closed*

'Third' is translated by *tiers*:

> **Un tiers** des étudiants ont des dettes
> *A third of students are in debt*
> **Les deux tiers** des blessés ont été évacués
> *Two-thirds of the injured were evacuated*

NB: *le tiers monde* 'the Third World'.

'Quarter' is translated by *quart*:

> **Un quart** seulement des accidents ont lieu sur les autoroutes
> *Only a quarter of accidents happen on motorways*

Les trois quarts étaient des hommes
Three-quarters were men

NB: Il est deux heures et **quart**   or   Il est deux heures **un quart**
It's quarter past two

Il est deux heures moins **le quart**
It's quarter to two

cinq kilos et **quart**   or   cinq kilos **un quart**
five and a quarter kilos

(See 6.7 for time.)

6.3.3 Verb agreement with fractions

Verbs are usually plural when fractions are subjects and refer to plural entities:

Le cinquième (des élèves) **ont** été recalés
A fifth (of the pupils) have failed

La moitié (des conducteurs) **ont** dépassé la limite de vitesse
Half (of all drivers) have broken the speed limit

Un tiers (des étudiants) **ont** des dettes
A third (of students) are in debt

Verbs are singular when fractions are subjects and refer to singular entities:

La moitié (de l'année) **est** déjà passée
Half (of the year) has already passed

Un tiers (du livre) **reste** à écrire
A third (of the book) remains to be completed

6.4 Some differences in the use of cardinal and ordinal numbers in French and English

6.4.1 Dates

While English uses ordinal numbers in dates French uses cardinal numbers, with the exception of 'first', which is *premier*:

le **premier** janvier	*the first of January*
le **deux** février	*the second of February*
le **trois** mars	*the third of March*

In letter headings the normal way of writing dates is:

le 1ᵉʳ janvier 2001
le 2 février 2001
le 3 mars 2001

or where the day is included:

le lundi 1ᵉʳ janvier 2001	or	lundi, le 1ᵉʳ janvier 2001
le vendredi 2 février 2001	or	vendredi, le 2 février 2001

NB: Months and days are written with a lower case initial letter in French, but with a capital letter in English.

6.4.2 Kings, queens and popes
As with dates, where English uses ordinal numbers, French uses cardinal numbers, with the exception of 'first' *premier*:

François I	François **premier**	*Francis the First*
Elizabeth I	Elizabeth **première**	*Elizabeth the First*
Henri II	Henri **deux**	*Henry the Second*
Louis XIV	Louis **quatorze**	*Louis the Fourteenth*
Jean XXIII	Jean **vingt-trois**	*Pope John the Twenty-third*

6.4.3 Ordinal number abbreviations
The abbreviated forms of *premier, première* are:

1er, 1ère *1st*

where ^{er} and ^{ère} are superscripts. The abbreviation for all other ordinal numbers is an *e* which can either be a superscript or a simple lower case letter:

2^e	2e	*2nd*
3^e	3e	*3rd*
4^e	4e	*4th* etc.

6.4.4 Order of cardinal numbers and adjectives
In English, cardinal numbers follow adjectives:

*the **last nine** chapters*
*the **other four** guests*
*the **first three** winners*

In French they precede adjectives:

les **neuf derniers** chapitres
les **quatre autres** invités
les **trois premiers** gagnants

6.4.5 Page numbers, bus numbers, etc.
As in English, French page numbers, bus numbers and so on are cardinal numbers which follow the noun; *un* is invariable in this usage. A definite article always accompanies the noun in French:

à **la** page un	*on page one*
Prenez **le** trente-deux	*Catch the number 32*
Le train part **du** quai vingt	*The train leaves from platform twenty*

6.4.6 Addresses
Like English, address numbers are cardinal numbers in French. But the French for 'a', 'b', 'c' is *bis, ter, quater*:

12, rue Lamarck
12bis, rue Lamarck
12ter, rue Lamarck

NB: In addresses, *rue, avenue, boulevard*, etc., usually begin with lower case letters.

6.4.7 'hundreds', 'thousands', 'millions' and 'billions'
The numeral nouns *centaine, millier, million, milliard* are always followed by *de* when they are followed by other nouns:

des centaines **de** personnes	*hundreds of people*
des milliers **de** personnes	*thousands of people*
un million **de** dollars	*a million dollars*
des millions **de** personnes	*millions of people*
cinq milliards **de** dollars	*five billion dollars*
des milliards **de** personnes	*billions of people*
des centaines **de** milliers **de** personnes	*hundreds of thousands of people*
des centaines **de** millions **de** personnes	*hundreds of millions of people*

6.4.8 *mille, milliers, milliards*

These numbers are often confused by English speakers:

mille 'thousand' is directly followed by a noun: *mille francs* 'a thousand francs'

des milliers 'thousands' is followed by *de* when followed by another noun: ***des milliers de** francs* 'thousands of francs'

des milliards 'billions' is also followed by *de* when followed by another noun: ***des milliards de** francs* 'billions of francs'

6.4.9 'once', 'twice', 'three times', etc.; 'both', 'all three', 'all four', etc.

Whereas English has the forms 'once', 'twice', then a regular pattern from 'three' onwards: 'three times', 'four times' etc., French has a fully regular pattern from 'one' on:

une fois	*once*
deux fois	*twice*
trois fois	*three times*
quatre fois	*four times*
. . .	

French has alternative forms for 'both', 'all three', 'all four', one with a definite article and one without (found only in formal written French); but from 'all five' onwards the definite article must be used:

tous/toutes les deux	tous/toutes deux	*both*
tous/toutes les trois	tous/toutes trois	*all three*
tous/toutes les quatre	tous/toutes quatre	*all four*
tous/toutes les cinq	NOT *tous/toutes cinq	*all five*
tous/toutes les six	NOT *tous/toutes six	*all six*
. . .		

Tous les deux sont arrivés	*Both have arrived*
Je les ai invitées **toutes les six**	*I invited all six*

NB: These expressions cannot precede a noun directly. To translate phrases like 'both players', 'all six singers', either use the definite article and a numeral alone: *les deux joueurs, les six chanteuses*:

Les deux joueurs sont arrivés
J'ai invité **les six chanteuses**

or, when the phrase is in subject position, move the *tous/toutes (les)* X to a position after the verb marked for tense:

Les joueurs sont **tous deux** arrivés

(See also 6.9.5.)

6.5 Measurements and comparisons

6.5.1 Numbers with length, height, depth etc.

With the verb *être*, numbers specifying length, height, depth, width, distance and so on, are preceded by *de*:

> La piscine est longue **de** 50 mètres
> La longueur de la piscine est **de** 50 mètres
> *The swimming pool is 50 metres long*
>
> Cette tour est haute **de** 20 mètres
> La hauteur de cette tour est **de** 20 mètres
> *This tower is 20 metres high*
>
> Le lac est profond **de** 300 mètres
> La profondeur du lac est **de** 300 mètres
> *The lake is 300 metres deep*
>
> Le fleuve est large **de** 2 kilomètres à cet endroit
> La largeur du fleuve à cet endroit est **de** 2 kilomètres
> *The river is 2 kilometres wide at this point*
>
> La distance de Londres à Paris est **de** 500 kilomètres
> *The distance from London to Paris is 500 kilometres*

An alternative way of describing some of these measurements is with the verbs *faire* and *avoir*; in this case *de* precedes *long, haut, large*, etc., which remain invariable in form:

> La piscine fait/a 50 mètres **de long**
> Cette tour fait/a 20 mètres **de haut**
> Le fleuve fait/a 2 kilomètres **de large**

In talking about how tall people are, the verbs *mesurer, faire* are usually used:

> Je mesure 1,97 mètres   *I am 1.97 metres tall*
> Elle fait 1,80 mètres   *She is 1.80 metres tall*

The verbs *mesurer, faire* are the equivalent of English 'is' in describing dimensions:

> La table **mesure** (or **fait**) trois mètres sur deux
> *The table is three metres by two*

6.5.2 Numbers in comparisons

When numbers figure in comparisons with the verb *être*, they are often preceded by *de*:

> Elle est mon aînée **de** six ans
> *She is six years older than me*
>
> La fenêtre est trop grande **de** cinq centimètres
> *The window is five centimetres too big*
>
> Elle est plus lourde **de** huit kilos
> *She is eight kilograms heavier*

In some of these cases alternative expressions with *avoir* are possible:

> Elle a six ans **de** plus que moi
> J'ai six ans **de** moins qu'elle

Translating 'more than' and 'less than' into French often causes English speakers some difficulty, because there are two possibilities:

> plus de   plus que
> moins de   moins que

plus de, moins de imply that there is a specific benchmark against which something is measured as being 'more than' or 'less than', and this is often a number:

> Elle gagne **plus de** 30 000FF par mois
> *She earns more than 30,000 francs a month*
> (*30 000FF* is the benchmark – she earns more than this)

> Il travaille **moins de** deux heures par jour
> *He works less than two hours a day*
> (*deux heures* is the benchmark – he works less than this)

> Interdit aux **moins de** 15 ans
> *Not suitable for children under fifteen*
> (*15 ans* is the benchmark – below this age, children are not allowed)

plus que, moins que imply a comparison between one person or thing and another, without a specific benchmark being mentioned:

> Elle gagne **plus que** moi
> *She earns more than me*
> (how much I earn isn't specified – but she earns more)

> Il travaille **moins que** son frère
> *He works less than his brother*
> (how much his brother works isn't specified – but he works less)

The difference between the two can be illustrated in the following pair of sentences:

> Elle a réuni **plus de** cinquante de ses collègues pour la fête
> *She got more than fifty of her colleagues together for the party*
> (*cinquante de ses collègues* is the benchmark – she managed to persuade more colleagues than this to come)

> Elle a gagné **plus que** tous ses collègues ensemble pendant l'année
> *She earned more than all her colleagues during the year*
> (her colleagues earned an unspecified amount during the year – however much it was, she earned more than this)

NB: The following expressions compare one measurement with another:

quatre mètres **sur** trois	*four metres by three*
un Français **sur** sept	*one French person in seven*
une chose **à** la fois	*one thing at a time*
20% **par** an	*20% a year*
deux heures **par** jour	*two hours a day*

'miles per gallon' is measured in French by the number of litres consumed per hundred kilometres: *dix litres aux cent (kilomètres)* (roughly 30 miles per gallon).

6.5.3 Numeral nouns and approximations

The following numeral nouns describe approximate, rather than specific, numbers:

une dizaine	*ten or so*
une quinzaine	*fifteen or so*
une vingtaine	*twenty or so*
une trentaine	*thirty or so*
une quarantaine	*forty or so*
une cinquantaine	*fifty or so*
une soixantaine	*sixty or so*
une centaine	*a hundred or so*

Je reviendrai dans **une quinzaine (une huitaine)** de jours
I'll come back in about a fortnight (a week) or so

Il a environ **la trentaine**
He is thirty something

Elle a **une quarantaine** d'années
She is in her forties

J'approche de **la cinquantaine**
I'm approaching my fifties

une douzaine (une demi-douzaine), however, means 'a dozen (a half-dozen)' exactly: *une douzaine d'œufs* 'a dozen eggs'.

A variety of other expressions, when used with numbers, also express approximations:

Ça coûte **environ** 300F/**à peu près** 300F/**dans les** 300F/**près de** 300F
That costs around/about/nearly 300 francs

Il a cinquante ans **et quelques**	*He is over fifty*
Il a **autour de** cinquante ans	*He is around fifty*
Elle va **sur ses** vingt-six ans	*She is going on twenty-six*

Le train arrive **vers** 11h/**aux alentours de** 11h/**aux environs de** 11 heures
The train arrives around 11 a.m.

NB: *ans* is always present when describing a person's age.

6.6 Dates, days, years

6.6.1 Dates

Dates always begin with *le* (which does not contract to *l'* even before numbers beginning with a vowel: *le huit mars, le onze septembre*):

le 1er janvier
le 2 mai
le 8 mars
lundi **le** 11 juin

Quelle est la date d'aujourd'hui? C'est **le** 2 janvier
On est **le** combien? On est **le** 2 janvier

NB: When writing dates, months always begin with lower case letters.

6.6.2 Days

When days of the week are used without a determiner, they usually refer to a specific day:

Je viendrai vous voir **lundi**   *I'll come and see you on Monday*

(But in dates, days of the week are preceded by *le: le lundi 8 août*.)

When days of the week are preceded by a definite article they usually describe what habitually happens:

Le magasin est fermé **le** lundi (or tous les lundis)
*The shop is closed **on** Mondays*

le matin, l'après-midi, le soir, la nuit are used in the same way:

Elle se lève tôt **le** matin
She gets up early in the mornings

(versus *Elle s'est levée tôt lundi matin* 'She got up early on Monday morning'.)

Seasons can be used in a similar way:

faire du ski **l'hiver** (also **en hiver**)   *to go skiing in winter*
jouer au tennis **l'été** (also **en été**)   *to play tennis in summer*

But the definite article may be used to stress that an event occurred on a particular day:

Le concours s'est déroulé **le** lundi
The competition took place on the Monday

Note the following expressions:

dimanche en huit   *a week on Sunday*
vendredi en quinze   *a fortnight on Friday*
tous les deux jours   *every other day*

6.6.3 Years

In referring to years in a date, *cent* is obligatory (while 'hundred' is often omitted in English):

1945	dix-neuf or mille neuf cent quarante-cinq *nineteen (hundred and) forty-five*
le 2 mai 1993	le deux mai dix-neuf cent quatre-vingt-treize *the second of May nineteen (hundred and) ninety-three*
'BC' is *av. J-C (avant Jésus-Christ)*:	50 av. J-C
'AD' is *ap. J-C (après Jésus-Christ)*:	500 ap. J-C

If *mille* is used in AD dates, it can be written optionally *mille* or (very rarely) *mil*:

> en **mille** neuf cent quinze or en **mil** neuf cent quinze
> *in nineteen fifteen*

an is used in *l'an 2000* 'the year 2000', *en l'an 1789* 'in the year 1789', etc.; but *année* is used in *les années 60* 'the 60s', *les années 30* 'the 30s', etc. (See Chapter 1.4 for *an/année*.)

6.7 Clock time

In telling time, 'it is' is always *il est*, never **c'est*:

> Quelle heure **est-il**? (Or Quelle heure avez-vous?)
> *What time is it?*

*heures i*s obligatory:

> Il est deux **heures** vingt; il est trois **heures** moins vingt
> *It's two twenty; it's twenty to three*

et links *quart* and *demi* to the hour in times past the hour – *demi* agrees in gender with the noun:

onze heures et quart	*a quarter past eleven*
midi et quart	*a quarter past midday*
minuit et quart	*a quarter past midnight*
onze heures et demie	*half past eleven*
midi et demi	*half past midday*
minuit et demi	*half past midnight*

'a quarter to' the hour is *moins le quart* (or *moins un quart*):

> onze heures moins le quart   *a quarter to eleven*

As in English, one can equally say *onze heures quinze* 'eleven fifteen', *midi trente* 'thirty minutes past midday', etc.

In French timetables, times are usually written as *21h35* or *21:35*.

NB: | | |
|---|---|
| à l'heure | *on time* |
| à temps | *in time* |

à deux heures	précises	*at two o'clock precisely* (official report)
	justes	*exactly two o'clock* (looking at watch)
	sonnantes	*bang on two o'clock* (for effect)
	tapantes	*spot on two* (for effect, more informal)

vers deux heures/vers les deux heures/autour de deux heures/ *about two*
à deux heures environ/dans les environs de deux heures   *o'clock*

Je peux faire mes comptes dans une heure *I can do my accounts in an hour's time*
Je peux faire mes comptes en une heure   *I can do my accounts within an hour*

(See Chapters 13.14.4 and 13.26.3.)

6.8 Money

franc is always present in quoting prices, but *centime* is optional:

> huit francs cinquante (centimes)
> *eight francs fifty (centimes)*

> deux cents francs quatre-vingts (centimes)
> *two hundred francs eighty (centimes)*

Foreign currencies are described in the same way:

> deux livres cinquante
> *two pounds fifty*

> trois dollars cinquante
> *three dollars fifty*

Prices can be written in various ways:

> F8,50
> FF8,50
> 8,50F
> 8,50FF
> 8F50 (usually found on price labels)

> Ça va chercher dans les quatre cents francs
> *That'll fetch around four hundred francs*
> (informal spoken style)

6.9 Quantifiers

6.9.1 Common quantifiers

Quantifiers, like numbers, determine 'how much' there is of something, but are less specific than numbers:

assez de		*enough*	
autant de		*as many*	
beaucoup de		*many*	
bien des	clients(s)	*many*	*customer(s)*
certains		*particular*	
chaque		*every*	
chacun des		*each one of the*	

une majorité de		*a majority of*	
une minorité de		*a minority of*	
moins de		*fewer*	
nombre de		*a lot of*	
une partie des		*a portion of*	
peu de		*few*	
pas mal de (informal French)		*quite a lot of*	
la plupart des	clients(s)	*most*	customer(s)
plus de		*more*	
plusieurs		*several*	
quantité de		*a lot of*	
quelques		*some, a few*	
le reste des		*the rest of the*	
tous les		*all the*	

6.9.2 Direct object quantifiers and *en*

When a quantifier on its own is a direct object, *en* must be inserted in front of the verb, as in the case of numbers (see 6.1.7):

J'**en** ai encore certains	*I still have some*
Ils n'**en** consomment qu'une partie	*They only consume a portion*
Il **en** a vendu la plupart	*He has sold most of it*

NB: When *quelques* 'some, a few' stands alone, it becomes *quelques-un(e)s*:

Il y avait **quelques** clients dans le magasin	*There were a few customers in the shop*
Il y en avait **quelques-uns** dans le magasin	*There were a few in the shop*

6.9.3 *de* or *du, de la, des* after quantifiers

The indefinite article *des* and the partitive articles *du, de la, des* (see Chapter 2.3.1 and 2.4) are omitted when a noun phrase follows one of the quantifiers listed with *de* in 6.9.1:

assez **de** *enough*	+	**des** clients *customers*	→ →	assez **de** clients *enough customers*	
autant **de** *as much*	+	**de** l'argent *money*	→ →	autant **d'**argent *as much money*	
peu **de** *not much*	+	**du** travail *work*	→ →	peu **de** travail *not much work*	

Quantifiers listed in 6.9.1 with *des*, however, are those which are followed by *des, du* or *de la:*

> bien **des** clients
> *many customers*

> la plupart **de l'**argent
> *most of the money*

> une partie **du** travail
> *part of the work*

When the quantifiers listed with *de* in 6.9.1 are followed by a noun with a definite article, this is not omitted. Compare:

> Beaucoup **d'**étudiants (indefinite) dorment moins qu'ils ne le souhaitent
> *Many students sleep less than they would wish*

> Beaucoup **des** étudiants interviewés (definite) dorment moins qu'ils ne le souhaitent
> *Many of the students interviewed sleep less than they would wish*

See also Chapter 2.3.2 and 2.4.

6.9.4 Quantifiers and personal pronouns

certains			some		them
beaucoup			many		
		eux			them
peu			few		
	d'entre	elles		of	us
plusieurs			several		
		nous			you
la plupart			most		
		vous			
chacun			each		

The preposition *d'entre* is used with quantifiers which precede stressed pronouns (for stressed pronouns see Chapter 3.3):
One can also find *certains parmi eux* 'some of them', *chacun de nous* 'each of us'.

6.9.5 *tout* and *chaque*

tous/toutes, like other quantifiers, can appear with the nouns they quantify or on their own:

> **Toutes les assiettes** sont sales/**Toutes** sont sales
> *All the plates are dirty/All are dirty*

> J'ai cassé **toutes les assiettes**/Je les ai **toutes** cassées
> *I broke all the plates/I broke them all*

When *tous/toutes* quantifies a subject, it can be optionally moved to a position after the verb:

> **Tous** les invités sont maintenant arrivés or Les invités sont maintenant **tous** arrivés
> *All the guests have arrived now/The guests have all arrived now*

When *tous/toutes* is used alone as a direct object, it can be optionally moved to a position after the verb:

> Je les ai **tous** vus   Je les ai vus **tous**   *I saw them all*

chaque means 'each, every':

> **Chaque** passager est prié de se présenter à la porte 12
> *Every passenger is requested to go to gate 12*

chaque cannot stand alone: it becomes *chacun(e):*

> Chaque assiette est peinte à la main/**Chacune** est peinte à la main
> *Every plate is hand painted/Every one is hand painted*

(For adverbial use of *tout*, as in *toute blanche, tout blanc*, see Chapter 5.6.7.)

6.9.6 Subject-verb agreement when subject quantifiers are present

With some quantifiers, the verb agrees not with the quantifier but with the noun:

> Beaucoup de professeurs **sont** surmenés
> *Many teachers are overworked*

Similar quantifiers are:

> *bien des, nombre de, pas mal de, peu de, la plupart de, quantité de, trop de*

With other quantifiers, however, the verb may agree with the noun or with the quantifier:

> La majorité de nos étudiants **ont/a** moins de quarante ans
> *The majority of our students are under forty*

> Une bonne partie de ses clients **viennent/vient** de l'étranger
> *A good portion of his customers come from abroad*

Similar quantifiers are: *une minorité de, le reste de, la moitié de, un tiers de,* and numeral nouns like *une dizaine de, une vingtaine*, etc. (See Chapter 9.1.5.)

7
Verb forms

7.1 Introduction

As in many languages, verbs in French have different forms for the different functions they perform in sentences. It is traditional (and easiest for reference) to present verb forms in **paradigms** (i.e. lists), and this is what we do in this chapter. We follow Judge and Healey (1983) in dividing the paradigms into **simple forms**, **compound forms** and **double compound forms**. Simple forms are made up of **stems** to which **endings** are attached (see 7.3 for stems and endings). Compound forms are made up of forms of the auxiliary verbs *avoir* and *être* plus a past participle. Double compound forms are made up of forms of the compound auxiliary verbs *avoir eu* or *avoir été* plus a past participle. The set of verb forms that this produces is illustrated below, using the third person singular form of the verb *donner* 'to give' (stems are in normal type, endings are in bold).

Not all books and teachers use the terminology we employ here, so we have added other terms in common use in brackets:

Simple tenses	Example
Present	Il donn-**e**
Imperfect	Il donn-**ait**
Simple past (past historic)	Il donn-**a**
Future	Il donn-**era**
Conditional	Il donn-**erait**
Present subjunctive	Qu'il donn-**e**
Imperfect subjunctive	Qu'il donn-**ât**

Simple non-finite forms

Simple infinitive	donn-**er**
Present participle	donn-**ant**
Past participle	donn-**é**
Imperative	donn-**e**
	donn-**ez**
	donn-**ons**

Compound tenses

Compound past (perfect)	Il **a** donné
Pluperfect	Il **avait** donné
Past anterior	Il **eut** donné
Compound future (future perfect)	Il **aura** donné
Compound conditional (conditional perfect)	Il **aurait** donné
Compound past subjunctive	Qu'il **ait** donné
Pluperfect subjunctive	Qu'il **eût** donné

Compound non-finite forms

Compound infinitive	**avoir** donné
Compound present participle	**ayant** donné
Compound past participle	**eu** donné
Compound imperative	**aie** donné
	ayez donné
	ayons donné

Double compound tenses

Double compound past	Il **a eu** donné
Compound pluperfect	Il **avait eu** donné
Double compound future	Il **aura eu** donné
Double compound conditional	Il **aurait eu** donné
Double compound past subjunctive	Qu'il **eût eu** donné

Double compound non-finite forms

Double compound infinitive	**avoir eu** donné
Double compound participle	**ayant eu** donné

7.2 Conjugations

For the purposes of systematic presentation, French verbs are best grouped into four **conjugations**. These are:

(1) Verbs whose infinitive ends in *-er* (e.g. *donner, chanter, parler*). This is by far the largest group.

(2) Verbs whose infinitive ends in *-ir*. Within this group there are two sub-groups:

    (a) verbs whose stems sometimes end in *-iss-* (e.g. *finir: fin-iss-ons, fin-iss-ant, fin-iss-aient*, etc.);

    (b) verbs whose stems do not add *-iss-* (e.g. *dormir, mentir*).

(3) Verbs whose infinitive ends in *-re* (e.g. *vendre, rendre*).

(4) Verbs whose infinitive ends in *-oir* (e.g. *recevoir*).

Verbs which differ from this pattern are included in the list of irregular verbs under 7.6.8.

7.2.1 Organization of the paradigms

The paradigms which follow in this chapter are divided into eight sections:

> 7.6.1 and 7.6.2 describe the forms of *avoir* and *être*, because these two verbs are essential to all the compound forms.
>
> 7.6.3 describes the forms of regular verbs belonging to the *-er* conjugation (e.g. *donner, chanter, parler*).
>
> 7.6.4 and 7.6.5 describe the forms of regular verbs belonging to the *-ir* conjugation. These subdivide into those whose stem sometimes ends in *-iss-* (like *finir: fin-iss-ons, fin-iss-ant, fin-iss-aient*, etc. – these are the majority of verbs in the *-ir* conjugation), and those whose stem does not add *-iss* (like *dormir: dorm-ons, dorm-ant, dorm-aient*, etc.). There are only about 30 of these verbs.
>
> 7.6.6 describes the forms of regular verbs belonging to the *-re* conjugation (e.g. *vendre, rendre*).
>
> 7.6.7 describes the forms of regular verbs belonging to the *-oir* conjugation (e.g. *recevoir, décevoir, concevoir*).
>
> 7.6.8 lists the forms of irregular verbs (i.e. those whose stems change idiosyncratically at various points in the paradigm).

7.3 Easy ways of generating some parts of the paradigms

A number of the parts of the verb paradigms can be productively generated using a few simple rules. It is sometimes easier to learn these rules than learning every verb form individually. However, be aware that these only work with regular verbs – irregular verbs have idiosyncratic forms which have to be learned.

7.3.1 An easy way of generating the present tense

For regular verbs ending in *-er* (like *donner*), *-ir* (the *finir* kind whose stems sometimes end in *-iss-*: *fin-iss-ons, fin-iss-ant, fin-iss-aient*, etc., but NOT the *dormir* kind – see 7.6.4 and 7.6.5) or *-re* (like *vendre*), take the infinitive form of the verb, omit the ending *-er, -ir* or *-re* (this creates a stem: *donn-, fin-, vend-*) and add the following endings:

	je	tu	il/elle	nous	vous	ils/elles
-er verbs	-e	-es	-e	-ons	-ez	-ent
-ir verbs (most verbs – see 7.6.4)	-is	-is	-it	-issons	-issez	-issent
-re verbs	-s	-s	–	-ons	-ez	-ent

For example:

Infinitive	Stem	Present tense
donner	donn-	je donn- e, etc.
finir	fin-	je fin- is, etc.
vendre	vend-	je vend- s, etc.

7.3.2 An easy way of generating the imperfect tense

For all regular verb conjugations, take the first person plural *nous* form of the present tense, omit *-ons* and add the following endings:

je	tu	il/elle	nous	vous	ils/elles
-ais	-ais	-ait	-ions	-iez	-aient

For example:

Infinitive	First person plural	Stem	Imperfect tense
donner	donnons	donn-	je donn- ais, etc.
commencer	commençons	commenç-	je commenç- ais, etc.
partager	partageons	partage-	je partage- ais, etc.
finir	finissons	finiss-	je finiss- ais, etc.
dormir	dormons	dorm-	je dorm- ais, etc.
vendre	vendons	vend-	je vend- ais, etc.
recevoir	recevons	recev-	je recev- ais, etc.

7.3.3 An easy way of generating the simple past (past historic)

For -*er* verbs, take the first person plural *nous* form of the present tense, omit -*ons* and add the following endings: -*ai, -as, -a, -âmes, -âtes, -èrent*.

For -*ir* (both *finir* and *dormir* types – see 7.6.4 and 7.6.5) and -*re* verbs, take the past participle, omit the final vowel, and add the following endings: -*is, -is, -it, -îmes, -îtes, -irent*.

For -*oir* verbs, take the past participle, omit the final vowel, and add the following endings: -*us, -us, -ut, -ûmes, -ûtes, -urent*.

	je	tu	il/elle	nous	vous	ils/elles
-*er* verbs (most verbs – see 7.6.3)	-ai	-as	-a	-âmes	-âtes	-èrent
-*ir* verbs -*re* verbs	-is	-is	-it	-îmes	-îtes	-irent
-*oir* verbs	-us	-us	-ut	-ûmes	-ûtes	-urent

For example:

Infinitive	First person plural	Stem	Simple past tense
donner	donnons	donn-	je donn- ai, etc.
commencer	commençons	commenç-	je commenç- ai, etc.
partager	partageons	partage-	je partage- ai, etc.
	Past participle		
finir	fini	fin-	je fin- is, etc.
dormir	dormi	dorm-	je dorm- is, etc.
vendre	vendu	vend-	je vend- is, etc.
recevoir	reçu	reç-	je reç- us, etc.

7.3.4 An easy way of generating the future and conditional

Take the infinitive form of -*er*, -*ir* and -*re* verbs (deleting the final *e* in the latter case) and add the following endings:
For example:

	je	tu	il/elle	nous	vous	ils/elles
Future	-ai	-as	-a	-ons	-ez	-ont
Conditional	-ais	-ais	-ait	-ions	-iez	-aient

Infinitive	Stem	Future/conditional
donner	donner-	je donner- ai, etc. je donner- ais, etc.
finir	finir-	je finir- ai, etc. je finir- ais, etc.
dormir	dormir-	je dormir- ai, etc. je dormir- ais, etc.
vendre	vendr-	je vendr- ai, etc. je vendr- ais, etc.

(For the doubling of consonants in verbs like *je jetterai, j'appellerai*, the change from *e* to *è* in verbs like *j'achèterai, il gèlera*, and the change from *é* to *è* in verbs like *j'espèrerai, je complèterai*, etc., see 7.4.)

7.3.5 An easy way of generating the present subjunctive

For all regular verb conjugations, take the third person plural *ils/elles* form of the present tense, omit *-ent* and add the endings:

je	tu	il/elle	nous	vous	ils/elles
-e	-es	-e	-ions	-iez	-ent

For example:

Infinitive	Third person plural	Stem	Present subjunctive
donner	donnent	donn-	je donn- e, etc.
finir	finissent	finiss-	je finiss- e, etc.
dormir	dorment	dorm-	je dorm- e, etc.
vendre	vendent	vend-	je vend- e, etc.
recevoir	reçoivent	reçoiv-	je reçoiv- e, etc.

NB: The stem *reçoiv-* changes when the ending does not begin with *-e*: *reçoive*, but *recevions, receviez*.

7.3.6 An easy way of generating the imperfect subjunctive

For all regular verb conjugations, take the first person singular *je* form of the simple past tense, omit the last letter and add the endings:

je	tu	il/elle	nous	vous	ils/elles
-sse	-sses	-^t	-ssions	-ssiez	-ssent

For example:

Infinitive	First person simple past	Stem	Imperfect subjunctive
donner	donnai	donna-	je donna- sse, etc.
commencer	commençai	commença-	je commença- sse, etc.
partager	partageai	partagea-	je partagea- sse, etc.
finir	finis	fini-	je fini- sse, etc.
dormir	dormis	dormi-	je dormi- sse, etc.
vendre	vendis	vendi-	je vendi- sse, etc.
recevoir	reçus	reçu-	je reçu- sse, etc.

7.3.7 An easy way of generating the imperative

For all verbs (with four exceptions – see below) take the second person singular *tu* form, the second person plural *vous* form and the first person plural *nous* form of the present tense, delete the subject and the final *-s* of any verb which ends in *-es* or *-as*. For example:

Infinitive	Present tense	Imperative
donner	tu donnes	donne!
	vous donnez	donnez!
	nous donnons	donnons!
aller	tu vas	va!
	vous allez	allez!
	nous allons	allons!

finir	tu finis	finis!
	vous finissez	finissez!
	nous finissons	finissons!
dormir	tu dors	dors!
	vous dormez	dormez!
	nous dormons	dormons!
vendre	tu vends	vends!
	vous vendez	vendez!
	nous vendons	vendons!
recevoir	tu reçois	reçois!
	vous recevez	recevez!
	nous recevons	recevons!

NB: The final *-s* which disappears from second person singular verbs ending in *-es* or *-as* reappears where the pronouns *y* or *en* follow the imperative:

aller	Va!	Vas-y!
parler	Parle!	Parles-en!

Four exceptions:

Infinitive	Present tense	Imperative
être	tu es	sois!
	vous êtes	soyez!
	nous sommes	soyons!
avoir	tu as	aie!
	vous avez	ayez!
	nous avons	ayons!
savoir	tu sais	sache!
	vous savez	sachez!
	nous savons	sachons!
vouloir	tu veux	veuille
	vous voulez	veuillez
	nous voulons	not used

(Both *veuille* and *veuillez* mean 'please'.)

NB: Although *vouloir* has irregular imperative forms, the related verb *en vouloir à qn* 'to hold a grudge against sb' has regular forms:

Tu ne lui en veux pas	Ne lui en veux pas!
Vous ne lui en voulez pas	Ne lui en voulez pas!
Nous ne lui en voulons pas	Ne lui en voulons pas!

7.4 Changes in the stem form of some *-er* conjugation verbs

The stems of a number of verbs of the *-er* conjugation change their form when they are followed by an *e*. (See also listings under irregular verbs, Table 7.H.)

The majority of verbs ending in *-eler* or *-eter* double the final consonant of the stem when it is followed by *-e* in the present, future, conditional and present subjunctive:

appeler

Present	j'appelle, tu appelles, il/elle appelle, ils/elles appellent
Future	j'appellerai, . . ., nous appellerons, etc.
Conditional	j'appellerais, . . ., nous appellerions, etc.
Present Subjunctive	que j'appelle, que tu appelles, qu'il/elle appelle, qu'ils/elles appellent

jeter
Present   je jette, . . . etc.
Future   je jetterai, . . . etc.
Conditional   je jetterais, . . . etc.
Present subjunctive que je jette, . . . etc.

The following verbs, however, do not double the final stem consonant, but change the first *e* to *è*: *acheter, celer, ciseler, corseter, crocheter, démanteler, écarteler, fureter, geler, haleter, marteler, modeler, peler* (together with verbs derived from these like *congeler, dégeler*, etc.):

acheter
Present   j'achète, . . . etc.
Future   j'achèterai, . . . etc.

Other verbs which have an unstressed *e* in the syllable before the final *-er* also change that vowel to *è* in the same circumstances, for example *mener, semer*:

mener
Present   je mène, . . . etc.
Future   je mènerai, . . . etc.

Verbs which have an *é* in the syllable before the final *-er* change that vowel to *è* in the same circumstances, for example *espérer, révéler*:

espérer
Present   j'espère, . . . etc.
Future   j'espèrerai, . . . etc.

Verbs of the *-er* conjugation whose stem ends in *-y*, for example *employer, nettoyer, essayer*, change the *y* to *i* in the same circumstances:

employer
Present   j'emploie, . . . etc.
Future   j'emploierai, . . . etc.

7.4.1 The forms of *créer, nier, scier, rire*, etc.

Verbs whose stems end in *-é* or *-i* behave just like any other verb: the final vowel does not change, for example:

je cr**ée** (present tense)
j'ai cr**éé** (compound past)
l'entreprise que j'ai cr**éée** (past participle agreement with a preceding feminine direct object – see Chapter 9.3.)
nous r**ions** (present tense)
nous r**iions** (imperfect tense or present subjunctive)
etc.

7.5 Verbs whose stems end in c- or g-

Verbs whose stems end in *c-* (pronounced [s]) change to *ç-* before an ending beginning with *-a, -o,* or *-u*, e.g. *commenc-er, rec-evoir*:

commenc-er   nous commenç- ons (present)
              je commenç- ais (imperfect)
              nous commenç- âmes (simple past) etc.
rec-evoir   je reç- ois (present)
              nous reç- ûmes (simple past) etc.

Verbs whose stems end in a *g-* (pronounced like '*je*') change to *ge-* before an ending beginning with *-a* or *-o*, e.g. *partag-er, protég-er*:

partag-er	nous partage- ons (present)
	je partage- ais (imperfect)
	nous partage- âmes (simple past) etc.

7.6 Verb paradigms

7.6.1 The irregular verb *avoir*

TABLE 7.A

Infinitive:	avoir	Compound infinitive:	avoir eu
Past participle:	eu	Compound present	
Present participle:	ayant	participle:	ayant eu

Simple forms		**Compound forms**	
Present:		Compound past:	
J'ai	Nous avons	J'ai eu	Nous avons eu
Tu as	Vous avez	Tu as eu	Vous avez eu
Il a	Ils ont	Il a eu	Ils ont eu
Imperfect:		Pluperfect:	
J'avais	Nous avions	J'avais eu	Nous avions eu
Tu avais	Vous aviez	Tu avais eu	Vous aviez eu
Il avait	Ils avaient	Il avait eu	Ils avaient eu
Simple past (past historic):		Past anterior:	
J'eus	Nous eûmes	J'eus eu	Nous eûmes eu
Tu eus	Vous eûtes	Tu eus eu	Vous eûtes eu
Il eut	Ils eurent	Il eut eu	Ils eurent eu
Future:		Compound future:	
J'aurai	Nous aurons	J'aurai eu	Nous aurons eu
Tu auras	Vous aurez	Tu auras eu	Vous aurez eu
Il aura	Ils auront	Il aura eu	Ils auront eu
Conditional:		Compound conditional:	
J'aurais	Nous aurions	J'aurais eu	Nous aurions eu
Tu aurais	Vous auriez	Tu aurais eu	Vous auriez eu
Il aurait	Ils auraient	Il aurait eu	Ils auraient eu

TABLE 7.A *(continued)*

Present subjunctive:		Compound past subjunctive:	
que j'aie	que nous ayons	que j'aie eu	que nous ayons eu
que tu aies	que vous ayez	que tu aies eu	que vous ayez eu
qu'il ait	qu'ils aient	qu'il ait eu	qu'ils aient eu
Imperfect subjunctive:		**Pluperfect subjunctive:**	
que j'eusse	que nous eussions	que j'eusse eu	que nous eussions eu
que tu eusses	que vous eussiez	que tu eusses eu	que vous eussiez eu
qu'il eût	qu'ils eussent	qu'il eût eu	qu'ils eussent eu
Imperative:		**Compound imperative:**	
aie		not used	
ayons			
ayez			

7.6.2 The irregular verb *être*

TABLE 7.B

Infinitive:	être	Compound infinitive:	avoir été
Past participle:	été	Compound past participle:	eu été
Present participle:	étant	Compound present participle:	ayant été

Simple forms		**Compound forms**	
Present:		Compound past:	
Je suis	Nous sommes	J'ai été	Nous avons été
Tu es	Vous êtes	Tu as été	Vous avez été
Il est	Ils sont	Il a été	Ils ont été
Imperfect:		Pluperfect:	
J'étais	Nous étions	J'avais été	Nous avions été
Tu étais	Vous étiez	Tu avais été	Vous aviez été
Il était	Ils étaient	Il avait été	Ils avaient été
Simple past (past historic):		Past anterior:	
Je fus	Nous fûmes	J'eus été	Nous eûmes été
Tu fus	Vous fûtes	Tu eus été	Vous eûtes été
Il fut	Ils furent	Il eut été	Ils eurent été
Future:		Compound future:	
Je serai	Nous serons	J'aurai été	Nous aurons été
Tu seras	Vous serez	Tu auras été	Vous aurez été
Il sera	Ils seront	Il aura été	Ils auront été

TABLE 7.B *(continued)*

Conditional:		Compound conditional:	
Je serais	Nous serions	J'aurais été	Nous aurions été
Tu serais	Vous seriez	Tu aurais été	Vous auriez été
Il serait	Ils seraient	Il aurait été	Ils auraient été
Present subjunctive:		**Compound past subjunctive:**	
que je sois	que nous soyons	que j'aie été	que nous ayons été
que tu sois	que vous soyez	que tu aies été	que vous ayez été
qu'il soit	qu'ils soient	qu'il ait été	qu'ils aient été
Imperfect subjunctive:		**Pluperfect subjunctive:**	
que je fusse	que nous fussions	que j'eusse été	que nous eussions été
que tu fusses	que vous fussiez	que tu eusses été	que vous eussiez été
qu'il fût	qu'ils fussent	qu'il eût été	qu'ils eussent été
Imperative:		**Compound imperative:**	
sois		not used	
soyons			
soyez			

7.6.3 Conjugation I: verbs whose infinitive ends in *-er*

TABLE 7.C

Infinitive:	parler	Compound infinitive:	avoir parlé
Past participle:	parlé	Compound past participle:	eu parlé
Present participle:	parlant	Compound present participle:	ayant parlé
Simple forms		**Compound forms**	
Present:		Compound past:	
Je parle	Nous parlons	J'ai parlé	Nous avons parlé
Tu parles	Vous parlez	Tu as parlé	Vous avez parlé
Il parle	Ils parlent	Il a parlé	Ils ont parlé
Imperfect:		Pluperfect:	
Je parlais	Nous parlions	J'avais parlé	Nous avions parlé
Tu parlais	Vous parliez	Tu avais parlé	Vous aviez parlé
Il parlait	Ils parlaient	Il avait parlé	Ils avaient parlé
Simple past (past historic):		Past anterior:	
Je parlai	Nous parlâmes	J'eus parlé	Nous eûmes parlé
Tu parlas	Vous parlâtes	Tu eus parlé	Vous eûtes parlé
Il parla	Ils parlèrent	Il eut parlé	Ils eurent parlé

TABLE 7.C *(continued)*

Future:		Compound future:	
Je parlerai	Nous parlerons	J'aurai parlé	Nous aurons parlé
Tu parleras	Vous parlerez	Tu auras parlé	Vous aurez parlé
Il parlera	Ils parleront	Il aura parlé	Ils auront parlé
Conditional:		Compound conditional:	
Je parlerais	Nous parlerions	J'aurais parlé	Nous aurions parlé
Tu parlerais	Vous parleriez	Tu aurais parlé	Vous auriez parlé
Il parlerait	Ils parleraient	Il aurait parlé	Ils auraient parlé
Present subjunctive:		Compound past subjunctive:	
que je parle	que nous parlions	que j'aie parlé	que nous ayons parlé
que tu parles	que vous parliez	que tu aies parlé	que vous ayez parlé
qu'il parle	qu'ils parlent	qu'il ait parlé	qu'ils aient parlé
Imperfect subjunctive:		Pluperfect subjunctive:	
que je parlasse	que nous parlassions	que j'eusse parlé	que nous eussions parlé
que tu parlasses	que vous parlassiez	que tu eusses parlé	que vous eussiez parlé
qu'il parlât	qu'ils parlassent	qu'il eût parlé	qu'ils eussent parlé
Imperative:		Compound imperative:	
parle (but parles-en)			
parlons			
parlez			

NB: Verbs whose stem ends in *c* or *g* are written *ç* and *ge* respectively before endings which begin with *a* or *o*: e.g. *nous commençons, je mangeais* – see 7.5.

NB: Verbs of the *-er* conjugation whose stem changes, like *compléter, espérer* (and other verbs ending in *-éter, -érer*), *appeler, mener, jeter, employer, nettoyer* (and other verbs ending in *-oyer* – see 7.4) are individually listed under irregular verbs.

7.6.4 Conjugation 2 (a): verbs whose infinitives end in *-ir*, and whose stems end in *-iss-* in certain paradigms

TABLE 7.D

Infinitive:	finir	Compound infinitive:	avoir fini
Past participle:	fini	Compound past participle:	eu fini
Present participle:	finissant	Compound present participle:	ayant fini

Simple forms		Compound forms	
Present:		**Compound past:**	
Je finis	Nous finissons	J'ai fini	Nous avons fini
Tu finis	Vous finissez	Tu as fini	Vous avez fini
Il finit	Ils finissent	Il a fini	Ils ont fini
Imperfect:		**Pluperfect:**	
Je finissais	Nous finissions	J'avais fini	Nous avions fini
Tu finissais	Vous finissiez	Tu avais fini	Vous aviez fini
Il finissait	Ils finissaient	Il avait fini	Ils avaient fini
Simple past (past historic):		**Past anterior:**	
Je finis	Nous finîmes	J'eus fini	Nous eûmes fini
Tu finis	Vous finîtes	Tu eus fini	Vous eûtes fini
Il finit	Ils finirent	Il eut fini	Ils eurent fini
Future:		**Compound future:**	
Je finirai	Nous finirons	J'aurai fini	Nous aurons fini
Tu finiras	Vous finirez	Tu auras fini	Vous aurez fini
Il finira	Ils finiront	Il aura fini	Ils auront fini
Conditional:		**Compound conditional:**	
Je finirais	Nous finirions	J'aurais fini	Nous aurions fini
Tu finirais	Vous finiriez	Tu aurais fini	Vous auriez fini
Il finirait	Ils finiraient	Il aurait fini	Ils auraient fini
Present subjunctive:		**Compound past subjunctive:**	
que je finisse	que nous finissions	que j'aie fini	que nous ayons fini
que tu finisses	que vous finissiez	que tu aies fini	que vous ayez fini
qu'il finisse	qu'ils finissent	qu'il ait fini	qu'ils aient fini
Imperfect subjunctive:		**Pluperfect subjunctive:**	
que je finisse	que nous finissions	que j'eusse fini	que nous eussions fini
que tu finisses	que vous finissiez	que tu eusses fini	que vous eussiez fini
qu'il finît	qu'ils finissent	qu'il eût fini	qu'ils eussent fini

TABLE 7.D *(continued)*

Imperative: finis finissons finissez	Compound imperative: aie fini ayons fini ayez fini

NB: Verbs which approximate to this pattern but which have significant differences are: *fleurir, haïr*. These are listed as irregular verbs.

7.6.5 Conjugation 2 (b): verbs whose infinitives end in *-ir*, and whose stems do not end in *-iss-* (e.g. *dormir*)

TABLE 7.E

Infinitive:	dormir	Compound infinitive:	avoir dormi
Past participle:	dormi	Compound past participle:	eu dormi
Present participle:	dormant	Compound present participle:	ayant dormi

Simple forms		**Compound forms**	
Present:		Compound past:	
Je dors	Nous dormons	J'ai dormi	Nous avons dormi
Tu dors	Vous dormez	Tu as dormi	Vous avez dormi
Il dort	Ils dorment	Il a dormi	Ils ont dormi
Imperfect:		Pluperfect:	
Je dormais	Nous dormions	J'avais dormi	Nous avions dormi
Tu dormais	Vous dormiez	Tu avais dormi	Vous aviez dormi
Il dormait	Ils dormaient	Il avait dormi	Ils avaient dormi
Simple past (past historic):		Past anterior:	
Je dormis	Nous dormîmes	J'eus dormi	Nous eûmes dormi
Tu dormis	Vous dormîtes	Tu eus dormi	Vous eûtes dormi
Il dormit	Ils dormirent	Il eut dormi	Ils eurent dormi
Future:		Compound future:	
Je dormirai	Nous dormirons	J'aurai dormi	Nous aurons dormi
Tu dormiras	Vous dormirez	Tu auras dormi	Vous aurez dormi
Il dormira	Ils dormiront	Il aura dormi	Ils auront dormi
Conditional:		Compound conditional:	
Je dormirais	Nous dormirions	J'aurais dormi	Nous aurions dormi
Tu dormirais	Vous dormiriez	Tu aurais dormi	Vous auriez dormi
Il dormirait	Ils dormiraient	Il aurait dormi	Ils auraient dormi

TABLE 7.E *(continued)*

Present subjunctive:		Compound past subjunctive:	
que je dorme	que nous dormions	que j'aie dormi	que nous ayons dormi
que tu dormes	que vous dormiez	que tu aies dormi	que vous ayez dormi
qu'il dorme	qu'ils dorment	qu'il ait dormi	qu'ils aient dormi
Imperfect subjunctive:		Pluperfect subjunctive:	
que je dormisse	que nous dormissions	que j'eusse dormi	que nous eussions dormi
que tu dormisses	que vous dormissiez	que tu eusses dormi	que vous eussiez dormi
qu'il dormît	qu'ils dormissent	qu'il eût dormi	qu'ils eussent dormi
Imperative:		Compound imperative:	
dors		aie dormi	
dormons		ayons dormi	
dormez		ayez dormi	

NB: *S'endormir, servir, desservir, mentir, démentir, partir, repartir, se repentir, sentir, consentir, ressentir, sortir* and *ressortir* conjugate like *dormir* BUT *asservir, impartir, répartir, assortir,* conjugate like *finir.*

Verbs which are similar to one or other of these *-ir* conjugations are: *cueillir, accueillir, recueillir, assaillir, tressaillir, couvrir, découvrir, recouvrir, offrir, ouvrir, rouvrir, souffrir* but they have special characteristics. They are listed individually as irregular verbs.

7.6.6 Conjugation 3: verbs with infinitives which end in *-re* (e.g. *vendre*)

TABLE 7.F

Infinitive:	vendre	Compound infinitive:	avoir vendu
Past participle:	vendu	Compound past participle:	eu vendu
Present participle:	vendant	Compound present participle:	ayant vendu
Simple forms		**Compound forms**	
Present:		Compound past:	
Je vends	Nous vendons	J'ai vendu	Nous avons vendu
Tu vends	Vous vendez	Tu as vendu	Vous avez vendu
Il vend	Ils vendent	Il a vendu	Ils ont vendu
Imperfect:		Pluperfect:	
Je vendais	Nous vendions	J'avais vendu	Nous avions vendu
Tu vendais	Vous vendiez	Tu avais vendu	Vous aviez vendu
Il vendait	Ils vendaient	Il avait vendu	Ils avaient vendu

TABLE 7.F (*continued*)

Simple past (past historic):		Past anterior:	
Je vendis	Nous vendîmes	J'eus vendu	Nous eûmes vendu
Tu vendis	Vous vendîtes	Tu eus vendu	Vous eûtes vendu
Il vendit	Ils vendirent	Il eut vendu	Ils eurent vendu
Future:		**Compound future:**	
Je vendrai	Nous vendrons	J'aurai vendu	Nous aurons vendu
Tu vendras	Vous vendrez	Tu auras vendu	Vous aurez vendu
Il vendra	Ils vendront	Il aura vendu	Ils auront vendu
Conditional:		**Compound conditional:**	
Je vendrais	Nous vendrions	J'aurais vendu	Nous aurions vendu
Tu vendrais	Vous vendriez	Tu aurais vendu	Vous auriez vendu
Il vendrait	Ils vendraient	Il aurait vendu	Ils auraient vendu
Present subjunctive:		**Compound past subjunctive:**	
que je vende	que nous vendions	que j'aie vendu	que nous ayons vendu
que tu vendes	que vous vendiez	que tu aies vendu	que vous ayez vendu
qu'il vende	qu'ils vendent	qu'il ait vendu	qu'ils aient vendu
Imperfect subjunctive:		**Pluperfect subjunctive:**	
que je vendisse	que nous vendissions	que j'eusse vendu	que nous eussions vendu
que tu vendisses	que vous vendissiez	que tu eusses vendu	que vous eussiez vendu
qu'il vendît	qu'ils vendissent	qu'il eût vendu	qu'ils eussent vendu
Imperative:		**Compound imperative:**	
vends		aie vendu	
vendons		ayons vendu	
vendez		ayez vendu	

A few verbs follow this pattern in its entirety, especially those ending in *-andre, -endre, -ondre, -erdre, -ordre*, e.g. *épandre, répandre, attendre, défendre, descendre, détendre, entendre, étendre, fendre, prétendre, rendre, tendre, vendre, confondre, correspondre, fondre, pondre, répondre, tondre, mordre, perdre, tordre*.

Other verbs which have sufficient differences to be listed individually as irregular verbs are: *prendre* (and compounds of *prendre*), *rompre* (and compounds of *rompre*), *battre* (and compounds of *battre*), *vaincre* (and compounds of *vaincre*), verbs ending in *-a/e/oindre: contraindre, craindre, plaindre, enfreindre, éteindre, étreindre, astreindre, atteindre, ceindre, dépeindre, déteindre, enceindre, feindre, geindre, peindre, restreindre, teindre, joindre,* and verbs ending in *-aître: apparaître, connaître, disparaître, méconnaître, paraître, reconnaître, repaître, accroître, décroître, croître*.

A distinct group of verbs end in *-uire*, e.g. *conduire, construire, cuire, déduire,* *détruire, enduire, introduire, produire, séduire, traduire.* These all follow the same pattern which is illustrated by *construire* in the table of irregular verbs.

7.6.7 Conjugation 4: verbs with infinitives which end in *-oir* (e.g. *recevoir*)

TABLE 7.G

Infinitive:	recevoir	Compound infinitive:	avoir reçu
Past participle:	reçu	Compound past participle:	eu reçu
Present participle:	recevant	Compound present participle:	ayant reçu

Simple forms		**Compound forms**	
Present:		Compound Past:	
Je reçois	Nous recevons	J'ai reçu	Nous avons reçu
Tu reçois	Vous recevez	Tu as reçu	Vous avez reçu
Il reçoit	Ils reçoivent	Il a reçu	Ils ont reçu
Imperfect:		Pluperfect:	
Je recevais	Nous recevions	J'avais reçu	Nous avions reçu
Tu recevais	Vous receviez	Tu avais reçu	Vous aviez reçu
Il recevait	Ils recevaient	Il avait reçu	Ils avaient reçu
Simple past (past historic):		Past anterior:	
Je reçus	Nous reçûmes	J'eus reçu	Nous eûmes reçu
Tu reçus	Vous reçûtes	Tu eus reçu	Vous eûtes reçu
Il reçut	Ils reçurent	Il eut reçu	Ils eurent reçu
Future:		Compound future:	
Je recevrai	Nous recevrons	J'aurai reçu	Nous aurons reçu
Tu recevras	Vous recevrez	Tu auras reçu	Vous aurez reçu
Il recevra	Ils recevront	Il aura reçu	Ils auront reçu
Conditional:		Compound conditional:	
Je recevrais	Vous recevrions	J'aurais reçu	Nous aurions reçu
Tu recevrais	Vous receviez	Tu aurais reçu	Vous auriez reçu
Il recevrait	Ils recevraient	Il aurait reçu	Ils auraient reçu
Present subjunctive:		Compound past subjunctive:	
que je reçoive	que nous recevions	que j'aie reçu	que nous ayons reçu
que tu reçoives	que vous receviez	que tu aies reçu	que vous ayez reçu
qu'il reçoive	qu'ils reçoivent	qu'il ait reçu	qu'ils aient reçu
Imperfect subjunctive:		Pluperfect subjunctive:	
que je reçusse	que nous reçussions	que j'eusse reçu	que nous eussions reçu
que tu reçusses	que vous reçussiez	que tu eusses reçu	que vous eussiez reçu
qu'il reçût	qu'ils reçussent	qu'il eût reçu	qu'ils eussent reçu

TABLE 7.G *(continued)*

Imperative:	Compound imperative:
reçois	aie reçu
recevons	ayons reçu
recevez	ayez reçu

NB: A number of verbs, e.g. *voir* and derivatives, do not follow this pattern. They are listed individually as irregular verbs.

7.6.8 Irregular verbs

TABLE 7.H

Infinitive:	**Present indicative:**		**Participles:**	abattant	abattu
abattre	j'abats	nous abattons	**Future:**	j'abattrai	
to knock down	tu abats	vous abattez	**Simple past:**	j'abattis	
	il abat	ils abattent	**Imperfect:**	j'abattais	
			Subj (pres):	que j'abatte	
			Subj (imp):	que j'abattisse	

Infinitive:	**Present indicative:**		**Participles:**	absolvant	absous/
absoudre	j'absous	nous absolvons	**Future:**	j'absoudrai	absoute (f)
to absolve	tu absous	vous absolvez	**Simple past:**	-	
	il absout	ils absolvent	**Imperfect:**	j'absolvais	
			Subj (pres):	que j'absolve	
			Subj (imp):	-	

Infinitive:
s'abstenir de *to abstain from*: see tenir

Infinitive:
abstraire *to abstract*: see traire

Infinitive:
accourir *to run up*: see courir

Infinitive:	**Present indicative:**		**Participles:**	accroissant	accru
accroître	j'accrois	nous accroissons	**Future:**	j'accroîtrai	
to increase	tu accrois	vous accroissez	**Simple past:**	j'accrus	
	il accroît	ils accroissent	**Imperfect:**	j'accroissais	
			Subj (pres):	que j'accroisse	
			Subj (imp):	que j'accrusse	

Infinitive:
accueillir *to welcome*: see cueillir

Infinitive:	**Present indicative:**		**Participles:**	achetant	acheté
acheter	j'achète	nous achetons	**Future:**	j'achèterai (è in all forms)	
to buy	tu achètes	vous achetez	**Simple past:**	j'achetai	
	il achète	ils achètent	**Imperfect:**	j'achetais	
			Subj (pres):	que j'achète	
				que nous achetions	
				que vous achetiez	
			Subj (imp):	que j'achetasse	

TABLE 7.H *(continued)*

Infinitive:
achever *to finish*: is like *acheter* in the distribution of *è*

Infinitive:	**Present indicative:**		**Participles:**	acquérant acquis
acquérir	j'acquiers	nous acquérons	**Future:**	j'acquerrai
to acquire	tu acquiers	vous acquérez	**Simple past:**	j'acquis
	il acquiert	ils acquièrent	**Imperfect:**	j'acquérais
			Subj (pres):	que j'acquière
			Subj (imp):	que j'acquisse

Infinitive:
adjoindre *to join with*: see joindre

Infinitive:
admettre *to let in*: see mettre

Infinitive:
advenir *to occur*: see venir

Infinitive:	**Present indicative:**		**Participles:**	allant allé
aller	je vais	nous allons	**Future:**	j'irai
to go	tu vas	vous allez	**Simple past:**	j'allai
	il va	ils vont	**Imperfect:**	j'allais
			Subj (pres):	que j'aille
			Subj (imp):	que j'allasse

Infinitive:
amener *to bring*: is like *mener* in the distribution of *è* in certain forms

Infinitive:	**Present indicative:**		**Participles:**	apparaissant apparu
apparaître	j'apparais	nous apparaissons	**Future:**	j'apparaîtrai
to appear	tu apparais	vous apparaissez	**Simple past:**	j'apparus
	il apparaît	ils apparaissent	**Imperfect:**	j'apparaissais
			Subj (pres):	que j'apparaisse
			Subj (imp):	que j'apparusse

Infinitive:
appartenir *to belong*: see tenir

Infinitive:	**Present indicative:**		**Participles:**	appelant appelé
appeler	j'appelle	nous appelons	**Future:**	j'appellerai (ll in all forms)
to call	tu appelles	vous appelez	**Simple past:**	j'appelai
	il appelle	ils appellent	**Imperfect:**	j'appelais
			Subj (pres):	que j'appelle
				que nous appelions
				que vous appeliez
			Subj (imp):	que j'appelasse

Infinitive:
apprendre *to learn, to teach*: see prendre

TABLE 7.H *Irregular verbs (continued)*

Infinitive:	Present indicative:		Participles:	assaillant assailli
assaillir	j'assaille	nous assaillons	Future:	j'assaillirai
to assail	tu assailles	vous assaillez	Simple past:	j'assaillis
	il assaille	ils assaillent	Imperfect:	j'assaillais
			Subj (pres):	que j'assaille
			Subj (imp):	que j'assaillisse
			Imperative:	assaille (assailles before *y* and *en*)

Infinitive:	Present indicative:		Participles:	s'asseyant assis
s'asseoir	je m'assieds	nous nous asseyons	Future:	je m'assiérai (or je m'assoirai)
to sit down	tu t'assieds	vous vous asseyez		
	il s'assied	ils s'asseyent	Simple past:	je m'assis
			Imperfect:	je m'asseyais (or je m'assoyais)
			Subj (pres):	que je m'asseye
(Also possible are:			Subj (imp):	que je m'assisse
	je m'assois	nous nous assoyons		
	tu t'assois	vous vous assoyez		
	il s'assoit	ils s'asseoient)		

Infinitive:	Present indicative:		Participles:	astreignant astreint
astreindre	j'astreins	nous astreignons	Future:	j'astreindrai
to oblige	tu astreins	vous astreignez	Simple past:	j'astreignis
	il astreint	ils astreignent	Imperfect:	j'astreignais
			Subj (pres):	que j'astreigne
			Subj (imp):	que j'astreignisse

Infinitive:	Present indicative:		Participles:	atteignant atteint
atteindre	j'atteins	nous atteignons	Future:	j'atteindrai
to attain	tu atteins	vous atteignez	Simple past:	j'atteignis
	il atteint	ils atteignent	Imperfect:	j'atteignais
			Subj (pres):	que j'atteigne
			Subj (imp):	que j'atteignisse

Infinitive:	Present indicative:		Participles:	avançant avancé
avancer	j'avance	nous avançons	Future:	j'avancerai
to advance	tu avances	vous avancez	Simple past:	j'avançai
	il avance	ils avancent	Imperfect:	j'avançais
			Subj (pres):	que j'avance
			Subj (imp):	que j'avançasse

NB: Always ç before an 'a' or 'o'

Infinitive:	Present indicative:		Participles:	battant battu
battre	je bats	nous battons	Future:	je battrai
to beat	tu bats	vous battez	Simple past:	je battis
	il bat	ils battent	Imperfect:	je battais
			Subj (pres):	que je batte
			Subj (imp):	que je battisse

Infinitive:	Present indicative:		Participles:	buvant bu
boire	je bois	nous buvons	Future:	je boirai
to drink	tu bois	vous buvez	Simple past:	je bus
	il boit	ils boivent	Imperfect:	je buvais
			Subj (pres):	que je boive
			Subj (imp):	que je busse

TABLE 7.H *(continued)*

Infinitive: bouillir *to boil*	Present indicative: je bous nous bouillons tu bous vous bouillez il bout ils bouillent	Participles: **Future:** **Simple past:** **Imperfect:** **Subj (pres):** **Subj (imp):**	bouillant bouilli je bouillirai je bouillis je bouillais que je bouille que je bouillisse
Infinitive: braire *to bray*	Present indicative: il brait ils braient	Participles: **Future:** **Simple past:** **Imperfect:** **Subj (pres):** **Subj (imp):**	brayant - il braira - il brayait - -
Infinitive: bruire *to buzz (of insects)*	Present indicative: il bruit ils bruissent	Participles: **Future:** **Simple past:** **Imperfect:** **Subj (pres):** **Subj (imp):**	- - il bruira - - - -

Infinitive: céder *to give up*: is like *espérer* and *compléter* in the way *é* and *è* are distributed

Infinitive: ceindre *to put sth around sth (rare)*	Present indicative: je ceins nous ceignons tu ceins vous ceignez il ceint ils ceignent	Participles: **Future:** **Simple past:** **Imperfect:** **Subj (pres):** **Subj (imp):**	ceignant ceint je ceindrai je ceignis je ceignais que je ceigne que je ceignisse
Infinitive: choir *to fall* (rare)	Present indicative: je chois - tu chois - il choit ils choient	Participles: **Future:** **Simple past:** **Imperfect:** **Subj (pres):** **Subj (imp):**	chu je choirai je chus - - -

Infinitive: circonscrire *to circumscribe*: see écrire

Infinitive: circonvenir *to circumvent*: see venir

Infinitive: clore *to conclude, close*	Present indicative: je clos - tu clos - il clôt ils closent	Participles: **Future:** **Simple past:** **Imperfect:** **Subj (pres):** **Subj (imp):**	- je clorai - - que je close -

TABLE 7.H *(continued)*

Infinitive:	Present indicative:		Participles:	combattant combattu
combattre	je combats	nous combattons	Future:	je combattrai
to fight	tu combats	vous combattez	Simple past:	je combattis
	il combat	ils combattent	Imperfect:	je combattais
			Subj (pres):	que je combatte
			Subj (imp):	que je combattisse

Infinitive:
commettre *to commit*: see mettre

Infinitive:
comparaître *to appear before a court*: see paraître

Infinitive:
complaire à *to humour*: see plaire

Infinitive:	Present indicative:		Participles:	complétant complété
compléter	je complète	nous complétons	Future:	je compléterai
to complete	tu complètes	vous complétez	Simple past:	je complétai
	il complète	ils complètent	Imperfect:	je complétais
			Subj (pres):	que je complète
				que nous complétions
				que vous complétiez
			Subj (imp):	que je complétasse

Infinitive:
comprendre *to understand*: see prendre

Infinitive:
compromettre *to compromise*: see mettre

Infinitive:	Present indicative:		Participles:	concluant conclu
conclure	je conclus	nous concluons	Future:	je conclurai
to conclude	tu conclus	vous concluez	Simple past:	je conclus
	il conclut	ils concluent	Imperfect:	je concluais
			Subj (pres):	que je conclue
			Subj (imp):	que je conclusse

Infinitive:
concourir *to converge*: see courir

Infinitive:
conduire *to drive*: see construire

Infinitive:	Present indicative:		Participles:	confisant confit
confire	je confis	nous confisons	Future:	je confirai
to preserve in	tu confis	vous confisez	Simple past:	je confis
fat or sugar	il confit	ils confisent	Imperfect:	je confisais
			Subj (pres):	que je confise
			Subj (imp):	-

TABLE 7.H *(continued)*

Infinitive:	Present indicative:		Participles:	connaissant connu
connaître	je connais	nous connaissons	**Future:**	je connaîtrai
to know	tu connais	vous connaissez	**Simple past:**	je connus
	il connaît	ils connaissent	**Imperfect:**	je connaissais
			Subj (pres):	que je connaisse
			Subj (imp):	que je connusse

Infinitive:
conquérir *to conquer*: see acquérir

Infinitive:	Present indicative:		Participles:	construisant construit
construire	je construis	nous construisons	**Future:**	je construirai
to build	tu construis	vous construisez	**Simple past:**	je construisis
	il construit	ils construisent	**Imperfect:**	je construisais
			Subj (pres):	que je construise
			Subj (imp):	que je construisisse

Infinitive:
contenir *to contain*: see tenir

Infinitive:	Present indicative:		Participles:	contraignant contraint
contraindre	je contrains	nous contraignons	**Future:**	je contraindrai
to constrain	tu contrains	vous contraignez	**Simple past:**	je contraignis
	il contraint	ils contraignent	**Imperfect:**	je contraignais
			Subj (pres):	que je contraigne
			Subj (imp):	que je contraignisse

Infinitive:
contredire *to contradict*: see interdire

Infinitive:
contrefaire *to imitate*: see faire

Infinitive:
contrevenir *to contravene*: see venir

Infinitive:
convaincre *to convince*: see vaincre

Infinitive:
convenir *to agree*: see venir

Infinitive:	Present indicative:		Participles:	corrompant corrompu
corrompre	je corromps	nous corrompons	**Future:**	je corromprai
to corrupt	tu corromps	vous corrompez	**Simple past:**	je corrompis
	il corrompt	ils corrompent	**Imperfect:**	je corrompais
			Subj (pres):	que je corrompe
			Subj (imp):	que je corrompisse

Infinitive:	Present indicative:		Participles:	cousant cousu
coudre	je couds	nous cousons	**Future:**	je coudrai
to sew	tu couds	vous cousez	**Simple past:**	je cousis
	il coud	ils cousent	**Imperfect:**	je cousais
			Subj (pres):	que je couse
			Subj (imp):	que je cousisse

TABLE 7.H *(continued)*

Infinitive: courir *to run*	Present indicative: je cours nous courons tu cours vous courez il court ils courent	Participles: courant couru Future: je courrai Simple past: je courus Imperfect: je courais Subj (pres): que je coure Subj (imp): que je courusse
Infinitive: couvrir *to cover*	Present indicative: je couvre nous couvrons tu couvres vous couvrez il couvre ils couvrent	Participles: couvrant couvert Future: je couvrirai Simple past: je couvris Imperfect: je couvrais Subj (pres): que je couvre Subj (imp): que je couvrisse Imperative: couvre (couvres before *y* and en)
Infinitive: craindre *to fear*	Present indicative: je crains nous craignons tu crains vous craignez il craint ils craignent	Participles: craignant craint Future: je craindrai Simple past: je craignis Imperfect: je craignais Subj (pres): que je craigne Subj (imp): que je craignisse
Infinitive: créer *to create* (regular verb)	Present indicative: je crée nous créons tu crées vous créez il crée ils créent	Participles: créant créé Future: je créerai Simple past: je créai Imperfect: je créais Subj (pres): que je crée Subj (imp): que je créasse
Infinitive: croire *to believe*	Present indicative: je crois nous croyons tu crois vous croyez il croit ils croient	Participles: croyant cru Future: je croirai Simple past: je crus Imperfect: je croyais Subj (pres): que je croie Subj (imp): que je crusse
Infinitive: croître *to increase*	Present indicative: je croîs nous croissons tu croîs vous croissez il croît ils croissent	Participles: croissant crû (crue) Future: je croîtrai Simple past: je crûs Imperfect: je croissais Subj (pres): que je croisse Subj (imp): que je crûsse
Infinitive: cueillir *to pick*	Present indicative: je cueille nous cueillons tu cueilles vous cueillez il cueille ils cueillent	Participles: cueillant cueilli Future: je cueillerai Simple past: je cueillis Imperfect: je cueillais Subj (pres): que je cueille Subj (imp): que je cueillisse Imperative: cueille (cueilles before *y* and *en*)

NB: The future and conditional have *cueiller* as a base and not *cueillir*. The same is true of *accueillir* and *recueillir* (but not *assaillir*).

TABLE 7.H *(continued)*

Infinitive: débattre *to discuss*	Present indicative: je débats tu débats il débat	nous débattons vous débattez ils débattent	Participles: Future: Simple past: Imperfect: Subj (pres): Subj (imp):	débattant débattu je débattrai je débattis je débattais que je débatte que je débattisse
Infinitive: déchoir *to decline*	Present indicative: je déchois tu déchois il déchoit	nous déchoyons vous déchoyez ils déchoient	Participles: Future: Simple past: Imperfect: Subj (pres): Subj (imp):	– déchu je déchoirai je déchus – que je déchoie que nous déchoyions que vous déchoyiez que je déchusse

Infinitive: découdre *to unstitch*: see coudre

Infinitive: découvrir *to discover*	Present indicative: je découvre tu découvres il découvre	nous découvrons vous découvrez ils découvrent	Participles: Future: Simple past: Imperfect: Subj (pres): Subj (imp): Imperative:	découvrant découvert je découvrirai je découvris je découvrais que je découvre que je découvrisse découvre (découvres before *y* and *en*)

Infinitive: décrire *to describe*: see écrire

Infinitive: décroître *to decrease*	Present indicative: je décrois tu décrois il décroît	nous décroissons vous décroissez ils décroissent	Participles: Future: Simple past: Imperfect: Subj (pres): Subj (imp):	décroissant décru je décroîtrai je décrus je décroissais que je décroisse que je décrusse

Infinitive: se dédire de *to go back on*: see interdire

Infinitive: déduire *to deduce*: see construire

Infinitive: défaillir *to become feeble*: see assaillir

Infinitive: défaire *to undo*: see faire

Infinitive: démettre *to dislocate*: see mettre

TABLE 7.H *(continued)*

Infinitive:	Present indicative:		Participles:	dépeignant	dépeint
dépeindre	je dépeins	nous dépeignons	**Future:**	je dépeindrai	
to describe	tu dépeins	vous dépeignez	**Simple past:**	je dépeignis	
	il dépeint	ils dépeignent	**Imperfect:**	je dépeignais	
			Subj (pres):	que je dépeigne	
			Subj (imp):	que je dépeignisse	

Infinitive:
déplaire à *to displease*: see plaire

Infinitive:
désapprendre *to unlearn*: see prendre

Infinitive:	Present indicative:		Participles:	déteignant	déteint
déteindre	je déteins	nous déteignons	**Future:**	je déteindrai	
to fade	tu déteins	vous déteignez	**Simple past:**	je déteignis	
	il déteint	ils déteignent	**Imperfect:**	je déteignais	
			Subj (pres):	que je déteigne	
			Subj (imp):	que je déteignisse	

Infinitive:
détenir *to be in possession of*: see tenir

Infinitive:
détruire *to destroy*: see construire

Infinitive:
dévêtir *to undress*: see vêtir

Infinitive:	Present indicative:		Participles:	devant	dû (due)
devoir	je dois	nous devons	**Future:**	je devrai	
must	tu dois	vous devez	**Simple past:**	je dus	
	il doit	ils doivent	**Imperfect:**	je devais	
			Subj (pres):	que je doive	
			Subj (imp):	que je dusse	

Infinitive:	Present indicative:		Participles:	disant	dit
dire	je dis	nous disons	**Future:**	je dirai	
to say	tu dis	vous dites	**Simple past:**	je dis	
	il dit	ils disent	**Imperfect:**	je disais	
			Subj (pres):	que je dise	
			Subj (imp):	que je disse	

Infinitive:
disconvenir à *to be unsuited to*: see venir

Infinitive:
discourir *to hold forth*: see courir

Infinitive:
disjoindre *to sever*: see joindre

TABLE 7.H (*continued*)

Infinitive: disparaître *to disappear*	**Present indicative:** je disparais tu disparais il disparaît	nous disparaissons vous disparaissez ils disparaissent	**Participles:** **Future:** **Simple past:** **Imperfect:** **Subj (pres):** **Subj (imp):**	disparaissant disparu je disparaîtrai je disparus je disparaissais que je disparaisse que je disparusse

Infinitive: dissoudre *to dissolve*: see absoudre

Infinitive: distraire *to distract*: see traire

Infinitive: s'ébattre *to frolic*: see battre

Infinitive: échoir *to fall due*	**Present indicative:** - - il échoit	- - ils échoient	**Participles:** **Future:** **Simple past:**	échéant échu il échoira il échut

Infinitive: éclore *to blossom*: see clore

Infinitive: écrire *to write*	**Present indicative:** j'écris tu écris il écrit	nous écrivons vous écrivez ils écrivent	**Participles:** **Future:** **Simple past:** **Imperfect:** **Subj (pres):** **Subj (imp):**	écrivant écrit j'écrirai j'écrivis j'écrivais que j'écrive que j'écrivisse

Infinitive: élire *to elect*: see lire

Infinitive: émettre *to emit*: see mettre

Infinitive: émouvoir *to excite*	**Present indicative:** j'émeus tu émeus il émeut	nous émouvons vous émouvez ils émeuvent	**Participles:** **Future:** **Simple past:** **Imperfect:** **Subj (pres):** **Subj (imp):**	émouvant ému j'émouvrai j'émus j'émouvais que j'émeuve que j'émusse

Infinitive: employer *to use*	**Present indicative:** j'emploie tu emploies il emploie	nous employons vous employez ils emploient	**Participles:** **Future:** **Simple past:** **Imperfect:** **Subj (pres):** **Subj (imp):**	employant employé j'emploierai j'employai j'employais que j'emploie que j'employasse

Infinitive: empreindre *to stamp*: see craindre

TABLE 7.H *(continued)*

Infinitive:	
s'en aller *to go away*: see aller	

Infinitive:	
enceindre *to surround*: see ceindre	

Infinitive:	
enclore *to fence in*: see clore	

Infinitive:	
encourir *to incur*: see courir	

Infinitive:	
enduire *to coat, render*: see construire	

Infinitive:	**Present indicative:**		**Participles:**	enfreignant enfreint
enfreindre	j'enfreins	nous enfreignons	**Future:**	j'enfreindrai
to infringe	tu enfreins	vous enfreignez	**Simple past:**	j'enfreignis
	il enfreint	ils enfreignent	**Imperfect:**	j'enfreignais
			Subj (pres):	que j'enfreigne
			Subj (imp):	que j'enfreignisse

Infinitive:	
s'enfuir *to flee*: see fuir	

Infinitive:	
enjoindre *to call upon*: see joindre	

Infinitive:	
enlever *to remove*: is like *mener* in the use of *è* in some forms of the verb	

Infinitive:	
s'enquérir *to make enquiries*: see acquérir	

Infinitive:	
s'ensuivre *to result, follow*: see suivre	
An impersonal verb used only in the infinitive and third singular form	

Infinitive:	
s'entremettre *to intervene*: see mettre	

Infinitive:	
entreprendre *to undertake*: see prendre	

Infinitive:	
entretenir *to maintain*: see tenir	

Infinitive:	
entrevoir *to make out*: see voir	

Infinitive:	
entrouvrir *to half-open*: see ouvrir	

TABLE 7.H *(continued)*

| Infinitive:
envoyer
to send | Present indicative:
j'envoie
tu envoies
il envoie |
nous envoyons
vous envoyez
ils envoient | Participles:
Future:
Simple past:
Imperfect:
Subj (pres):
Subj (imp): | envoyant
j'enverrai
j'envoyai
j'envoyais
que j'envoie
que j'envoyasse | envoyé |

Infinitive: épeler *to spell*: is like *appeler* in the distribution of single '*l*' and double '*ll*'

Infinitive: s'éprendre de *to fall in love with*: see prendre

Infinitive: équivaloir à *to be equivalent to*: see valoir

| Infinitive:
espérer
to hope | Present indicative:
j'espère
tu espères
il espère |
nous espérons
vous espérez
ils espèrent | Participles:
Future:
Simple past:
Imperfect:
Subj (pres):
Subj (imp): | espérant
j'espèrerai
j'espérai
j'espérais
que j'espère
que j'espérasse | espéré |

| Infinitive:
éteindre
to extinguish | Present indicative:
j'éteins
tu éteins
il éteint |
nous éteignons
vous éteignez
ils éteignent | Participles:
Future:
Simple past:
Imperfect:
Subj (pres):
Subj (imp): | éteignant
j'éteindrai
j'éteignis
j'éteignais
que j'éteigne
que j'éteignisse | éteint |

| Infinitive:
étreindre
to embrace | Present indicative:
j'étreins
tu étreins
il étreint |
nous étreignons
vous étreignez
ils étreignent | Participles:
Future:
Simple past:
Imperfect:
Subj (pres):
Subj (imp): | étreignant
j'étreindrai
j'étreignis
j'étreignais
que j'étreigne
que j'étreignisse | étreint |

Infinitive: exclure *to exclude*: see conclure

Infinitive: extraire *to extract*: see traire

| Infinitive:
faillir
to almost do, nearly do

e.g. | Present indicative:
-

j'ai failli/il a failli, etc., tomber
I/he nearly fell

Je ne faillirai pas à mon devoir
I won't fail in my duty | Participles:
Future:
Simple past:
Imperfect:
Subj (pres):
Subj (imp): | -
je faillirai
je faillis
je faillais
-
- | failli |

TABLE 7.H *(continued)*

Infinitive:	Present indicative:		Participles:	faisant	fait
faire	je fais	nous faisons	Future:	je ferai	
to do	tu fais	vous faites	Simple past:	je fis	
	il fait	ils font	Imperfect:	je faisais	
			Subj (pres):	que je fasse	
			Subj (imp):	que je fisse	

Infinitive:	Present indicative:	Participles:	-	fallu
falloir	il faut	Future:	il faudra	
to be necessary,		Simple past:	il fallut	
'must'		Imperfect:	il fallait	
		Subj (pres):	qu'il faille	
		Subj (imp):	qu'il fallût	

Infinitive:	Present indicative:		Participles:	feignant	feint
feindre	je feins	nous feignons	Future:	je feindrai	
to feign	tu feins	vous feignez	Simple past:	je feignis	
	il feint	ils feignent	Imperfect:	je feignais	
			Subj (pres):	que je feigne	
			Subj (imp):	que je feignisse	

Infinitive:
fleurir: has two present participles depending on meaning: *fleurissant* for the meaning of 'coming into flower', but *florissant* for 'flourishing' as in 'a flourishing business'.

Infinitive:	Present indicative:	Participles:	-	frit
frire	je fris	Future:	je frirai	
to fry	tu fris	Simple past:	-	
	il frit	Imperfect:	-	
		Subj (pres):	-	
		Subj (imp):	-	

Infinitive:	Present indicative:		Participles:	fuyant	fui
fuir	je fuis	nous fuyons	Future:	je fuirai	
to flee	tu fuis	vous fuyez	Simple past:	je fuis	
	il fuit	ils fuient	Imperfect:	je fuyais	
			Subj (pres):	que je fuie	
			Subj (imp):	que je fuisse	

Infinitive:	Present indicative:		Participles:	geignant	geint
geindre	je geins	nous geignons	Future:	je geindrai	
to groan	tu geins	vous geignez	Simple past:	je geignis	
	il geint	ils geignent	Imperfect:	je geignais	
			Subj (pres):	que je geigne	
			Subj (imp):	que je geignisse	

Infinitive:
geler *to freeze*: is like *mener* in the use of *è* in some forms

Infinitive:	Present indicative:		Participles:	gisant	-
gésir	je gis	nous gisons	Future:	-	
to be at rest,	tu gis	vous gisez	Simple past:	-	
(as in grave),	il gît	ils gisent	Imperfect:	je gisais	
lie about (as clothes			Subj (pres):	-	
on floor)	NB: ci-gît ... *here lies* ...		Subj (imp):	-	

TABLE 7.H *(continued)*

Infinitive:	Present indicative:		Participles:	haïssant	haï
haïr	je hais	nous haïssons	**Future:**	je haïrai	
to hate	tu hais	vous haïssez	**Simple past:**	je haïs	
	il hait	ils haïssent	**Imperfect:**	je haïssais	
			Subj (pres):	que je haïsse	
			Subj (imp):	que je haïsse	

NB: The ï (i with trema) indicates two syllables. The verb is regular apart from the use of the trema.

Infinitive:
induire *to induce*: see construire

Infinitive:
inscrire *to inscribe*: see écrire

Infinitive:
instruire *to instruct*: see construire

Infinitive:	Present indicative:		Participles:	interdisant	interdit
interdire	j'interdis	nous interdisons	**Future:**	j'interdirai	
to forbid	tu interdis	vous interdisez	**Simple past:**	j'interdis	
	il interdit	ils interdisent	**Imperfect:**	j'interdisais	
			Subj (pres):	que j'interdise	
			Subj (imp):	que j'interdisse	

Infinitive:
intervenir *to intervene*: see venir

Infinitive:
introduire *to insert*: see construire

Infinitive:	Present indicative:		Participles:	jetant	jeté
jeter	je jette	nous jetons	**Future:**	je jetterai	
to throw	tu jettes	vous jetez	**Simple past:**	je jetai	
	il jette	ils jettent	**Imperfect:**	je jetais	
			Subj (pres):	que je jette	
				que nous jetions	
				que vous jetiez	
			Subj (imp):	que je jetasse	

Infinitive:	Present indicative:		Participles:	joignant	joint
joindre	je joins	nous joignons	**Future:**	je joindrai	
to join	tu joins	vous joignez	**Simple past:**	je joignis	
	il joint	ils joignent	**Imperfect:**	je joignais	
			Subj (pres):	que je joigne	
			Subj (imp):	que je joignisse	

Infinitive:	Present indicative:		Participles:	lisant	lu
lire	je lis	nous lisons	**Future:**	je lirai	
to read	tu lis	vous lisez	**Simple past:**	je lus	
	il lit	ils lisent	**Imperfect:**	je lisais	
			Subj (pres):	que je lise	
			Subj (imp):	que je lusse	

TABLE 7.H *(continued)*

Infinitive:	
luire *to shine*: is similar to *construire*, except that its past participle is *'lui'* and it normally does not have a simple past or an imperfect subjunctive.	

Infinitive:
maintenir *to maintain*: see tenir

Infinitive:	**Present indicative:**		**Participles:**	mangeant	mangé
manger	je mange	nous mangeons	**Future:**	je mangerai	
to eat	tu manges	vous mangez	**Simple past:**	je mangeai	
	il mange	ils mangent	**Imperfect:**	je mangeais	
			Subj (pres):	que je mange	
			Subj (imp):	que je mangeasse	

NB: Insert 'e' after 'g' before 'a' or 'o' to ensure correct pronunciation.

Infinitive:	**Present indicative:**		**Participles:**	maudissant	maudit
maudire	je maudis	nous maudissons	**Future:**	je maudirai	
to curse	tu maudis	vous maudissez	**Simple past:**	je maudis	
	il maudit	ils maudissent	**Imperfect:**	je maudissais	
			Subj (pres):	que je maudisse	
			Subj (imp):	que je maudisse	

Infinitive:	**Present indicative:**		**Participles:**	méconnaissant	méconnu
méconnaître	je méconnais	nous méconnaissons	**Future:**	je méconnaîtrai	
to	tu méconnais	vous méconnaissez	**Simple past:**	je méconnus	
misunderstand	il méconnaît	ils méconnaissent	**Imperfect:**	je méconnaissais	
			Subj (pres):	que je méconnaisse	
			Subj (imp):	que je méconnusse	

Infinitive:	**Present indicative:**		**Participles:**	menant	mené
mener	je mène	nous menons	**Future:**	je mènerai	
to lead	tu mènes	vous menez	**Simple past:**	je menai	
	il mène	ils mènent	**Imperfect:**	je menais	
			Subj (pres):	que je mène	
				que nous menions	
				que vous meniez	
			Subj (imp):	que je menasse	

NB: è in cases where the following syllable contains a 'silent' 'e'.

Infinitive:
se méprendre *to be mistaken*: see prendre

Infinitive:	**Present indicative:**		**Participles:**	mettant	mis
mettre	je mets	nous mettons	**Future:**	je mettrai	
to put	tu mets	vous mettez	**Simple past:**	je mis	
	il met	ils mettent	**Imperfect:**	je mettais	
			Subj (pres):	que je mette	
			Subj (imp):	que je misse	

TABLE 7.H *(continued)*

Infinitive: moudre *to grind*	Present indicative: je mouds nous moulons tu mouds vous moulez il moud ils moulent	Participles: Future: Simple past: Imperfect: Subj (pres): Subj (imp):	moulant moulu je moudrai je moulus je moulais que je moule que je moulusse
Infinitive: mourir *to die*	Present indicative: je meurs nous mourons tu meurs vous mourez il meurt ils meurent	Participles: Future: Simple past: Imperfect: Subj (pres): Subj (imp):	mourant mort je mourrai je mourus je mourais que je meure que je mourusse
Infinitive: mouvoir *to move*	Present indicative: je meus nous mouvons tu meus vous mouvez il meut ils meuvent	Participles: Future: Simple past: Imperfect: Subj (pres): Subj (imp):	mouvant mû (mue, mus) je mouvrai je mus je mouvais que je meuve que je musse
Infinitive: naître *to be born*	Present indicative: je nais nous naissons tu nais vous naissez il naît ils naissent	Participles: Future: Simple past: Imperfect: Subj (pres): Subj (imp):	naissant né je naîtrai je naquis je naissais que je naisse que je naquisse
Infinitive: nettoyer *to clean*	Present indicative: je nettoie nous nettoyons tu nettoies vous nettoyez il nettoie ils nettoient	Participles: Future: Simple past: Imperfect: Subj (pres): Subj (imp):	nettoyant nettoyé je nettoierai je nettoyai je nettoyais que je nettoie que je nettoyasse

Infinitive:
nuire *to harm*: is similar to construire, except that its past participle is 'nui' and it normally does not have a simple past or an imperfect subjunctive.

Infinitive:
obtenir *to obtain*: see tenir

Infinitive: offrir *to give*	Present indicative: j'offre nous offrons tu offres vous offrez il offre ils offrent	Participles: Future: Simple past: Imperfect: Subj (pres): Subj (imp): Imperative:	offrant offert j'offrirai j'offris j'offrais que j'offre que j'offrisse offre (offres before *y* and *en*)

Infinitive:
omettre *to omit*: see mettre

TABLE 7.H *(continued)*

Infinitive:	Present indicative:		Participles:	ouvrant ouvert
ouvrir	j'ouvre	nous ouvrons	**Future:**	j'ouvrirai
to open	tu ouvres	vous ouvrez	**Simple past:**	j'ouvris
	il ouvre	ils ouvrent	**Imperfect:**	j'ouvrais
			Subj (pres):	que j'ouvre
			Subj (imp):	que j'ouvrisse
			Imperative:	ouvre (ouvres before *y* and *en*)

Infinitive:	Present indicative:		Participles:	paraissant paru
paraître	je parais	nous paraissons	**Future:**	je paraîtrai
to seem	tu parais	vous paraissez	**Simple past:**	je parus
	il paraît	ils paraissent	**Imperfect:**	je paraissais
			Subj (pres):	que je paraisse
			Subj (imp):	que je parusse

Infinitive:
parcourir *to travel through*: see courir

Infinitive:
parfaire *to perfect*: see faire

Infinitive:
parvenir *to reach*: see venir

Infinitive:	Present indicative:		Participles:	peignant peint
peindre	je peins	nous peignons	**Future:**	je peindrai
to paint	tu peins	vous peignez	**Simple past:**	je peignis
	il peint	ils peignent	**Imperfect:**	je peignais
			Subj (pres):	que je peigne
			Subj (imp):	que je peignisse

Infinitive:
permettre *to allow*: see mettre

Infinitive:
peser *to weigh*: is like *mener* in the use of *è* in some forms

Infinitive:	Present indicative:		Participles:	se plaignant se plaint
se plaindre	je me plains	nous nous plaignons	**Future:**	je me plaindrai
to complain	tu te plains	vous vous plaignez	**Simple past:**	je me plaignis
	il se plaint	ils se plaignent	**Imperfect:**	je me plaignais
			Subj (pres):	que je me plaigne
			Subj (imp):	que je me plaignisse

Infinitive:	Present indicative:		Participles:	plaisant plu
plaire	je plais	nous plaisons	**Future:**	je plairai
to please	tu plais	vous plaisez	**Simple past:**	je plus
	il plaît	ils plaisent	**Imperfect:**	je plaisais
			Subj (pres):	que je plaise
			Subj (imp):	que je plusse

TABLE 7.H *(continued)*

Infinitive: pleuvoir *to rain* (impersonal)	Present indicative: il pleut		Participles: Future: Simple past: Imperfect: Subj (pres): Subj (imp):	pleuvant plu il pleuvra il plut il pleuvait qu'il pleuve qu'il plût
Infinitive: poursuivre *to pursue*: see suivre				
Infinitive: pourvoir *to provide*	**Present indicative:** je pourvois tu pourvois il pourvoit	nous pourvoyons vous pourvoyez ils pourvoient	**Participles:** **Future:** **Simple past:** **Imperfect:** **Subj (pres):** **Subj (imp):**	pourvoyant pourvu je pourvoirai je pourvus je pourvoyais que je pourvoie que je pourvusse
Infinitive: pouvoir *to be able to*	**Present indicative:** je peux tu peux il peut (alternative: je puis)	nous pouvons vous pouvez ils peuvent	**Participles:** **Future:** **Simple past:** **Imperfect:** **Subj (pres):** **Subj (imp):**	pouvant pu je pourrai je pus je pouvais que je puisse que je pusse
Infinitive: prédire *to predict*: see interdire				
Infinitive: prendre *to take*	**Present indicative:** je prends tu prends il prend	nous prenons vous prenez ils prennent	**Participles:** **Future:** **Simple past:** **Imperfect:** **Subj (pres):** **Subj (imp):**	prenant pris je prendrai je pris je prenais que je prenne que nous prenions que vous preniez que je prisse

NB: Two 'n's when 'n' is followed by a 'silent' 'e': *prenne, prennes, prennent.*

Infinitive: prescrire *to prescribe*: see écrire				
Infinitive: prévaloir *to prevail*: see valoir				
Infinitive: prévenir *to anticipate*: see venir				
Infinitive: prévoir *to foresee*	**Present indicative:** je prévois tu prévois il prévoit	nous prévoyons vous prévoyez ils prévoient	**Participles:** **Future:** **Simple past:** **Imperfect:** **Subj (pres):** **Subj (imp):**	prévoyant prévu je prévoirai je prévis je prévoyais que je prévoie que je prévisse

TABLE 7.H *(continued)*

Infinitive: produire *to produce*: see construire	

Infinitive:
produire *to produce*: see construire

Infinitive:
projeter *to plan*: is like *jeter* in the use of single 't' and double 'tt'.

Infinitive:
promettre *to promise*: see mettre

Infinitive:
proscrire *to outlaw*: see écrire

Infinitive:
protéger *to protect*: is like *espérer*, *compléter* in the distribution of *é* and *è*

Infinitive:
provenir de *to arise from*: see venir

Infinitive:
r-, re-, ré-: for derived verbs with these prefixes, e.g. rasseoir, reconstruire, réélire, etc., see the entry for the non-prefixed counterpart, i.e. s'asseoir, construire, lire, etc.

Infinitive:	Present indicative:		Participles:	rabattant rabattu
rabattre	je rabats	nous rabattons	**Future:**	je rabattrai
to pull down	tu rabats	vous rabattez	**Simple past:**	je rabattis
(e.g. hat)	il rabat	ils rabattent	**Imperfect:**	je rabattais
			Subj (pres):	que je rabatte
			Subj (imp):	que je rabattisse

Infinitive:
(se) rappeler *to recall*: is like appeler in the distribution of single 'l' and double 'll'

Infinitive:	Present indicative·		Participles:	reconnaissant reconnu
reconnaître	je reconnais	nous reconnaissons	**Future:**	je reconnaîtrai
to recognize	tu reconnais	vous reconnaissez	**Simple past:**	je reconnus
	il reconnaît	ils reconnaissent	**Imperfect:**	je reconnaissais
			Subj (pres):	que je reconnaisse
			Subj (imp):	que je reconnusse

Infinitive:	Present indicative:		Participles:	recouvrant recouvert
recouvrir	je recouvre	nous recouvrons	**Future:**	je recouvrirai
to cover	tu recouvres	vous recouvrez	**Simple past:**	je recouvris
	il recouvre	ils recouvrent	**Imperfect:**	je recouvrais
			Subj (pres):	que je recouvre
			Subj (imp):	que je recouvrisse

Infinitive:
refléter *to reflect*: is like *espérer* and *compléter* in the distribution of *é* and *è*

Infinitive:
rejeter *to throw back*: is like *jeter* in the use of single 't' and double 'tt'

TABLE 7.H *(continued)*

Infinitive:	Present indicative:		Participles:	renvoyant renvoyé
renvoyer	je renvoie	nous renvoyons	**Future:**	je renverrai
to sack, send back	tu renvoies	vous renvoyez	**Simple past:**	je renvoyai
	il renvoie	ils renvoient	**Imperfect:**	je renvoyais
			Subj (pres):	que je renvoie
			Subj (imp):	que je renvoyasse

Infinitive:
repétér *repeat*: is like *espérer* and *compléter* in the distribution of *é* and *è* (second syllable)

Infinitive:	Present indicative:		Participles:	résolvant résolu
résoudre	je résous	nous résolvons	**Future:**	je résoudrai
to resolve	tu résous	vous résolvez	**Simple past:**	je résolus
	il résout	ils résolvent	**Imperfect:**	je résolvais
			Subj (pres):	que je résolve
			Subj (imp):	que je résolusse

Infinitive:	Present indicative:		Participles:	restreignant restreint
restreindre	je restreins	nous restreignons	**Future:**	je restreindrai
to restrain	tu restreins	vous restreignez	**Simple past:**	je restreignis
	il restreint	ils restreignent	**Imperfect:**	je restreignais
			Subj (pres):	que je restreigne
			Subj (imp):	que je restreignisse

Infinitive:	Present indicative:		Participles:	riant ri
rire	je ris	nous rions	**Future:**	je rirai
to laugh	tu ris	vous riez	**Simple past:**	je ris
	il rit	ils rient	**Imperfect:**	je riais
			Subj (pres):	que je rie
			Subj (imp):	que je risse

Infinitive:	Present indicative:		Participles:	rompant rompu
rompre	je romps	nous rompons	**Future:**	je romprai
to break	tu romps	vous rompez	**Simple past:**	je rompis
	il rompt	ils rompent	**Imperfect:**	je rompais
			Subj (pres):	que je rompe
			Subj (imp):	que je rompisse

Infinitive:
satisfaire *to satisfy*: see faire

Infinitive:	Present indicative:		Participles:	sachant su
savoir	je sais	nous savons	**Future:**	je saurai
to know	tu sais	vous savez	**Simple past:**	je sus
	il sait	ils savent	**Imperfect:**	je savais
			Subj (pres):	que je sache
			Subj (imp):	que je susse

Infinitive:
secourir *to help*: see courir

Infinitive:
séduire *to seduce*: see construire

TABLE 7.H *(continued)*

Infinitive: semer *to sow*: is like *mener* in the distribution of *è* in certain forms				

Infinitive:	**Present indicative:**		**Participles:**	souffrant	souffert
souffrir	je souffre	nous souffrons	**Future:**	je souffrirai	
to suffer	tu souffres	vous souffrez	**Simple past:**	je souffris	
	il souffre	ils souffrent	**Imperfect:**	je souffrais	
			Subj (pres):	que je souffre	
			Subj (imp):	que je souffrisse	

Infinitive:
soumettre *to submit*: see mettre

Infinitive:
sourire *to smile*: see rire

Infinitive:
souscrire *to sign*: see écrire

Infinitive:
soustraire *to withdraw*: see traire

Infinitive:
soutenir *to support*: see tenir

Infinitive:
se souvenir de *to remember*: see venir

Infinitive:
subvenir *to subsidize*: see venir

Infinitive:	**Present indicative:**	**Participles:**	suffisant	suffi
suffire	il suffit	**Future:**	il suffira	
to suffice		**Simple past:**	il suffit	
(impersonal)		**Imperfect:**	il suffisait	
		Subj (pres):	qu'il suffise	
		Subj (imp):	qu'il suffît	

Infinitive:	**Present indicative:**		**Participles:**	suivant	suivi
suivre	je suis	nous suivons	**Future:**	je suivrai	
to follow	tu suis	vous suivez	**Simple past:**	je suivis	
	il suit	ils suivent	**Imperfect:**	je suivais	
			Subj (pres):	que je suive	
			Subj (imp):	que je suivisse	

Infinitive:
surprendre *to surprise*: see prendre

TABLE 7.H *(continued)*

Infinitive: surseoir *to postpone*	Present indicative: je sursois nous sursoyons tu sursois vous sursoyez il sursoit ils sursoient	Participles: Future: Simple past: Imperfect: Subj (pres): Subj (imp):	sursoyant sursis je surseoirai je sursis je sursoyais que je sursoie que je sursisse
Infinitive: survenir *to happen*: see venir			
Infinitive: survivre à *to survive*: see vivre			
Infinitive: se taire *to be quiet*	Present indicative: je me tais nous nous taisons tu te tais vous vous taisez il se tait ils se taisent	Participles: Future: Simple past: Imperfect: Subj (pres): Subj (imp):	se taisant tu je me tairai je me tus je me taisais que je me taise que je me tusse
Infinitive: teindre *to dye*	Present indicative: je teins nous teignons tu teins vous teignez il teint ils teignent	Participles: Future: Simple past: Imperfect: Subj (pres): Subj (imp):	teignant teint je teindrai je teignis je teignais que je teigne que je teignisse
Infinitive: tenir *to hold*	Present indicative: je tiens nous tenons tu tiens vous tenez il tient ils tiennent	Participles: Future: Simple past: Imperfect: Subj (pres): Subj (imp):	tenant tenu je tiendrai je tins je tenais que je tienne que je tinsse
Infinitive: traduire *to translate*: see construire			
Infinitive: traire *to milk*	Present indicative: je trais nous trayons tu trais vous trayez il trait ils traient	Participles: Future: Simple past: Imperfect: Subj (pres): Subj (imp):	trayant trait je trairai - je trayais que je traie que nous trayions que vous trayiez -
Infinitive: transcrire *to transcribe*: see écrire			
Infinitive: transmettre *to transmit*: see mettre			
Infinitive: transparaître *to show through*: see paraître			

TABLE 7.H *(continued)*

Infinitive:	Present indicative:		Participles:	vainquant	vaincu
vaincre	je vaincs	nous vainquons	**Future:**	je vaincrai	
to defeat	tu vaincs	vous vainquez	**Simple past:**	je vainquis	
	il vainc	ils vainquent	**Imperfect:**	je vainquais	
			Subj (pres):	que je vainque	
			Subj (imp):	que je vainquisse	

Infinitive:	Present indicative:		Participles:	valant	valu
valoir	je vaux	nous valons	**Future:**	je vaudrai	
to be worth	tu vaux	vous valez	**Simple past:**	je valus	
	il vaut	ils valent	**Imperfect:**	je valais	
			Subj (pres):	que je vaille	
			Subj (imp):	que je valusse	

Infinitive:	Present indicative:		Participles:	venant	venu
venir	je viens	nous venons	**Future:**	je viendrai	
to come	tu viens	vous venez	**Simple past:**	je vins	
	il vient	ils viennent	**Imperfect:**	je venais	
			Subj (pres):	que je vienne	
			Subj (imp):	que je vinsse	

Infinitive:	Present indicative:		Participles:	vêtant	vêtu
vêtir	je vêts	nous vêtons	**Future:**	je vêtirai	
to clothe	tu vêts	vous vêtez	**Simple past:**	je vêtis	
	il vêt	ils vêtent	**Imperfect:**	je vêtais	
			Subj (pres):	que je vête	
			Subj (imp):	que je vêtisse	

Infinitive:	Present indicative:		Participles:	vivant	vécu
vivre	je vis	nous vivons	**Future:**	je vivrai	
to live	tu vis	vous vivez	**Simple past:**	je vécus	
	il vit	ils vivent	**Imperfect:**	je vivais	
			Subj (pres):	que je vive	
			Subj (imp):	que je vécusse	

Infinitive:	Present indicative:		Participles:	voyant	vu
voir	je vois	nous voyons	**Future:**	je verrai	
to see	tu vois	vous voyez	**Simple past:**	je vis	
	il voit	ils voient	**Imperfect:**	je voyais	
			Subj (pres):	que je voie	
			Subj (imp):	que je visse	

Infinitive:	Present indicative:		Participles:	voulant	voulu
vouloir	je veux	nous voulons	**Future:**	je voudrai	
to want	tu veux	vous voulez	**Simple past:**	je voulus	
	il veut	ils veulent	**Imperfect:**	je voulais	
			Subj (pres):	que je veuille	
			Subj (imp):	que je voulusse	

8

Verb constructions

8.1 Relations between verbs and their complements

Verbs can be classified by the kinds of complement they take. Table 8.A outlines the main types dealt with in this chapter.

TABLE 8.A *Classification of verbs by the complements they take*

	Complement type	
Verb type	**Direct object**	**Prepositional object**
Intransitive (8.2) e.g. *partir* *Jeanne partira*	No —	No —
Directly Transitive (8.3) e.g. *fermer* *Il ferme*	Yes *les yeux*	No —
Indirectly Transitive (8.4) e.g. *hériter* *Yvon hérite*	No —	Yes *d'une fortune*
Ditransitive (8.5) e.g. *planter* *Hervé a planté*	Yes *le jardin*	Yes *de roses*
Pronominal (8.7) (a) *se* is a direct object e.g. *s'évanouir* (b) *se* is an indirect object e.g. *se faire mal*	(a) *Marie s'est évanouie* —	— (b) *Elle s'est fait mal* (à elle-même)

8.2 Intransitive constructions

Intransitive verbs have no object:

Depuis janvier les prix ont augmenté	*Since January prices have gone up*
Il a acquiescé	*He agreed*
L'eau scintillait	*The water sparkled*
La neige tombe	*Snow is falling*

La fête continue	*The party is going on*
Elle avait disparu	*She had disappeared*
Vous descendez?	*Are you going down?*
Il ne souffrira pas	*He won't suffer*

They may be accompanied (usually optionally, but sometimes obligatorily) by adverbs (see Chapter 5). Examples shown in brackets indicate that the adverb is optional:

Elle part (**en vacances**)	*She is going (on holiday)*
Un léger brouillard montait (**de la mer**)	*A mist rose (from the sea)*
Il a respiré **fortement**	*He breathed deeply*
Christian serait tombé (**du haut de la falaise**)	*Christian apparently fell (from the cliff)*
Elle est descendue (**péniblement**)	*She went down (gingerly)*
Cet homme avait vécu **plus de 90 ans**	*That man had lived into his nineties*
Louis tremblait (**de tous ses membres**)	*Louis was trembling (all over)*
Les minutes passaient (**lentement**)	*The minutes passed (slowly)*

8.2.1 Intransitive verbs and auxiliary *avoir*

Most intransitive verbs employ the auxiliary *avoir* in compound tenses:

Depuis janvier les prix **ont** augmenté	*Since January prices have gone up*
Il **aurait** acquiescé	*He agreed, apparently*
La fête **avait** continué	*The party had gone on*
Elle **avait** disparu	*She had disappeared*
Il n'**a** pas souffert	*He didn't suffer*
La situation **aura** probablement empiré	*The situation will probably have got worse*

A small set of verbs, including *commencer, changer, disparaître, vieillir*, normally appear with the auxiliary *avoir* in compound tenses, but their past participles may be used with *être* to describe a state of affairs. In this case the past participle is used in very much the same way as an adjective (for adjectives, see Chapter 4). Compare the following sentences:

Il **a** commencé à lire ce roman	*He began to read this novel*
La pièce **est** commencée	*The play has begun*

Il **a** changé les pneus de sa voiture	*He changed the tyres on his car*
Depuis dix ans elle **est** vraiment changée	*She has really changed in ten years*

NB: With *être* and a state of affairs, there will be agreement between the past participle and the subject. With *avoir* and an action there will not. (See Chapter 9.2 and 9.3.)

8.2.2 Intransitive verbs and auxiliary *être*

Intransitive verbs with *être*

A small set of intransitive verbs, some very frequently used, appear with the auxiliary *être* in compound tenses:

Un léger brouillard **est** monté de la mer	*A mist rose from the sea*
Christian **est** tombé du haut de la falaise	*Christian fell from the cliff*
Elle **était** descendue	*She had gone down*
Marie-Christine **est** née en 1968	*Marie-Christine was born in 1968*

The verbs which take *être* in this way are:

aller	*to go*	naître	*to be born*
arriver	*to arrive*	partir	*to leave*
décéder	*to die*	rentrer	*to go home*
demeurer	*to remain*	rester	*to stay*
descendre	*to go down*	retourner	*to return*
devenir	*to become*	revenir	*to come back*
entrer	*to enter*	sortir	*to go out*
monter	*to go up*	tomber	*to fall*
mourir	*to die*	venir	*to come*

and verbs derived from the above: *redescendre, remonter, renaître, repartir, retomber, parvenir* and *survenir*.

Intransitive verbs with *avoir* or *être*

A further set of intransitive verbs, e.g. *accourir, apparaître, passer,* can appear either with *avoir* or with *être* in compound tenses. It would seem that the use of *être* is now more common and *avoir* may appear dated:

Quand il a appris la nouvelle il **est** accouru	*When he heard the news he came quickly*
Il nous **est** apparu que le gardien avait menti	*It became apparent to us that the porter had lied*
Il **est** passé nous voir	*He came to see us*

(See 8.3.4. for intransitive verbs which can be used with *avoir* when used transitively.)

8.3 Directly transitive verbs

Directly transitive verbs have direct objects:

lire **la nouvelle** dans le journal	*to read the item in the newspaper*
quitter **le Pays de Galles**	*to leave Wales*
composter **un billet**	*to punch a ticket*
fumer **une cigarette**	*to smoke a cigarette*
ouvrir **la portière**	*to open the (car, train) door*
prendre **le train**	*to take the train*
rencontrer **un ami**	*to meet a friend*
expliquer **les faits**	*to explain the facts*
étouffer **un juron**	*to stifle an oath*
lever **la tête**	*to raise one's head*

8.3.1 Directly transitive verbs without objects

Sometimes the objects of transitive verbs may be omitted. When this happens the object is still 'understood', but with a general or non-specific interpretation:

Clément boit	*Clément drinks* ('alcohol' understood)
La vitesse tue	*Speed kills* ('people' understood)
Gustave enseigne	*Gustave teaches* ('pupils' understood)
Il ne sait pas conduire	*He can't drive* ('cars' understood)
On attend	*We're waiting* ('for something to happen' understood)

8.3.2 Directly transitive verbs take the auxiliary *avoir*

All transitive verbs take the auxiliary *avoir* in compound tenses, whether the object is present or omitted:

Elle **a** quitté le Pays de Galles	*She has left Wales*
J'**ai** rencontré un ami	*I met a friend*
Dans la bousculade Laurent **avait** reçu des coups	*In the confusion Laurent had been hit*
On **a** attendu	*We waited*

8.3.3 Verbs with intransitive and transitive uses

Some verbs can be used intransitively (without an object) and transitively (with an object):

Les prix augmentent	*Prices are going up*
La chaîne augmente ses prix	*The store is increasing its prices*
Il rentre	*He is going home*
Il rentre la voiture au garage	*He is putting the car in the garage*
Elle sort	*She is going out*
Elle sort son appareil-photo	*She is getting her camera out*
Le moteur a calé	*The engine stalled*
Alain a calé le moteur	*Alain stalled the engine*

8.3.4 *être* and *avoir* with verbs used intransitively and transitively

Intransitive verbs which take the auxiliary *être* in compound tenses take *avoir* when they are used transitively:

Pierre **est** descendu	*Pierre went down*
BUT	
Pierre **a** descendu les valises	*Pierre has taken the suitcases down*
Marie **est** montée prendre son maillot de bain	*Marie has gone up to fetch her swimming costume*
BUT	
Marie **avait** monté un sac de charbon	*Marie had taken a sack of coal up*
Mickey **est** sorti	*Mickey has gone out*
BUT	
Mickey **a** sorti une pièce d'identité	*Mickey got out some identification*
Bernard **sera** rentré	*Bernard will have gone home*
BUT	
Bernard **avait** rentré la voiture au garage	*Bernard had put the car in the garage*
Eliane **était** retournée à la banque	*Eliane had gone back to the bank*
BUT	
Eliane **a** retourné tout l'appartement	*Eliane has turned the flat upside down*

The verbs *descendre* and *monter* also take the auxiliary *avoir* in compound tenses when they are used with adverbials of place like *l'escalier, la rue, la côte*:

Il **a** descendu l'escalier/la rue	*He went down the stairs/the street*
Elle **a** monté la côte	*She went up the hill*

Compare with:

Il **est** descendu vers la rue	*He went down towards the street*
Elle **est** monté à l'échelle	*She climbed up the ladder*

8.3.5 Verbs which are directly transitive in French but whose translation equivalents involve the object of a preposition in English

English speakers should pay special attention to the following verbs. Unlike their English counterparts, their objects are not preceded by a preposition:

approuver **un choix**	to approve **of** a choice
attendre **le train**	to wait **for** the train
chercher **une enveloppe**	to look **for** an envelope
demander **un verre d'eau**	to ask **for** a glass of water
descendre **la rue**	to go **down** the street
écouter **la radio**	to listen **to** the radio
espérer **une récompense**	to hope **for** a reward
habiter **une maison**, **une ville**,	to live **in** a house, **in** a town, **in** a
une région	region
longer **la falaise**	to go **along** the cliff
monter **la côte**	to go **up** the hill
payer **un tour de manège**	to pay **for** a ride on a roundabout
payer **une tournée**	to pay **for** a round (of drinks)
présider **une séance**	to be the chairperson **of** a session
regarder **le soleil**	to look **at** the sun
viser **la cible**	to aim **at** the target

habiter also appears in constructions like: *habiter à la campagne, habiter en ville, habiter en France*. Here *à la campagne, en ville* and *en France* are not objects but adverbials; they can co-occur with direct objects: *habiter une petite maison à la campagne, habiter un bon quartier en ville*, etc.

Examples:

Il approuve mon choix	(NOT *Il approuve de mon choix)
J'attends le train	(NOT *J'attends pour le train)
Nous cherchons la gare	(NOT *Nous cherchons pour la gare)
Cette publicité vise les jeunes	(NOT *Cette publicité vise aux jeunes)

(See Chapter 3.2 to see how this influences the choice of object pronouns.)

8.4 Indirectly transitive verbs

Indirectly transitive verbs take an object introduced by a preposition:

Introduced by *à*

assister **à** une réunion	to be present at a meeting
compatir **à** la douleur de quelqu'un	to feel for somebody in their sorrow
croire **au** diable	to believe in the devil
en vouloir **à** son cousin	to hold a grudge against one's cousin
participer **aux** activités	to take part in the activities
penser **à** son avenir	to think about one's future
pourvoir **aux** besoins de quelqu'un	to provide for somebody's needs
réfléchir **à** son passé	to reflect on one's past
songer **à** un voyage en Italie	to envisage a trip to Italy
veiller **au** bon règlement d'une affaire	to see to the proper handling of a matter

NB: **(a)** *Croire à* is used to mean 'to believe in the existence of some phenomenon': *croire aux fées* 'to believe in fairies', *croire au bonheur* 'to believe in (human) happiness'. *Croire* can also take direct objects: *Je crois cette histoire* 'I believe this story', *Elle le croit* 'She believes him'. *Croire en* means 'to believe in' in the sense of 'to have faith in': *croire en Dieu* 'to believe in God', *croire en ses co-équipiers* 'to believe in one's team-mates'.

(b) *Penser* can also take an object preceded by *de* with the meaning 'to have an opinion about something': *Qu'est-ce que vous pensez de son article?* 'What do you think of his article?'

(c) *veiller sur quelqu'un* means 'to watch over somebody'.

Introduced by *de*

déborder **d'**eau	*to overflow with water*
déjeuner **de** fruits	*to lunch on fruit*
dépendre **des** circonstances	*to depend on the circumstances*
dîner **de** moules et **de** frites	*to dine on mussels and french fries*
fourmiller **d'**abeilles	*to swarm with bees*
gémir **de** douleur	*to groan with pain*
grouiller **de** fourmis	*to swarm with ants*
parler **de** ses amis	*to speak of one's friends*
regorger **de** richesses	*to abound in wealth*
répondre **de** son ami	*to answer for one's friend*
rire **de** ses compagnons	*to laugh at one's friends*
rougir **de** honte	*to go red with shame*
tenir **de** sa mère	*to take after one's mother*
trembler **de** peur	*to tremble with fear*
triompher **de** son adversaire	*to overcome one's opponent*
vivre **de** l'air du temps	*to live on fresh air alone*
vivre **de** presque rien	*to live on next to nothing*

(For pronominal verbs which take prepositional objects (*s'habituer à, s'éloigner de*, etc.) see 8.7.3.)

8.4.1 Verbs which are indirectly transitive in French but whose translation equivalents are directly transitive in English

Special attention should be given to the following verbs because, while they are indirectly transitive in French, their English counterparts are directly transitive.

Objects introduced by *à*

contravenir **à** la réglementation	*to break the rule*
convenir **à** Julie	*to suit Julie*
(dé)plaire **à** son professeur	*to (dis)please one's teacher*
(dés)obéir **à** ses parents	*to (dis)obey one's parents*
échapper **à** la police	*to evade capture by the police*
échouer **à** un examen	*to fail an exam*
jouer **au** football, **au** rugby, **au** tennis	*to play football, rugby, tennis*
nuire **à** la réputation de quelqu'un	*to harm somebody's reputation*
parvenir **au** sommet	*to reach the summit*
plaire **à** quelqu'un	*to please somebody*
remédier **à** la situation	*to rectify the situation*
renoncer **à** l'alcool	*to give up alcohol*
résister **à** une force	*to resist a force*
ressembler **à** son chien	*to look like one's dog*
subvenir **aux** besoins de quelqu'un	*to look after somebody financially*
succéder **à** son père	*to succeed one's father*

survivre **à** un accident	*to survive an accident*
téléphoner **à** quelqu'un	*to telephone somebody*
toucher **aux** affaires de quelqu'un	*to mess about with somebody's things*

While *échapper à* means 'to evade capture', *s'échapper de* means 'to escape from': *s'échapper de la prison*.

Examples:

Il joue **au** football	(NOT *Il joue football)
Il a téléphoné **à** sa femme	(NOT *Il a téléphoné sa femme)
Elle ressemble beaucoup **à** sa mère	(NOT *Elle ressemble beaucoup sa mère)
Le nouveau poste plaisait **à** Antoine	(NOT *Le nouveau poste plaisait Antoine)

See Chapter 3.2 for the relevance of this distinction to the choice of object pronoun.

Objects introduced by *de*

abuser **de** son héritage	*to misuse one's inheritance*
douter **de** la vérité d'une histoire	*to doubt the truth of a story*
hériter **d'**une fortune	*to inherit a fortune*
jouer **du** piano/**du** violon/**de** la flûte	*to play the piano/violin/flute*
jouir **de** privilèges sans précédent	*to enjoy unprecedented privileges*
médire **de** son voisin	*to slander one's neighbour*
redoubler **d'**efforts	*to double one's efforts*

Note that *entrer* is usually followed by *dans*: *entrer dans la maison*. *Grimper* is usually followed either by *sur* or by *à*: *grimper sur un escabeau* 'to climb a step-ladder', *grimper à l'échelle* 'to climb a ladder'.

Examples:

Elle espère hériter **d'**une fortune	(NOT *Elle espère hériter une fortune)
Elle jouait **du** piano	(NOT *Elle jouait le piano)

(For pronominal verbs which take prepositional objects – *s'apercevoir de, se servir de*, etc. – see 8.7.3.)

8.5 Ditransitive verbs

Ditransitive verbs take a direct object and an object introduced by a preposition.

Introduced by *à* and corresponding typically to English 'to'

accoutumer un apprenti **au** métier	*to get an apprentice used to a trade*
admettre un invité **à** la fête	*to admit a guest to the party*
appeler quelqu'un **au** téléphone	*to call somebody to the phone*
apprendre le français **à** des élèves	*to teach French to pupils*
avouer un crime **à** la police	*to confess to the police about a crime*
condamner un malfaiteur **à** une peine de prison	*to condemn a criminal to prison*
conduire les hôtes **à** leur chambre	*to take the guests to their room*
contraindre les rebelles **à** l'obéissance	*to force the rebels into obedience*
convier des amis **à** une fête	*to invite friends to a party*
dire ses quatre vérités **à** quelqu'un	*to shout the bare truth at somebody*

destiner son fils **à** une belle carrière	*to arrange a great career for one's son*
dire des mensonges **à** sa famille	*to tell lies to one's family*
emmener les invités **à** leur hôtel	*to take guests to their hotel*
exposer sa famille **à** des dangers	*to expose one's family to danger*
forcer les citoyens **à** la révolution	*to drive the citizens to revolution*
habituer les motocyclistes **au** port du casque	*to get motorcycle riders used to wearing a helmet*
inciter les ouvriers **à** la révolte	*to incite workers to revolt*
inviter les syndicalistes **à** une réunion	*to invite the trade union representatives to a meeting*
jurer l'amour éternel **à** quelqu'un	*to swear eternal love to somebody*
louer une voiture **à** un touriste	*to rent a car to a tourist*
obliger ses créanciers **au** remboursement	*to force one's debtors to pay up*
ordonner la retraite **à** ses troupes	*to order one's troops to retreat*
provoquer quelqu'un **à** une réaction trop vive	*to provoke somebody into a hasty reaction*
réduire quelqu'un **à** la mendicité	*to reduce somebody to beggary*
rendre le magnétoscope **à** son voisin	*to return the video recorder to one's neighbour*
suggérer une idée **à** un collègue	*to suggest an idea to a colleague*

NB: *louer une voiture à un garagiste* is likely to mean: 'to hire a car **from** a garage owner'.

Introduced by *à* and corresponding typically to English 'from' or 'for'

acheter un camion **à** un garagiste	*to buy a lorry from a garage owner*
arracher de l'argent **à** un avare	*to prise money from a miser*
cacher la catastrophe **à** sa famille	*to hide the disaster from one's family*
dérober de l'argent **à** ses enfants	*to steal money from one's children*
emprunter cinq cents francs **à** un ami	*to borrow five hundred francs from a friend*
enlever le pistolet **au** voleur	*to take the revolver away from the thief*
ôter une écharde **à** quelqu'un	*to remove a splinter from somebody's flesh*
louer une camionette **au** garagiste	*to hire a van from the garage owner*
préparer la famille **à** de bien tristes nouvelles	*to prepare the family for very sad news*
reprocher une liaison **à** son mari	*to be angry with one's husband for having had an affair*
réserver des sièges **aux** invités	*to reserve some seats for the guests*
retirer son permis **au** conducteur	*to take the driver's licence away from him*
soustraire une grosse somme **à** une vieille dame	*to swindle an old lady out of a large sum*
voler une bague **à** sa cousine	*to steal a ring from one's cousin*

Introduced by *de* and corresponding typically to English 'with' or 'in' or, less frequently, 'from' or 'on'

accabler son amie **de** cadeaux	*to overwhelm one's girl friend with presents*
accompagner ses commentaires **de** sarcasme	*to bring sarcasm into one's comments*
affranchir une population **de** l'esclavage	*to free a population from slavery*
armer ses soldats **de** mitrailleuses	*to arm one's soldiers with machine guns*
charger un voisin **d'**une commission	*to entrust an errand to a neighbour*
coiffer un enfant **d'**un chapeau de paille	*to put a straw hat on a child's head*
combler ses invités **de** gentillesses	*to cover one's guests in kindness*

couvrir sa petite amie **de** cadeaux	*to drown one's girl friend in presents*
cribler un corps **de** balles	*to riddle a body with bullets*
éloigner sa fille **de** ses admirateurs	*to remove one's daughter from her admirers*
encombrer la voiture **d'**affaires de sport	*to clutter up the car with sports equipment*
entourer la famille **de** bons amis	*to surround the family with good friends*
envelopper le cadeau **d'**un papier de soie	*to wrap the present in tissue paper*
habiller son mari **de** vêtements sport	*to buy casual styles of clothes for one's husband*
menacer ses employés **d'**une réduction de salaire	*to threaten one's employees with reduction in salary*
munir les étudiants **du** savoir nécessaire	*to provide students with the necessary knowledge*
orner le parebrise **d'**autocollants	*to decorate the windscreen with stickers*
planter le jardin **de** roses	*to plant the garden with roses*
pourvoir un réfugié **d'**un faux passeport	*to provide a refugee with a false passport*
remplir l'auditoire **de** terreur	*to fill the audience with terror*
semer un champ **de** haricots	*to sow a field with beans*
souiller un drap **de** sang	*to soil a sheet with blood*
tacher un pantalon **de** graisse	*to stain trousers with grease*
tapisser la chambre **d'**un papier peint rose	*to paper the bedroom in pink*
vêtir un cardinal **d'**une robe de pourpre	*to dress a cardinal in a purple robe*

8.5.1 In French, unlike English, double object constructions with no preposition are impossible

Some ditransitive verbs in English allow the preposition introducing the second object to be omitted and the order of the objects to be switched around. This is not possible in French:

to give a present to one's uncle		*to give one's uncle a present*
offrir un cadeau **à** son oncle	BUT NOT	*offrir son oncle un cadeau
to pass the salt to one's neighbour		*to pass one's neighbour the salt*
passer le sel **à** son voisin	BUT NOT	*passer son voisin le sel

(See 8.6.3 for the consequences of this in forming a passive.)

8.6 The passive

By use of the passive, emphasis may be placed on the receiver of an action (usually what would be the object in the equivalent active sentence) rather than on the agent of the action (usually the subject).

8.6.1 Formation of the passive

Passives are produced from directly transitive sentences by moving the object noun phrase into the position of the grammatical subject, introducing the verb *être* and, optionally, moving the erstwhile subject into a phrase introduced by *par* or *de*:

Nantes a battu Paris St Germain
Nantes beat Paris St Germain

becomes:

> Paris St Germain a été battu (par Nantes)
> *Paris St Germain were beaten (by Nantes)*

> Quand elle est arrivée au commissariat, son mari l'accompagnait
> *When she got to the police station, her husband was with her*

becomes:

> Quand elle est arrivée au commissariat, elle était accompagnée de son mari
> *When she got to the police station, she was in the company of her husband*

Note that the rules of agreement for the past participle are those of *être* (see Chapter 9.2.2): i.e. it agrees with the subject:

> **Delphine** a été battu**e** au tennis (par Suzanne)
> *Delphine was beaten at tennis by Suzanne*

> **Georges** a été batt**u** au tennis par Jean-Claude
> *George was beaten at tennis by Jean-Claude*

NB: The use of the preposition *par* to introduce the subject usually implies some degree of voluntary involvement; the use of *de* suggests more a state of affairs. See also Chapter 13.15.5.

8.6.2 Problems in the formation of the passive arising from different kinds of direct objects

Most verbs which have a direct object (directly transitive verbs – see 8.3) will convert into a passive, but there are limitations to whether the meaning is sensible or not. *Aimer* can be turned into a sensible passive:

> Juliette aime Georges
> *Juliette loves George*

> Georges est aimé par Juliette
> *George is loved by Juliette*

but *lire* produces a less natural sentence:

> Je lis ce livre
> *I am reading this book*

> Ce livre est lu par moi (???)
> *This book is being read by me (???)*

Usually passives which make an inanimate direct object a subject and put an animate subject in a *par* or *de* phrase are unnatural.

NB: The verb *avoir* is used in the passive only in the colloquial *J'ai été eu* 'I have been had' in the sense of 'swindled'.

8.6.3 Possible confusions between English and French over what is a direct object: English 'double object' verbs

English has a set of verbs which allow two structures for a similar meaning: one has a direct object and a prepositional object, the other has two non-prepositional objects and the word order is different:

John gave flowers to Naomi
John gave Naomi flowers

In both sentences 'Naomi' is the indirect object of the verb 'give' and 'flowers' is the direct object, but in the 'double object' construction 'Naomi' directly follows the verb, which gives the impression that it is the direct object.

English allows either object to become the subject in a passive sentence:

Flowers were given to Naomi by John
Naomi was given flowers by John

French, however, only allows the prepositional object construction *offrir quelque chose à quelqu'un*: Jean a offert des fleurs à Naomi (NOT *Jean a offert Naomi des fleurs*) Furthermore, French only allows **the direct object** to become the subject in a passive sentence. Thus:

Des fleurs furent offertes à Naomi par Jean
Flowers were given to Naomi by Jean

is an acceptable French sentence, but

*Naomi fut offerte des fleurs par Jean

is entirely unacceptable.

Sentences constructed with similar verbs run into the same problems:

English
To teach somebody something: I taught French to John
                                                 I taught John French
                                                 French was taught to John by me
                                                 John was taught French by me

French
Enseigner **quelque chose à quelqu'un**:   J'ai enseigné le français à Jean
                           But   *J'ai enseigné Jean le français
                                             is **unacceptable**
                 Therefore   Le français fut enseigné à Jean par
                                             moi is **acceptable**
                           But   *Jean fut enseigné le français par
                                             moi is **unacceptable**

English
To tell somebody something: I told a story to John
                                                 I told John a story
                                               A story was told to John by me
                                               John was told a story by me

French
Raconter **quelque chose à quelqu'un**:   J'ai raconté une histoire à Jean
                           But   *J'ai raconté Jean une histoire
                                               is **unacceptable**
                 Therefore   Une histoire fut racontée à Jean
                                             par moi is **acceptable**
                           But   *Jean fut raconté une histoire par
                                             moi is **unacceptable**

Common French verbs whose prepositional objects must keep the preposition and cannot be made the subject of a passive are listed below:

accorder qc à qn   *to grant sb sth*
apprendre qc à qn   *to teach sb sth*

commander qc à qn	*to order sb to do sth/to order sth from sb*
conseiller qc à qn	*to advise sb to do sth*
défendre qc à qn	*to forbid sb sth*
demander qc à qn	*to ask sb sth*
donner qc à qn	*to give sb sth*
écrire qc à qn	*to write sb sth*
enseigner qc à qn	*to teach sb sth*
laisser qc à qn	*to leave sb sth*
montrer qc à qn	*to show sb sth*
offrir qc à qn	*to offer sb sth, treat sb to sth*
pardonner qc à qn	*to forgive sb sth*
passer qc à qn	*to pass sb sth*
permettre qc à qn	*to allow sb sth*
prescrire qc à qn	*to prescribe sb sth*
prêter qc à qn	*to lend sb sth*
promettre qc à qn	*to promise sb sth*
refuser qc à qn	*to refuse sb sth*

8.7 Pronominal verbs

Pronominal verbs are accompanied by an unstressed pronoun which agrees with the subject, and is one of *me, te, se, nous, vous*. This can function as a direct object:

Direct object

se laver 'to wash (oneself)'

je **me** lave	nous **nous** lavons
tu **te** laves	vous **vous** lavez
Paul **se** lave	ils **se** lavent
Virginie **se** lave	elles **se** lavent

or as an indirect object:

Indirect object

se laver le visage 'to wash one's face' (literally: 'to wash the face to oneself')

je **me** lave le visage	nous **nous** lavons le visage
tu **te** laves le visage	vous **vous** lavez le visage
Paul **se** lave le visage	ils **se** lavent le visage
Virginie **se** lave le visage	elles **se** lavent le visage

Some verbs exist in both a pronominal and non-pronominal form, as *laver* does: *laver la voiture* 'to wash the car', *se laver le visage* 'to wash one's face'. Others are always pronominal, for example *s'évanouir* 'to faint', *s'enorgueillir de* 'to take pride in', *s'évertuer à* 'to try very hard to'.

All pronominal verbs are conjugated with *être* in compound tenses. (For the agreement of past participles with pronominal verbs see 8.7.7 and Chapter 9.4.)

8.7.1 Pronominal verbs used reflexively

When pronominal verbs are used to describe something which the subject does to herself, himself, themselves, etc., they are being used reflexively:

Je me vois dans la glace	*I can see myself in the mirror*
Je me déteste	*I hate myself*

Il s'est fait mal	*He hurt himself*
Elle s'était cassé la jambe	*She had broken her leg*

Note that English translations of pronominal verbs used reflexively do not always require a form of *-self*. In French, however, the reflexive pronoun is always required:

Je me lave	*I am washing (myself)*
Il se rase	*He is shaving (himself)*
Il s'est roulé par terre	*He rolled (himself) on the ground*

The pronoun itself may be the direct or indirect object of the verb. If the verb in its non-pronominal form is directly transitive, the pronoun will be a direct object. If the verb in its non-pronominal form is indirectly transitive, the pronoun will be an indirect object pronoun. For example, *laver* takes a direct object: *laver la voiture*. Therefore in *Je me lave* the pronoun is direct. But *parler (parler à qn)* takes an indirect object, e.g. *parler à une amie*. Therefore in *Je me parle* the pronoun is indirect.

The reflexive pronoun is the direct object

Je me lave à l'eau froide	*I wash in cold water*
Elle est maladroite et se blesse fréquemment	*She is clumsy and often injures herself*
Il se coiffe pendant des heures	*He spends hours doing his hair*
Tu te baignes tous les jours?	*Do you have a swim every day?*
Suzanne s'habille très mal	*Suzanne dresses very badly*
Jean-Pierre se nourrit très bien	*Jean-Pierre has a healthy diet*
Marianne se cache dans l'armoire	*Marianne is hiding in the cupboard*

The reflexive pronoun is the indirect object

Je me parle constamment en me promenant	*I constantly talk to myself when I go for a walk*
En répétant des confidences on ne peut que se nuire	*By repeating secrets you only succeed in doing yourself harm*
Tu t'achèteras un nouveau blouson pour la rentrée	*You'll buy yourself a new jacket to go back to school*
Je me reproche ces bêtises	*I feel bad about this foolishness*
Je me jure de continuer à travailler	*I promise myself that I will continue to work*
Il faut bien s'admettre la vérité	*We just have to accept the truth*
Marianne se cache la vérité	*Marianne is hiding the truth from herself*

The difference between direct object reflexives and indirect object reflexives is clear from the last example in each set:

Marianne se cache dans l'armoire
Marianne se cache la vérité

In the first example the *se* is the person who is hidden: *Marianne cache **Marianne** dans l'armoire*. In the second example it is *la vérité* which is hidden and the *se* is the indirect object: *Marianne cache la vérité à **Marianne**.* These differences are significant when it comes to past participle agreement (see 8.7.7 below and Chapter 9.4).

Many ordinarily directly transitive, indirectly transitive and ditransitive verbs can be used pronominally as reflexives, for example:

Il critique **son patron**
He criticizes his boss

Il **se** critique
He criticizes himself

Je juge **le prisonnier** coupable
I consider the prisoner guilty

Je **me** juge coupable
I consider myself guilty

Elle regarde **son amie**
She is looking at her girl friend

Elle **se** regarde
She is looking at herself

Tu offres un cadeau **à Philippe**
You are giving a present to Philip

Tu **t'**offres un cadeau
You are giving a present to yourself

Il parle **à sa mère**
He's talking to his mother

Il **se** parle
He's talking to himself

Elle cache la vérité **à son mari**
She is hiding the truth from her husband

Elle **se** cache la vérité
She is hiding the truth from herself

8.7.2 Pronominal verbs and body parts

The normal way of describing events in which subjects do things to their own bodies is to use a pronominal verb and the part of the body preceded by a definite or indefinite article, and not by a possessive determiner as in English:

Je **me** lave toujours **les mains** avant de déjeuner
I always wash my hands before lunch

Elle va **se** couper **le doigt** si elle ne fait pas attention
She will cut her finger if she's not careful

Nathan **s'**est cassé **la jambe** en jouant au football
Nathan broke his leg playing football

Tu as encore oublié de **te** brosser **les dents**!
You forgot to brush your teeth again!

J'aime bien **me** brosser **les cheveux**
I like brushing my hair

Elle **s'**est cassé **une dent de devant**
She broke one of her front teeth

(See also Chapter 2.2.8 for the use of the definite article with parts of the body.)

8.7.3 Pronominal verbs without a reflexive interpretation

Some verbs include a pronoun but it is impossible to see in what way they can be assigned a reflexive interpretation, e.g. *s'abstenir, se douter, s'en aller, s'enfuir, s'évanouir, se repentir, se taire* etc.:

Je **m'abstiendrai** de tout commentaire
I will refrain from making any comment

Tu **t'es** toujours **douté** qu'il lui ferait faux bond
You always guessed he would let her down

Il reste encore aujourd'hui mais il **s'en va** demain
He's staying today but he is going tomorrow

A la vue de tout ce sang, ils **se sont évanouis**
At the sight of so much blood they fainted

Il **s'est** toujours **repenti** de ces paroles
He always regretted those words

Ils **se sont tus** pour protéger leur camarade
They kept quiet to protect their friend

Common pronominal verbs which do not have a reflexive interpretation:

s'abstenir de tout commentaire	*to refrain from making any comment*
s'accouder au parapet	*to lean on one's elbows on the parapet*
s'accoutumer à conduire la nuit	*to get used to driving at night*
s'accroupir derrière un arbre	*to crouch behind a tree*
s'affaiblir lentement	*to get slowly weaker*
s'affaisser/s'affaler/s'écrouler par terre	*to collapse on the ground*
s'agenouiller près de quelqu'un	*to kneel down next to somebody*
s'amuser en vacances	*to have fun on holiday*
s'apercevoir de qch	*to notice something*
s'appeler Dupont	*to be called Dupont*
s'approcher de qn	*to approach somebody*
s'appuyer au rebord de la fenêtre	*to lean on the windowsill*
s'arrêter aux feux	*to stop at the lights*
s'asseoir dans un fauteuil	*to sit down in an armchair*
s'assoupir au volant	*to doze off at the wheel*
s'avancer vers la montagne	*to advance towards the mountain*
se blottir contre sa mère	*to cuddle up to one's mother*
se briser/se casser en miettes	*to break into pieces*
se charger d'une tâche	*to take on a task*
se comporter mal	*to behave badly*
se contenter d'une carrière médiocre	*to make do with a mediocre career*
se coucher tôt	*to go to bed early*
se dépêcher de poser sa candidature	*to hurry to apply for the job*
se déshabiller dans le noir	*to get undressed in the dark*
se diriger vers la maison	*to go towards the house*
se distinguer par son intelligence	*to stand out by one's intelligence*
se douter de qc	*to suspect something*
se dresser contre une injustice	*to protest against an injustice*
s'écarter du chemin	*to stray from the track*
s'échapper/s'évader d'une prison	*to escape from a prison*
s'écouler vite	*to pass quickly (of time)*
s'écrier	*to shout, exclaim*
s'éloigner de la ville	*to move away from the town*
s'emparer de son adversaire	*to get hold of one's opponent*
s'en aller ailleurs	*to go away somewhere else*
s'endormir dans la voiture	*to go to sleep in the car*
s'enfuir dans les bois	*to flee into the woods*
s'ennuyer à la campagne	*to become bored in the country*
s'enquérir auprès de l'ambassade	*to enquire at the Embassy*
s'étonner de la vitesse de la voiture	*to be surprised at the speed of the car*
s'évanouir	*to faint*
se fâcher de qc	*to get annoyed at something*
se fatiguer facilement	*to get easily tired*
se fermer doucement	*to close gently*
se fier à ses collègues	*to trust one's colleagues*
s'habiller en tenue de soirée	*to wear evening dress*
s'habituer à un nouvel emploi	*to get used to a new job*
s'intéresser au latin	*to be interested in Latin*
se lever tard	*to get up late*
se méfier de la police	*to distrust the police*
se mêler à la conversation	*to join in the conversation*
se mettre debout	*to stand up*
se moquer de qn	*to make fun of somebody*

se nourrir de pain	*to live on bread*
s'occuper de ses enfants	*to look after one's children*
se passer de cigarettes	*to go without cigarettes*
se plaindre du temps	*to complain about the weather*
se rappeler une amie	*to remember a friend*
se raviser brusquement	*to change one's mind suddenly*
se réfugier sous les arbres	*to take refuge under the trees*
se repentir de ses paroles	*to regret one's words*
se retourner	*to turn around*
se réunir le dimanche	*to meet on Sundays*
se réveiller	*to wake up*
se servir d'une scie	*to use a saw*
se soucier de la santé de qn	*to worry about somebody's health*
se souvenir d'une amie	*to remember a friend*
se taire	*to keep quiet*
se tenir droit	*to stand straight*
se tromper	*to be wrong*

8.7.4 *se faire* and *se laisser*

se faire and *se laisser* are used to convey the idea that the subject causes some event to befall himself or herself without necessarily intending that it should:

Julie **s'est fait écraser** par un camion	*Julie was run over by a lorry*
Pierre **s'est fait sortir** du terrain	*Pierre got (himself) sent off the field*
Jean **s'est fait embrasser** par Christine	*Jean got Christine to kiss him*
Elle **s'est laissé convaincre** par son père	*She let herself be persuaded by her father*
Il **se laissait guider**	*He let himself be led*
Guido **s'est laissé pousser** les moustaches	*Guido allowed his moustache to grow*

(See Chapter 9.4 for agreement of the past participle of *faire* and *laisser* in this construction.)

8.7.5 Pronominal verbs used reciprocally

When a pronominal verb is used in the plural and describes a situation where several subjects are doing things **to each other**, it is being used reciprocally:

D'ordinaire, les journalistes **se consultent** avant de publier un article de ce genre
Journalists usually consult each other before publishing this kind of article

Ils **se rencontreront** à Paris	*They will meet (each other) in Paris*
Nous **nous connaissons**	*We know each other*
Les enfants **se disputent**	*The children are arguing (with each other)*

The pronoun can be a direct object, as in the above examples, or an indirect object, as in the following examples:

Souvent les participants **s'écrivent** et restent en contact après la conférence
Participants often write to one another and keep in touch after the conference

Il a ensuite été demandé aux élèves de **se poser** des questions sans le secours du professeur
Pupils were then required to ask each other questions without the teacher's help

Nous **nous envoyons** des cadeaux à Noël chaque année
We send each other presents every year at Christmas

Sometimes there is a possible ambiguity between a reflexive interpretation of the pronoun and a reciprocal interpretation, for example:

> Les boxeurs **se sont blessés**
> *The boxers hurt each other* or
> *The boxers hurt themselves* (i.e. each hurt himself but not the other)

> Les participants **se sont posé** des questions
> *The participants asked each other questions* or
> *The participants asked questions of themselves*

One way to make the reciprocal interpretation entirely clear is to add the expression *l'un l'autre* 'each other' in its appropriate form. For example, where a direct object is involved:

> Les boxeurs se sont blessés **l'un l'autre**
> *The boxers hurt each other*

But where an indirect object is involved:

> Les participants se sont posé des questions **l'un à l'autre**
> *The participants asked each other questions*

l'un l'autre also varies for gender and number. If the subjects are feminine in gender *l'une l'autre* is required:

> On s'aide **l'une l'autre** pour la garde des enfants
> *We help each other out with looking after the children*

If more than just two subjects are involved a plural form of *l'un l'autre* is required:

> Les universitaires du monde entier peuvent se contacter **les uns les autres** par courrier électronique
> *Academics all over the world can contact each other by electronic mail*

(For agreement of the past participle see 8.7.7 and Chapter 9.4.)

8.7.6 Pronominal verbs used as passives

Pronominal verbs are increasingly used with a meaning equivalent to an English passive:

> Les jeux électroniques **se vendent** comme des petits pains
> *Computer games are selling like hot cakes*

> Ces verbes **se conjugent** avec 'être'
> *These verbs are conjugated with 'être'*

> Le français **se parle** au Canada et en Afrique
> *French is spoken in Canada and in Africa*

> Les baskets **s'achètent** dans les magasins de sport
> *Trainers can be bought in sports shops*

> Les valeurs **se maintiennent** à la Bourse
> *Stocks and shares are holding up on the Stock Exchange*

Cela ne **se fait** pas	*That is just not done*
Ce vin **se boit** chambré	*This wine is drunk at room temperature*
La vengeance est un plat qui **se mange** froid	*Revenge is a meal to be eaten cold*
C'est une revue qui **se lit** facilement	*This journal is easy to read*

8.7.7 Pronominal verbs, the auxiliary *être* and the agreement of the past participle

Pronominal verbs are always conjugated with *être* in their compound tenses, and the question arises as to when the past participle is marked for agreement. Whereas the past participle of non-pronominal verbs which take *être* always agrees with the subject (*elle est arrivée, nous sommes arrivés, elles sont arrivées* – see Chapter 9.2), the participle with pronominal verbs only agrees with a direct object pronoun. For example:

(a) Where the meaning of the pronoun is reflexive and it is a direct object:

Je (fem) **me** suis lav**ée** à l'eau froide
I washed in cold water

Elle était maladroite et **s'**était fréquemment bless**ée**
She was clumsy and often injured herself

Suzanne **s'**est très mal habill**ée**
Suzanne dressed very badly

Marianne **s'**est cach**ée** dans l'armoire
Marianne hid in the cupboard

(See also 8.7.1)

(b) Where the meaning of the pronoun is reciprocal and it is a direct object:

Les deux équipes **se** sont rencontr**ées** à Paris
The two teams met (each other) in Paris

Nous **nous** sommes attendu**s** les uns les autres avant de rentrer
We waited for each other before going home

Jean-Pierre et Richard **se** sont rencontr**és** à Lyon
Jean-Pierre and Richard met in Lyons

Marianne et sa mère **se** sont attend**ues** à la gare
Marianne and her mother waited for each other at the station

(c) Where the pronoun has no detectable reflexive or reciprocal meaning, but is an integral part of the verb, and is a direct object:

A la vue de tout ce sang, elles **se** sont évanou**ies**
At the sight of so much blood, they fainted

Ils **se** sont toujours repenti**s** de ces paroles
They always regretted those words

Ils **se** sont tu**s** dès qu'ils ont vu le directeur
They kept quiet as soon as they saw the headmaster

This includes when the pronominal verb is used as a passive:

Les jeux vidéo **se** sont vendu**s** comme des petits pains
Video games sold like hot cakes

BUT the past participle will not agree in any case where the pronoun is an indirect object (see 8.7.1). In particular this will be the case:

(i) where the non-pronominal version of the verb has a prepositional indirect object e.g. *nuire à qn, cacher qch à qn, écrire à qn* and therefore the *se* is seen as an indirect object:

Elle **s'est nui** en faisant de telles demandes
She did herself harm by these requests

Marianne **s'est caché** la vérité
Marianne hid the truth from herself

Les participants **se sont écrit**
The participants wrote to each other

(ii) where the pronoun is indirect, given that the direct object is a body part (as in 8.7.2):

Je (fem) **me** suis lavé les mains avant de déjeuner
I washed my hands before lunch

Elle **s'est coupé** le doigt parce qu'elle ne faisait pas attention
She cut her finger because she was careless

Nathan **s'est cassé** la jambe en jouant au football
Nathan broke his leg playing football

NB: Where the pronoun is an indirect object (and hence the participle does not agree with it), the participle may nevertheless agree with a **preceding** direct object, as in:

Les deux **valises qu'**il s'est achet**ées** sont cassées
The two suitcases he bought are broken

Combien de valises s'est-il achet**ées**?
How many suitcases did he buy?

(See Chapter 9 for the general rules of past participle agreement.)

8.8 Impersonal verbs

A number of verbs only exist in an impersonal (and infinitive) form. They only take the pronoun *il* as their subject, which in this case does not refer to a person or thing: i.e. it is an impersonal use.

8.8.1 Weather verbs

The best-known group of impersonal verbs describe the weather:

Il pleut	*It's raining*
Il pleut des cordes	*It's raining cats and dogs*
Il neige	*It's snowing*
Il grêle	*It's sleeting*
Il tonne	*There's thunder about*
Il vente	*It's windy*
Il bruine	*It's drizzling*

More generally climatic conditions can be expressed by an impersonal use of *faire* followed by an adjective or a noun:

Il fait beau	*It's a nice day*
Il fait du soleil	*It's sunny*
Il fait mauvais	*It's not a nice day*
Il fait chaud	*It's hot*
Il fait lourd	*The weather is oppressive*
Il fait sec	*It's very dry*
Il fait humide	*It's very humid*
Il fait du brouillard	*It's foggy*

| Il fait de l'orage | *It's stormy* |
| Il fait un froid de canard | *It's very cold* |

8.8.2 *falloir*

falloir only exists in impersonal forms (see the list of irregular verbs in Chapter 7). It may be followed by a noun, by an infinitive, by a clause – with the verb in the subjunctive – and it may be preceded by a pronoun acting as indirect object:

Il faut du temps	*Time is needed*
Il faut partir	*It is time to leave*
Il faut que nous partions	*We must leave*
Il nous faut partir	*We must leave*
Il nous faudra revenir dans trois semaines	*We must come back in three weeks*
Il a fallu trois mois pour que nous nous décidions	*It took us three months to make up our minds*
Il faudrait être certain que cela soit la bonne décision	*We need to be sure that this is the right decision*

8.8.3 *il y a*

il y a ('there is' or 'there are') also exists only in the impersonal form. It is usually followed directly by a noun but may also be followed by an infinitive introduced by *à* or by *de quoi*. It is frequently used in spoken French in the construction: *il y a* + noun + relative clause. In spoken French the pronunciation often reduces to /ja/:

Il y a quelques problèmes au garage
There are a few problems at the garage

Il y a eu de bons gouvernements, autrefois
There have been good governments, in the past

Il y avait toujours quelque chose à faire
There was always something to be done

Il y a à faire dans la cuisine
There are things to do in the kitchen

Il y a à boire et à manger dans le frigo
There's something to eat and drink in the fridge

Il y a de quoi vous occuper ici
There's lots to do here

Il y avait de quoi vous faire peur la nuit
It was enough to make you afraid at night

Il y a des gens qui vous attendent dehors
There are people waiting for you outside

Il y a ceux qui prétendent tout savoir
There are those who think they know everything

Il y en a qui disent du mal des autres
Some people say bad things about others

8.8.4 *il s'agit de*

il s'agit de is only ever used impersonally. It may be followed by a noun, by an infinitive and, rarely, by a clause. English-speaking learners frequently attempt to use it with a personal subject, e.g. **ce livre s'agit de.* . . . This is **impossible**.

Il s'agit de votre frère
It's about your brother

Il s'agit de faire ce qui vous intéresse
You have to do what interests you

Il s'agit de convàincre votre tante
It is a matter of convincing your aunt

Il s'agissait de vous faire changer d'avis
It was an attempt to make you change your mind

Tout au long de cette affaire il s'est agi de mon honnêteté
Throughout this matter it has been a question of my honesty

Il ne s'agit pas que vous preniez toute la responsabilité sur vous
There is no question of your taking on the whole responsibility

Il ne s'agit pas de prendre du retard
We'd better not get behind schedule

8.8.5 Verbs which take a personal subject can also on occasions be used impersonally

Il se passe ici des choses qui vous intéresseront sûrement
There are things going on here which will probably interest you

Il est arrivé hier soir un événement très curieux
A very unusual event took place yesterday evening

Il convient d'être très circonspect de nos jours
It is sensible to be very careful these days

Il nous arrive assez souvent de recevoir des personnalités importantes
We quite often have important people as guests

Il manque des couverts à cette table
This table has not been laid properly

Il y va de sa vie
His life is at stake

Il nous manque plusieurs de nos camarades ce soir
Several of our comrades are missing tonight

Il ne me souvient pas d'avoir été présenté à cette personne
I don't (seem to) remember having been introduced to this person (formal language)

être can also be used impersonally, either in set expressions or more formally as an alternative to *il y a*:

Il est grand temps que nous partions	*It is high time we went*
Il n'est absolument pas question d'attendre	*There can be no question of waiting*
Il est dommage d'avoir attendu si longtemps	*It is a pity to have waited so long*
Est-il besoin de vous le rappeler?	*Is there any need to remind you?* (formal style)
Il est des jours où l'on souhaiterait être ailleurs	*There are days when one would wish to be elsewhere*

There are two set phrases used to introduce fairy stories:

Il était une fois . . .   and
Il y avait une fois . . .
Once upon a time . . .

8.9 Verbs which take noun + adjective or noun + noun complements

A small number of verbs allow an adjective or predicative noun (*président*, *directeur*, etc.) to follow the noun which is the direct object:

boire qc frais	*to drink sth chilled*
considérer qc peu probable	*to consider sth unlikely*
croire qn heureux	*to believe sb happy*
élire qn président	*to elect sb president*
estimer qn inapte	*to reckon sb unsuitable*
juger qn maladroit	*to judge sb clumsy*
laisser qn tranquille	*to leave sb alone*
manger qc chaud	*to eat sth hot*
nommer qn directeur	*to appoint sb director*
rendre qn malade	*to make sb ill*
trouver qc difficile	*to find sth difficult*

Note that 'to make somebody happy, sad, etc.' or 'to make something difficult, easy, etc.' is the verb *rendre*, and NOT *faire: rendre qn heureux, rendre qn triste, rendre qc difficile, rendre qc facile.*

9

Verb and participle agreement

9.1 Subject-verb agreement

As in English, French verbs agree with their subject in person and number:

Je ne voul**ais** pas jouer
I didn't want to play

Elle voul**ait** partir en vacances
She wanted to go on holiday

Les garçons voul**aient** tous participer au match
The boys all wanted to take part in the match

9.1.1 Agreement with more than one subject linked by et

If one of the subjects is a **first person pronoun**, the verb will be in the first person plural form:

Hubert et moi **sommes** allés vous chercher
Hubert and I went to look for you

Ma sœur et moi **serons** dans la même famille en France
My sister and I are staying with the same family in France

Toi/Vous et moi **sommes** toujours d'accord
You and I always agree

If one of the subjects is a **second person pronoun** and there is no first person pronoun, the verb will be in the second person plural form:

Toi et ton copain **avez** intérêt à nettoyer cette pièce avant que tes parents ne rentrent.
You and your friend had better clean this room before your parents get back

Vous et vos amis **devrez** vous dépêcher si vous voulez prendre le train de 15 heures
You and your friends will have to hurry if you want to catch the 3 o'clock train

If all the subjects are **third person,** the verb will be in a third person plural form:

Jeanne et Suzanne **sont** venues toutes les deux
Jeanne and Suzanne both came

Le groupe Alsthom et le groupe GEC **sont** arrivés à un accord pour le développement d'une nouvelle locomotive
Alsthom and GEC have reached agreement on the development of a new train

(See also Chapter 3.3.5 for coordinated stressed pronouns.)

9.1.2 Agreement with more than one subject linked by: *ni ... ni*, 'neither ... nor', *soit ... soit*, 'either ... or' and *ou*, 'or'

French tends to make a distinction between the two kinds of meaning which may be conveyed by these methods of coordination. If the meaning emphasizes the individual and does not 'add them together', the verb may well be singular:

Ni Simon ni Steven n'**a** pu me dire où se trouvaient les autres
Neither Simon nor Steven was able to tell me where the others were

C'est soit lui soit sa sœur qui **doit** te téléphoner
Either he or his sister must be responsible for telephoning you

If, on the other hand, the intention is to consider the two elements as a group, the verb will be plural:

Ni Lord Byron ni Chateaubriand n'**ont** pu comprendre l'inutilité des rêveries romantiques
Neither Lord Byron nor Chateaubriand could understand how useless romantic dreams are

The same principle underlies agreement with *ni l'un ni l'autre*. Where they are 'additive' the verb is likely to be plural, where they act as 'alternative individuals' the verb is likely to be singular:

Ni Alberte ni Suzanne n'**avaient** pu rencontrer le peintre
Neither Alberte nor Suzanne managed to meet the painter

Ni l'une ni l'autre n'**ont** pu rencontrer le peintre
Neither the one nor the other was able to meet the painter

Ni Alberte ni Suzanne ne **viendra**
Neither Alberte nor Suzanne will come

Ni l'une ni l'autre ne **viendra**
Neither the one nor the other will come

9.1.3 Verb agreement with collective noun subjects

Normally collective nouns which are singular require the verb to be in a singular form, unlike English where speakers use either a singular or plural verb form:

Le gouvernement **a** décidé de modifier la loi sur la nationalité
The government has/have decided to change the nationality law

Le comité **a** proposé une réunion pour 16 heures
The committee has/have suggested a meeting at 4 o'clock

La famille **passe** les vacances de Noël en Bretagne
The family is/are spending the Christmas holidays in Brittany

NB: *Tout le monde* always agrees with a singular verb:

Tout le monde **vient** passer le weekend chez moi
Everybody's coming to my place for the weekend

This may change, however, when the collective noun is followed by a plural complement. The verb may then be in the singular or the plural (although some speakers still have a preference for the singular):

> L'équipe de footballeurs anglais **a** (*or* **ont**) dû quitter la ville très rapidement
> *The team of English football players had to leave town in a hurry*

> La foule des supporters **ont** (*or* **a**) été rapidement dispersé(e)(s)
> *The crowd of supporters were rapidly dispersed*

Note that in English there is a preference for a plural verb in these cases.

9.1.4 Verb agreement with fractions

When fractions (see Chapter 6.3) are subjects and have plural complements, whether they are present or implied, verbs normally agree with those complements:

> La moitié (**des gens)** se **sont** exprimés
> *Half (of the people) made their views known*

> Un tiers (de **ceux** qui étaient présents) se **sont** exprimés
> *A third (of those present) made their views known*

But when the fraction has a singular complement, whether present or implied, verbs agree with the fraction:

> **La moitié** (de la population) s'**est** exprimée
> *Half (the population) made their view known*

> **Un tiers** (de la maison) a été détruit
> *A third (of the house) was destroyed*

NB: *les deux tiers* and percentages usually agree with a plural verb:

> Les deux tiers des électeurs **ont** voté pour la droite
> *Two-thirds of the electorate voted for the right*

> 66% **ont** voté pour la droite
> *66% voted for the right*

9.1.5 Verb agreement with numeral nouns and quantifiers

When numeral nouns like *une dizaine* 'ten or so', *une vingtaine* 'twenty or so' *une douzaine* 'a dozen' etc. (see Chapter 6.5.3) are subjects, the verb can agree with the numeral noun or its complement, depending on where the emphasis lies:

> Nous sommes vingt ce midi à la maison: **une douzaine** d'œufs ne nous **suffira** pas
> *There are twenty of us having lunch at home today: a dozen eggs won't be enough*

> Une vingtaine de **policiers ont** été blessés
> *Twenty or so policemen were injured*

When most quantifiers (like *la plupart de* 'most', *(un grand) nombre de* 'a large number of', *quantité de* 'a lot of', *beaucoup de* 'many') are subjects, the verb agrees with their complement, whether it is present or implied:

> La plupart (des **habitants**) **partagent** mes sentiments
> *Most (of the inhabitants) share my feelings*

La plupart (d'entre **eux**) **sont** prêts à nous aider
Most (of them) are ready to help us

Un grand nombre (de **locataires**) **sont** déjà allés se plaindre
A large number (of the tenants) have already been to complain

Beaucoup (de **manifestants**) se **présenteront** à la mairie cet après-midi
A lot (of demonstrators) will go to the Town Hall this afternoon

With *la majorité de* 'the majority of', *une minorité de* 'a minority of', *le reste de* 'the rest of', the verb can agree either with the quantifier or its complement:

La majorité (de nos étudiants) **ont/a** moins de quarante ans
The majority (of our students) are under forty

Plus d'un tends to be singular:

Plus d'un ami m'**a** incité à me présenter au premier tour
More than one friend suggested I should stand in the first round

But *moins de* tends to be plural:

Moins de dix personnes m'**ont** indiqué leur désaccord
Fewer than ten people told me they disagreed

9.1.6 Agreement with the verb *être*

Where two nouns are linked by the verb *être*, the verb normally agrees with the preceding subject, although some speakers will make it agree with what follows:

Mon problème **était** mes enfants, car je n'avais personne pour les garder
My problem was my children, for I had no-one to look after them

When *ce* is the subject of *être*, there is a choice between using *c'est* or *ce sont*. Whereas most nouns and pronouns follow *c'est*, for example:

C'est moi/nous	*It's me/us*
C'est toi/vous/lui/elle	*It's you/him/her*
C'est le facteur	*It's the postman*

In formal French, plural nouns and third person plural pronouns are supposed to follow *ce sont*:

Ce sont mes parents	*It's my parents*
Ce sont eux	*It's them*

However, most speakers (and even writers) of formal French use *c'est* in these cases these days:

C'est mes parents
C'est eux

Where numbers are involved, *c'est* is always used:

C'est 1 000 francs que je vous dois
It's 1,000 francs that I owe you

The *c'est/ce sont* construction is often used with relative clauses, and it is important to remember that the verb in the relative clause agrees in person and number with the complement of *c'est/ce sont*:

> C'est **moi** qui **suis** le plus âgé
> *It's me who's the oldest*

> C'est **nous** qui **sommes** les responsables
> *We are the ones responsible*

> C'est **vous** qui **avez** pris ma serviette de bain
> *It's you who has taken my towel*

> Ce sont **elles** qui **ont** fait cela
> *They are the ones who did that*

9.2 Agreement of the past participle with the subject of *être*

There are three cases where the past participle agrees with the subject of *être*: (a) with intransitive verbs which select the auxiliary *être* in compound tenses; (b) in passives; (c) where the past participle functions like an adjective.

9.2.1 Agreement of the past participle with the subject of intransitive verbs which select auxiliary *être* in compound tenses

The past participles of *aller* 'to go', *monter* 'to go up', *mourir* 'to die', *naître* 'to be born', *sortir* 'to go out', *tomber* 'to fall', etc (see Chapter 8.2.2 for the full list) agree with the subject in gender and number in compound tenses:

Les Durand étaient allé**s** à Morlaix	*The Durands had gone to Morlaix*
Suzanne est sorti**e**	*Suzanne went out*
Elles sont tombé**es**	*They fell over*
Jean-Paul et Janine sont monté**s** au troisième	*Jean-Paul and Janine went up to the third floor*

NB: Some intransitive verbs which select auxiliary *être* in compound tenses can also be used transitively (see Chapter 8.3.4). In this case they select the auxiliary *avoir* in compound tenses and there is no agreement between the subject and the past participle:

> Jean-Paul et Janine ont monté les valises au troisième
> *Jean-Paul and Janine took the cases up to the third floor*

9.2.2 Agreement of the past participle following *être* with the subject of a passive

Passives are constructed from transitive verbs by turning the direct object into the subject and making the verb an *être* + past participle construction (see Chapter 8.6). The past participle agrees with the subject in gender and number in these cases:

> **La guerre** a été déclenché**e** par un malentendu
> *The war was started by a misunderstanding*

> **Les bourgeois** de Calais ont été choqué**s** par l'œuvre de Rodin
> *The burghers of Calais were shocked by Rodin's work of art*

9.2.3 Past participles used as adjectives with *être*

When past participles are used like adjectives and follow *être*, they agree with the subject:

La piscine est couverte   *The swimming pool is indoors*
Les guichets sont fermés   *The (ticket office) windows are closed*

9.3 Agreement of the past participle of verbs conjugated with *avoir* with a preceding direct object

There are three cases where past participles agree with preceding direct objects in the compound tenses of verbs conjugated with *avoir*: (a) when the preceding direct object is an unstressed pronoun like *le, la, les, me, te* etc., e.g. *Je les ai vus* 'I saw them'; (b) when the preceding direct object is the head of a relative clause: e.g. *La lettre que j'ai écrite* 'The letter which I wrote'; (c) in questions, when the direct object has been moved to a position preceding the past participle, e.g. *Quelle lettre a-t-il écrite?*

9.3.1 Agreement of the past participle with preceding direct object pronouns

In compound tenses, the past participle of verbs conjugated with *avoir* normally agrees with preceding unstressed direct object pronouns:

J'ai vu Marie: Je **l**'ai vu**e**
I saw Marie: I saw her

Les policiers avaient repéré les voleurs: Les policiers **les** avaient repéré**s**
The police had found the thieves: The police had found them

Les voisins ont appelé ma sœur et moi (fem): Les voisins **nous** ont appelé**es**
The neighbours called my sister and me: The neighbours called us

NB: *le* used to refer to a clause is invariably masculine (see Chapter 3.2.8), and so there is no agreement with the past participle:

Sa mère est malade; il **l**'a souvent di**t**
His mother is ill; he has often said so

Past participles do NOT agree with any other preceding pronouns, nor with indirect objects, nor with *en*:

J'ai parlé à Marie: Je **lui** ai parlé (NOT *parlée)
I spoke to Marie: I spoke to her

J'ai indiqué le chemin à Jean-Claude et Paul: Je **leur** ai indiqué (NOT *indiqués) le chemin
I told Jean-Claude and Paul how to get there: I told them how to get there

Ce matin il y a eu des vaches qui sont passées dans le champ du voisin. J'**en** ai **vu** (NOT * vues) hier aussi
This morning there were some cows which got into the neighbour's field. I saw some yesterday as well

9.3.2 Recognizing when an unstressed pronoun is a direct object

Whilst English speakers may learn to remember to make the agreement between a preceding direct object pronoun and the past participle without too much difficulty, they often still have problems in recognizing when a preceding pronoun is a direct object and when it is not. This is particularly the case where the pronouns are *me, te, nous, vous* which can function either as direct object or indirect object pronouns, and when the verbs involved are directly transitive in English but have indirectly transitive counterparts in French (see Chapter 8.4.1). For example, there is no agreement in the following cases because the pronouns are all indirect objects:

convenir à qn	La situation nous a conven**u**	*The situation suited us*
désobéir à qn	Lucien vous a désobé**i**	*Lucien disobeyed you*
nuire à qn	Hubert m'a nu**i**	*Hubert did me* (fem) *some damage*
succéder à qn	Suzanne m'a succéd**é**	*Suzanne succeeded me* (fem)
téléphoner à qn	Les voisins vous ont téléphon**é**	*The neighbours phoned you*
résister à qn	Les voleurs nous ont résist**é**	*The thieves resisted us*

9.3.3 Agreement with a preceding direct object pronoun when the participle is followed by infinitives

When a verb is preceded by a direct object pronoun and followed by an infinitive, it is usually said that the participle only agrees when the pronoun is **the subject of the infinitive and is the direct object of the verb containing the participle**. There will be **no agreement when it is the object of the infinitive**. This means that there will be agreement in cases like the following:

Nathalie a vu **une voiture** écraser son chien
Nathalie saw a car run her dog over
(*une voiture* is the subject of *écraser* and the object of *vu*)

Nathalie l'a v**ue** écraser son chien
Nathalie saw it run her dog over

Hubert-Jean a regardé **sa fille** gagner la course
Hubert-Jean watched his daughter win the race
(*sa fille* is the subject of *gagner* and the object of *regardé*)

Hubert-Jean l'a regard**ée** gagner la course
Hubert-Jean watched her win the race

On a entendu **les voix** résonner dans la caverne
We heard the voices echoing in the cave
(*les voix* is the subject of *résonner* and the object of *entendu*)

On les a entend**ues** résonner dans la caverne
We heard them echoing in the cave

But no agreement in cases like the following:

Nathalie a vu écraser **sa maison** par une énorme roche
Nathalie saw her house crushed by a huge rock
(*sa maison* is the object of *écraser)*

Nathalie l'a v**u** écraser par une énorme roche
Nathalie saw it crushed by a huge rock

Hubert-Jean a regardé détruire **la forêt** par des bulldozers
Hubert-Jean watched the forest being destroyed by bulldozers
(*la forêt* is the object of *détruire*)

Hubert-Jean l'a regard**é** détruire par des bulldozers
Hubert-Jean watched it being destroyed by bulldozers

Derrière la haie, j'ai entendu chanter **une vieille chanson**

> *Behind the hedge I heard (someone) singing an old song*
> (*une vielle chanson* is the object of *chanter*)

> Derrière la haie, je l'ai entendu chanter
> *Behind the hedge I heard (someone) singing it*

Verbs which are likely to be preceded by direct object pronouns and followed by infinitives are perception verbs like *écouter* 'to listen to', *entendre* 'to hear', *voir* 'to see', etc. (see Chapter 12.3.8).

Verbs of movement like *amener* 'to bring', *emmener* 'to take', *envoyer* 'to send' may also be followed by infinitives with subjects which give rise to agreement:

> J'ai emmené **les invités** prendre le petit déjeuner à l'hôtel
> *I took the guests to have breakfast at the hotel*
> (*les invités* is the subject of *prendre* and the object of *emmené*)

> Je **les** ai emmen**és** prendre le petit déjeuner à l'hôtel
> *I took them to have breakfast at the hotel*

> Jean-Claude a envoyé **les secrétaires** chercher du papier à lettres
> *Jean-Claude sent the secretaries to look for some typing paper*
> (*les secrétaires* is the subject of *chercher* and the object of *envoyer*)

> Jean-Claude **les** a envoy**ées** chercher du papier à lettres
> *Jean-Claude sent them to look for some typing paper.*

The verb *laisser* follows the same pattern:

> Nous avons laissé **les enfants** partir en vacances tout seuls
> *We let the children go on holiday on their own*
> (*les enfants* is the subject of *partir* and the object of *laisser*)

> Nous **les** avons laiss**és** partir en vacances tout seuls
> *We let them go on holiday on their own*

> Les voisins ont laissé **les chiens** jouer dans le jardin
> *The neighbours let the dogs play in the garden*
> (*les chiens* is the subject of *jouer* and the object of *laissé*)

> Les voisins **les** ont laiss**és** jouer dans le jardin
> *The neighbours let them play in the garden*

(But see 9.4 for agreement of *se laisser*.)

Faire, however, is an exception. When it is followed by an infinitive, its past participle never agrees with a preceding direct object:

> Nous **les** avons fait (NOT *faits) partir en vacances tout seuls
> *We made them go on holiday on their own*

> Les voisins **les** ont fait (NOT *faits) jouer dans le jardin

(See also Chapter 12.3.9. For object pronouns in this construction see Chapter 3.2.32. See 9.4 for agreement of *se faire*.)

NB: Perception verbs and *laisser* may allow a following infinitive with either a preceding or following subject:

J'ai entendu **les voisins** parler *or*
J'ai entendu parler **les voisins**
I heard the neighbours talk(ing)

J'ai laissé **les enfants** partir *or*
J'ai laissé partir **les enfants**
I let the children leave

In either case, if the subject of the infinitive is turned into an unstressed pronoun, it will give rise to agreement with the past participle:

Je **les** ai entend**us** parler
I heard them talk(ing)

Je **les** ai laiss**és** partir
I let them go

(See Chapter 3.2.32 for position of pronouns.)

9.3.4 Agreement of past participles with preceding direct objects in relative clauses

When the head of a relative clause (see Chapter 15.1) is the implied direct object of that clause, and it precedes the verb, a past participle agrees with it in gender and number:

Voilà **l'homme** que j'ai rencontr**é** à la gare hier
There's the man I met at the station yesterday

Voilà **la femme** que j'ai rencontr**ée** à la gare hier
There's the woman I met at the station yesterday

Voilà **les enfants** que j'ai rencontr**és** à la gare hier
There are the children I met at the station yesterday

Voilà **les jeunes filles** que j'ai rencontr**ées** à la gare hier
There are the girls I met at the station yesterday

NB: The past participles of impersonal verbs (see Chapter 8.8), like *il y a* 'there is/are', never agree with a preceding complement:

Il y a eu des problèmes
There were problems

Les problèmes qu'il y a **eu** (NOT *eus) ont été vite oubliés
The problems that there were were quickly forgotten

It is important to distinguish this **impersonal** use from the **personal** use where agreement would take place:

Les problèmes **qu'il a eus** ont été vite oubliés
The problems which he had have been quickly forgotten

9.3.5 Recognizing when the head of a relative clause is a direct object

Sometimes it is not easy to determine whether the head of a relative clause is a direct object or not. Verbs like *courir* 'to run', *coûter* 'to cost', *dormir* 'to sleep', *marcher* 'to walk', *mesurer* 'to measure', *payer* 'to pay', *peser* 'to weigh', *valoir* 'to be worth', *vivre* 'to live' can take complements which look like direct objects, but are in fact measure adverbs:

Ce livre m'a coûté **cinquante francs**
This book cost me fifty francs

La valise pèse **vingt kilos**
The suitcase weighs twenty kilos

Il a marché **une dizaine de kilomètres**
He walked ten kilometres or so

Elle a dormi **deux heures**
She slept for two hours

In each of these cases the phrase in bold is a measure adverb and not a direct object. One test you can use to find out if the complement of a verb is a direct object or not is to try to make it the subject of a passive sentence – most direct objects can be turned into passive subjects. None of the above examples can be: you cannot say **Cinquante francs ont été coûté par ce livre*, nor **Une dizaine de kilomètres ont été marché*, etc.

If the head of a relative clause is an adverb, there is no agreement between it and the past participle:

Les cinquante francs que ce livre m'a coûté...
The fifty francs that this book cost me...

Les deux heures qu'elle a dormi...
The two hours she slept...

But to make matters more confusing, some of these verbs can also take direct objects. When direct objects are the heads of relative clauses there is agreement with the past participle:

J'ai pesé **la valise**   (direct object)
I weighed the suitcase

La valise a pesé **vingt kilos**   (adverb)
The suitcase weighed twenty kilos

La valise que j'ai pes**ée**...
Les vingts kilos que la valise a pesé...

9.3.6 Agreement with a preceding direct object in a relative clause when the participle is followed by an infinitive

As in the case of preceding direct object pronouns (see 9.3.3), when a verb is preceded by a direct object which is the head of a relative clause and followed by an infinitive, the participle only agrees when that head is the implied direct object of the verb containing the participle and the subject of the infinitive. This means that there will be agreement in cases like the following:

Nathalie a vu **une énorme roche** écraser sa maison
Nathalie saw a huge rock crush her house

Voilà **l'énorme roche que** Nathalie a v**ue** écraser sa maison
There's the huge rock which Nathalie saw crush her house

On a entendu **les voix** résonner dans la caverne
We heard the voices echoing in the cave

> Ce sont **les voix qu'** on a entend**ues** résonner dans la caverne
> *Those are the voices we heard echoing in the cave*

But no agreement in cases like the following:

> Nathalie a vu écraser **sa maison** par une énorme roche
> *Nathalie saw her house crushed by a huge rock*

> C'est **sa maison que** Nathalie a v**u** écraser par une énorme roche
> *It's her house that Nathalie saw crushed by a huge rock*

> Hubert-Jean a regardé détruire **la forêt** par des bulldozers
> *Hubert-Jean watched the forest being destroyed by bulldozers*

> Voilà **la forêt que** Hubert-Jean a regard**é** détruire par des bulldozers
> *There's the forest that Hubert-Jean watched being destroyed by bulldozers*

As in the case of preceding direct object pronouns, the types of verb which give rise to these contexts are perception verbs, movement verbs and *laisser* (but not *faire*) (see 9.3.3).

9.3.7 Agreement of past participles with preceding direct objects in questions

Questions can be formed in various ways (see Chapter 14). When they are constructed in such a way that the direct object precedes the past participle in compound tenses, the past participle agrees with it in gender and number:

> **Quel livre** as-tu achet**é?**
> *Which book did you buy?*

> **Quelle voiture** as-tu achet**ée?**
> *Which car did you buy?*

> **Laquelle** a-t-il chois**ie?**
> *Which one did he buy?*

> **Lesquels** ont-ils accept**és?**
> *Which ones did they accept?*

> **Combien de citrons** as-tu achet**és?**
> *How many lemons did you buy?*

> **Combien de bouteilles** de vin as-tu achet**ées?**
> *How many bottles of wine did you buy?*

NB: The past participles of impersonal verbs (see Chapter 8.8), like *il y a* 'there is/are', never agree with a preceding questioned complement:

> **Quels problèmes** y a-t-il **eu** (NOT *eus)?
> *What problems were there?*

This must be distinguished from the personal use where agreement would take place:

> **Quels problèmes** a-t-il **eus?**
> *What problems did he have?'*

9.3.8 Recognizing when a questioned phrase is a direct object

Sometimes it is not easy to determine whether a questioned phrase is a direct object or not. Verbs like *courir* 'to run', *coûter* 'to cost', *dormir* 'to sleep', *marcher* 'to walk', *mesurer* 'to measure', *payer* 'to pay', *peser* 'to weigh', *valoir* 'to be worth', *vivre* 'to live' can take complements which look like direct objects, but are in fact measure adverbs. Where such phrases are questioned there is no agreement with a past participle (see also 9.3.5):

> Elle a dormi deux heures
> *She slept for two hours*
>
> **Combien d'heures** a-t-elle dormi (NOT *dormi**es**)?
> *How many hours did she sleep?*
>
> Ce livre m'a coûté cinquante francs
> *This book cost me fifty francs*
>
> **Combien de francs** ce livre a-t-il coûté (NOT *coûté**s**)?
> *How many francs did this book cost?*

9.3.9 Agreement with a preceding questioned direct object when the participle is followed by an infinitive

As in the case of preceding direct object pronouns (see 9.3.3), when a verb is preceded by a questioned direct object and followed by an infinitive, the participle only agrees when the questioned phrase is the implied direct object of the verb containing the participle and is the subject of the infinitive. This means that there will be agreement in cases like the following:

> Nathalie a vu **une voiture** écraser son chien
> *Nathalie saw a car run her dog over*
>
> **Quelle voiture** Nathalie a-t-elle vu**e** écraser son chien?
> *Which car did Nathalie see run her dog over?*
>
> On a entendu **les voix** résonner dans la caverne
> *We heard voices echoing in the cave*
>
> **Quelles voix** avez-vous entendu**es** résonner dans la caverne?
> *What voices did you hear echoing in the cave?*

But no agreement in cases like the following:

> Nathalie a vu écraser **sa maison** par une énorme roche
> *Nathalie saw her house crushed by a huge rock*
>
> **Quelle maison** Nathalie a-t-elle v**u** écraser par une énorme roche?
> *Which house did Nathalie see crushed by a huge rock?*
>
> Hubert-Jean a regardé détruire **la forêt** par des bulldozers
> *Hubert-Jean watched the forest being destroyed by bulldozers*
>
> **Quelle forêt** Hubert-Jean a-t-il regard**é** détruire par des bulldozers?
> *Which forest did Hubert-Jean see destroyed by bulldozers?*

As in the case of preceding direct object pronouns, the types of verb which give rise to these contexts are perception verbs, movement verbs and *laisser* (but not *faire*).

9.4 Agreement of the past participle of pronominal verbs in compound tenses

Pronominal verbs (see Chapter 8.7) include an unstressed object pronoun which agrees with the subject:

Je me rase	*I'm shaving*
Elle se lève	*She's getting up*

In compound tenses the past participle agrees with this preceding object pronoun only if it is a direct object. The problem is determining when it is a direct object and when it is not.

With verbs where the pronoun is not understood as a reflexive (that is, where it does not mean anything, but is just a part of the verb – see Chapter 8.7.3), the participle always agrees, with one exception:

Elle **s'**est lev**ée**	*She got up*
Ils **se** sont tus	*They fell silent*
Nous **nous** sommes abstenus de tout commentaire	*We refrained from making any comment*

Exception: *se rire de* 'to make light of': *Ils **se** sont **ri** de vos menaces* 'They made light of your threats'.

Where a pronominal verb is used reflexively (see Chapter 8.7.1), it will have a non-reflexive counterpart. If the verb has a direct object in its non-reflexive counterpart, the reflexive pronoun is a direct object, and a past participle will agree with it in compound tenses:

Reflexive use	**Non-reflexive counterpart**
Je **me** rase	Le coiffeur rase **son client**
I am shaving	*The barber is shaving his client*
Elle **se** sert la première	Elle sert **sa fille** la première
She serves herself first	*She serves her daughter first*

Ils **se** sont ras**és** de bonne heure
They shaved early
Elle **s'**est serv**ie** la première
She served herself first

If the verb has an indirect object in its non-reflexive counterpart, the reflexive pronoun is an indirect object, and there will be no agreement with a past participle:

Reflexive use	**Non-reflexive use**
Elle **s'**offre un gâteau	Elle offre un gâteau **à Jean**
She treats herself to a cake	*She treats Jean to a cake*
Nous **nous** cachons la vérité	Nous cachons la vérité **à nos amis**
We hide the truth from ourselves	*We hide the truth from our friends*

> Elle **s'**est offer**t** (NOT *offer**te**) un gâteau
> *She treated herself to a cake*

> Nous **nous** sommes caché (NOT *caché**s**) la vérité
> *We hid the truth from ourselves*

The past participles of pronominal verbs used with parts of the body do not agree with the preceding pronoun where the body part is a direct object:

> Elle **s'**est coup**é** (NOT *coup**ée**) **le doigt** (= Elle a coupé le doigt à elle-même, although you cannot say this)
> *She cut her finger* (can even mean 'Her finger was cut off')

But where the body part is an indirect object, the pronoun is a direct object and a past participle agrees with it:

> Elle **s'**est coup**ée au doigt** (= Elle a coupé sa main au doigt, although again you cannot say this)
> *She cut her finger* (can only mean a surface cut)

There is no agreement between the past participle and the preceding pronoun with *se laisser* + infinitive, *se faire* + infinitive or *se voir* + infinitive:

> Elle s'est laiss**é** (NOT *laiss**ée**) convaincre
> *She let herself be persuaded*

> Julie s'est fai**t** (NOT *fai**te**) écraser par un camion
> *Julie got run over by a lorry*

> Jeanette s'est v**u** (NOT *v**ue**) offrir des fleurs par Georges
> *Jeanette has been given flowers by Georges*

10

Tense

10.1 Introduction

One of the essential functions of verbs is to express distinctions in time. Tenses serve (a) to situate events as taking place in the Present, Past or Future; (b) to indicate the time at which events occur relative to other events. The verb forms for each of the tenses mentioned in this chapter are given in full in Chapter 7.

10.2 The present

(a) The present tense is used to refer to an action or a state of affairs which exists at the time of speaking:

> Je ne **peux** pas lui parler parce que je **suis** dans mon bain
> *I can't speak to him because I'm in the bath*

> Il vous **téléphone** pour demander votre aide
> *He's phoning to ask for your help*

(b) It is used to express timeless facts:

> L'eau **se transforme** en vapeur quand elle bout
> *Water turns to steam when it boils*

> La terre **tourne** autour du soleil
> *The earth goes round the sun*

(c) It is used to refer to an action which is habitual:

> Je **prends** un bain tous les matins à huit heures
> *I take a bath every morning at eight o'clock*

> Il **vient** me voir toutes les semaines pour s'assurer que tout va bien
> *He comes to see me every week to check that everything's OK*

(d) In certain contexts, notably when the context provides a clear temporal reference to the future, it can refer to the future:

> Je **viens** demain, c'est sûr
> *I'll come tomorrow for sure*

> Demain, il **part** pour Paris
> *Tomorrow he will be leaving for Paris*

(e) Some writers use the present tense to refer to past events when they wish to render the past event more immediate. This can be found particularly in the writings of historians, journalists, novelists, and so on:

Grâce au vignoble, les villes **sont** prospères dès le 16e siècle
The vineyard enabled the towns to prosper from the 16th century

10.2.1 Differences between French and English in the use of the present tense

French simple present for the English progressive

English indicates that an event is in progress via a special form of the verb called the 'progressive': 'be + V-ing', e.g. 'I am thinking'. French does not have an equivalent special form for this. The English present progressive will normally be translated into French by the simple present:

Je **réfléchis**
I think or *I am thinking*

However, if it is important to stress the length of time, or the simultaneity of the event, French can use *en train de*:

Je **suis en train** de réfléchir
I am thinking

Thus, when French uses a present tense, this may correspond either to the simple present or the present progressive of English. The meaning will depend on the context. For example, *Je promène mon chien* will be 'I walk my dog' in the first example below, but 'I am walking my dog' in the second:

Je promène mon chien tous les matins aux Champs Elysées
I walk my dog in the Champs Elysées every morning
(Simple present in English because it expresses an habitual action)

Qu'est-ce que vous faites?
What are you doing?
Je promène mon chien
I am walking my dog
(Progressive form in English because it stresses the ongoing nature of the current action)

French simple present for English perfect

English has a form of the verb called the 'perfect': 'have + V-ed/V-en', e.g. 'I have walked', 'He has spoken'. It is used for reference to an event which happened in the past, but whose consequences continue into the present. In some cases the English perfect will be translated by the simple present in French:

J'**envisage** souvent de partir
I have often thought of leaving

Je vous **apporte** des fraises
I have brought you some strawberries

10.3 The past

Three forms are available to express PAST events:

The imperfect:	Je jouais du piano
The simple past (past historic):	Je jouai du piano
The compound past (perfect):	J'ai joué du piano

10.3.1 The imperfect

(a) This tense is used to describe ongoing past events without reference to a time of starting or finishing:

Pierre **lisait**	*Pierre was reading*
Il **était** tard	*It was late*
La ville **dormait**	*The town was sleeping*

In narratives, the imperfect typically provides a background of ongoing events against which particular completed events are acted out. If the narrative is written, these completed events will be in the compound past and/or simple past; if the narrative is spoken, they will be in the compound past (see 10.3.3):

Il **était** tard. M. Dupont **arrêta** sa voiture devant un café
It was late. M. Dupont pulled up in front of a café

Les voleurs **faisaient** beaucoup de bruit. Les gendarmes **se glissèrent** dans la pièce sans se faire remarquer
The thieves were making a great deal of noise. The policemen slipped into the room without being noticed

Je **somnolais** tranquillement quand quelqu'un **a sonné** à la porte
I was dozing quietly when someone rang the door bell

(b) It also typically refers to an habitual action in the past. This is generally described in English through the use of the forms 'used to' or 'would':

M. Dupont **s'arrêtait** toujours au café quand il avait le temps
M. Dupont always used to stop at the café when he had the time or
M. Dupont would always stop at the café when he had the time

Since 'would' can also express the conditional in English, it is important for the English speaker to distinguish the 'would' which corresponds to the French imperfect from the 'would' which corresponds to the French conditional. If 'would' is imperfect, it should be possible to replace it with 'used to' and still have a grammatical sentence. If substitution of 'would' by 'used to' produces an ungrammatical sentence, it is a conditional:

Le dimanche, j'**allais** manger dans un restaurant à Paris
On Sundays, I would ('used to' is OK) go to a restaurant in Paris

Si tu me donnais de l'argent, j'**irais** manger dans un restaurant à Paris dimanche
*If you gave me some money, I would (NOT *'used to', therefore a conditional) go to a restaurant in Paris on Sunday*

(See 10.4.2 for the conditional tense. See Chapter 11.3.1 for the use of 'would'.)

(c) It can be used to describe completed past events where the speaker or writer wishes to make the past event more immediate by presenting it as if it were in progress:

Je **courais** jusqu'à la voiture. J'**attendais** un instant, puis je **faisais** marche arrière. Je **roulais** en me répétant: « Fais attention »
I ran to the car. I waited a moment, then I put it into reverse. I drove, repeating to myself: 'Be careful'

10.3.2 The simple past (past historic)

The simple past tense refers to completed events in the past which are not seen as having any particular relevance to the present from the point of view of the speaker. Nowadays the use of the simple past (past historic) is restricted to written or very formal spoken French (e.g. very formal speeches):

> Les Jeux Olympiques **eurent** lieu à Montréal en 1982
> *The Olympic Games took place in Montreal in 1982*

> Les dinosaures **vécurent** au jurassique
> *Dinosaurs lived in the Jurassic period*

> Le président **partit** à 22h pour New York
> *The president left at 10 p.m. for New York*

10.3.3 The compound past (perfect)

The compound past tense refers to a completed event in the past. In contrast to the simple past (past historic), however, it may refer to an action in the past whose effect continues into the present. It is available both in spoken and written French:

> Nous **sommes arrivés** hier de Dijon
> *We came in from Dijon yesterday*

> Ils **ont vendu** leur maison et ils **sont partis** à l'étranger
> *They sold their house and went abroad*

> Ils **ont acheté** six croissants pour notre petit déjeuner
> *They bought six croissants for our breakfast*

In some texts the simple past and the compound past are used together. The simple past refers to completed events which do not give rise to consequences continuing into the present, from the perspective of the writer. The compound past, by contrast, refers to past events whose consequences do continue to have present relevance, from the perspective of the writer. For example, the following extract from a newspaper article marking the fiftieth anniversary of the death of the French airman and novelist Antoine de Saint-Exupéry, opens with the following passage:

> Le 31 juillet 1944, quand un officier **porta** [*simple past*] officiellement disparu le Lightning P38 no. 223 piloté par Antoine de Saint-Exupéry, un colosse trop à l'étroit dans sa combinaison d'aviateur **est entré** [*compound past*] dans la légende
>
> *On 31 July 1944, when an officer officially reported as lost the Lightning P38 no. 223 piloted by Antoine de Saint-Exupéry, a giant of a man, too big for his aviator's suit, became a legend*

The simple past *porta* describes an event which is seen as over and done with; the compound past *est entré* describes an event which is seen as having a continuing consequence for the present, from the perspective of the writer: Saint-Exupéry became **and still is** a legendary figure.

10.3.4 An illustration of the working of the past tenses in context

Compound past (perfect) and imperfect

Here is a literary example taken from the novel *L'Eté meurtrier* by Sébastien Japrisot. The completed events are in the compound past because, although written, this particular piece of narrative is told in the first person from the point of view of one of the characters, giving the effect of a spoken narrative. These events are set against a descriptive background defined by the imperfect:

> J'**ai connu** Gabriel [*compound past – completed event*] en avril 1945, quand nous **avons fui** Berlin [*compound past – completed event*], et que je **suivais** [*imperfect – background context*] avec ma mère et d'autres réfugiés, les colonnes des soldats qui **allaient** [*imperfect – background context*] vers le sud. C'**était** dans un village [*imperfect – background context*] un matin très tôt, près de Chemnitz. Nous **avions** déjà **perdu** ma cousine Herta [*pluperfect – see 10.4.1 – earlier completed event*] qui **avait** trois ans de plus que moi [*imperfect – background context*] entre Torgën et Leipzig, parce qu'elle **avait trouvé** un camion et nous un autre [*pluperfect – see 10.5.1 – earlier completed event*]. Et c'est ce matin-là que j'**ai perdu** ma mère [*compound past – completed event*]. Je crois qu'elle **a changé** de direction [*compound past – completed event*], qu'elle **est allée** vers Kassel [*compound past – completed event*], à l'ouest, où elle **avait** des amis [*imperfect – background context*]…

> *I met Gabriel in April 1945 when we fled from Berlin, and when I was following, with my mother and other refugees, the columns of soldiers going south. It was in a village very early one morning, near Chemnitz. We had lost my cousin Herta, who was three years older than me, between Torgën and Leipzig because she had found one lorry, and we another. And it was the same morning that I lost my mother. I believe she changed direction, and that she went towards Kassel, to the West, where she had friends …*

Simple past (past historic)

The simple past tense refers to completed events in the past which are not seen as having any particular relevance to the present from the point of view of the speaker. For example, consider the following narrative from another novel by Sébastien Japrisot, *La Dame dans l'auto avec des lunettes et un fusil*. Here a series of events are over and done with at some point prior to when the narrator is speaking:

> Elle **ramassa** ses vêtements épars [*simple past – completed event with no consequences continuing into the present from the perspective of the narrator*]. Elle les **rangea** soigneusement dans sa valise noire [*simple past – completed event with no continuing consequences*]. Elle ne **prit** pas la route déserte [*simple past – completed event with no continuing consequences*] par où ils **étaient venus** [*pluperfect – see 10.5.1 – earlier completed event*]. Elle **gravit** à nouveau la colline [*simple past – completed event with no continuing consequences*] et, sur la roche plate où ils **s'étaient assis** [*pluperfect – see 10.5.1 – earlier completed event*], elle **étala** [*simple past – completed event with no continuing consequences*], ouvert en deux, le sac en papier qui **avait enveloppé** [*pluperfect – see 10.5.1 – earlier completed event*] ses nu-pieds neufs. Elle **écrivit** dessus [*simple past – completed event with no continuing consequences*] …

> *She picked up her scattered clothes. She packed them carefully into her black suitcase. She didn't take the deserted road along which they had come. She climbed the hill again and, on the flat rock where they had sat, she spread the opened-out paper bag which had contained her new flip-flops. She wrote on it …*

In modern French the simple past tense is restricted to written French. It is found in literary texts (novels, plays, poems) and in newspaper articles. It is used typically in passages of **impersonal third person narration**, as in the above example. Engel (1990) has conducted a survey of the use of the simple past in newspaper articles. Among other things, she found that the simple past was likely to be used in formal, objectivity-seeking articles, in sports reports, in *faits divers* (reports of accidents, fires, rescues, etc.), and in items on the arts.

As noted above, the simple past is not found in all contexts in written French, even in literary French. Where a narrative is told from a personal, first person perspective (and hence is more like spoken French than written) it is very likely that it will be told in the compound past. Japrisot, for example, in the novel quoted from above, has passages narrated in the third person and simple past tense, and passages narrated in the first person and compound past. The extract cited above would become the following if recounted from the point of view of the woman in question:

> J'**ai ramassé** mes vêtements épars. Je les **ai rangés** dans ma valise noire. Je n'**ai** pas **pris** la route déserte par où nous **étions venus**. J'**ai gravi** à nouveau la colline et, sur la plate roche où nous nous **étions assis**, j'**ai étalé**, ouvert en deux, le sac en papier qui **avait enveloppé** mes nu-pieds neufs. J'**ai écrit** dessus...

10.3.5 Differences between French and English in the use of past tense forms

French compound past/simple past and imperfect for English simple past

The English simple past is used in a range of contexts where French distinguishes between the compound past/simple past on the one hand and the imperfect on the other. Take, for example, the English sentence 'He slept all afternoon'. This can describe a one-off, completed past event, in which case the French equivalent would be a compound past or a simple past form of the verb:

> (Hier) il **a dormi** tout l'après-midi
> (Hier) il **dormit** tout l'après-midi
> (compound past or simple past (past historic) because it is a completed action in the past)
> *(Yesterday) he slept all afternoon*

Or it can describe an habitual action, in which case the French equivalent would be an imperfect form of the verb:

> (Quand il était plus jeune,) il **dormait** tout l'après-midi
> *(When he was younger,) he slept all afternoon (= he used to sleep ...)*

Note that there is a distinction between viewing an action as habitual and viewing it as repeated. Repeated actions which are completed are described by verbs in the compound past/simple past in French:

> Tous les jours de cette année-là elle a travaillé d'arrache-pied/elle travailla d'arrache-pied
> (compound past or simple past because each of the repeated actions, i.e. the work carried out each day, is envisaged as a completed action in the past)
> *Every day that year she worked like mad*

French imperfect for English past progressive

English indicates that an event was in progress in the past via a special form of the verb known as the 'progressive': 'was/were V-ing', e.g. 'He was sleeping'. French does not have an equivalent special form for this. The English past progressive will normally be translated into French by the imperfect tense:

> Quand je l'ai trouvé, il **dormait** paisiblement sur la plage
> *When I found him he was sleeping peacefully on the beach*

> Nous **allions** vers l'Arc de Triomphe quand les avions sont passés/passèrent au-dessus de nous
> *We were going towards the Arc de Triomphe when the planes flew over us*

If there is a need to emphasize the duration, *en train de* can be used:

> Elle **était en train de** mettre la dernière touche à son dessin quand on a frappé/frappa à la porte
> *She was putting the finishing touches to her drawing when someone knocked at the door*

10.4 The future

Two tenses are used to refer to future time: the future and the conditional, although the conditional also expresses meanings which are not simply related to future time.

10.4.1 The future tense

The future tense has three main functions:

(a) It is used to describe events which take place in the future:

> Quand il ira à Paris il m'**achètera** des livres
> *When he goes to Paris he will buy me books*

(b) As in English, it can be used as a more polite alternative to the imperative to give orders:

> Vous **fermerez** la porte, s'il vous plaît
> *Will you close the door, please*

> Je **prendrai** un kilo de vos prunes jaunes
> *I'll have a kilo of your yellow plums*

> Vous m'**excuserez**
> *Will you excuse me*

(c) It is sometimes the equivalent of English 'may', when a speaker is speculating about possible causes or outcomes:

> Elle **aura** encore sa migraine
> *She may have her headache again*

> Peut-être qu'elle **viendra**
> *She may perhaps come*

(See Chapter 11.3.4 for more on 'may'.)

NB: The future can be replaced by a present tense form of the verb *aller* + an infinitive where a greater certainty about the likelihood of an event taking place is implied than is given by the future. In many contexts the future and *aller* + an infinitive can be interchanged, e.g.:

Tu **vas** y aller, je le sais bien *or* Tu **iras**, je le sais bien
I'm quite sure you will go

But in some contexts there is a clear difference in meaning between the two:

Elle **va avoir** un bébé
She will have a baby or She's having a baby (i.e. She's pregnant)

Compared with:

Elle **aura** un bébé (un jour, mais elle n'est pas pressée)
She will have a baby (one day, but she is in no hurry)

10.4.2 The conditional tense

The conditional has six main functions:

(a) It refers to events which **would** take place in the future if certain conditions were met:

Il m'**achèterait** des livres à Paris si je lui donnais l'argent
He would buy me books in Paris if I gave him the money

Je l'**accompagnerais** volontiers si je ne devais pas retourner à Dijon
I would love to go with him if I didn't have to go back to Dijon

(b) In reported speech (see 10.7) it is the equivalent of a future tense in direct speech:

Il a dit: 'Je viendrai' Il a dit qu'il **viendrait**
He said: 'I will come' *He said he would come*

Je lui ai demandé: `Est-ce tu pourras venir?'
I asked him, 'Will you be able to come?'

Je lui ai demandé s'il **pourrait** venir
I asked him if he could come

(c) The conditional is used, especially in journalistic language, to state something as an 'alleged' fact, i.e. one which the writer doesn't wish to state as definitely true and often one attributed to other sources:

Selon des sources bien informées, le Prince de Galles **rejoindrait** le reste de la famille royale aux sports d'hiver la semaine prochaine
According to reliable sources, the Prince of Wales will be joining the rest of the royal family for a skiing holiday next week

D'après notre correspondant à Tel Aviv, un accord de paix **serait** réalisable dans la semaine à venir
According to our correspondent in Tel Aviv, a peace agreement will be possible in the coming week

(d) The conditional (and even the compound conditional – see 10.5.5) can be used in French as 'could' and 'would' are in English to make a request sound more polite:

> Je **voudrais** réserver deux places, s'il vous plaît
> *I would like to book two seats, please*

> Je **voudrais** vous demander un renseignement
> J'**aurais voulu** vous demander un renseignement
> *I was wondering if I could ask you for information*

(e) Sometimes the conditional can be the equivalent of English 'might' when the speaker is speculating about possible causes or outcomes – it expresses greater uncertainty than the future tense used for the same purpose:

> Elle **aurait** encore sa migraine
> *She might have her headache again*

> Peut-être qu'elle **viendrait**
> *She might come, perhaps*

(See Chapter 11.3.5 for more on 'might'.)

(f) In formal French the conditional can be used as an alternative to a clause with *si* (see also Chapter 17.3.7):

> Il me **proposerait** un million de francs que je n'irais pas!
> *Even if he offered me a million francs I still wouldn't go!*

(For tenses in *si* clauses see 10.8 and Chapter 17.3.6.)

10.4.3 Differences between French and English in the use of future and conditional tenses

In English, verbs in clauses introduced by conjunctions like 'when', 'as soon as', 'as long as', 'after', 'once' are usually in a present or past tense verb form:

> *When she **comes** I'll tell her*

> *He will arrive as soon as **I have left**

Where such clauses refer to events which are yet to happen (as they mostly do), in French you must use a future, conditional, compound future or compound conditional, as appropriate. These clauses are introduced by conjunctions like: *quand, lorsque, aussitôt que, dès que, sitôt que, dès lors que, tant que, après que, une fois que.*

> Quand elle **viendra** (NOT *vient), je le lui dirai

> Il arrivera dès que je **serai parti** (NOT *suis parti)

> **Une fois que** nous **serons passés** à l'hôtel je pourrai enfin me débarrasser de ces valises
> *Once we've been to the hotel I will finally be able to get rid of these suitcases*

A good indicator that the event has yet to happen is the verb in the other clause, which will be in a future tense, conditional tense, etc., in English: 'He **will** arrive as soon as I have left'. (See also Chapter 17.3.2.)

10.4.4 Use of tenses with *depuis, il y a* and *pendant*

depuis

In clauses containing the preposition *depuis* 'for' or 'since', the tense of the verb differs systematically between French and English.

(a) In the case of the present, there are two points in time, now and an event in the past. Where the consequences of the event in the past continue into the present, from the perspective of the speaker, French uses a present tense, while English uses the perfect:

> Je **suis** ici depuis plus d'un an
> *I **have been** here for more than a year*
> (My being here continues at the time I am speaking)

> Elle **habite** notre village depuis Pâques
> *She **has been** living in our village since Easter*
> (She is still living there at the time of speaking)

However, if the event does **not** have consequences which continue into the present, a past tense form of the verb will be used in French:

> Il n'**est** pas **venu** ici depuis plus d'un an
> *He hasn't been here for more than a year*
> (The last time he was here was over a year ago, so the event does not continue at the time of speaking)

> Il **a arrêté** de fumer depuis plus d'un an
> *He has stopped smoking for more than a year*
> (His giving up smoking was an event which was completed more than a year ago, and so does not continue at the time of speaking)

Compare with:

> Il **fume** depuis plus d'un an
> *He has been smoking for more than a year*
> (His smoking started more than a year ago and continues into the present)

(b) In the case of the past, there are also two points in time, one in the past and one further back in the past. If the consequences of the event further back in the past continue forwards to the event in the past, French uses the imperfect tense where English uses the pluperfect:

> J'**étais** là depuis plus d'un an
> *I **had been** there for more than a year*

But if the more distant event does not have continuing consequences, a pluperfect form of the verb will be used in French:

> Il **avait arrêté** de fumer depuis plus d'un an quand il est tombé malade
> *He had stopped smoking for more than a year when he became ill*

(For *depuis que* see Chapter 17.3.4.)

il y a

By contrast *il y a* 'ago' focuses on the completion of an event in the past, and the tense used in French is a past tense, just as it is in English:

> Je **suis arrivé** il y a un an
> *I arrived a year ago*

> Elle **a commencé** à habiter notre village il y a six mois
> *She began living in our village six months ago*

> Nous y **sommes allés** il y a plus de dix ans
> *We went there more than ten years ago*

pendant

pendant 'for', enables the speaker to indicate the length of time associated with an event, whether it is in the present, future or is a completed event in the past:

> Jean-Paul prétend qu'il **veut** maintenir son silence pendant trois semaines
> *Jean-Paul says that he wants to keep quiet about it for three weeks*

> Ensuite nous **irons** passer des vacances en Irlande pendant quinze jours
> *After that we will spend a fortnight on holiday in Ireland*

> J'y **suis resté** pendant trois semaines l'année dernière
> *I stayed there for three weeks last year*

(For *il y a un mois que* ... 'it's a month since ...', *voilà/voici plusieurs ans que* ... 'it's several years since ...', see Chapter 17.3.4.)

10.5 Other tenses indicating the time at which events occur relative to other events

10.5.1 The pluperfect tense

Whereas the simple past and compound past tenses refer to events completed in the past from the perspective of the speaker or writer, the pluperfect describes events completed at some point even before these past events:

> La police laissa une balise pour indiquer où l'accident **était arrivé**
> *The police left a marker to show where the accident happened/had happened*
> (Pluperfect – an event which occurred prior to the police marking the spot)

> Je n'ai pas pris la route déserte par où nous **étions venus**
> *I didn't take the very quiet road along which we had come*
> (Pluperfect – an event which occurred prior to me taking a different road)

10.5.2 The past anterior tense

The past anterior is not used very frequently and can only occur in texts in which the simple past is used. It has two functions:

(a) It refers to a past event which **immediately** precedes another past event described by the simple past (as opposed to one past event preceding another without any specification of the length of the period between the two events – in this case a pluperfect would be used). A typical context for the past anterior is a clause introduced by the conjunctions *quand, lorsque* 'when', *aussitôt que, dès que, sitôt que, dès lors que* 'as soon as', *tant que* 'as long as', *après que* 'after', *une fois que* 'once':

> Après qu'elle **fut sortie**, il **enleva** la nappe
> *After she left, he removed the tablecloth*
> (Her leaving immediately preceded his removing the tablecloth)

> Dès que j'**eus fini**, je **me rendis** chez moi
> *As soon as I had finished, I went home*
> (My finishing immediately preceded my going home)

(b) It is used with adverbs like *vite* 'quickly', *bientôt* 'soon' where the idea of speed or urgency is expressed, and the verb would otherwise be in the pluperfect:

> Elle **eut** bientôt écrit la lettre
> *She had soon written the letter*

> Il **fut** vite envoyé chercher un médecin
> *He had quickly been sent to fetch a doctor*

(See also Chapter 17.3.3.)

10.5.3 The double compound past and compound pluperfect tenses

The double compound past tense and compound pluperfect tense can be used in spoken French where the past anterior is used in written French, to describe an event which immediately precedes another past event (typically in clauses introduced by *quand, lorsque* 'when', etc. – see 10.5.2), or to express speed or urgency. Where the verb describing the main past event is in a compound past tense form, the verb describing the preceding event is in a double compound past form:

> Ils ont gardé le silence pendant tout mon discours, mais ils **ont applaudi** quand j'**ai eu fini**
> *They were quiet throughout my speech but they applauded when I had finished*
> (The main past event is their applauding, and the verb is in a compound past form; my finishing the speech immediately precedes their applauding, and is in a double compound past form)

Where the verb describing the main past event is in a pluperfect tense form, the verb describing the preceding event is in a compound pluperfect form:

> Quand ils **avaient eu fini** de préparer leurs questions, ils les **avaient données** au Président de séance
> *When they had finished preparing their questions, they had given them to the Chair of the session*
> (The main past event is their having given the questions to the Chair, and the verb is in a pluperfect form; their finishing preparing the questions immediately precedes their giving the questions to the Chair, and is in a compound pluperfect form)

In expressing speed or urgency, only the double compound past tense is possible:

> J'**ai eu** vite **fini** le livre
> *I quickly finished the book*

The use of the double compound past and compound pluperfect tenses is not obligatory and is in fact relatively rare. Ordinary compound past and pluperfect tenses are the normal forms to use in these contexts.

10.5.4 The compound future tense (future perfect)

Typically the compound future tense describes a future event from the perspective of its completion (as opposed to the future tense, which views an event simply from the perspective of its futurity). It usually corresponds to English 'will have':

> J'**aurai fini** mon travail dès lundi
> *I will have finished my work from Monday*
> (versus: *Je finirai mon travail lundi* 'I will finish my work on Monday')

Given this perspective, a compound future can describe an event which takes place before another event in the future:

> J'**aurai fini** mon travail avant de partir en vacances
> *I will have finished my work before going on holiday*

The compound future can also be the equivalent of English 'may have', when a speaker is speculating about an event which may have occurred before another in the past:

> Elle **aura fini** peut-être ses devoirs avant de vous téléphoner
> *She may perhaps have finished her homework before she telephoned you*

10.5.5 The compound conditional tense (conditional perfect)

The compound conditional has four main functions:

(a) It refers to events which **would have** taken place if certain conditions had been met (but weren't):

> Ç'**aurait été** la chute du gouvernement, s'il y avait eu des élections à ce moment-là
> *The government would have fallen if there had been elections at that time*

> Tu l'**aurais vu** partir si tu étais venu plus tôt
> *You would have seen him leave if you had come earlier*

(b) In reported speech (see 10.7) it is the equivalent of a compound future in direct speech:

Direct speech:	Il a dit: 'J'aurai fini mon travail avant de partir en vacances' *He said: 'I will have finished my work before going on holiday'*
Reported speech:	Il a dit qu'il **aurait fini** son travail avant de partir en vacances' *He said he would have finished his work before going on holiday*

(c) The compound conditional can be used to indicate that the speaker is stating something as a possible fact and not as a certainty, most often a fact asserted by others:

> Le Président **serait** déjà **parti** pour l'Allemagne
> *(It is said that) the President may have already left for Germany*
> (i.e. I have been told he has but I am not repeating it as a fact)

> Selon mes collègues, j'**aurais dit** que le président allait prendre sa retraite
> *According to my colleagues, I said that the chairman was going to retire*

This is widely used in the press to express unsubstantiated or alleged facts:

> On ne sait donc toujours pas si l'assassin présumé, qui **aurait avoué** son crime, était bien le seul tireur ou s'il avait été aidé de plusieurs complices
> *We therefore still do not know whether the suspected killer, who **has allegedly admitted** his crime, was indeed the only one who fired or whether he was helped by several accomplices*

(d) In formal French the compound conditional can be used as an alternative to a *si* clause containing a verb in the pluperfect (see also Chapter 17.3.7):

> Il me l'**aurait dit** plus tôt, j'aurais pu m'y prendre autrement
> S'il me l'**avait dit** plus tôt, j'aurais pu m'y prendre autrement
> *If he'd told me earlier, I could have done it another way*

10.5.6 The double compound future
The double compound future can be used (but need not be) to describe an event completed in the future **immediately** before another future event. Typical contexts where it might be found are clauses introduced by *dès que, quand, lorsque, aussitôt que*, and so on (see 10.5.2 for the list):

> Dès qu'ils **auront eu bu** leur café, il faudra qu'ils se dépêchent de partir
> *As soon as they have drunk their coffee, they will have to hurry up and leave*

10.6 Combining tenses

When it is necessary to use tenses to indicate one moment in time relative to another, French is much more precise than English. In many sentences one clause establishes the main tense and another situates a second event in relation to it. When this is the case, it is essential to express the relative time relationship clearly in French by use of the appropriate tense as exemplified below.

10.6.1 Time relative to the present
(a) Assuming that one clause of a sentence relates to the present, events which precede the present will be in:

> the **imperfect** if one wishes to stress the duration of the action;

> the **compound past (perfect)** if one wishes to link the past action to the present or to leave that possibility open;

> and in the **simple past (past historic)** if one wishes to indicate, in written French, that the action is definitely completed.

The English sentence:

> *She often played the violin, now she plays the piano*

could be rendered into French in each of the following ways, depending on which of three possible meanings is intended:

(i) If 'played' refers to an habitual action in the past compared with the situation now, then the imperfect will be the appropriate tense:

> Elle **jouait** souvent du violon, maintenant elle joue du piano
> (*jouait* indicates that she was in the habit of playing the violin: a meaning which could have been conveyed by the English `used to' or 'would')

(ii) If 'played' refers to an event completed in the past but possibly still relevant to the present, then the compound past (perfect) will be the appropriate tense:

> Elle **a souvent joué** du violon, maintenant elle joue du piano
> (*a joué* indicates that on several occasions in the past, she played the violin: it is neutral about whether she still plays it or not but leaves open that possibility)

(iii) If 'played' refers to an event (or a repeated set of events) seen as completed in the past and with no relevance to the present, the simple past (past historic) will be the appropriate tense in writing:

> Elle **joua** souvent du violon, maintenant elle joue du piano
> (*joua* suggests that for a specified period in the past (e.g. up to the age of ten), she played the violin but that the event is sharply cut off from the present)

(b) Assuming that one clause of the sentence relates to the present, events which follow the present will be expressed through the future:

> J'exige une excellente performance de mes employés aujourd'hui, et je l'**exigerai** encore demain
> *I demand a high-level of performance from my employees now and I will continue to do so in the future*

> Il pleut aujourd'hui et il **va** pleuvoir encore demain
> *It's raining today and it will rain again tomorrow*

(c) An event which occurs immediately before an event which is in the present, can be expressed by the present tense of *venir de*. The English translation usually involves 'just':

> Mais non! Tu ne fais que répéter ce que je **viens de** te dire!
> *Not at all! You are simply repeating what I have just told you!*

> Nous **venons de** présenter nos idées aux clients
> *We have just presented our ideas to the clients*

> Nous reviendrons sur la question que nous **venons d'**évoquer
> *We will come back again to the topic we have just been discussing*

10.6.2 Time relative to the past

(a) Assuming that one clause of a sentence indicates that an event has taken place in the past, the following forms are used to indicate events further in the past than the given past event. Where the past event is expressed by the compound past (perfect) or the simple past (past historic), an event further in the past will be expressed by the pluperfect (see 10.5.1), or, in certain styles, the past anterior (see 10.5.2). These differences are frequently not expressed in the equivalent English sentences where simple past forms are used:

> Elle **a voulu** revendre le meuble dès qu'elle l'**avait** acheté
> *She wanted to sell the piece of furniture as soon as she bought it*

> Quand elle **eut fini** de jouer du violon elle **joua** du piano
> *When she finished playing the violin, she played the piano*

It is frequently possible for English to use the pluperfect 'had bought', 'had finished playing', etc. but most often users prefer the simpler forms and leave the interpretation to the reader: normally it is clear in context what is meant. However, despite the fact that English frequently does not mark these temporal distinctions, they **cannot** be left vague in French:

> Papa veut savoir à quelle heure elle **est** rentrée hier soir
> *Dad wants to know at what time she **came** in last night*

> Papa a voulu savoir à quelle heure elle **était** rentrée hier soir
> *Dad wanted to know at what time she **came** in last night*

> On déposa des fleurs sur le trottoir pour indiquer où l'accident **était** arrivé
> *Flowers were left (or people left flowers) on the pavement to show where the accident happened*

> Quand je suis entré dans la pièce je me suis rendu compte que Jean **était** arrivé avant moi
> *When I went into the room I realized that John **was** there before me*

(b) The double compound past is used in cases where it is required that the event further in the past is marked as completed:

> Ils ont gardé le silence pendant tout mon discours, mais ils ont applaudi quand j'**ai eu fini**
> *They were quiet throughout my speech but they applauded when I **had finished***

(c) The compound conditional is used to refer to a hypothetical event related to an event in the past:

> Nous **aurions acheté** votre maison si nous en avions entendu parler à temps
> *We would have bought your house if we had heard of it in time*

> Vous **auriez pu** l'acheter si vous aviez voulu
> *You could have bought it if you had wanted to*

(d) The imperfect of *venir de* can be used when one event is indicated as just having been completed prior to another one already expressed in the past tense. Note that the French imperfect must be translated by an English pluperfect 'had told/presented etc.':

Il ne faisait que répéter ce que je **venais de** lui dire
He simply repeated what I had just told him

Nous **venions de** conclure notre présentation quand la panne d'électricité est survenue
We had just finished our presentation when there was a power cut

La question que nous **venions d'**évoquer avait soulevé beaucoup de controverse
The matter we had just discussed raised a great deal of controversy

10.6.3 Time relative to the future

(a) A sequential relationship between two events in the future can be expressed through the compound future:

Est-ce qu'elle **aura fini** ses devoirs **avant de partir** demain matin?
Will she have finished her homework before she leaves tomorrow morning?

marks a future action which **precedes** the indicated future point in time.

Est-ce qu'elle **finira** ses devoirs **après avoir pris** sa douche demain matin?
Will she finish her homework after having her shower tomorrow morning?

marks a future action which **follows** the indicated future point in time. (Note the preferred translation with '-ing'.)

Une fois que nous **serons passés** à l'hôtel je **pourrai** enfin me débarrasser de ces valises
Once we've been to the hotel I will finally be able to get rid of these suitcases

Lorsqu'il m'**aura fourni** des explications valables, nous **pourrons** nous mettre d'accord sur la solution à adopter
Once he has provided me with a satisfactory explanation, we shall be able to agree on the solution to be chosen

both mark a future action which **precedes** another future action. (Note the translation into English by a present perfect.)

(b) The double compound future is used to indicate the completed nature of the event preceding another event in the future:

Quand vous **aurez eu fini** de préparer vos questions, vous les **présenterez** au Président de séance
When you have finished preparing your questions, you (will) give them to the Chair of the session

10.7 Tenses in direct and reported descriptions of events

When descriptions of events (e.g. *Le prisonnier s'est évadé par la fenêtre* 'The prisoner escaped through the window') or the utterances of others ('direct speech' – e.g. *«Je viens demain»* 'I'm coming tomorrow') are **reported** to a third party, the tense of the verb in the original sentence can change in certain circumstances, and there may also be consequential changes in any associated time adverbs:

Direct description:	Le prisonnier **s'est évadé** par la fenêtre
	The prisoner escaped through the window
Reported description:	La police croyait que le prisonnier **s'était évadé** par la fenêtre
	The police thought that the prisoner had escaped through the window
Direct speech:	Je **viens demain**
	I'm coming tomorrow
Reported speech:	Il a dit qu'il **venait le lendemain**
	He said that he was coming the following day

(For the choice of appropriate time adverbs see Chapter 5.6.8.)

Verbs which introduce reported descriptions or reported speech are those like *dire que* 'to say that', *expliquer que* 'to explain that', *penser que, croire que* 'to think, believe that', *maintenir que* 'to maintain that', *prétendre que* 'to claim that', and so on.

Mostly, the tense of the verb in the **reported** clause is the same as the tense of the verb in the original statement or utterance. But where the **reporting** verb is in a past tense – imperfect, compound past/simple past or pluperfect – the following systematic changes occur in the tense of the reported verb:

Original tense		Reported tense
present	→	imperfect
(compound) future	→	(compound) conditional
compound/simple past	→	pluperfect

Table 10.A illustrates the pattern.

TABLE 10.A *Tenses following a reporting verb in a past tense*

Direct description	Reporting verb (imperfect, compound or simple past, pluperfect)	Reported verb
Elle parle (present) *She is speaking*	Ils croyaient qu' Ils ont cru/crurent qu' *They thought that* Ils avaient cru qu' *They had thought that*	elle parlait (imperfect) *she was speaking/spoke*
Elle parlera (future) *She will speak*	Ils croyaient qu' Ils ont cru/crurent qu' *They thought that*	elle parlerait (conditional) *she would speak*
Elle aura parlé (compound future) *She will have spoken*	Ils avaient cru qu' *They thought that*	elle aurait parlé (compound conditional) *she would have spoken*
Elle a parlé (compound past) *She spoke/has spoken* Elle parla (simple past) *She spoke*	Ils croyaient qu' Ils ont cru/crurent qu' *They thought that* Ils avaient cru qu' *They had thought that*	elle avait parlé (pluperfect) *she had spoken*

Other tenses of reported verbs remain the same as the original. To take some typical examples:

Direct description	Reported
Elle parlait	Ils avaient cru qu'elle parlait *They had thought that she was speaking*
Elle aurait parlé	Ils ont cru qu'elle aurait parlé *They thought that she would have spoken*
Elle avait parlé	Ils croyaient qu'elle avait parlé *They thought that she had spoken*

And where the **reporting** verb is in a non-past tense (i.e. present or any form of the (compound) future or (compound) conditional) the tense of the reported verb remains the same as the original:

Direct description	Reported
Elle parle	Ils croiraient qu'elle parle *They would think that she is speaking*
Elle parlera	Ils croient qu'elle parlera *They think that she will speak*
Elle a parlé	Ils auraient cru qu'elle a parlé *They would have thought that she spoke*

10.8 Tenses with *si*

si has two distinct functions. One is to introduce indirect questions, and corresponds to English 'if' when it can also mean 'whether': *Elle m'a demandé si je voulais y aller* 'She asked me **if/whether** I wanted to go there'. Tenses following indirect question *si* are determined in exactly the same way as for reported speech, as described in 10.7. (See also Chapter 17.3.6.)

The other function of *si* is to introduce 'hypothetical clauses'. In this use it corresponds to English 'if' when it cannot alternate with 'whether', e.g. 'I won't stay if (NOT *whether) he comes' *Je ne resterai pas s'il vient*. The tense of the verb in the hypothetical *si* clause can **never** be in the (compound) future or (compound) conditional tense. Rather, it will typically obey one of the following patterns:

Je ne **reste** pas s'il **vient**
I'm not staying if he comes

Je ne **resterai** pas s'il **vient**
I won't stay if he comes

Je ne **resterais** pas s'il **venait**
I wouldn't stay if he came

Je ne **serais** pas **resté** s'il **venait/était venu**
I wouldn't have stayed if he came/had come

Je ne **restais** pas s'il **venait**
I wasn't staying if he was coming

11

The subjunctive, modal verbs, exclamatives and imperatives

11.1 The attitude of the subject to events: the subjunctive

The **subjunctive** is expressed by a particular set of forms which verbs can typically take only in subordinate clauses (but see 11.4.4 for an exception). The selection of the subjunctive in a subordinate clause (rather than the normal indicative) is always determined by the nature of the clause on which it is dependent.

> It should be noted that in many cases **there is no choice** about whether to use the subjunctive or indicative: certain types of main clause ALWAYS select subjunctive in a dependent subordinate clause; others ALWAYS select the indicative. However, some main clause constructions are ambiguous, and allow the verb in a dependent subordinate clause to be either subjunctive or indicative: the choice of one or the other produces different meanings.

The majority of main clause constructions which select the subjunctive have a general property in common, and it is useful to consider the subjunctive from this perspective. The subjunctive is selected in a subordinate clause where the subject of the main clause views the event described in the subordinate clause **with a significant degree of personal interpretation.** This notion of 'personal interpretation' can be broken down into three types, which are illustrated below:

(a) The subject judges an event to be more towards the 'unlikely' end of a scale going from 'probable' to 'unlikely'.
(b) The subject projects his or her personal desires or feelings on to an event.
(c) The subject cannot present an event as probable from his or her point of view, because it is in some way conditional on other events, is hypothetical, is unknowable or is simply vague.

Subjunctive: dependent on the subject's belief that an event is unlikely to occur

Where the subject of the main clause expresses a belief in the relative probability of an event's occurring (whether in the past or the future), the indicative will be used. For example, expressions like the following give rise to the indicative in dependent subordinate clauses:

Jean affirme que				Jean declares that		
Jean pense que	}	Pierre **est venu**		Jean thinks that	}	Pierre came
Jean imagine que				Jean reckons that		

In the case of impersonal subjects – *il est certain que, il est probable que*, etc. – or with verbs where the subject is in the first person – *je crois que, j'imagine que*, etc. – it is the speaker of the sentence who expresses a belief in the **probability** of an event's occurring and this equally gives rise to the indicative:

Je crois que				I believe that		
Je juge que				I reckon that		
Je pense que	}	Pierre **viendra**		I think that	}	Pierre will come
Je suppose que				I suppose that		
Il est certain que				It's certain that		
Il est probable que				It's probable that		

BUT where the main clause expresses the subject's belief that an event is **unlikely** to occur or to have occurred, the **subjunctive** is required. For example, where the above expressions are negated or questioned, or when other terms suggesting less certainty are used, the event becomes more 'unlikely' than 'probable'. This gives rise to the subjunctive in dependent subordinate clauses:

Jean ne pense pas que				Jean doesn't think that		
Jean n'imagine pas que		Pierre **soit venu**		Jean doesn't imagine that		Pierre came
etc.				etc.		

Je ne crois pas que				I don't believe that		
Il n'est pas certain que		Pierre **vienne**		It's not certain that		Pierre will come
Il est possible que				It's possible that		
etc.				etc.		

Est-il certain que				Is it certain that . . .		
Crois-tu que		Pierre **vienne?**		Do you think that		Pierre will come?
etc.				etc.		

Est-ce que Jean				Does Jean think that . . .		
pense que						
Est-ce que Jean		Pierre **soit venu?**		Does Jean imagine that		Pierre came?
imagine que				etc.		
etc.						

Subjunctive: dependent on the subject's attitude to an event

Where the construction which introduces the subordinate clause inherently presents the event as simply a matter of fact, the indicative will be used. For example, after the verb *savoir que* 'to know that' the indicative will always be used because *savoir que* states the subject's view of an event as a matter of fact, uncoloured by a significant degree of personal interpretation:

> Il sait que Pierre est venu
> (*il sait que* states 'Pierre's having come' as a factual reality)

BUT where the construction which introduces the subordinate clause inherently expresses the subject's personal desires or feelings, the subjunctive will be required. For example, after the verb *regretter que* 'to be sorry that', the subjunctive will always be used because *regretter* places the event in the context of an emotional, personal interpretation by the subject:

> Il regrette que Pierre **soit venu**
> ('Pierre's having come' is not in doubt, but *il regrette que* expresses a personal attitude towards that event)

Thus, where a subject places a particular personal interpretation on an event described in a subordinate clause, the **subjunctive** is likely to be used – even if the factual reality of the event is not in doubt. It is the attitude towards the event, the way the subject wishes it to be seen, which is more important than the reality or otherwise of the event. For example, Josette Alia, writing in the *Nouvel Observateur* in 1990 about the beginning of the feminist movement wrote:

> L'essentiel, pour nous, était que le scandale **fût** là
> *The most important thing for us was that there **should have been** a scandal*

To have written the following, equally grammatical, sentence would have changed the meaning in an important way:

> L'essentiel, pour nous, était que le scandale **fut** là
> *The most important thing for us was that there **was** a scandal*

In using the subjunctive Josette Alia does not lay the stress on the concept that there actually was a scandal (although she certainly thinks that there was) because that, from her point of view, is not what is important: she wishes to stress that the important thing was for the early feminists (with whom she identifies herself) to have created one – hence the subjunctive.

Subjunctive: dependent on the subject's view of an event as conditional, hypothetical, unknowable or vague

In cases where the idea of conditionality is expressed overtly through the conditional word *si*, the indicative is always used (for tenses with *si* see 10.8):

> **Si** tu **viens** demain nous pourrons nous promener au bord du lac
> *If you come tomorrow, we will be able to go for a walk beside the lake*

> **S'ils avaient répondu** à ma première lettre, j'aurais cessé de les importuner
> *If they had replied to my letter, I would have stopped bothering them*

BUT certain expressions introducing dependent clauses place a condition on an event; the subject can then only present it as something which, from his or her point of view, is possible in certain circumstances, but no more than that. Therefore with expressions such as *à condition que* 'on the condition that' and *à moins que* 'unless', the subjunctive is obligatory:

> Je veux bien y aller, à condition qu'on **prenne** l'avion
> *I'd be very pleased to go, as long as we take the plane*

> Jean-Charles devra changer ses habitudes à moins qu'il **veuille** qu'on le prenne pour un imbécile
> *Jean-Charles will have to change his ways unless he wants people to think he is a complete idiot*

When time constraints make the outcome of events unknowable by the subject, references to events in an unknown time scale tend to be in the subjunctive: *avant que* 'before' and *jusqu'à ce que* 'until' must be followed by the subjunctive:

> Avant que tu (ne) me le **dises**, je te promets que je serai là à l'heure
> *Before you say anything to me, I promise that I will be there on time*

> Je veux attendre ici jusqu'à ce qu'il **soit arrivé** chez lui
> *I want to stay here until he has got home*

When subjects are confronted with a degree of vagueness which means that they do not know enough about the situation to be certain of anything they say, the subjunctive is used: *quoi que, quel(le(s)) que* 'whichever, whatever' must be followed by the subjunctive:

> Quoi qu'il **fasse**, il ne mettra plus jamais les pieds chez moi
> *Whatever he does, he will never set foot in my house again*

> Quels que **soient** ses problèmes, je ne vois pas très bien comment je pourrais l'aider
> *Whatever her problems may be, I can't easily see how I could help her*

SUMMARY
Contexts which give rise to the subjunctive

(a) The subjunctive is used mainly in subordinate clauses (but see 11.4.4).

(b) The subordinate clause is dependent on constructions which express **a significant degree of personal interpretation of events: these interpretations present events as more unlikely than probable, and/or in a way which is coloured by the desires or feelings of the subject, and/or as conditional, hypothetical or unknowable.**

NB: **(a)** As noted above, in the great majority of cases where the subjunctive is used, there is no choice: it is required after the relevant expression. However, in some limited subordinate contexts there is a genuine choice between using the indicative and the subjunctive because the construction on which the subordinate clause is dependent can be used with more than one meaning. This is the case in the example from Josette Alia used above. It is also the case in the following examples (the first from Judge and Healey, 1983:131).

A speaker trying to find a student who speaks Chinese might say:

> Je cherche un étudiant qui **sait** parler chinois
> *I'm looking for a student who can speak Chinese*

This would be used if the speaker is reasonably sure that there is such a student in a known group (i.e. 'I know one of the students speaks Chinese – I'm looking for that student'). By contrast, if the speaker said:

> Je cherche un étudiant qui **sache** parler chinois
> *I'm looking for a student who can speak Chinese*

he or she would be expressing reservations about whether such a student is likely to be available (i.e. 'I'm looking for any student who speaks Chinese – I don't know whether any of them do').

An irate parent waiting for a teenager who is coming in late might say:

> Je suppose que tu **vas** me dire que tu es allé au cinéma avec ta copine
> *I suppose you're going to tell me that you went to the cinema with your girl friend.*

The indicative is used because the parent wants to express his or her certainty about what excuses are likely to be offered.

By contrast, an insurance agent wanting to sell holiday insurance to a client might say:

> Supposez toujours que vous **soyez** aux Etats-Unis et que vous tombiez malade, qu'est-ce que vous allez faire sans assurance?
> *Just suppose that you are in the United States and you fall ill, how could you manage without health insurance?*

Here the whole issue is hypothetical. Hence the subjunctive.

(b) Although the subjunctive is typically marked in verbs in subordinate clauses introduced by *que*, **not every subordinate clause introduced by *que* requires the verb to be in the subjunctive** – in fact most of them don't! It is only when the subordinate clause is dependent on a construction which expresses a significant degree of subjective interpretation of the event along the lines described above, usually through the use of one of the specific ways of introducing the subordinate clause, that the subjunctive is used.

11.1.1 Forms of the subjunctive

The conjugation of verbs in the subjunctive is described fully in Chapter 7. Here is a brief summary of the way that regular verbs form the subjunctive in the various tenses (but see Chapter 7 for irregular verbs).

Present subjunctive

For many verbs, take the third person plural, present tense form of the indicative, delete *-ent*:

for example:

(ils)	parlent	→	parl-
	finissent	→	finiss
	dorment	→	dorm-
	vendent	→	vend-
	reçoivent	→	reçoiv-

and add the endings:

-e
-es
-e
-ions
-iez
-ent

for example:

> parle, parles, parle, parlions, parliez, parlent
> finisse, finisses, finisse, finissions, finissiez, finissent
> etc.

NB: The stem *reçoiv-* changes when the ending does not begin with *-e*: *reçoive, reçoives, reçoive, **recevions, receviez**, reçoivent*.

Imperfect subjunctive

For many verbs, take the first person singular, simple past tense form of the indicative, delete the last letter: for example:

(je)	parlai	→	parla-
	finis	→	fini-
	dormis	→	dormi-
	vendis	→	vendi-
	reçus	→	reçu-

and add the endings:

> *-sse*
> *-sses*
> *-^t*
> *-ssions*
> *-ssiez*
> *-ssent*

for example:

> parlasse, parlasses, parlât, parlassions, parlassiez, parlassent
> finisse, finisses, finît, finissions, finissiez, finissent
> reçusse, reçusses, reçût, reçussions, reçussiez, reçussent
> etc.

Compound past and pluperfect subjunctive

The compound past subjunctive is formed from the present subjunctive forms of *avoir* or *être*, as appropriate, followed by the past participle. The pluperfect subjunctive is formed from the imperfect subjunctive of *avoir* or *être*, as appropriate, followed by the past participle. (See Chapter 7 for details.)

11.1.2 Which tense of the subjunctive should be used?

In formal written French it is still possible to use all of the tenses of the subjunctive: present, imperfect, compound past and pluperfect. In such cases the tense to use is determined in a broadly similar way to the choice of tenses with indicative forms of the verb (see Chapter 10). The only difference is that because there is no future or conditional subjunctive, the present tense form of the subjunctive is normally used in contexts where the future or conditional would be appropriate.

However, in less formal written French, and generally in spoken French, only the present tense and the compound past tense of the subjunctive are used. In this case, the present tense forms of the subjunctive typically cover all cases where present, imperfect, simple past, future or conditional tenses of the indicative would be used. For example:

Nous préférons qu'il **soit** au courant
We prefer him to know about it
(Compare: *Nous savons qu'il est au courant* – present tense)

Le professeur se plaignait que ses élèves ne **sachent** pas employer correctement le subjonctif
The teacher used to complain that his pupils didn't know how to use the subjunctive correctly
(Compare: *Le professeur disait que ses élèves ne savaient pas employer correctement le subjonctif* – imperfect tense)

Il était heureux dans le bureau jusqu'à ce que le patron **embauche** une nouvelle secrétaire
He was happy in the office until the boss hired a new secretary
(Compare: *Il était heureux dans le bureau. Mais alors le patron embaucha une nouvelle secrétaire* – simple past tense)

Je démissionnerai tout de suite à moins que vous ne la **renvoyiez**
I'll resign immediately unless you sack her
(Compare: *Vous ne la renverrez pas? Alors je démissionnerai* – future tense)

Il serait peu probable que nos amis **sachent** que nous sommes partis
It would be unlikely that our friends would know that we have left
(Compare: *Il serait probable que nos amis sauraient que nous sommes partis* – conditional tense)

The compound past tense forms of the subjunctive typically cover all cases where compound past, pluperfect, compound future or compound conditional tenses of the indicative would be used. For example:

Quoiqu'ils **aient fait** de gros efforts, l'entreprise reste en difficulté
Although they have made considerable efforts, the company is still in difficulty
(Compare: *Ils ont fait de gros efforts, mais l'entreprise reste en difficulté* – compound past tense)

N'ont-ils pas cru que l'autre équipe **ait été** éliminée?
Didn't they think that the other team had been eliminated?
(Compare: *Ils ont cru que l'autre équipe avait été éliminée* – pluperfect tense)

Quoi que mes parents **aient décidé**, je n'y consentirai pas
Whatever my parents have decided, I won't agree to it
(Compare: *Mes parents auront décidé, mais je n'y consentirai pas* – compound future tense)

Crois-tu que les élèves **aient obtenu** d'aussi bonnes notes si quelqu'un d'autre avaient été leur professeur?
Do you believe that the pupils would have got such good marks if someone else had been their teacher?
(Compare: *Je crois que les élèves auraient obtenu d'aussi bonnes notes si quelqu'un d'autre avait été leur professeur* – compound conditional tense)

11.1.3 Subjunctive after verbs, adjectives and nouns which express the personal desires, orders, expectations, fears, regrets or other emotional states of the subject in relation to the event

Verbs and adjectives
Verbs and adjectives of wishing, ordering, expressing fears and other emotional states are normally followed by subjunctive subordinate clauses. The verb in

subordinate clauses dependent on the following verbs is almost always in the subjunctive:

aimer que	*to wish that*
attendre que	*to wait for*
s'attendre à ce que	*to expect that*
avoir envie que	*to really want that*
commander que	*to order that*
consentir que	*to agree or to accept that*
être content que	*to be pleased that*
craindre que	*to fear that*
demander que	*to ask that*
désirer que	*to wish that*
être désolé que	*to be sorry that*
être dommage que	*to be a pity or to be regretted that*
douter que	*to doubt that*
s'étonner que	*to be surprised that*
exiger que	*to require that*
être heureux que	*to be happy that*
insister pour que	*to insist that*
ordonner que	*to order that*
permettre que	*to allow that*
avoir peur que	*to be afraid that*
préférer que	*to prefer that*
être ravi que	*to be delighted that*
regretter que	*to regret that*
se réjouir que	*to rejoice that*
souhaiter que	*to wish that*
être surpris que	*to be surprised that*
tenir à ce que	*to be anxious that*
être triste que	*to be sad that*
veiller à ce que	*to be careful that*
vouloir que	*to want that*

J'aimerais que tous les étudiants **puissent** trouver du travail en fin d'études.
I would like all the students to be able to obtain a job at the end of their period of study

'Attendez que ma joie **revienne** et que **soit** mort le souvenir . . .' (chanson de Barbara)
'Wait until I can be happy again and for the memory to die . . .'

Je consens que tu **fasses** ce stage de photo mais n'oublie pas que tu devras quand-même aller à tes cours
I agree that you can go on this photography course, but don't forget that you will still have to go to your lectures

Je crains que cela (ne) **soit** vrai
I'm afraid that may be true

Il est dommage que le gouvernement n'**ait** pas pu obtenir la libération des otages plus tôt
It is to be regretted that the government was not able to obtain the release of the hostages at an earlier date

Personnellement, je ne doute pas que leur version **soit** véridique mais ils auront du mal à convaincre leurs parents
I don't doubt that their version is true but they will find it difficult to convince their parents

Je m'étonne que nous n'**ayons** pas encore **reçu** la marchandise
I'm surprised that we haven't yet received the goods

Il a exigé que nous l'**emmenions** jusqu'à Paris
He demanded that we should take him all the way to Paris

Elle était ravie que ses copains **aient obtenu** l'autorisation de passer dans la classe supérieure
She was very happy that her friends had been allowed to move up to the next class

J'ordonne que les prisonniers **soient libérés** tout de suite
I order that the prisoners should be freed immediately

J'ai peur que la vérité **soit** différente
I'm afraid that the truth might be different

Nous préférons qu'il **soit** au courant
We prefer him to know about it

Je suis ravi que tu **aies trouvé** l'âme sœur
I am delighted that you have found your partner for life

Je veux que tu **sois** là à la naissance
I want you to be present at the birth

(For the use of non-negative *ne* in subordinate clauses see Chapter 16.16.)

Nouns

The subjunctive is normally required in clauses dependent on nouns which express similar meanings to the verbs listed above, i.e. wishing, ordering, being pleased, sad, surprised, etc.: *l'attente que, la crainte que, le désir que, l'ordre que, la peur que, le souhait que:*

La crainte qu'il **soit relâché** a provoqué une manifestation devant la prison
The fear that he might be freed gave rise to a demonstration in front of the prison

Yvonne et Pierre ont exprimé le désir qu'elle **soit invitée**
Yvonne and Pierre have said that they want her to be invited

L'ordre qu'il **soit executé** a été donné au plus haut niveau
The order that he should be executed was given at the highest level

NB: Where the subject of the main clause is unspecified, as in a passive, or is the same as the subject of the subordinate clause, the subjunctive can be avoided by the use of an infinitive with *la crainte de, le désir de, la peur de, l'ordre de* etc.:

L'ordre **qu'il soit executé** a été donné au plus haut niveau
L'ordre **de l'executer** a été donné au plus haut niveau

11.1.4 Subjunctive after verbs of saying, thinking and believing in negatives and questions

Verbs of saying, thinking and believing – *affirmer que* 'to state that', *croire que* 'to believe that', *déclarer que* 'to declare that', *imaginer que* 'to imagine that', *penser que* 'to think that', *trouver que* 'to find that', and so on – normally present an event simply as a fact and, where they are followed by a dependent subordinate clause, the verb in this clause is in the indicative:

Ils ont cru que l'autre équipe **avait été éliminée**
They thought that the other team had been eliminated

But when such verbs are **negated or questioned**, this introduces uncertainty about the likelihood of the event occurring, and verbs in the dependent clause are in the subjunctive:

N'ont-ils pas cru que l'autre équipe **ait été éliminée**?
Didn't they think that the other team had been eliminated?

Nous n'affirmons pas que l'accident **soit** de votre faute, mais les circonstances prêtent à croire que cela pourrait être le cas
We are not saying that the accident was your fault, but the circumstances lead us to believe that this might be the case

Croyez-vous que la guerre froide **soit** vraiment terminée?
Do you think the cold war is really over?

Peut-on dire que cette statue **soit** un bon exemple du style de Michel-Ange?
Would you say that this statue is a good example of Michelangelo's style?

Je ne pense pas que cela **soit** vrai
I don't think that is correct

Je ne trouve pas que votre plaisanterie **soit** de mauvais goût, mais simplement déplacée dans ce contexte
I don't think that your joke was in bad taste but merely out of place in this context

Similarly, when verbs of saying, thinking and believing are used to introduce hypothetical cases, verbs in clauses dependent on them will be in the subjunctive:

Imaginez quelle **ait été** sa surprise
Just imagine what her surprise must have been

Supposons que nous **ayons gagné** la loterie nationale
Let's suppose that we won the national lottery

On imagine mal que ce film **ait été tourné** par Godard
It's difficult to imagine that this film was made by Godard

NB: Note that *espérer que* 'to hope that' does NOT give rise to the subjunctive in a dependent clause, even when negated or questioned:

Ils espéraient que l'autre équipe **avait été éliminée**
They hoped the other team had been eliminated

N'espéraient-ils pas que l'autre équipe **avait été éliminée**?
Didn't they hope that the other team had been eliminated?

11.1.5 Subjunctive after impersonal verbs expressing the belief that an event is unlikely as opposed to probable

Some impersonal verbs and expressions present the occurrence of events described in dependent subordinate clauses as probable: verbs in these clauses are in the indicative. Examples of such cases are: *il est certain que* 'it is certain that', *il s'ensuit que* 'it follows that', *il est évident que* 'it is obvious that', *il est probable que* 'it is probable that', *il me semble que* 'I think that', *il est vrai que* 'it is true that':

Il est probable que nous **arriverons** à Paris après-demain
It is probable that we will arrive in Paris the day after tomorrow

Il me semble que tout ce travail **valait** la peine
I think that all this work was worth it

But others present the events as less probable, only possible or even impossible; these require the subjunctive in dependent clauses: *il n'est pas certain que* 'it is not certain that'; *il est douteux que* 'it is doubtful that'; *il est impossible que* 'it is impossible that'; *il est invraisemblable que* 'it is unbelievable that'; *il se peut que, il est possible que* 'it is possible that'; *il est peu probable que* 'it is unlikely that'; *il n'est pas sûr que* 'it is not sure that'; *il n'est pas vrai que* 'it is not true that'.

Note particularly the following contrasts:

il est certain que + indicative	il n'est pas certain que + subjunctive
il est probable que + indicative	il est peu probable que + subjunctive
il est sûr que + indicative	il n'est pas sûr que + subjunctive
il est vrai que + indicative	il n'est pas vrai que + subjunctive

Il n'est pas certain que tes explications **soient acceptées** par tous
It is not certain that your explanations would be accepted by everyone

Il est douteux que le contrat **ait été** signé à temps
It is doubtful the contract will have been signed on time

Il est invraisemblable qu'ils **aient pu** s'enfuir sans être remarqués
It is incredible that they should have been able to escape without anyone noticing

Il se peut que nous **rencontrions** nos camarades à la sortie de la ville
We may meet up with our friends on the outskirts of town

Il est possible que nous **puissions** trouver une solution à votre problème
It is possible that we may be able to find a solution to your problem

Il est peu probable que vous **réussissiez** le permis la première fois
It is not very likely that you'll pass your driving test first time

Il n'est pas sûr que nous **ayons choisi** la meilleure solution
We can't be sure that we have chosen the best solution

Il n'est pas vrai que Juliette nous **ait proposé** de rester sur place
It is not true that Juliette proposed that we should stay where we were

Some impersonal constructions express the subjective desires or feelings of the speaker of the sentence: *il faut que* 'it is necessary that' (often equivalent to 'must'); *il est important que* 'it is important that'; *il est nécessaire que* 'it is necessary that'; *il est regrettable que* 'it is regrettable that'; *il semble que* 'it seems that'; *il est temps que* 'it is time that'; *il vaut mieux que* 'it is better if'.

Il faut qu'ils **soient** prêts à partir tout de suite
They must be ready to leave immediately

Il est important que tous **comprennent** la nécessité d'améliorer la productivité
It is important that everyone understands the need to increase productivity

Il est nécessaire que vous **partiez** avec eux: il serait trop dangereux de les laisser voyager seuls
It is necessary for you to go with them: it would be too dangerous to let them travel on their own

Il est regrettable que nous n'**ayons** pas **pu** transmettre ces renseignements
It is a pity that we were not able to pass on this information

Il semble que l'ennemi **soit** mieux préparé
It seems that the enemy is better prepared

Il est temps que nous nous **préparions** à aider les sans-abri
It is time for us to get ready to help the homeless

Il vaut mieux que ce **soit** Jean-Claude qui fournisse les explications
It is better that it should be Jean-Claude who puts forward the explanations

NB: Note in particular the contrast:

il me semble que + indicative	Il me semble que l'ennemi **est** mieux préparé *I think that the enemy is better prepared*
il semble que + subjunctive	Il semble que l'ennemi **soit** mieux préparé *It seems that the enemy is better prepared*

11.1.6 Subjunctive after certain conjunctions

Some subordinating conjunctions introduce hypothetical situations or establish conditions: these are normally followed by verbs in the subjunctive in the subordinate clause:

afin que pour que	*in order that*
en attendant que	*whilst waiting for*
non que ce n'est pas que	*not that*
à moins que	*unless*
à supposer que supposé que en supposant que en admettant que	*supposing that*
bien que quoique encore que malgré que	*although*
de façon que de manière que de sorte que si bien que	*so that, in such a way that*
de peur que de crainte que	*for fear that*
pour peu que si peu que	*however little that*
pourvu que à condition que	*provided that*
sans que	*without*

soit que   *whether*

tel que   *such as*

Couvrez vos cahiers **afin qu'**ils ne se **salissent** pas
Cover your exercise books so that they won't get dirty

Ils sont allés habiter à Paris **pour que** leur fils **puisse** suivre des cours à
Henri IV
They moved to Paris so that their son could study at the 'lycée Henri IV'

En attendant que le beau temps **revienne**, on passait les soirées à lire au coin
du feu
Waiting for the fine weather to return, we spent the evenings reading by the fireside

Je lui ai demandé de modifier le manuscrit; **non que** je **sois déçu**, mais je
voudrais qu'il y ait plus de dialogue
*I asked her to change the manuscript; it's not that I am disappointed, but I would like
there to be more dialogue*

Je passe te prendre à six heures **à moins que** tu ne **m'appelles** avant
I'll call by to pick you up at six unless you ring me beforehand

A supposer que la réponse **soit** favorable, qu'est-ce que vous allez faire?
Supposing that the reply is positive, what will you do?

Bien que ces arguments **soient** en partie valables, ils ne justifient pas votre
comportement
*Although these arguments are valid to a certain degree, I do not think that they justify
your behaviour*

Quoique les ouvrières **aient fourni** de gros efforts, la compagnie est toujours en
difficulté
*Although the workers have made considerable efforts, the company is still in
difficulty*

J'ai branché le répondeur **de crainte qu'**on ne **me dérange** pendant la réunion
*I've switched on the answering machine for fear that I might be interrupted during the
meeting*

Ils ont fait mettre leur numéro sur la liste rouge **de peur qu'**on ne les **dérange**
chez eux
They have gone ex-directory for fear of being disturbed at home

Je te montrerai comment cela fonctionne **de façon que** tu **puisses** l'expliquer à
Georges plus tard
I'll show you how it works so that you can explain it to George later

Je mets les chaises au jardin **de manière que** tu **puisses** lire au soleil
I'll set out the garden chairs in such a way that you can read in the sun

Expliquez-moi ce que vous avez décidé **de sorte que** je **sois** en mesure de
rédiger un rapport
Let me know in detail what you have decided, so that I may write a report

Je veux bien vous conduire jusqu'à Lyon **à condition que** vous **payiez** mon
billet de retour
I am quite willing to drive you to Lyons as long as you pay for me to come back

Nous nous offrirons des vacances cette année, **pourvu que** nos marges
bénéficiaires nous le **permettent**
We will take some holidays this year, provided that we make sufficient profit

Elle aurait bien pu quitter le village **sans que** je **m'en aperçoive**
She could well have left the village without my noticing

Et s'il avait créé un scandale **tel que** vous **ayez** été obligé de céder, vous auriez perdu beaucoup d'argent
And if he had created such a scandal that you had been obliged to give in, you would have lost a lot of money

The conjunctions *de façon que, de manière que, de sorte que, si bien que* 'so that' have two distinct meanings. On the one hand they express a wish that something which has not yet happened might happen. With this meaning they have the force of 'creating the conditions for another event to occur' and are followed by the subjunctive:

Je te montrerai comment cela fonctionne **de façon que** tu **puisses** l'expliquer à Georges
I'll show you how it works so that ('creating the conditions for you to') you can explain it to George

Dis-m'en un peu plus sur ce qui se passe au bureau, **de sorte que** je **puisse** te conseiller
Tell me a little more about what's happening at the office so that ('creating the conditions for me to') I can advise you

On the other hand, they can describe a causal effect of one event on another. With this meaning they have the force of 'with the result that' and are followed by the indicative:

Le mécanicien a réglé le fonctionnement des vitesses **de façon que** tu **peux** t'en servir de nouveau
The mechanic has adjusted the gears so that ('with the result that') you can use them again

Tu ne me racontes plus jamais ce qui se passe au bureau, **de sorte que** je **suis** incapable de te conseiller
You never tell me any more about what's happening at the office so that ('with the result that') I cannot advise you

(See also Chapter 17.3.8.)

11.1.7 Subjunctive after time conjunctions

With the time conjunctions: *avant que* 'before' and *jusqu'à ce que* 'until' the subjunctive is always used:

Il faut réagir rapidement, **avant que** le problème ne **devienne** insurmontable
We must react quickly before the problem becomes impossible to deal with

Sébastien va s'assurer de sa situation financière **avant qu'**il ne **démissionne**
Sébastien will sort out his financial position before he resigns

Il a persisté **jusqu'à ce qu'**elle **sorte** avec lui
He kept on until she went out with him

avant que can be replaced by *avant de* when the subject of the verb in the subordinate clause is the same as that in the introducing clause:

Sébastien va s'assurer de sa situation financière **avant qu'il ne démissionne**
Sébastien va s'assurer de sa situation financière **avant de démissionner**

The conjunction *après que* 'after' is normally followed by the indicative and not the subjunctive:

> Nous avons commencé après qu'ils **étaient arrivés**
> *We began after they arrived*

However, presumably by analogy with *avant que*, you will often hear people using the subjunctive after *après que*. (See also Chapter 17.3.1.)

(For the use of non-negative *ne* in dependent clauses see Chapter 16.16, and for non-negative *ne* in clauses dependent on conjunctions see Chapter 17.3.8.)

11.1.8 Subjunctive in clauses dependent on expressions which claim a unique status for an entity

Verbs in clauses which are dependent on superlatives, on nouns modified by one of the adjectives *dernier, premier, seul, unique,* or on *personne* or *rien,* are in the subjunctive if the sentence makes the claim that the entity referred to is 'peerless' (i.e. is the biggest, best, worst, first, last, only one of its kind ever):

> Ce chou-fleur est **le plus gros** que j'**aie** jamais **vu**
> *This cauliflower is the biggest I have ever seen*

> Jennifer est **la meilleure** spécialiste que j'**aie entendue** sur ce sujet
> *Jennifer is the best specialist I have heard on this subject*

> Jeanne est **la seule** qui **soit** capable de le faire
> *Jeanne is the only woman who could do it*

> Mon frère est **l'unique** candidat qui **ait été selectionné**
> *My brother is the only candidate who has been selected*

> Je ne connais **personne** qui **soit** mieux qualifié que lui pour exprimer les espoirs de la jeune génération
> *I don't know anyone better qualified than him to express the aspirations of the young*

> Il possède **la dernière** des voitures qui **soit** équipée d'un moteur spécial
> *He owns the last of the cars which have a special engine*

However, where there is no claim about the 'peerless' quality of the entity (e.g. when it is described as the biggest, best, worst, first etc. of a particular set, but there may be other bigger, better, worse, etc., entities in the world) the verb is in the indicative:

> C'est le premier film que j'**ai** vu
> *That's the first film I saw*

There is nothing peerless about this. It is simply the assertion of a fact. Other people see their first film as well. But compare with:

> C'était la première personne qui **ait fait** l'ascension du Matterhorn
> *He was the first person to scale the Matterhorn*

This was a 'peerless' first, and so the subjunctive is used. Similarly, compare:

> Je ne connais personne qui **soit** plus doué pour le piano que vous
> *I don't know anyone more gifted for the piano than you (peerless)*

> Je ne connais personne qui **sait** jouer du violon
> *I don't know anyone who plays the violin*
> (not peerless – there are plenty of people in the world who can play the violin;
> it's just that one of them is not in my set of acquaintances)

Other examples of non-peerless cases:

> C'est la dernière fois que je **viens** vous voir
> *This is the last time I am coming to see you*

> La première fois que je t'**ai vu**, je t'ai trouvé un peu farfelu
> *The first time I saw you I thought you were a bit eccentric*

> Le livre de cuisine est le seul qui **est tombé** de l'étagère
> *The cook book is the only one which fell off the shelf*

(See also Chapter 15.11.3.)

11.1.9 Use of the indicative in clauses introduced by an adverb

When an adverb, like *peut-être que* 'perhaps', *heureusement que* 'luckily', *certainement que* 'of course', *apparemment que* 'apparently', is used in the first part of a clause, despite the fact that they often express the meanings which in other clauses give rise to the subjunctive, the subjunctive is NOT used:

> Peut-être qu'il **viendra**, peut-être qu'il viendra pas
> *Maybe he'll make it, maybe not*

> Heureusement que tu **étais** là, sinon j'aurais eu peur
> *Lucky you were here otherwise I'd have been afraid*

> Certainement que ton copain **peut** coucher ici
> *Of course your friend can sleep here*

NB: This construction is more frequent in informal than formal French.

11.1.10 Use of the subjunctive in hypothetical clauses coordinated by et *que*

When a hypothetical clause introduced by *si* is extended by a coordinated clause, the second clause is introduced by *que* and the verb is usually in the subjunctive:

> S'il retéléphone demain et qu'il **veuille** savoir où j'étais, dis-lui que j'étais chez ma mère
> *If he rings again tomorrow and he wants to know where I was, tell him I was at my mother's*

> Si Hélène hérite de la maison et qu'elle la **vende**, tante Zoë sera furieuse
> *If Helen inherits the house and sells it, Aunt Zoë will be furious*

> C'est curieux, mais, si Paris St Germain gagne le championnat et qu'ils **perdent** la Coupe d'Europe, ils seront mieux placés pour la saison suivante
> *It's odd but, if Paris St Germain win the league and lose the European cup, they will be in a better position for next season*

(See also Chapter 17.5.)

A related construction is an adverbial clause introduced by *que* which also requires the subjunctive, and is translated by 'whether . . . or' in English:

> **Que** Jeanne **vienne ou ne vienne pas,** il faudra inviter sa fille
> *Whether Jeanne comes or not, we will have to invite her daughter*

> **Que** tu **sois** présent **ou que** tu **sois absent,** cela m'indiffère totalement
> *Whether you are present or absent is all the same to me*

11.1.11 Subjunctive in subject clauses

When a clause, rather than a noun phrase, is the subject of a sentence, the verb in that clause is in the subjunctive:

> **Que** des Allemands **soient présents** à la cérémonie du souvenir ne peut que renforcer la solidarité européenne
> *European solidarity can only be reinforced by the fact that Germans are present at the commemoration*

> **Que** Suzanne et Jean-Paul **aient choisi** le mariage religieux a pu paraître choquant à certains de leurs amis
> *(The fact) That Suzanne and Jean-Paul chose to get married in church may have been a shock for some of their friends*

The subjunctive is also used when such subject clauses are introduced by *le fait que* 'the fact that', or *l'idée que* 'the idea that':

> Le fait que Suzanne et Jean-Paul **aient accepté** de se marier . . .
> L'idée que tu **veuilles** assister à cette cérémonie . . .

Note that the subjunctive is required in subject clauses even with verbs and adjectives which normally require the indicative when subordinate clauses are not in subject position. Compare:

> Il est probable que nous **arriverons** à Paris après-demain
> (indicative)
> *It is likely that we will arrive in Paris the day after tomorrow*

> Que nous **arrivions** à Paris après-demain est probable
> (subjunctive)
> *That we shall arrive in Paris the day after tomorrow is likely*

> Il me semble certain qu'il **est parti**
> (indicative)
> *I think it certain that he has left*

> Qu'il **soit parti** me semble certain
> (subjunctive)
> *That he has left seems certain*

11.1.12 Use of the subjunctive in clauses dependent on indefinite expressions

Verbs in subordinate clauses following the indefinite expressions *qui que* 'whoever', *quoi que* 'whatever', *où que* 'wherever', *quelque + [noun] que* 'whichever, whatever [noun]', *quel que* 'whatever', *quelque/si/aussi/pour + [adjective] que* 'however [adjective]', are in the subjunctive:

> Qui que vous **soyez**, je n'accepterai pas ce comportement
> *Whoever you are, I won't accept that behaviour*

> Quoi qu'en **disent** mes parents, j'ai décidé d'y aller
> *Whatever my parents say, I have decided to go there*

> Où qu'il **se cache**, je le trouverai
> *Wherever he is hiding, I will find him*

> Quelques bêtises que tu **aies faites**, ton père et moi te pardonnons
> *Whatever stupid things you may have done, your father and I forgive you*

> Quelles que **soient** les raisons qui vous ont amené chez nous, je suis heureux de vous accueillir
> *Whatever might be the reasons which have brought you to us, I am happy to welcome you*

> Quelque rares que **soient** ces pierres, on arrivera quand même à les vendre
> *However rare these stones may be, we will manage to sell them anyway*

Note that in this last example *quelque* does not agree with *rares* or *pierres*. (For more on these constructions see Chapter 15.10 and 15.11.1.)

More generally, where a subordinate clause is dependent on an indefinite expression which describes a hypothetical, rather than real, state of affairs, the verb in the subordinate clause is likely to be in the subjunctive:

> S'il connaissait **un endroit** qui **convienne**, il le dirait
> *If he knew of a place which was suitable, he would say so*
> (There is no particular place that he knows of)

> Elle veut acheter **une maison** qui **ait** une piscine
> *She wants to buy a house with a swimming pool*
> (She has no particular house in mind)

Compare with:

> S'il connaît **un endroit** qui **convient**, allons-y
> *If he knows of a suitable place, let's go there*

> Elle veut acheter **une maison** qui **a** une piscine
> (Which suggests that there is a specific house with a swimming pool which she wants to buy)

(See also Chapter 15.11.2 and 15.11.4.)

11.2 The use of *devoir, pouvoir, savoir, falloir*

The modal verbs *devoir, pouvoir, savoir* and *falloir* enable a speaker to express a number of attitudes about events and the participants in events: the likelihood of an event occurring; the ability of a participant to perform some action; how obligated a participant is in an event. Modal verbs are also used in granting permission and in formulas expressing politeness.

In this section we describe the various uses of these four verbs. Then in 11.3

we take a different perspective and describe how the English modals would',
'should', 'could', 'may', 'might', 'ought to' and 'must' are rendered in French.

11.2.1 *devoir*

devoir expresses four main meanings:

(a) something which the speaker sees as very probable, usually because it is
logical;
(b) something which the speaker sees as a moral obligation;
(c) something which the speaker thinks of as planned or agreed;
(d) something which the speaker thinks of as an act, usually in the past, which
was a necessary outcome of events.

Probability (logical necessity)

> Les nouveaux joueurs sont les premiers sélectionnés du département, donc
> l'équipe **devrait** maintenant faire de meilleures performances
> *The new players are the best in the département, so the team should now produce some*
> *better performances*

> Cela **doit** être vrai
> *It must be true*

> Il **doit** être revenu puisqu'il recommence le travail demain
> *He must have come back because he starts work again tomorrow*

> Il pleut depuis trois semaines presque constamment. Nous **devrons** nous
> attendre à des inondations
> *It has been raining almost constantly for three weeks. We must expect floods*

> J'**ai dû** payer la facture puisque je n'ai reçu aucun courrier de relance
> *I must have paid the bill since I haven't had a reminder*

Moral obligation

> Il est absolument essentiel que je parle à Sylvain. Vous savez où il est et vous
> **devez** me le dire
> *It is absolutely essential that I should speak to Sylvain. You know where he is and you*
> *must tell me*

> Tu **dois** revenir demain sinon maman sera très déçue
> *You must come back tomorrow or Mum will be very disappointed*

> Vous êtes allés dîner chez eux, maintenant vous **devrez** les inviter chez vous
> *You have been to dinner at their house, now you will have to invite them to yours*

> Ce toit est dangereux; vous **devriez** en parler au propriétaire
> *This roof is dangerous; you should speak to the landlord about it*

A planned event (usually which did not or will not happen)

> Ils **devaient** annoncer le nom du gagnant à 18 heures mais une panne
> d'électricité est survenue
> *They were about to reveal the name of the winner when the power cut happened*

> Le jour de l'accident je **devais** accompagner mon père à Paris
> *The day of the accident I was to accompany my father to Paris*

A necessary outcome of events

Plus tard, il **devait** souvent repenser à ces quelques instants
Later on he was often to reflect on these few moments

Même si elle avait voulu occulter ces faits, elle ne le pouvait plus. Elle **devait** en tirer les conséquences
Even if she had wanted to remain unaware of these facts, she could no longer do so. She was obliged to accept what followed from them

50 ans après la fin de la guerre, son héroïsme **devait** être reconnu par le gouvernement
Fifty years after the end of the war his heroism was to be recognised by the government

11.2.2 *pouvoir*

pouvoir expresses five main meanings:

(a) The granting or refusing of permission by the speaker;
(b) An indication that the speaker believes someone else is capable of doing something;
(c) An indication that the speaker feels that something is probable in the future;
(d) A general assertion by the speaker about what may happen;
(e) An expression of politeness by the speaker.

The granting or refusing of permission by the speaker

Vous **pouvez** disposer!
You are dismissed!

Non, tu ne **peux** pas aller chez ce garçon
No, you cannot go to this boy's house

Il **pourra** m'en parler quand il voudra
He may talk to me about it when he wishes

Vous **pourrez** partir dès que la réunion sera terminée mais pas avant
You may go as soon as the meeting is over but not before

An indication that the speaker believes someone is capable of doing something

Elle a déjà fait la cuisine pour toute la famille: elle **peut** très bien s'occuper du repas de nos invités
She has already cooked for the whole family: she is quite capable of preparing the meal for our guests

Un grand garçon comme toi! Bien sûr que tu **pourras** porter ma valise jusqu'à ma chambre
A big boy like you! Of course you will be able to carry my case up to my room

Nous ne **pourrons** prendre notre décision que lorsque les experts nous aurons remis leur rapport
We will only be able to take our decision once the experts have put in their report

An indication that the speaker feels that something is quite probable in the future

Votre lettre **peut** très bien arriver lundi matin; elle a sans doute été retardée à cause des fêtes de Noël
Your letter may very well arrive on Monday morning; it has probably been delayed by the Christmas holidays

S'ils continuent à jouer comme ça, ils **pourraient** gagner le championnat
If they go on playing like that, they could well win the title

Tu passes trop de temps devant ton écran d'ordinateur: tu **peux** t'abîmer la vue
You spend too much time working on your computer: you could damage your eyesight

La gouttière fuit: si cela continue, l'eau **pourrait** abîmer le mur
The gutter's leaking: if it goes on, the water could ruin the wall

Il faut soigner cette égratignure, elle **pourrait** s'infecter
Treat this scratch, it could get infected

A general assertion by the speaker about what may happen

On **peut** toujours faire mieux
It is always possible to do better

Dans une pièce où il y a une cheminée, une étincelle **peut** toujours mettre le feu
In a room with an open hearth, a spark can always cause a fire

Il n'est pas trop tard; il **peut** encore venir
It is not too late; he may still come

Comme papa a trouvé du travail, on **va pouvoir** déménager
Since dad has got a job we'll be able to move house

An expression of politeness by the speaker

Puis-je vous demander de m'aider?
May I request your assistance?

Pourriez-vous m'indiquer le chemin de Douaumont?
Could you show me the way to Douaumont?

On **pourrait** voir les choses sous cet angle, mais personnellement je pense que l'important est ailleurs
It would be possible to see things in this way but I personally think that there is a much more important point

11.2.3 *savoir*

savoir expresses two main meanings:

(a) 'to know' in the sense of 'to possess knowledge about';
(b) 'to know' in the sense of 'to know how to do something'.

'to know' (possess knowledge)

Je **sais** mes leçons par cœur
I know my lessons by heart

Jean et Marie **savent** où nous trouver
Jean and Marie know where to find us

Monet **savait** beaucoup de choses sur l'utilisation de la couleur en peinture
Monet knew a lot about the use of colour in painting

'to know' (know how to ...)

N'ayez pas peur. Je **sais** nager
Don't worry. I can swim

Elle n'a que quatre ans mais déjà elle **sait** lire
She is only four but already she can read

Tu n'as pas besoin de parler si lentement. Ils **savent** parler français
You don't need to speak so slowly. They can speak French

Nous n'avons pas peur d'y aller. Nous **savons** nous défendre
We are not frightened to go there. We know how to look after ourselves

NB: There can be confusion between *pouvoir* and *savoir* in this area. *Savoir* is 'to know how to in principle' and *pouvoir* is 'to be able to do it in a particular situation':

Oui je **sais** réparer le moteur mais je ne peux pas le faire sans outils
Yes I can (= I know how to) repair the engine, but I can't do it (= I am unable to do so here and now) without tools

If people were feeling threatened in some way, they might say:

Nous **savons** nous défendre
We can look after ourselves

to indicate that they have necessary skills (karate, boxing, a willingness to fight etc.). In a situation where they may have to make use of these skills, they would say:

Nous **pourrons** nous défendre contre les attaques de l'extrême droite
We can defend ourselves against attacks by the extreme right

to indicate that they think they will be able to apply these skills in these circumstances.

11.2.4 *falloir*

falloir (impersonal) expresses one main meaning: it is equivalent to English: 'must', or 'ought to':

Il **faut** qu'ils viennent m'aider
They must come and help me

Il **aurait fallu** que les Anglais restent en dehors de l'Union Européenne
The English should have stayed out of the European Union

11.3 The French equivalents of the English modal verbs: 'would', 'should', 'could', 'may', 'might', 'ought to', and 'must'

As can be seen from the translations in the preceding section, *devoir, pouvoir, savoir* and *falloir* can be translated in a number of ways depending on the context. The most frequent translations are 'would', 'should', 'can', 'could', 'may', 'might', 'ought to', and 'must'. The problems which arise in this area for English speakers are mainly to do with errors in establishing how these forms relate to the English modal verbs which express many of the same meanings.

The English modal verbs also, however, express a number of other meanings. For correct usage, it is essential that learners should be able to distinguish the meanings of the English modals in order to know which French forms to use. In some cases one of the French modal verbs is appropriate; in other cases, a sentence with *si*, a conditional tense, an imperfect tense, a present or future tense or a subjunctive may be the appropriate form.

11.3.1 'would'

'would' has three main meanings:

(a) 'would' may be used in English to express possible future behaviour which is dependent on some condition. It will usually be rendered by the conditional form of the verb in French:

> Je **viendrais** à ton anniversaire si j'avais assez d'argent pour me payer le train
> *I **would** come to your birthday party if I had enough money to pay the train fare*
> (the conditional form *viendrais* is used to denote a possible future action envisaged IF certain other events take place)

(b) 'would' may be used to indicate something which is desired or not desired. In this case it is often rendered by a form of the verb *vouloir*:

> Elle n'**a** pas **voulu** me dire où le trouver
> *She **wouldn't** tell me where to find him*
> (the 'wouldn't' in English is quite close in meaning to 'did not want to': it is therefore rendered as *n'a pas voulu*)

(c) 'would' may also indicate an habitual action in the past. This is generally rendered by the imperfect form of the verb in French:

> Ces événements **avaient** souvent lieu pendant les vacances d'été
> *These events **would** often take place during the summer holidays*

(The imperfect tense is used to indicate an habitual action in the past – see Chapter 10.3.1.)

11.3.2 'should'

'should' has four main meanings:

(a) 'should' may indicate a moral obligation. This is usually rendered by the use of *devoir*:

> Tu **devrais** téléphoner chez toi plus souvent
> *You **should** phone home more often*
> (*devoir* in the conditional form to indicate the moral duty)

Note also that the English 'should have' is rendered by *aurait dû* plus an infinitive and not by a participle form of the main verb:

> Tu **aurais dû** me dire (not *avoir dit) cela plus tôt
> *You **should have** told me that before*

falloir is also possible here:

> Il **aurait fallu** me le dire plus tôt

(b) 'should' may convey a conditional. This is usually rendered by a conditional form of the verb in French:

> Si j'avais su cela, je ne **serais** pas venu
> *If I had known about that I **should** not have come*

(c) 'should' may express a probable future action. Depending on the degree of probability, this may be rendered by a form of *devoir* or by a future tense:

> Le livre **devrait** sortir le mois prochain
> Le livre **devra** sortir le mois prochain
> Le livre **sortira** le mois prochain
> *The book **should** be coming out next month*

These three sentences indicate an increasing degree of probability going from top to bottom.

(d) 'should' can also indicate a chance event. This may be translated by some means of expression other than the verb:

> Si **par hasard** vous entendez parler d'un appartement à louer, dites-le moi
> *If you **should** hear of a flat to let, do let me know*
> (a present tense plus an adverb expressing the idea of chance conveys the meaning of 'should')

Sometimes a simple present tense will convey the meaning of 'should':

> Si Jean **téléphone**, dis-lui que je le rappellerai
> *If John **should** telephone, tell him I'll call him back*

Where one wants to stress the improbability of the chance event occurring, a form of *devoir* can be used:

> Si Jean **devait** téléphoner, il faudrait lui dire que je le rappellerai
> *In the unlikely event of John telephoning, tell him I'll call him back*

(For more on the use of tenses with *si* see Chapter 10.8 and Chapter 17.3.6.)

11.3.3 'could'
'could' has four main meanings:

(a) 'could' may be a simple past tense of the verb 'can' i.e. 'was able to'. This is particularly frequent in reported speech. There is little difficulty here in using *pouvoir*:

> Malgré tout le mal qu'on s'est donné, il n'**a** quand même pas **pu** venir
> *After all the trouble we had taken he still **couldn't** come*

> Il a dit: 'Je **peux** venir'
> *He said: 'I **can** come'*

and in reported speech:

> Il a dit qu'il **pouvait** venir
> *He said he **could** come*

(See Chapter 10.7.)

(b) 'could' may indicate a possibility. This will normally be a conditional or a form of the impersonal verb *il se peut que*:

> Il faut que tu fasses attention; cela **pourrait** être un piège
> *You must be careful; it **could** be a trap*

> Cela fait plusieurs jours que je ne le vois plus: il **se peut qu'**il soit parti
> *I haven't seen him for a few days: he **could** have left*

(c) 'could' may indicate that permission has been given. This may be rendered by the use of *pouvoir* or by another verb, such as *permettre*:

> Sa mère a dit qu'il **pouvait** venir
> Sa mère lui **a permis** de venir
> *Her mother said he **could** come*

(d) 'could' may imply that something should be done or should have been done: this can be rendered by a suitable tense of *pouvoir*:

> Elle **aurait pu** me dire qu'elle ne **pourrait** pas le faire
> *She could have told me that she couldn't do it*

11.3.4 'may'
'may' has four main meanings:

(a) 'may' indicates something which is simply envisaged. Sometimes, especially in informal speech, an adverb will suffice. Or the impersonal forms *cela se peut*, *il se peut que* + *subjunctive*:

> Peut-être qu'elle **viendra**, ou peut-être qu'elle ne **viendra** pas
> *She **may** come or she **may** not*

> Cela **se peut** mais nous ne pouvons en être certains
> *That **may** be the case but we can't be sure*

> Il **se peut** que ce soit lui le coupable mais cela reste à prouver
> *He **may** be the guilty party but it has yet to be proved*

The subjunctive on its own is used very often when possible consequences are feared:

> Je fais photocopier le certificat de peur que tu **ne le perdes**
> *I am photocopying the certificate because I am frightened you may lose it*

(b) 'may' can indicate permission. This is most often rendered by the use of *pouvoir*:

> Cendrillon **peut** aller au bal, dit la méchante belle-mère
> *'Cinderella **may** go to the ball', said the wicked stepmother*

> Vous **pouvez** rester jusqu'à onze heures
> *You **may** stay till eleven*

(c) 'may' can be a kind of blessing. This will normally be rendered by a subjunctive in the main clause:

> Que Dieu vous **bénisse** tous
> ***May** God bless you all*

> Que Dieu nous **protège**
> ***May** God protect us*

(d) 'may' can indicate an open-ended possibility. This is often rendered by a subjunctive:

> Quoi qu'il en **soit**, je n'ai toujours pas récupéré mon argent
> *That's as **may** be, I still haven't got my money back*

> Quoi qu'il **dise,** je ne le croirai pas
> *Whatever he **may** say I won't believe him*

11.3.5 'might'
'might' has three main meanings:

(a) 'might' is sometimes simply a past 'may' as in giving permission in indirect speech. In this case a form of *pouvoir* is to be expected:

> Elle a dit: Vous **pouvez** y aller
> *She said: You **may** go*

> Elle a dit qu'on **pouvait** y aller si on finissait nos devoirs d'abord
> *She said we **might** go if we finished our homework first*

(b) 'might' indicates something which is envisaged. The French equivalents are the same as for 'may' (see 11.3.4.(a)). Sometimes, especially in informal speech, an adverb will suffice. Or the impersonal form *il se peut que + subjunctive* may be used. Or the subjunctive on its own may be used when possible consequences are feared:

> **Peut-être** qu'elle viendra, ou peut-être pas
> Il **se peut** qu'elle vienne, (on ne sait pas)
> *She **might** come or she might not*

> Je surveillais les enfants de peur qu'ils ne **se fassent mal**
> *I kept an eye on the children for fear that they **might** hurt themselves*

(c) 'might' can be a polite form. This usually corresponds to a form of *pouvoir*, or a use of *permettre*:

> **Puis**-je vous suggérer d'essayer autre chose?
> ***Might** I suggest that you try something else?*

Permettez-moi de vous demander pourquoi vous êtes venu?
Might I ask why you have come?

11.3.6 'ought to'

'ought to' conveys one main meaning:

'ought to' expresses a moral obligation. It is usually rendered by *devoir*, often in a conditional form:

Vous **devriez** sortir davantage
*You **ought to** get out more*

Tu **devrais** renouveler ta garde-robe
*You **ought to** buy some new clothes*

falloir is also possible:

Il **faut que** tu sortes davantage
Il **faut que** tu rcnouvelles ta garde-robe

11.3.7 'must'

'must' has two main meanings:

(a) 'must' can express moral obligation. This usually requires *devoir* or *falloir*:

Vous **devez** venir: nous ne pourrions pas prendre de décision sans vous
Il **faut que** vous veniez: nous ne pourrions pas prendre de décision sans vous
Il vous **faut** venir: nous ne pourrions pas prendre de décision sans vous
*You **must** come: we couldn't decide without you*

(b) 'must' can indicate a logical possibility/certainty. This is usually rendered by *devoir*:

Si elle le dit, c'est que ça **doit** être vrai . . .
*If she says so, then it **must** be the case . . .*

Vous **avez dû** sortir l'atlas de la voiture parce qu'il n'y est plus
*You **must have** got the road map out of the car because it isn't there now*

11.4 Exclamatives

Exclamatives are the direct expression of a speaker's surprise, disgust, anger, fervour and analogous emotions:

Comme elle a grandi!	*How she's grown!*
Que de monde!	*What a lot of people!*
Que le diable l'emporte!	*The devil take him!*
Vive la France!	*Long live France!*

There are four types of exclamative in French.

11.4.1 Exclamatives formed with *comme* or *que* + the indicative

Sentences can be turned into exclamations simply by putting *comme* or *que* in front of them, and without changing word order. The verb remains in the indicative:

Pierre a changé	**Comme** Pierre a changé!
Pierre has changed	**Que** Pierre a changé!
	How Pierre has changed!
Il se plaignait	**Comme** il se plaignait!
He used to complain	**Qu'**il se plaignait!
	How he used to complain!
C'est dégoûtant	**Comme** c'est dégoûtant!
It's disgusting	**Que** c'est dégoûtant!
	How disgusting it is!
Elle parle vite	**Comme** elle parle vite!
She speaks quickly	**Qu'**elle parle vite!
	How quickly she speaks!

NB: In informal French, *ce que* and *qu'est-ce que* are common alternatives to *comme* and *que*: *Ce que Pierre a changé! Qu'est-ce qu'il se plaignait!*, etc.

When exclamations are reported – that is when they follow verbs like *savoir, raconter, dire,* and so on – *comme/que* are replaced by *combien*:

Elle sait **combien** Pierre a changé
She knows how Pierre has changed

Ils ont raconté **combien** il se plaignait
They recounted how he used to complain

11.4.2 Exclamatives formed with *quel*

Exclamations can bear specifically on nouns. French uses *quel* to perform this function. Where a sentence is involved, the *quel*-phrase is placed at the beginning of the sentence and *quel* agrees in gender and number with the noun:

Quel vent!	*What a wind!*
Quelle surprise!	*What a surprise!*
Quels progrès ces étudiants ont faits!	*What progress these students have made!*
Avec **quelle** adresse il a résolu le problème!	*With what skill he solved the problem!*

When the direct object is the focus of the exclamation, in formal French it is possible optionally to invert the subject and the verb (in an operation known as 'stylistic inversion' – see Chapter 14.3.7), providing that there is no other material following the verb:

Quels progrès ces étudiants ont faits!
Quels progrès ont faits **ces étudiants**!

11.4.3 *que de* + noun meaning 'what a lot of X!'

que de followed by a noun is used to create an exclamative of the form 'what a lot of X!', or 'so much/so many X!':

Que de monde!	*What a lot of people!*
Que de difficultés!	*So many difficulties!*
Que de problèmes on doit affronter!	*What a lot of problems we have before us!*

11.4.4 The subjunctive used in two kinds of main clause exclamative

Although the subjunctive normally only occurs in subordinate clauses, it can be used in main clause exclamations like:

Vive la Bretagne!	*Long live Brittany!*
Dieu **soit** loué!	*Praise God!*
Sauve qui peut!	*Every man for himself!*
Puissiez-vous réussir!	*May you succeed!*

and also those headed by *que*:

Que la Sainte Vierge vous **bénisse**!
May the Holy Virgin bless you!

Que Dieu nous **protège**!
May God help us!

Qu'il **aille** au diable!
The devil take him!

Qu'il **aille** se faire voir ailleurs!
May he get lost!

Both of these types of exclamation are remnants from an earlier period in the history of French, and are rather formal and archaic. Only *Vive X!* and *Qu'il/elle/ils/elles V!* are used productively in modern French (*Vive les vacances!* 'Long live the holidays!', *Vive la révolution!* 'Long live the revolution!'; *Qu'il m'attende!* 'Let him wait for me!', *Qu'elle cherche ailleurs!* 'Let her look elsewhere!', etc.).

11.5 Imperatives

Imperatives in French are used very much as they are in English to give orders, express encouragement, give advice, and so on:

Asseyez-vous	*Sit down*
Allez la France!	*Come on, France!*
Allons-y	*Let's go*
Fais attention!	*Watch out!*

11.5.1 Form of imperatives

Imperatives are formed from the second person, singular and plural, and the first person plural of the present tense forms of verbs. Delete the subject and the final -*s* of any verb that ends in -*es* or -*as*:

tu parles	→	parle	*speak*
vous parlez		parlez	*speak*
nous parlons		parlons	*let's speak*
tu vas	→	va	*go*
vous allez		allez	*go*
nous allons		allons	*let's go*
tu ouvres	→	ouvre	*open*
vous ouvrez		ouvrez	*open*
nous ouvrons		ouvrons	*let's open*
tu finis	→	finis	*finish*
vous finissez		finissez	*finish*
nous finissons		finissons	*let's finish*
tu dors	→	dors	*sleep*
vous dormez		dormez	*sleep*
nous dormons		dormons	*let's sleep*
tu reçois	→	reçois	*receive*
vous recevez		recevez	*receive*
nous recevons		recevons	*let's receive*

There are four verbs with irregular imperative forms:

être		**avoir**	
sois	*be*	aie	*have*
soyez	*be*	ayez	*have*
soyons	*let's be*	ayons	*let's have*

savoir		**vouloir**	
sache	*know*	veuille	(used almost
sachez	*know*	veuillez	exclusively to
sachons	*let's know*	—	mean *please* –
			see 11.5.5)

Verbs which double a consonant in their present tense singular forms (like *appeler* – *tu appelles*, *jeter* – *tu jettes*) or change a vowel (like *acheter* – *tu achètes*, *espérer* – *tu espères*, *nettoyer* – *tu nettoies*) carry this change over to the imperative: *appelle!*, *jette!*, *nettoie!*, etc. (See Chapter 7.4 for these changes.)

The final *-s* which disappears from the second person singular of verbs ending in *-es* or *-as* reappears when the verb is followed by *y* or *en*:

parle	*speak*	parles-en	*speak about it*
va	*go*	vas-y	*go on*

The equivalent of English constrastive imperatives like 'you go (instead of me)', 'you shut up (instead of me)' are the forms *vous-même, toi-même*: *Allez-y* **vous-même**, *Tais-toi* **toi-même**.

11.5.2 Pronominal verbs in imperatives

Pronominal verbs like *se lever* 'to get up', *se réveiller* 'to wake up', *se servir* 'to help (serve) oneself', *se taire* 'to shut up', etc., drop their subjects in the imperative, but keep their object pronouns:

tu te lèves	→	lève-**toi**	*get up*
vous vous levez		levez-**vous**	*get up*
nous nous levons		levons-**nous**	*let's get up*
tu te sers	→	sers-**toi**	*help yourself*
vous vous servez		servez-**vous**	*help yourself*
nous nous servons		servons-**nous**	*let's help ourselves*

11.5.3 Location and order of pronouns with imperatives

In affirmative imperatives, direct and indirect object pronouns, and the pronouns *y* and *en*, come immediately after the verb which governs them. The pronouns *me* and *te* become the stressed forms *moi* and *toi*. Pronouns are linked to their governing verb in written French by hyphens (see also Chapter 3.2.5):

Prends-**les**	*Take them*
Suivez-**nous**	*Follow us*
Ecoutez-**moi**	*Listen to me*
Tais-**toi**	*Shut up*

NB: Pronouns governed by an infinitive following an imperative are NOT linked to the imperative by a hyphen:

Monte **les** chercher	*Go up and look for them*
	(*les* is the object of *chercher*)
Courez **lui** téléphoner	*Run and phone him*
	(*lui* is the indirect object of *téléphoner*)

When more than one pronoun is present the order is:

verb – direct object – indirect object – *y/en*

moi and *toi* become *m'*, *t'* if they are followed by *y* or *en*:

Donne-**le-moi**	*Give it to me*
Donnez-**le-lui**	*Give it to him*
Donne-**m'en**	*Give me some of it*
Accroche-**t'y**	*Hang on to it*

(See also Chapter 3.2.31.)

In negative imperatives pronouns precede the verb and the order is the same as in simple non-imperative sentences (see Chapter 3.2.5 and 3.2.31):

Ne **me le** donne pas	*Don't give it to me*
Ne **le lui** donnez pas	*Don't give it to him*
Ne **m'en** donne pas	*Don't give me any*
Ne **t'y** accroche pas	*Don't hang on to it*

11.5.4 Compound imperatives

Compound imperatives are formed from the imperative of *avoir* or *être*, as appropriate, and a past participle. They are used to express orders to be fulfilled in the future:

Ayez tapé cette lettre avant la fin de la journée
Type the letter before the end of the day

11.5.5 Toning down imperatives

Orders can be toned down by the use of *veuillez*, which is an equivalent of *s'il vous plaît*:

Asseyez-vous	*Sit down*
Veuillez vous asseoir	*Please sit down*
Asseyez-vous, s'il vous plaît	*Sit down, please*

or by the use of a non-imperative declarative sentence with a future tense:

Vous **fermerez** la porte, s'il vous plaît
Close the door, please

Vous me **donnerez** deux baguettes
Give me two baguettes (French loaves), please

11.5.6 Infinitives used as imperatives

Infinitives can be used in French as imperatives when the addressee is non-specific (e.g. in road signs addressed to all road users, or in instructions addressed to the purchasers of a food product):

Ralentir	*Slow down*
Ouvrir doucement	*Open carefully*

(See also Chapter 12.10.)

11.5.7 Third person imperatives

Third person imperatives which are formed in English by the use of 'let', are formed in French by the use of *que* + a verb in the subjunctive (see 11.4.4):

Qu'il **s'asseye**	*Let him sit down*
Qu'elle **descende** me commander une bière	*Let her go down and order me a beer*
Qu'ils te le **donnent**	*Let them give it to you*

12

The infinitive

12.1 Introduction: what are infinitives?

'Infinitive' means 'not expressing tense'. The infinitive forms of the verb are those like *aller* 'to go', *finir* 'to finish', *descendre* 'to go down', *recevoir* 'to receive'. Whereas in English the infinitive form of the verb is signalled by the presence of 'to': '**to** go', in French the infinitive is signalled by an infinitive ending: all*er*. There are four infinitive endings, and all French verbs take one of these endings in their infinitive form:

-er	e.g. *aimer, placer, arriver, étudier*
-ir	e.g. *finir, courir, venir, dormir*
-re	e.g. *vendre, rire, être, paraître*
-oir(e)	e.g. *s'asseoir, recevoir, avoir, boire, croire*

Most dictionaries, by convention, use the infinitive form of the verb as the headword for the entry for all parts of the verb.

There are FIVE main ways in which infinitives are used in French:

(a) As **complements to other verbs**:

Marie refuse de **sortir**   *Marie refuses to come out*

(b) As **complements to adjectives**:

C'est utile à **savoir**   *It's useful to know*

(c) As **complements to nouns**:

Défense de **fumer**   *No smoking*

(d) As **subordinate infinitive clauses**:

Se détendre le week-end, c'est important pour la santé
To relax at weekends is important for one's health

(e) As **polite commands**:

Ralentir   *Slow down*

Soulever, écarter doucement   *Lift and separate carefully*
(instructions for opening a packet of coffee)

12.2 Infinitives as complements to other verbs

Infinitives may immediately follow other verbs:

> Marie veut **partir**
> *Marie wants to leave*

or they may follow the direct object or the indirect object of another verb:

> Christine a encouragé Jean à **démissionner**
> (follows the direct object)
> *Christine has encouraged Jean to resign*

> Pierre a ordonné à Miguel de **revenir**
> (follows the indirect object)
> *Pierre ordered Miguel to come back*

In such cases it is important to know whether there is a **linking preposition**: ... *a encouragé Jean à démissionner*, ... *a ordonné à Miguel de revenir*, or **no preposition** at all: ... *veut partir*. This is a difficult area for English speakers because in English infinitives are only ever preceded by *to*.

It is not easy to give firm rules because usage is sometimes idiosyncratic. However, rough rules-of-thumb can be given by grouping verbs together into loose meaning classes. Each class tends to select one option or the other – *à*, *de* or no linking preposition – when followed by an infinitive. The classes are listed in the following sections. Within each section verbs are listed **alphabetically**, and at the end of the chapter there is a comprehensive, alphabetically ordered, quick reference **index** to all the verbs taking infinitive complements listed in this chapter. There are special rules dealing with the agreement of the past participle in verb + infinitive constructions. These are dealt with as part of the general treatment of the agreement of the past participle in Chapter 9.3.

12.3 Verbs which take infinitive complements without a linking preposition

12.3.1 'Movement' verbs without objects

Movement verbs which do not have objects typically take infinitive complements without a preceding preposition:

aller dîner quelque part	*to go and have dinner somewhere*
s'en aller vivre ailleurs	*to go and live somewhere else*
arriver réparer la machine à laver	*to come to repair the washing machine*
courir téléphoner à la police	*to run and phone the police*
descendre commander une bière	*to go down and order a beer*
monter chercher ses lunettes	*to go up and look for one's glasses*
partir s'installer à Paris	*to leave to go to live in Paris*
rentrer prendre son maillot de bain	*to go home and get one's swimming costume*
retourner faire des courses	*to go back to do some shopping*
revenir ouvrir les fenêtres	*to come back to open the windows*
sortir acheter un journal	*to go out to buy a newspaper*

The verb *être* in the past tense, with an infinitive complement, is sometimes used to mean 'go': *nous avons été la voir* 'we went to see her'.

12.3.2 'Movement' verbs with objects

Movement verbs with objects typically take infinitive complements without a preceding preposition:

amener un copain dîner chez soi	*to bring a friend home for dinner*
emmener ses enfants jouer au square	*to take one's children to play in the park*
envoyer Marie chercher le docteur	*to send Marie to fetch the doctor*
mener son oncle voir le château	*to take one's uncle to see the castle*

12.3.3 'Modal' verbs

Verbs of 'obligation', 'necessity' and 'possibility' – modal verbs – take infinitive complements without a preceding preposition (see also Chapter 11.2):

devoir parler au directeur	*to have to speak to the director*
oser critiquer son patron	*to dare to criticize one's boss*
pouvoir persuader son oncle	*to be able to persuade one's uncle*
savoir parler italien	*to be able to speak Italian*
vouloir construire un périphérique	*to want to build a ring-road*

12.3.4 Verbs of 'saying'

Verbs of saying typically take infinitive complements without a preceding preposition:

affirmer connaître le patron	*to state that one knows the boss*
confirmer avoir reçu le paquet	*to confirm that one received the package*
déclarer comprendre ce livre	*to declare that one understands this book*
dire s'intéresser à la psychologie	*to say that one is interested in psychology*
nier avoir brisé l'assiette	*to deny having broken the plate*
prétendre être heureux	*to claim to be happy*
reconnaître s'être trompé	*to admit that one was wrong*

dire, with an indirect object, can also be used as a verb of **ordering** (see 12.5.16). In this case it takes an infinitive complement preceded by the preposition *de*: *dire à quelqu'un **de** fermer la porte* 'to tell somebody to close the door'.

12.3.5 Verbs of 'thinking' and 'imagining'

Verbs of thinking and imagining typically take infinitive complements without a preceding preposition:

croire avoir fini	*to believe that one has finished*
estimer pouvoir prendre le train	*to reckon to be able to take the train*
(s')imaginer avoir gagné la partie	*to imagine having won the match*
penser rencontrer un ami	*to think one might meet a friend*
se rappeler avoir visité l'abbaye	*to remember having visited the abbey*

But *se souvenir* 'to remember' takes infinitive complements with the preposition *de*: *se souvenir **d**'avoir visité l'abbaye*.

12.3.6 Verbs expressing 'personal attitude' to something

Verbs which express 'liking', 'wishing' or 'inclination' typically take infinitive complements without a preceding preposition:

adorer dîner au restaurant	*to love eating out*
aimer travailler le soir	*to like to work in the evenings*
aimer autant rester chez soi	*to just as soon stay at home*
aimer mieux éviter les embouteillages	*to prefer to avoid traffic jams*
compter commencer bientôt	*to count on starting soon*
daigner donner son opinion	*to deign to give one's opinion*
désirer dormir un peu	*to want to sleep a little*
entendre être obéi	*to mean to be obeyed*
espérer partir en vacances	*to hope to go on holiday*
préférer manger seul	*to prefer to eat alone*
souhaiter faire la connaissance de quelqu'un	*to wish to make somebody's acquaintance*

aimer can sometimes be found with an infinitive complement preceded by *à*: *aimer à travailler le soir*.

12.3.7 Seem

sembler 'to seem', and verbs with similar meaning to *sembler* take infinitive complements without a preceding preposition:

s'avérer être efficace	*to turn out to be effective*
paraître dire la vérité	*to appear to be telling the truth*
se révéler avoir des conséquences inattendues	*to turn out to have unexpected consequences*
sembler préférer les légumes	*to seem to prefer vegetables*

12.3.8 'Perception' verbs

Verbs expressing the manner in which an event is perceived take infinitive complements without a preceding preposition:

écouter les enfants réciter une poésie	*to listen to the children reciting a poem*
entendre l'horloge sonner trois heures	*to hear the clock strike three o'clock*
regarder le chien manger	*to watch the dog eating*
sentir ses pieds s'enfoncer dans la boue	*to feel one's feet sink into the mud*
voir Paul partir	*to see Paul leave*

12.3.9 *faire* and *laisser*

The verbs *faire* and *laisser* take infinitive complements without a preceding preposition:

faire travailler Pierre	*to make Pierre work*
faire payer les gens	*to make people pay*
laisser Pierre travailler	*to let Pierre work*
laisser travailler Pierre	*to let Pierre work*
laisser tomber le football pour le rugby	*to drop football and take up rugby instead*

(For the placement of object pronouns in these constructions see Chapter 3.2.32.)

It is possible, but not necessary, to delete *se* in the verbs *se taire* 'to be quiet' and *s'asseoir* 'to sit down' when they follow *faire* (and sometimes also *laisser*):

> Il a fait (se) taire les enfants
> *He made the children be quiet*

> Elle a fait (s')asseoir tout le monde
> *She got everyone to sit down*

12.4 Verbs which take infinitive complements preceded by the preposition *à*

12.4.1 Verbs of 'beginning' and 'continuing'

Verbs which signal the beginning or continuation of an action typically take an infinitive complement preceded by *à*:

se mettre à rédiger un rapport	*to start to draft a report*
persister à demander une réponse	*to persist in asking for a reply*

Commencer and *continuer* are verbs which take an infinitive complement preceded interchangeably by *à* or by *de*:

commencer à/d'écrire ses mémoires	*to begin to write one's memoirs*
continuer à/de faire des efforts	*to continue to make an effort*

The following verbs can take infinitive complements preceded by *par*:

commencer par enlever le papier peint	*to begin by removing the wallpaper*
finir par vendre sa maison	*to finish by selling one's house*

These are nearly always rendered in English by a construction involving 'by + verb + ing', and contrast with the use of the same verbs with infinitives preceded by *à* or *de*:

commencer à/d'enlever le papier peint	*to begin to remove the wallpaper*
finir de tondre le gazon	*to finish mowing the lawn*

12.4.2 Verbs expressing 'manner'

Verbs which express the manner in which an action is conducted typically take an infinitive complement preceded by *à*:

s'abaisser jusqu'à demander de l'argent à ses proches	*to stoop to asking one's family and friends for money*
s'appliquer à apprendre le russe	*to apply oneself to learning Russian*
s'apprêter à parler	*to get ready to speak*
s'attarder à bavarder dans le restaurant	*to linger chatting in the restaurant*
se borner à considérer les points principaux	*to limit oneself to considering the main points*
concourir à assurer la défaite de l'ennemi	*to combine to defeat the enemy*
condescendre à faire quelque chose	*to condescend to do something*
conspirer à produire une catastrophe	*to conspire to produce a catastrophe*
s'entêter à découvrir la vérité	*to be bent on discovering the truth*
se limiter à corriger les plus grosses erreurs	*to limit oneself to correcting the worst errors*
s'obstiner à découvrir la vérité	*to be bent on discovering the truth*

s'oublier à lire un roman	*to become absorbed in reading a novel*
s'en tenir à changer quelques détails	*to stick to changing a few details*
travailler à se faire aimer	*to work to get oneself liked*

12.4.3 Pronominal verbs expressing an 'emotional reaction'

Pronominal verbs which express a subject's emotional reaction to an event typically take an infinitive complement preceded by *à*:

s'abêtir à trop travailler	*to become stupid by working too hard*
s'abrutir à regarder la télévision	*to become stupefied from watching television*
s'affoler à imaginer le pire	*to panic imagining the worst*
s'amuser à mettre le professeur en colère	*to have fun making the teacher angry*
se délecter à visiter Bruges	*to take delight in visiting Bruges*
s'énerver à rattacher constamment ses lacets	*to get annoyed constantly retying one's laces*
s'ennuyer à faire un travail monotone	*to get bored doing a monotonous job*
s'irriter à expliquer qc	*to get more and more annoyed as one tries to explain sth*
se plaire à tout critiquer	*to take pleasure in criticizing everything*

Exceptions:

s'étonner d'être si calme	*to be surprised to be so calm*
s'inquiéter de trouver la route bloquée	*to worry about finding the road blocked*
s'irriter d'avoir à expliquer chaque point 3 fois	*to be annoyed by having to explain each point three times*
se réjouir de/à écrire des contes pour enfants	*to take real pleasure in writing children's stories*

12.4.4 Pronominal verbs of 'effort'

Pronominal verbs which express the effort with which an action is undertaken typically take an infinitive complement preceded by *à*:

s'acharner à trouver une solution	*to be bent on finding a solution*
s'égosiller à appeler les enfants	*to go hoarse calling the children*
s'épuiser à travailler	*to exhaust oneself working*
s'éreinter à traîner une valise	*to tire oneself out dragging a suitcase along*
s'essoufler à monter la côte	*to get out of breath climbing the hill*
s'évertuer à conclure l'affaire	*to do one's utmost to close the deal*
se fatiguer à répéter l'avertissement	*to tire oneself out repeating the warning*
se tuer à le dire	*to be sick and tired of saying it*
s'user à repeindre la maison	*to wear oneself out repainting the house*

12.4.5 Pronominal verbs expressing 'dedication'

Pronominal verbs which express the dedication with which an action is undertaken typically take an infinitive complement preceded by *à*:

s'attacher à traduire la pensée du maître	*to be careful to convey the master's thoughts*
s'aventurer à faire des suggestions	*to be so bold as to make suggestions*
se décider à prendre sa retraite	*to persuade oneself to retire*
s'essayer à gérer un restaurant	*to try one's hand at running a restaurant*
se hasarder à faire une course en montagne	*to venture to go up a mountain*
se résigner à tout perdre	*to resign oneself to losing everything*
se résoudre à changer d'emploi	*to come to terms with having to change jobs*
se risquer à jouer en Bourse	*to take risks by playing the Stock Exchange*

Note the following differences in meaning when some of these verbs are used with *à* and with *de*:

se décider à prendre sa retraite	*to persuade oneself to retire*
décider de prendre sa retraite	*to decide to retire*
s'essayer à gérer un restaurant	*to try one's hand at running a restaurant*
essayer de gérer un restaurant	*to try to run a restaurant*
se risquer à investir à l'étranger	*to take risks by investing abroad*
risquer de tout perdre	*to risk losing everything*
se résoudre à changer d'emploi	*to accept having to change jobs*
résoudre de changer d'emploi	*to resolve to change jobs*

12.4.6 Verbs expressing 'aspiration' and 'success'

Verbs which express the aspiration to do something, or success in achieving it, typically take an infinitive complement preceded by *à*:

arriver à obtenir gain de cause	*to manage to get one's way*
aspirer à dominer sa peur	*to aspire to overcome fear*
chercher à faire fortune	*to seek to make one's fortune*
être disposé à favoriser qn	*to be inclined to favour sb*
incliner à quitter son emploi	*to be inclined to give up one's job*
parvenir à battre un adversaire	*to succeed in beating one's opponent*
réussir à gagner la course	*to succeed in winning the race*
tendre à éviter les problèmes	*to have a tendency to avoid problems*
tenir à lire un livre	*to be bent on reading a book*
viser à remporter la victoire	*to aim to be victorious*

12.4.7 Verbs expressing 'unwillingness'

Verbs which express an unwillingness to do something typically take an infinitive complement preceded by *à*:

hésiter à critiquer qn	*to hesitate to criticize sb*
rechigner à vendre ses livres	*to baulk at selling one's books*
renoncer à tout relire	*to give up on the idea of re-reading everything*
répugner à tout faire soi-même	*to be very reluctant to do the work oneself*

12.4.8 Verbs of 'forcing'

Verbs which express the pressure put on someone to do something typically take an infinitive complement preceded by *à*:

condamner qn à vivre sans ressources	*to condemn sb to live in poverty*
contraindre Julie à revenir	*to force Julie to come back*
forcer une entreprise à baisser ses prix	*to make a company reduce its prices*
obliger Pierre à partir	*to make Pierre leave*

Note that the following verbs, when used in the passive, take an infinitive complement preceded by *de*:

être contraint de démissionner	*to be obliged to resign*
être forcé de rentrer	*to have to go home*
être obligé de travailler à l'étranger	*to be forced to work abroad*

12.4.9 Verbs of 'inviting'

Verbs which invite someone to do something typically take an infinitive complement preceded by *à*:

appeler un tiers à arbitrer	*to call on a third party to arbitrate*
assigner le témoin à comparaître	*to call on the witness to appear*
autoriser les clients à s'en servir	*to authorize the clients to make use of it*
inviter Robert à donner son avis	*to invite Robert to give his opinion*

12.4.10 Verbs of 'training' and 'teaching'

Verbs which train or teach someone to do something typically take an infinitive complement preceded by *à*:

accoutumer un malade à prendre moins de calmants	*to get a sick person used to taking fewer painkillers*
apprendre à ses élèves à parler italien	*to teach one's pupils to speak Italian*
dresser un chien à aller chercher le journal	*to train a dog to fetch the newspaper*
enseigner à Jacques à jouer au tennis	*to teach Jacques to play tennis*
habituer un citadin à travailler en plein air	*to get a town-dweller used to working in the open air*
préparer quelqu'un à traverser une période de chômage	*to prepare somebody for a period of unemployment*

Note that *apprendre, enseigner* are the only two verbs in French which take both an indirect object preceded by *à* and an infinitive preceded by *à*:

apprendre à quelqu'un à faire quelque chose	*to teach somebody to do something*
enseigner à quelqu'un à faire quelque chose	*to teach somebody to do something*

Verbs which English speakers often think have indirect objects, but which in fact have direct objects, are:

aider quelqu'un à faire quelque chose	*to help somebody to do something*
inviter quelqu'un à faire quelque chose	*to invite somebody to do something*
obliger quelqu'un à faire quelque chose	*to make somebody do something*

12.4.11 Verbs of 'encouragement' and 'cajoling'

Verbs which encourage or cajole someone to do something typically take an infinitive complement preceded by *à*:

amener Jean à reparler de l'accident
to bring Jean to talk about the accident again

conduire quelqu'un **à** se repentir
to bring somebody to repent

convier son frère **à** réfléchir
to suggest that somebody's brother should think something over

décider quelqu'un **à** changer de cap
to make somebody decide to change direction

déterminer quelqu'un **à** s'inscrire à l'université
to make somebody decide to go to university

encourager sa secrétaire **à** chercher un nouvel emploi
to encourage one's secretary to find another job

engager quelqu'un **à** repenser un projet
to bring somebody to reconsider a plan

entraîner des adolescents **à** voler des voitures
to encourage youngsters to steal cars

exhorter quelqu'un **à** mener campagne
to exhort somebody to campaign

inciter le gouvernement **à** agir
to incite the government to act

pousser Claudine **à** se marier
to push Claudine into getting married

Note also the following contrasts involving *décider*:

décider quelqu'un **à** partir	*to bring somebody to leave*
décider de partir	*to decide to leave*
se décider à partir	*to decide to leave* (after much thought)

12.4.12 Verbs expressing 'the dedication of time, money to doing something'

consacrer ses loisirs **à** faire des croquis	*to spend one's free time making sketches*
dépenser de l'argent **à** réparer sa voiture	*to spend money repairing one's car*
mettre deux heures **à** ranger ses affaires	*to take two hours to tidy one's things*
occuper son temps **à** lire des romans policiers	*to spend one's time reading crime novels*
passer son temps **à** faire des mots croisés	*to spend one's time doing crosswords*
utiliser ses connaissances **à** améliorer le sort de ses semblables	*to use one's knowledge to improve the lot of one's fellow beings*

12.4.13 Verbs of 'discovering'

attraper qn **à** pêcher sans permis	*to catch sb fishing without a licence*
prendre qn **à** fouiller dans un tiroir	*to catch sb going through a drawer*
surprendre qn **à** voler des livres	*to catch sb stealing books*

12.5 Verbs which take an infinitive complement preceded by *de*

There is no real community of meaning in the verbs which take an infinitive complement preceded by *de* but some grouping by meaning is possible.

12.5.1 Verbs of 'advising somebody to do or not to do something'

avertir qn **de** ne pas recommencer
to warn sb not to do it again

conjurer qn **de** laisser les choses comme elles sont
to plead with sb to leave things as they are

conseiller (à qn) **de** ne pas intenter de procès
to advise sb not to bring something to court

convaincre son employeur **de** hausser les salaires
to convince one's employer to raise salaries

déconseiller (à qn) **de** prendre l'autoroute
to advise sb not to take the motorway

désaccoutumer qn **de** fumer
to encourage sb to lose the habit of smoking

déshabituer qn **de** s'endormir en écoutant la radio
to get sb out of the habit of going to sleep whilst listening to the radio

dissuader qn **de** manifester dans la rue
to persuade sb not to demonstrate in the street

enjoindre à qn **de** s'inscrire à un parti politique
to suggest to sb that they join a political party

persuader qn **de** vendre sa maison
to persuade sb to sell his/her/their house

recommander (à qn) **de** ne pas trop insister
to suggest to sb not to insist too much

suggérer à qn **de** téléphoner
to suggest to sb that they telephone

Note that while *décourager* takes an infinitive complement preceded by *de*, *encourager* takes an infinitive complement preceded by *à*:

encourager sa secrétaire **à** démissionner
to encourage one's secretary to resign

12.5.2 Verbs of 'allowing', 'admitting' and 'agreeing'

accepter de sortir les poubelles	*to agree to put the dustbins out*
choisir de poursuivre ses études à Paris	*to choose to pursue one's studies in Paris*
convenir de retrouver qn à 20h	*to agree to meet up with sb at 8.00 p.m.*
décider de prendre sa retraite	*to decide to retire*
dispenser un étudiant **de** faire un test	*to exempt a student from a test*

entreprendre de rétablir des liens	*to undertake to re-establish links*
jurer à son père **de** lui rendre visite	*to swear to one's father to visit him*
obtenir de pouvoir sortir tôt	*to get permission to go out early*
permettre (à qn) **de** rembourser sans payer les intérêts	*to allow somebody to pay back without interest*
résoudre de ne plus boire de café	*to resolve to drink no more coffee*

12.5.3 Verbs expressing the idea of 'anger'

enrager d'avoir perdu son argent
to be very angry about having lost one's money

être furieux d'être exclu du groupe
to be furious at being excluded from the group

s'indigner de se voir refuser l'entrée du club
to be indignant at being refused entry to the club

menacer les grévistes **de** les licencier
to threaten the strikers with being sacked

12.5.4 Verbs of 'asking for' and of 'attempting to'

demander à Pierre **de** surveiller les enfants	*to ask Pierre to keep an eye on the children*
essayer de chanter une chanson	*to try to sing a song*
implorer qn **de** revenir	*to implore sb to come back*
parler de faire le tour du monde	*to speak of doing a world tour*
prier qn **de** bien vouloir partir	*to ask sb to kindly leave*
proposer à une municipalité **de** construire un théâtre	*to put to a town hall the idea of building a theatre*
supplier qn **de** faire attention	*to beg sb to be careful*
tâcher de terminer le travail à temps	*to try to finish the work on time*
tenter de résoudre le problème sans avoir recours à l'extérieur	*to attempt to resolve the problem without asking for outside help*

Note: *demander à qn de faire qc* 'to ask somebody to do something', but *demander à faire qc* 'to ask to do something'.

12.5.5 Verbs of 'blaming', 'making responsible for'

accuser qn **d'**avoir collaboré avec l'ennemi
to accuse sb of having collaborated with the enemy

blâmer qn **d'**avoir été négligent
to blame sb for having been careless

charger qn **d'**apporter à manger tous les jours
to make sb responsible for bringing in food every day

gronder son fils **d'**avoir perdu les clefs de la voiture
to tell your son off for having lost the car keys

reprocher à qn **d'**avoir perdu les clefs
to hold it against sb that they lost the keys

soupçonner qn **d'**avoir dissimulé la vérité
to suspect sb of not having told the truth

12.5.6 Verbs of '(self-)congratulation'

s'applaudir d'avoir écrit au président
to be pleased with oneself for having written to the president

féliciter qn **d'**avoir terminé sa thèse
to congratulate sb on finishing their thesis

se flatter d'être le meilleur joueur
to imagine that one is the best player

se glorifier d'avoir monté l'équipe tout seul
to be very proud of having put together the team unaided

louer qn **d'**avoir gagné une course
to praise sb for having won a race

mériter de gagner
to deserve to win

se vanter d'être le meilleur joueur de l'équipe
to boast of being the best player in the team

12.5.7 Verbs of 'denial'

s'abstenir de boire du vin	*to abstain from drinking wine*
se disculper d'avoir voulu supplanter qn	*to exonerate oneself from having wanted to take over from sb*
refuser de s'abaisser à un compromis	*to refuse to stoop to a compromise*

Exception: *nier* takes an infinitive complement without a linking preposition:

nier être impliqué dans l'affaire	*to deny being implicated in the affair*

12.5.8 Verbs of 'excusing' and 'pardoning'

excuser qn **d'**être arrivé en retard
to overlook sb's late arrival

pardonner (à qn) **d'**avoir fait souffrir la famille
to pardon sb for having caused the family pain

12.5.9 Verbs of 'forbidding'

défendre à qn **d'**afficher des avis au mur
to forbid sb to stick up notices on the wall

interdire (à qn**) de** coller des affiches
to prohibit bill posting

12.5.10 Verbs of 'being fearful'

appréhender de devoir se présenter devant un tribunal
to be fearful of having to appear before a court

avoir peur de conduire
to be afraid to drive

craindre de devoir partir à l'étranger
to be afraid of having to go abroad

frémir de penser à ce qui aurait pu arriver
to shudder to think what might have happened

s'inquiéter d'avoir à rentrer
to worry about having to go home

pâlir de voir un collègue promu avant soi
to blanch at seeing a colleague promoted before oneself

redouter de devoir rembourser les billets
to fear having to reimburse the tickets

se soucier de créer une bonne impression
to care about making a good impression

trembler de penser qu'on a failli se faire écraser
to tremble to think that one nearly got run over

12.5.11 Verbs of 'forgetting'

négliger de fermer la porte à clé
to neglect to lock the door

omettre de préciser à son hôte qu'on arrivera en retard
to forget to tell one's host that one will be late

oublier de signaler une absence
to forget to report an absence

12.5.12 Verbs of 'hurrying' or 'delaying'

se dépêcher d'aller chez le boulanger avant la fermeture
to hurry to get to the baker's before it shuts

se hâter de mettre en œuvre ses propres idées
to want to quickly put one's own ideas into operation

12.5.13 Verbs of 'delighting' or 'regretting'

avoir regret de ne pas avoir vu qn avant sa mort
to regret not having seen sb before he died

regretter d'avoir choisi la solution de facilité
to regret having chosen the easy way out

se réjouir d'avoir été élu
to be delighted at having been elected

se repentir d'avoir commis une erreur
to regret having made a mistake

12.5.14 Verbs of 'pretending'

affecter de ne pas être au courant de ce qui se passe
to pretend not to know what's happening

faire semblant de ne pas avoir entendu
to pretend not to have heard

feindre d'être malade
to pretend to be ill

12.5.15 Verbs of 'pre-planning'

envisager de vivre sur une île déserte	*to imagine living on a desert island*
méditer de changer de métier	*to think about changing jobs*
préméditer de quitter sa femme	*to plan on leaving one's wife*
projeter de quitter le pays	*to think about leaving the country*
proposer de partir tout seul dans le Midi	*to propose going to the south of France on one's own*
ruminer d'écrire ses mémoires	*to have it in mind to write one's memoirs*

12.5.16 Verbs of 'ordering'

chuchoter à qn **de** fermer la porte	*to whisper to sb to close the door*
commander à un bataillon **de** se préparer	*to order a batallion to get ready*
dire à Pierre **de** rejoindre la compagnie	*to tell Pierre to rejoin the company*
écrire à Marie **d'**aller voir sa mère	*to write to Marie to go and see her mother*
hurler à qn **de** passer le ballon	*to shout to sb to pass the ball*
ordonner à qn **de** quitter les lieux	*to order sb to leave the premises*
prescrire à qn **de** se reposer	*to order sb to rest*
répondre à qn **de** se taire	*to tell sb in response to be quiet*
sommer qn **de** venir aussi vite que possible	*to instruct sb to come as quickly as possible*
téléphoner à sa mère **d'**envoyer de l'argent	*to phone one's mother to send money*

12.5.17 Verbs of 'finishing' and of 'stopping somebody doing something'

s'abstenir de fumer pendant trois mois	*to refrain from smoking for three months*
achever de construire sa maison	*to finish building one's house*
arrêter de faire l'idiot en cours	*to stop playing the fool in class*
cesser de participer aux matchs de football	*to stop taking part in football matches*
empêcher qn **de** partir en vacances	*to stop sb going on holiday*
éviter de faire les mêmes erreurs	*to avoid making the same mistakes*
finir de se préparer	*to finish getting ready*

12.5.18 Verbs of 'thanking'

remercier qn **de** vous avoir invité à manger
to thank sb for having invited you for a meal

savoir gré à qn **de** bien vouloir répondre rapidement
to be grateful to sb for replying quickly

12.5.19 Impersonal verbs expressing 'personal reaction' to an event

Compare some of the the impersonal verbs below, which take *de*, with the same verbs used personally, which take *à* (see 12.4.3):

Ça m'**agace de** les voir sans occupation	*It annoys me to see them idle*
Ça m'**amuse de** le voir en colère	*It amuses me to see him angry*
Ça l'**attriste d'**apprendre qu'elle est malheureuse	*It saddens him to learn that she is unhappy*
Ça me **consterne de** l'apprendre	*It dismays me to learn that*
Ça me **dégoûte de** voir ce gaspillage	*It appals me to see this waste*

Ça m'**ennuie d'**être suivi par des journalistes   *I find it wearing to be followed by reporters*

Ça la **fâche d'**avoir à se justifer auprès de toi   *It irritates her to have to justify herself to you*

Ça les **fatigue de** faire la navette   *It tires them to commute*

Ça l'**intéresse de** voir le manuscrit   *It interests him to see the manuscript*

Ça l'**intrigue de** savoir ce qu'ils ont dit   *It intrigues him to know what they said*

Ça nous **irrite d'**avoir à refaire le travail   *It irritates us to have to do the work again*

12.5.20 Other verbs with infinitive complements preceded by *de*

s'affliger d'avoir causé de la peine à qn
to be sorry to have caused sb pain

ambitionner de paraître dans un film
to have ambitions to appear in a film

avoir droit de donner son avis
to have the right to give one's opinion

en avoir marre de tout faire à la maison
to be fed up with doing everything in the house

brûler de jouer dans l'équipe du collège
to have a great desire to play in the school team

comploter de renverser le gouvernement
to plot to overthrow the government

consoler qn **d'**avoir perdu un parent
to console sb for having lost a relative

se contenter de vivre à la campagne
to be happy to live in the country

dédaigner d'accorder un entretien à un journaliste
to be snooty about giving an interview to a journalist

défier qn **de** dire la vérité
to challenge sb to tell the truth

dégoûter qn **de** manger des fraises
to put sb off eating strawberries

désespérer de pouvoir sortir de prison
to despair of getting out of prison

douter de pouvoir faire qc
to doubt that one will be able to do sth

s'efforcer de manger du chou
to force oneself to eat cabbage

entreprendre de récupérer l'argent perdu
to undertake to get back the money

envier qn **d'**avoir démissionné
to envy sb for having resigned

être tenu de remplir ses obligations
to be obliged to meet one's obligations

se garder de raconter la vérité
to make sure not to tell the truth

gémir d'avoir à payer ses dettes
to groan at having to pay one's debts

se mêler de monter une affaire
to take it upon oneself to start a business

offrir de dédommager les victimes
to offer to recompense the victims

plaindre qn **de** ne pas avoir d'enfants
to pity sb because they don't have children

presser qn **de** s'acquitter de ses dettes
to put pressure on sb to pay off their debts

prévoir de gagner beaucoup d'argent
to foresee making lots of money

promettre d'emmener toute la famille aux Etats Unis
to promise to take the whole family to the United States

réclamer de pouvoir s'asseoir où on veut
to demand to be allowed to sit where one wishes

se remettre d'avoir été attaqué dans la rue
to recover from having been attacked in the street

se réserver de déterminer soi-même le jour de sa mort
to reserve the right to decide for oneself the day of one's death

rêver de devenir milliardaire
to dream of becoming a millionaire

rougir de devoir parler en public
to blush at having to speak in public

sourire de voir les enfants s'amuser dans le jardin
to smile at seeing the children playing in the garden

12.6 Omission of objects before infinitives

The direct or indirect objects of verbs with infinitive complements may be omitted in French when they have a non-specific or indefinite interpretation:

Le succès encourage ___ à continuer
Success encourages one to continue

Ce résultat force ___ à repenser le problème
This result forces us to rethink the problem

Dans cette région, c'est l'irrigation qui a permis ___ d'améliorer le rendement
agricole
The irrigation of the region has allowed farmers to improve crop yield

L'expérience enseigne ___ à être prudent
Experience teaches one to be careful

Cette déclaration autorise ___ à penser que les dirigeants ont changé d'avis
This declaration allows us to think that the leaders have changed their opinion

12.7 Infinitives as complements to adjectives

Adjectives take infinitive complements preceded either by *à* or *de*, never without a preposition.

12.7.1 Infinitives following adjectives in impersonal constructions

Adjectives used in impersonal constructions take an infinitive complement preceded by *de*:

Dans ce quartier il est dangereux **de** sortir le soir
In this part of the town it is dangerous to go out in the evening

Il ne sera pas évident **de** récupérer les papiers volés
It won't be easy to get the stolen papers back

Il serait étonnant **de** trouver Jules dans une boîte de nuit
It would be surprising to come across Jules in a night club

Il est nécessaire **de** demander des explications précises
It is necessary to ask for precise explanations

Il est rare **de** voir Jean-Marie jouer au rugby
It is rare to see Jean-Marie play rugby

Il est regrettable **de** ne pas avoir de recours contre la pollution par le bruit
It is unfortunate that there is no redress against noise pollution

Other common adjectives which can be used impersonally in this way are:

agréable **de** faire qc	*pleasant to do sth*
bon **de** faire qc	*good to do sth*
commode **de** faire qc	*convenient to do sth*
difficile **de** faire qc	*difficult to do sth*
facile **de** faire qc	*easy to do sth*
important **de** faire qc	*important to do sth*
(im)possible **de** faire qc	*(im)possible to do sth*
intéressant **de** faire qc	*interesting to do sth*
inutile **de** faire qc	*useless to do sth*
mauvais **de** faire qc	*bad to do sth*
merveilleux **de** faire qc	*amazing to do sth*
pénible **de** faire qc	*irksome to do sth*
simple **de** faire qc	*simple to do sth*
utile **de** faire qc	*useless to do sth*

12.7.2 Infinitives following adjectives used personally

When the adjectives in 12.7.1 are used personally (that is to describe a noun or personal pronoun) they take an infinitive complement preceded by *à*. Compare the personal and impersonal constructions in the following:

La pâte à pain est agréable **à** toucher
Dough is nice to handle

Il est agréable **de** toucher de la pâte à pain
It's nice to handle dough

Le foie de veau est bon **à** manger
Calf's liver is good to eat

Il est bon **de** manger du foie de veau
It's good to eat calf's liver

C'est difficile **à** faire
That's difficult to do

Il est difficile **de** le faire
It's difficult to do that

Cette voiture va être difficile **à** vendre
This car will be difficult to sell

Il va être difficile **de** vendre cette voiture
It will be difficult to sell this car

Avec tout ce que tu as mis dedans, les poubelles sont difficiles **à** sortir
With all that you've put in them, the dustbins are difficult to put out

Il est difficile **de** sortir les poubelles, avec tout ce que tu as mis dedans
It's difficult to put out the dustbins with all that you have put in them

Ces problèmes sont faciles **à** résoudre
These problems are easy to solve

Il est facile **de** résoudre ces problèmes
It is easy to solve these problems

Cette machine à laver est impossible **à** réparer
This washing machine is impossible to repair

Il est impossible **de** réparer cette machine à laver
It is impossible to repair this washing machine

La défaite est difficile **à** accepter
Defeat is hard to accept

Il est difficile **d'**accepter la défaite
It is hard to accept defeat

Since the pronouns *il* and *ce* can be used both impersonally and personally, this means that alternations like the following can be found:

Il est difficile **de** comprendre Pierre
It is difficult to understand Pierre

Il (i.e. Pierre) est difficile **à** comprendre
He is difficult to understand

C'est beau **de** voir tous ces enfants jouer ensemble
It's wonderful to see all these children playing together

C'est beau **à** voir
It's wonderful to see

(See also Chapter 3.1.22 for discussion of this construction.)

12.7.3 Infinitives following adjectives of 'manner' take *à*

Adjectives which describe the manner in which an action is carried out typically take an infinitive complement preceded by *à*:

Nous sommes prêts **à** accepter votre proposition
We are ready to accept your proposal

Vu ses qualifications il est propre **à** assumer ces fonctions
With his qualifications he is suitable for the job

Other common adjectives which behave in this way are:

être disposé/enclin/porté **à** faire qc	*to be inclined to do sth*
être habile **à** faire qc	*to be skilful in doing sth*
être prompt **à** faire qc	*to be prompt in doing sth*
être seul **à** faire qc	*to be alone in doing sth*

12.7.4 Infinitives following adjectives which take *de*

Most other adjectives which take an infinitive complement select the preposition *de*:

Nous sommes très heureux **d'**apprendre votre mariage
We are very happy to hear the news of your wedding

Nous vous sommes tous reconnaissants **d'**avoir bien voulu participer à nos activités
We are all grateful to you for having kindly agreed to take part in our activities

Vous êtes libre **d'**essayer	*You are free to try*
(but Libre à vous **d'**essayer	*Up to you to try)*

Other common adjectives which take *de*:

certain/sûr **de** faire qc	*sure to do sth*
content **de** faire qc	*pleased to do sth*
désireux **de** faire qc	*keen to do sth*
désolé **de** faire qc	*sorry to do sth*
étonné **de** faire qc	*astonished to do sth*
fier **de** faire qc	*proud to do sth*
impatient **de** faire qc	*impatient to do sth*
(in)capable **de** faire qc	*(in)capable of doing sth*
susceptible **de** faire qc	*likely to do sth*

12.8 Infinitives as complements to nouns

Nouns take infinitive complements preceded either by *à* or by *de*, never without a preposition.

12.8.1 Infinitives following nouns related to verbs and adjectives

Nouns related to verbs and adjectives which take an infinitive complement preceded by *à* or *de* typically take the same preposition:

inviter qn **à** faire qc	l'invitation **à** faire qc
disposé **à** faire qc	la disposition **à** faire qc
craindre **de** faire qc	la crainte **de** faire qc

défendre à qn de fumer	Défense **de** fumer
interdire à qn **de** faire qc	Interdiction **de** pénétrer en ces lieux
menacer qn **de** faire qc	la menace **de** faire qc
ordonner à qn **de** faire qc	l'ordre **de** faire qc
permettre à qn **de** faire qc	la permission **de** faire qc
désireux **de** faire qc	le désir **de** faire qc
impatient **de** faire qc	l'impatience **de** faire qc

12.8.2 Infinitives following nouns involved in the event described by an infinitive take *à*

Nouns which are understood as being involved in the event described by the infinitive (as subject, direct object, indirect object, instrument, or time when the event takes place) typically take an infinitive preceded by *à*:

une maison **à** rénover
('maison' is understood as the object of 'rénover')
a house to renovate

C'était un soir **à** se promener sur la plage
('soir' is understood as the time when walking takes place)
It was an evening for walking on the beach

Other common examples:

un appartement **à** louer	*an apartment to rent*
du bois **à** brûler	*firewood*
une chambre **à** coucher	*a bedroom*
un exemple **à** ne pas suivre	*an example not to be followed*
un fer **à** repasser	*an iron*
un homme **à** craindre	*a man to be feared*
une idée **à** examiner	*an idea to explore*
une maison à vendre	*a house for sale*
un pays **à** voir l'hiver	*a country to see in winter*
une poêle **à** frire	*a frying pan*
une pomme **à** cuire	*a cooking apple*
des repas **à** emporter	*take-away meals*
un roman **à** lire	*a novel to read*
une salle **à** manger	*a dining room*

12.8.3 Some common idioms in which the preposition is *à*

avoir intérêt **à** faire qc	*to have a stake in doing sth*
avoir du mal **à** faire qc	*to experience some difficulty in doing sth*
avoir plaisir **à** faire qc	*to take pleasure in doing sth*
être d'âge **à** faire qc	*to be old enough to do sth*
Nous sommes cinq **à** faire qc	*There are five of us doing sth*
être le dernier **à** faire qc	*to be the last to do sth*
être d'humeur **à** faire qc	*to be in a mood for doing sth*
être le premier **à** faire qc	*to be the first to do sth*
être le seul **à** faire qc	*to be the only one to do sth*
prendre plaisir **à** faire qc	*to take pleasure in doing sth*

12.8.4 Most other nouns take the preposition *de*

avoir l'air/l'apparence **de** faire qc	*to appear to be doing sth*
avoir besoin **de** faire qc	*to need to do sth*
avoir de la chance **de** faire qc	*to be lucky to do sth*
avoir le droit **de** faire qc	*to have the right to do sth*
avoir envie **de** faire qc	*to want to do sth*
avoir hâte **de** faire qc	*to be quick to do sth*
avoir honte **de** faire qc	*to be ashamed to do sth*
avoir raison **de** faire qc	*to be right to do sth*
avoir tort **de** faire qc	*to be wrong to do sth*
avoir le toupet/le culot **de** faire qc	*to have the cheek to do sth*
avoir la veine **de** faire qc	*to be lucky to do sth*
la façon/la manière **de** faire qc	*the manner of doing sth*
le moment **de** faire qc	*the moment to do sth*
les moyens **de** faire qc	*the means to do sth*
l'occasion **de** faire qc	*the opportunity to do sth*
le temps **de** faire qc	*the time to do sth*

12.9 Infinitives in subordinate clauses

Infinitives in subordinate clauses may play the role of subjects or objects. The examples we have quoted extensively above where infinitives follow the verb and/or are introduced by *à* and *de* mainly show infinitive clauses playing the role of objects in the sentence. They can also be subjects.

In some cases they are linked to the main clause by the use of *c'est*, in other cases they directly precede the main verb. In many cases both *c'est* and *est* are possible with minimal stylistic difference. *Voici* and *voilà* may also play a linking role:

Partir c'est mourir un peu
To leave is to die a little

Se cacher la vérité, **c'est** remettre le problème à plus tard
Hiding the truth from oneself is putting the problem off until later

Mettre les hommes politiques devant les réalités, **voilà** le problème
Getting politicians to face up to reality, that's where the problem is

S'accorder sur l'essentiel, **voilà** ce qu'on doit faire
What we must do is agree on the basics

Pleurer ne sert à rien
Crying won't get us anywhere

Se fâcher dans cette situation ne fera qu'aggraver les choses
In this situation getting angry will make matters worse

Manger trop de fraises peut rendre malade
Eating too many strawberries could make you ill

Courir chercher un médecin était la seule chose à faire
To run to get a doctor was the only thing to do

Habiter Paris est très agréable
Living in Paris is very pleasant

Jouer Molière était sa plus chère ambition
Acting in a play by Molière was his most cherished hope

Se détendre le weekend, **c'est** important pour la santé
For health reasons it is important to relax at weekends

12.10 Infinitives as polite commands

In certain cases, instructions are conveyed by means of infinitives rather than
the more forceful imperatives. This is particularly the case where the audience
is non-specific, as in road-users, consumers or students taking exams:

Ralentir: Enfants (or Attention: Ecole)   *Slow down. School*

Soulever, écarter doucement   *Lift and separate carefully*
(instructions for opening a packet
of coffee)

Ecrire les réponses au verso   *Write the answers on the back of this*
page

Ne **répondre** qu'à l'une des questions   *Answer only one question in this*
de la section ci-dessous   *section*

Ouvrir doucement   *Be careful when opening*
Ne pas **renverser**   *Don't spill*
Ne pas **retourner**   *Don't turn over*
A **manier** avec précaution   *Be careful when handling*
Remettre entre les mains de . . .   *Only to be given to . . . personally*
Appuyer sur le bouton   *Press the button*
Agiter avant d'ouvrir   *Shake before opening*

12.11 Quick-reference index to verbs taking infinitive complements

s'abaisser à faire qc **(12.4.2)**   *to stoop to doing sth*
s'abêtir, s'abrutir à faire qc **(12.4.3)**   *to become stupid from doing sth*
s'abstenir de faire qc **(12.5.7, 12.5.17)**   *to refrain from doing sth*
accepter de faire qc **(12.5.2)**   *to agree to do sth*
accoutumer qn à faire qc **(12.4.10)**   *to get sb used to doing sth*
accuser qn d'avoir fait qc **(12.5.5)**   *to accuse sb of having done sth*
s'acharner à faire qc **(12.4.4)**   *to be bent on doing sth*
achever de faire qc **(12.5.17)**   *to finish doing sth*
adorer faire qc **(12.3.6)**   *to adore doing sth*
affecter d'avoir fait qc **(12.5.14)**   *to pretend to have done sth*
affirmer avoir fait qc **(12.3.4)**   *to state that one has done sth*
s'affliger d'avoir fait qc **(12.5.20)**   *to be sorry to have done sth*
s'affoler à faire qc **(12.4.3)**   *to panic doing sth*
aider qn à faire qc **(12.4.10)**   *to help sb do sth*
aimer faire qc **(12.3.6)**   *to like doing sth*
aimer autant faire qc **(12.3.6)**   *to just as soon do sth*
aimer mieux faire qc **(12.3.6)**   *to prefer doing sth*
s'en aller faire qc **(12.3.1)**   *to go and do sth*
aller faire qc **(12.3.1)**   *to go and do sth*
ambitionner de faire qc **(12.5.20)**   *to have ambitions to do sth*
amener qn faire qc **(12.3.2)**   *to bring sb along to do sth*

amener qn à faire qc **(12.4.11)**	*to bring sb to the point of doing sth*
s'amuser à faire qc **(12.4.3)**	*to have fun doing sth*
appeler qn à faire qc **(12.4.9)**	*to call on sb to do sth*
s'applaudir d'avoir fait qc **(12.5.6)**	*to congratulate oneself on having done sth*
s'appliquer à faire qc **(12.4.2)**	*to apply oneself to doing sth*
appréhender de faire qc **(12.5.10)**	*to be fearful of doing sth*
apprendre à qn à faire qc **(12.4.10)**	*to teach sb to do sth*
s'apprêter à faire qc **(12.4.2)**	*to get ready to do sth*
arrêter de faire qc **(12.5.17)**	*to stop doing sth*
arriver faire qc **(12.3.1)**	*to come to do sth*
arriver à faire qc **(12.4.6)**	*to succeed in doing sth*
aspirer à faire qc **(12.4.6)**	*to aspire to do sth*
assigner qn à faire qc **(12.4.9)**	*to call on sb to do sth*
s'attacher à faire qc **(12.4.5)**	*to cling to doing sth*
s'attarder à faire qc **(12.4.2)**	*to linger doing sth*
attraper qn à faire qc **(12.4.13)**	*to catch sb doing sth*
s'attrister à faire qc **(8.4.3)**	*to be saddened doing sth*
autoriser qn à faire qc **(12.4.9)**	*to authorize sb to do sth*
s'aventurer à faire qc **(12.4.5)**	*to be so bold as to do sth*
s'avérer être qc **(12.3.7)**	*to turn out to be sth*
avertir qn de faire qc **(12.5.1)**	*to warn sb to do sth*
avoir droit de faire qc **(12.5.20)**	*to have the right to do sth*
en avoir marre de faire qc **(12.5.20)**	*to be fed up doing sth*
avoir peur de faire qc **(12.5.10)**	*to be afraid to do sth*
avoir regret d'avoir fait qc **(12.5.13)**	*to regret having done sth*
blâmer qn d'avoir fait qc **(12.5.5)**	*to blame sb for having done sth*
se borner à faire qc **(12.4.2)**	*to limit oneself to doing sth*
brûler de faire qc **(12.5.20)**	*to have a great desire to do sth*
cesser de faire qc **(12.5.17)**	*to stop doing sth*
charger qn de faire qc **(12.5.5)**	*to make sb responsible for doing sth*
chercher à faire qc **(12.4.6)**	*to seek to do sth*
choisir de faire qc **(12.5.2)**	*to choose to do sth*
chuchoter à qn de faire qc **(12.5.16)**	*to whisper to sb to do sth*
commander à qn de faire qc **(12.5.16)**	*to order sb to do sth*
commencer à/de faire qc **(12.4.1)**	*to start to do sth*
commencer par faire qc **(12.4.1)**	*to start by doing sth*
comploter de faire qc **(12.5.20)**	*to plot to do sth*
compter faire qc **(12.3.6)**	*to count on doing sth*
concourir à faire qc **(12.4.2)**	*to combine to do sth*
condamner qn à faire qc **(12.4.8)**	*to condemn sb to doing sth*
condescendre à faire qc **(12.4.2)**	*to condescend to do sth*
conduire qn à faire qc **(12.4.11)**	*to bring sb to do sth*
confirmer avoir fait qc **(12.3.4)**	*to confirm having done sth*
conjurer qn de faire qc **(12.5.1)**	*to plead with sb to do sth*
consacrer du temps à faire qc **(12.4.12)**	*to spend time doing sth*
conseiller à qn de faire qc **(12.5.1)**	*to advise sb to do sth*
consoler qn d'avoir fait qc **(12.5.20)**	*to console sb for having done sth*
conspirer à faire qc **(12.4.2)**	*to conspire to do sth*
se contenter de faire qc **(12.5.20)**	*to be happy to do sth*
continuer à/de faire qc **(12.4.1)**	*to continue to do sth*
contraindre qn à faire qc **(12.4.8)**	*to force sb to do sth*

convaincre qn de faire qc **(12.5.1)**	*to convince sb to do sth*
convenir de faire qc **(12.5.2)**	*to agree to do sth*
convier qn à faire qc **(12.4.11)**	*to invite sb to do sth*
courir faire qc **(12.3.1)**	*to run to do sth*
craindre de faire qc **(12.5.10)**	*to fear to do sth*
croire avoir fait qc **(12.3.5)**	*to believe to have done sth*
daigner faire qc **(12.3.6)**	*to deign to do sth*
décider de faire qc **(12.4.5, 12.4.11** and **12.5.2)**	*to decide to do sth*
décider qn à faire qc **(12.4.11)**	*to make sb decide to do sth*
se décider à faire qc **(12.4.5, 12.4.11)**	*to make up one's mind to do sth*
déclarer avoir fait qc **(12.3.4)**	*to declare that one has done sth*
déconseiller à qn de faire qc **(12.5.1)**	*to advise sb not to do sth*
dédaigner de faire qc **(12.5.20)**	*not to lower oneself to do sth*
défier qn de faire qc **(12.5.20)**	*to challenge sb to do sth*
défendre à qn de faire qc **(12.5.9)**	*to forbid sb to do sth*
dégoûter qn de faire qc **(12.5.20)**	*to put sb off doing sth*
se délecter à faire qc **(12.4.3)**	*to take delight in doing sth*
demander à qn de faire qc **(12.5.4)**	*to ask sb to do sth*
démentir avoir fait qc **(12.3.4)**	*to deny having done sth*
se dépêcher de faire qc **(12.5.12)**	*to hurry to do sth*
dépenser de l'argent à faire qc **(12.4.12)**	*to spend money doing sth*
désaccoutumer qn de faire qc **(12.5.1)**	*to wean sb off doing sth*
descendre faire qc **(12.3.1)**	*to go down and do sth*
désespérer de faire qc **(12.5.20)**	*to despair of doing sth*
déshabituer qn de faire qc **(12.5.1)**	*to wean sb off doing sth*
désirer faire qc **(12.3.6)**	*to want to do sth*
déterminer qn à faire qc **(12.4.11)**	*to make sb decide to do sth*
devoir faire qc **(12.3.3)**	*to have to do sth*
dire avoir fait qc **(12.3.4)**	*to say that one has done sth*
dire à qn de faire qc **(12.5.16)**	*to tell sb to do sth*
se disculper d'avoir fait qc **(12.5.7)**	*to exonerate oneself from having done sth*
dispenser qn de faire qc **(12.5.2)**	*to allow sb not to do sth*
dissuader qn de faire qc **(12.5.1)**	*to dissuade sb from doing sth*
douter de pouvoir faire qc **(12.5.20)**	*to doubt that one is able to do sth*
dresser un animal à faire qc **(12.4.10)**	*to train an animal to do sth*
écouter qn faire qc **(12.3.8)**	*to listen to sb doing sth*
écrire à qn de faire qc **(12.5.16)**	*to write to sb to do sth*
s'efforcer de faire qc **(12.5.20)**	*to force oneself to do sth*
s'égosiller à dire qc **(12.4.4)**	*to go hoarse saying sth*
emmener qn faire qc **(12.3.2)**	*to take sb to do sth*
empêcher qn de faire qc **(12.5.17)**	*to prevent sb from doing sth*
encourager qn à faire qc **(12.4.11, 12.5.1)**	*to encourage sb to do sth*
s'énerver à faire qc **(12.4.3)**	*to get annoyed doing sth*
engager qn à faire qc **(12.4.11)**	*to bring sb to do sth*
enjoindre à qn de faire qc **(12.5.1)**	*to suggest to sb that they do sth*
s'ennuyer à faire qc **(12.4.3)**	*to get bored doing sth*
enrager d'avoir fait qc **(12.5.3)**	*to be angry about having done sth*
enseigner à qn à faire qc **(12.4.10)**	*to teach sb to do sth*
entendre faire qc **(12.3.6)**	*to intend, mean to do sth*
entendre qn faire qc **(12.3.8)**	*to hear sb doing sth*
s'entêter à faire qc **(12.4.2)**	*to be bent on doing sth*

entraîner qn à faire qc **(12.4.11)**	*to cause sb to do sth*
entreprendre de faire qc **(12.5.20)**	*to undertake to do sth*
envier qn d'avoir fait qc **(12.5.20)**	*to envy sb for having done sth*
envisager de faire qc **(12.5.15)**	*to imagine doing sth*
envoyer qn faire qc **(12.3.2)**	*to send sb to do sth*
s'épuiser à faire qc **(12.4.4)**	*to exhaust oneself doing sth*
s'éreinter à faire qc **(12.4.4)**	*to tire oneself out doing sth*
espérer faire qc **(12.3.6)**	*to hope to do sth*
s'essayer à faire qc **(12.4.5)**	*to try one's hand at doing sth*
essayer de faire qc **(12.4.5, 12.5.4)**	*to try to do sth*
s'essouffler à faire qc **(12.4.4)**	*to get out of breath doing sth*
estimer avoir fait qc **(12.3.5)**	*to reckon to have done sth*
s'étonner de faire qc **(12.4.3)**	*to be surprised at doing sth*
être contraint de faire qc **(12.4.8)**	*to be obliged to do sth*
être disposé à faire qc **(12.4.6)**	*to be inclined to do sth*
être forcé de faire qc **(12.4.8)**	*to have to do sth*
être furieux d'avoir fait qc **(12.5.3)**	*to be furious at having done sth*
être obligé de faire qc **(12.4.8)**	*to be forced to do sth*
être tenu de faire qc **(12.5.20)**	*to be obliged to do sth*
s'évertuer à faire qc **(12.4.4)**	*to do one's utmost to do sth*
éviter de faire qc **(12.5.17)**	*to avoid doing sth*
excuser qn d'avoir fait qc **(12.5.8)**	*to excuse sb for having done sth*
exhorter qn à faire qc **(12.4.11)**	*to exhort sb to do sth*
faire faire qc à qn **(12.3.9)**	*to make sb do sth*
faire semblant de faire qc **(12.5.14)**	*to pretend to do sth*
se fatiguer à faire qc **(12.4.4)**	*to tire oneself out doing sth*
feindre d'avoir fait qc **(12.5.14)**	*to pretend to have done sth*
féliciter qn d'avoir fait qc **(12.5.6)**	*to congratulate sb on having done sth*
finir de faire qc **(12.4.1, 12.5.17)**	*to finish doing sth*
finir par faire qc **(12.4.1)**	*to finish by doing sth*
se flatter de faire qc **(12.5.6)**	*to imagine oneself doing sth*
forcer qn à faire qc **(12.4.8)**	*to make sb do sth*
frémir de faire qc **(12.5.10)**	*to shudder at doing sth*
se garder de faire qc **(12.5.20)**	*to make sure not to do sth*
gémir de faire qc **(12.5.20)**	*to groan at doing sth*
se glorifier d'avoir fait qc **(12.5.6)**	*to be proud of having done sth*
gronder qn d'avoir fait qc **(12.5.5)**	*to scold sb for having done sth*
habituer qn à faire qc **(12.4.10)**	*to get sb used to doing sth*
se hasarder à faire qc **(12.4.5)**	*to venture to do sth*
se hâter de faire qc **(12.5.12)**	*to hasten to do sth*
hésiter à faire qc **(12.4.7)**	*to hesitate to do sth*
hurler à qn de faire qc **(12.5.16)**	*to shout to sb to do sth*
s'imaginer faire qc **(12.3.5)**	*to imagine doing sth*
implorer qn de faire qc **(12.5.4)**	*to implore sb to do sth*
inciter qn à faire qc **(12.4.11)**	*to incite sb to do sth*
incliner à faire qc **(12.4.6)**	*to be inclined to do sth*
s'indigner d'avoir fait qc **(12.5.3)**	*to be furious at having done sth*
s'inquiéter de faire qc **12.4.3, 12.5.10)**	*to worry about doing sth*
interdire à qn de faire qc **(12.5.9)**	*to forbid sb to do sth*

inviter qn à faire qc **(12.4.9, 12.4.10)**	*to invite sb to do sth*
s'irriter de/à faire qc **(12.4.3)**	*to become irritated doing sth*
jurer (à qn) de faire qc **(12.5.2)**	*to swear (to sb) to do sth*
laisser qn faire qc **(12.3.9)**	*to let sb do sth*
se limiter à faire qc **(12.4.2)**	*limit oneself to doing sth*
louer qn d'avoir fait qc **(12.5.6)**	*to praise sb for doing sth*
méditer de faire qc **(12.5.15)**	*to think about doing sth*
se mêler de faire qc **(12.5.20)**	*to be mixed up in doing sth*
menacer (qn) de faire qc **(12.5.3)**	*to threaten to do sth (sb with doing sth)*
mener qn faire qc **(12.3.2)**	*to take sb to do sth*
mériter de faire qc **(12.5.6)**	*to deserve to do sth*
mettre x jours à faire qc **(12.4.12)**	*to take x days to do sth*
se mettre à faire qc **(12.4.1)**	*to start doing sth*
monter faire qc **(12.3.1)**	*to go up and do sth*
négliger de faire qc **(12.5.11)**	*to neglect to do sth*
nier avoir fait qc **(12.3.4)**	*to deny having done sth*
obliger qn à faire qc **(12.4.8, 12.4.10)**	*to make sb do sth*
s'obstiner à faire qc **(12.4.2)**	*to be bent on doing sth*
obtenir de qn de faire qc **(12.5.2)**	*to get permission from sb to do sth*
occuper son temps à faire qc **(12.4.12)**	*to spend one's time doing sth*
offrir à qn de faire qc **(12.5.20)**	*to offer sb (the chance of) doing sth*
omettre de faire qc **(12.5.11)**	*to omit to do sth*
ordonner à qn de faire qc **(12.5.16)**	*to order sb to do sth*
oser faire qc **(12.3.3)**	*to dare to do sth*
oublier de faire qc **(12.5.11)**	*to forget to do sth*
s'oublier à faire qc **(12.4.2)**	*to become absorbed in doing sth*
pâlir de faire qc **(12.5.10)**	*to blanch at doing sth*
paraître faire qc **(12.3.7)**	*to appear to do sth*
pardonner à qn d'avoir fait qc **(12.5.8)**	*to pardon sb for having done sth*
parler de faire qc **(12.5.4)**	*to speak of doing sth*
partir faire qc **(12.3.1)**	*to leave to do sth*
parvenir à faire qc **(12.4.6)**	*to succeed in doing sth*
passer son temps à faire qc **(12.4.12)**	*to spend one's time doing sth*
penser faire qc **(12.3.5)**	*to think one might do sth*
permettre à qn de faire qc **(12.5.2)**	*to allow sb to do sth*
persister à faire qc **(12.4.1)**	*to persist in doing sth*
persuader qn de faire qc **(12.5.1)**	*to persuade sb to do sth*
plaindre qn d'avoir fait qc **(12.5.20)**	*to pity sb for having done sth*
se plaire à faire qc **(12.4.3)**	*to take pleasure in doing sth*
pousser qn à faire qc **(12.4.11)**	*to push sb into doing sth*
pouvoir faire qc **(12.3.3)**	*to be able to do sth*
préférer faire qc **(12.3.6)**	*to prefer to do sth*
préméditer de faire qc **(12.5.15)**	*to think about doing sth beforehand*
prendre qn à faire qc **(12.4.13)**	*to catch sb doing sth*
préparer qn à faire qc **(12.4.10)**	*to prepare sb for doing sth*
prescrire à qn de faire qc **(12.5.16)**	*to order sb to do sth*
presser qn de faire qc **(12.5.20)**	*to put pressure on sb to do sth*

prétendre avoir fait qc **(12.3.4)** — *to claim to have done sth*
prévoir de faire qc **(12.5.20)** — *to foresee doing sth*
prier qn de faire qc **(12.5.4)** — *to ask sb politely to do sth*
projetter de faire qc **(12.5.15)** — *to think about doing sth*
promettre à qn de faire qc **(12.5.20)** — *to promise sb to do sth*
proposer (à qn) de faire qc **(12.5.4, 12.5.15)** — *to propose doing sth (to sb)*

se rappeler avoir fait qc **(12.3.5)** — *to remember having done sth*
rechigner à faire qc **(12.4.7)** — *to baulk at doing sth*
réclamer de faire qc **(12.5.20)** — *to demand to do sth*
recommander à qn de faire qc **(12.5.1)** — *to recommend sb to do sth*
reconnaître avoir fait qc **(12.3.4)** — *to admit to having done sth*
redouter de faire qc **(12.5.10)** — *to fear doing sth*
refuser de faire qc **(12.5.7)** — *to refuse to do sth*
regarder qn faire qc **(12.3.8)** — *to watch sb doing sth*
regretter d'avoir fait qc **(12.5.13)** — *to regret having done sth*
se réjouir de/à faire qc **(12.4.3, 12.5.13)** — *to take pleasure in doing sth*
remercier qn d'avoir fait qc **(12.5.18)** — *to thank sb for having done sth*
se remettre d'avoir fait qc **(12.5.20)** — *to recover from having done sth*
renoncer à faire qc **(12.4.7)** — *to give up doing sth*
rentrer faire qc **(12.3.1)** — *to go home and do sth*
se repentir d'avoir fait qc **(12.5.13)** — *to regret having done sth*
répondre à qn de faire qc **(12.5.16)** — *to tell sb in response to do sth*
reprocher à qn d'avoir fait qc **(12.5.5)** — *to reproach sb for having done sth*
répugner à faire qc **(12.4.7)** — *to be reluctant to do sth*
se réserver de faire qc **(12.5.20)** — *to reserve the right to do sth*
se résigner à faire qc **(12.4.5)** — *to resign oneself to doing sth*
résoudre de faire qc **(12.4.5, 12.5.2)** — *to resolve to do sth*
se résoudre à faire qc **(12.4.5)** — *to accept having to do sth*
retourner faire qc **(12.3.1)** — *to go back and do sth*
réussir à faire qc **(12.4.6)** — *to succeed in doing sth*
se révéler avoir/être qc **(12.3.7)** — *to turn out to have/be sth*
revenir faire qc **(12.3.1)** — *to come back and do sth*
rêver de faire qc **(12.5.20)** — *to dream of doing sth*
risquer de faire qc **(12.4.5)** — *to risk doing sth*
se risquer à faire qc **(12.4.5)** — *to take risks in doing sth*
rougir de faire qc **(12.5.20)** — *to blush at doing sth*
ruminer de faire qc **(12.5.15)** — *to think about doing sth*

savoir faire qc **(12.3.3)** — *to be able to do sth*
savoir gré à qn de faire qc **(12.5.18)** — *to be grateful to sb for doing sth*
sembler faire qc **(12.3.7)** — *to seem to do sth*
sentir qn faire qc **(12.3.8)** — *to feel sb do sth*
sommer qn de faire qc **(12.5.16)** — *to instruct sb to do sth*
sortir faire qc **(12.3.1)** — *to go out and do sth*
se soucier de faire qc **(12.5.10)** — *to care about doing sth*
souhaiter faire qc **(12.3.6)** — *to wish to do sth*
soupçonner qn d'avoir fait qc **(12.5.5)** — *to suspect sb of having done sth*
sourire de faire qc **(12.5.20)** — *to smile at doing sth*
se souvenir d'avoir fait qc **(12.3.5)** — *to remember having done sth*
suggérer à qn de faire qc **(12.5.1)** — *to suggest doing sth to sb*
supplier qn de faire qc **(12.5.4)** — *to beg sb to do sth*
surprendre qn à faire qc **(8.4.13)** — *to surprise sb doing sth*

tâcher de faire qc **(12.5.4)**	*to try to do sth*
téléphoner à qn de faire qc **(12.5.16)**	*to phone sb to do sth*
tendre à faire qc **(12.4.6)**	*to have a tendency to do sth*
tenir à faire qc **(12.4.6)**	*to be bent on doing sth*
s'en tenir à faire qc **(12.4.2)**	*to stick to doing sth*
tenter de faire qc **(12.5.4)**	*to try to do sth*
travailler à faire qc **(12.4.2)**	*to work at doing sth*
trembler de faire qc **(12.5.10)**	*to tremble to do sth*
se tuer à faire qc **(12.4.4)**	*to be sick and tired of doing sth*
s'user à faire qc **(12.4.4)**	*to wear oneself out doing sth*
utiliser ses connaissances à faire qc **(12.4.12)**	*to use one's knowledge in doing sth*
se vanter d'avoir fait qc **(12.5.6)**	*to boast of having done sth*
viser à faire qc **(12.4.6)**	*to aim to do sth*
voir qn faire qc **(12.3.8)**	*to see sb doing sth*
vouloir faire qc **(12.3.3)**	*to want to do sth*

13

Prepositions

13.1 Introduction

Prepositions are forms like *de, à, dans, en, sur, par, pour, avec, au-dessus de, du haut de, à cause de,* and so on. For many French prepositions one can normally find an English counterpart which is used in the same way in a majority of cases. For example. For example:

de ≈ 'of':	une boîte **d'**allumettes ≈ *a box **of** matches* trois kilos **de** sucre ≈ *three kilos **of** sugar*
à ≈ 'at':	**à** trois heures ≈ ***at** three o'clock* être **à** l'école ≈ *to be **at** school*
dans ≈ 'in':	**dans** sa chambre ≈ ***in** her room* **dans** les années trente ≈ ***in** the thirties*

However, there are many cases where there is no direct relation between the prepositions used in each language. For example:

un pichet rempli **de** cidre
*a pitcher filled **with** (NOT *of) cider*

tenir un livre **à** la main
*to hold a book **in** (NOT *at) one's hand*

*It's kind **of** you*
C'est gentil **à** (NOT *de) vous

*She is good **at** languages*
Elle est bonne **en** (NOT *aux) langues

This chapter lists the major French prepositions alphabetically, illustrates their main uses and gives their English equivalents in sections 13.2–13.58. English prepositions and their French counterparts are listed in section 13.59.

13.2 *à*

13.2.1 *à* = 'at'

Referring to place

Le camion ralentissait à chaque virage	*The lorry slowed down at every bend*
Elle est à l'école, au café, au cinéma	*She is at school, at the café, at the cinema*
à l'église, au restaurant, à la pharmacie	*at church, at the restaurant, at the chemist's*

Si on se réunissait au café?	*Shall we meet at the café?*
Il était assis au chevet de sa mère	*He was sitting at his mother's bedside*
Mis en bouteille à la source	*Bottled at the spring*
au bord du lac	*at the edge of the lake*

Referring to time

à trois heures, à minuit, à midi	*at three o'clock, at midnight, at midday*
à la nuit tombée, au crépuscule	*at nightfall, at dusk*

BUT *au petit matin* is translated by: '**in** the early morning'.

au petit déjeuner, au dîner	*at breakfast, at dinner*
à la fin, au début	*at the end, at the beginning*
une chose à la fois	*one thing at a time*
à toute vitesse	*at full speed*
Il est mort à 26 ans	*He died at 26*

13.2.2 *à* = 'to'

au nord, au sud, à l'est, à l'ouest	*to the north, to the south, to the east, to the west*

NB: l'Afrique du Sud: *South Africa;* au sud de l'Afrique: *to the south of Africa.*

Elle va à l'école, au café, au cinéma, à l'église, au restaurant, à la pharmacie	*She is going to school, to the café, to the cinema, to church, to the restaurant, to the chemist's*
monter à sa chambre	*to go up to one's room*
tourner à droite, à gauche	*to turn to the right, to the left*

'**to**' most countries of masculine gender is *à*:

au Japon	*to Japan*
au Danemark	*to Denmark*
au Portugal	*to Portugal*
au Canada	*to Canada*
aux Etats-Unis, aux USA	*to the United States, to the USA*

(For countries of feminine gender, and most countries of masculine gender beginning with a vowel, 'to' is *en: en France, en Grèce,* etc., see 13.26.1. See also Chapter 2.2.2. For the gender of countries see Chapter 1.2.6.)

'**to**' most small islands, and larger islands which are some distance away, is *à*:

à Malte, à Jersey, à Guernsey, à Chypre, à la Martinique, à la Réunion, à Madagascar, à Tahiti, aux Philippines
to Malta, to Jersey, to Guernsey, to Cyprus, to Martinique, to Reunion, to Madagascar, to Tahiti, to the Philippines

NB: 'to' larger islands close to Europe, and very large islands generally is *en*: *en Sicile, en Sardaigne, en Crète, en Nouvelle-Zélande,* etc.
'**to**' towns and cities is *à*:

à Paris, à Londres, à Berlin	*to Paris, to London, to Berlin*

13.2.3 *à* = 'in'

Referring to place

vivre à Paris	*to live in Paris*
à cet endroit (BUT **dans** ce lieu)	*in this place*
au village (BUT **en** ville)	*in the village (in town)*
se reposer au jardin, au parc, au salon	*to rest in the garden, in the park, in the sitting-room*

à in these cases is a simple statement of location; *dans* is used when the 'containing' properties of the location are given more emphasis, for example:

se promener au parc
to walk in the park (simple statement of location)

perdre ses clefs dans le parc
to lose one's keys in the park (the park is the area within which the keys were lost)

Compare:

Ils sont partis se promener au parc	*They have gone for a walk in the park*
On se promenait dans le parc quand on a perdu nos clefs	*We were walking in the park when we lost our keys*
vivre à Paris	*to live in Paris* (simple statement of location)
Il est difficile de se garer dans Paris	*It's difficult to park in Paris* (i.e. within Paris, as opposed to anywhere else)
au deuxième rang du parterre	*in the second row of the stalls*
à l'arrière	*in the back*
à l'intérieur	*inside*
tenir quelque chose à la main	*to hold something in one's hand*
porter une fleur au chapeau	*to wear a flower in one's hat*
au paradis (BUT **en** enfer)	*in heaven (in hell)*

'in' most countries of masculine gender is *à*:

au Japon	*in Japan*
au Danemark	*in Denmark*
au Portugal	*in Portugal*
au Canada	*in Canada*
aux Etats-Unis, aux USA	*in the United States, in the USA*

(For countries of feminine gender, and most countries of masculine gender beginning with a vowel, 'in' is *en*: *en France*, *en Iran*, etc. See 13.26.1 and 1.2.6.)

'in' or 'on' most small islands, and larger islands which are some distance away, is *à*:

à Malte, à Jersey, à Guernsey, à Chypre, à la Martinique, à la Réunion, à Madagascar, àTahiti, aux Philippines
in Malta, in Jersey, in Guernsey, in Cyprus, in Martinique, in Reunion, in Madagascar, in Tahiti, in the Philippines

NB: 'in' large islands close to Europe, and very large islands generally, is *en*: *en Sicile, en Sardaigne, en Crète, en Nouvelle-Zélande*, etc.

'in' towns and cities is *à*:

à Paris, à Londres, à Berlin, à Marseille	*in Paris, in London, in Berlin, in Marseilles*

Referring to time

la veille au soir	*in the evening of the day before*
à l'entracte	*in the interval*
vivre au 20e siècle	*to live in the 20th century*
arriver à temps	*to arrive in time*

13.2.4 *à* = 'on'

Je le ramasserai au retour	*I'll pick it up on my way back*
Il est arrivé à pied	*He arrived on foot*
Je l'ai appris au service militaire	*I learned it when I was on military service*
Elle a essayé de le contacter à plusieurs reprises	*She tried to contact him on several occasions*
à la page 2	*on page 2*
à la télévision/à la radio	*on (the) television/on (the) radio*
se mettre à genoux	*to get down on one's knees*
avoir une cicatrice à la jambe	*to have a scar on one's leg*
frapper à la porte, à la vitre	*to knock on the door, on the window*
les pommes étaient à terre	*the apples were on the ground*

Modes of transport

à bicyclette	*on a bicycle*
à pied	*on foot*
à cheval	*on horseback*
à dos de chameau	*on a camel*

BUT also: *en vélo, en taxi, en voiture, en ambulance*, etc. (See 13.26.5.)

13.2.5 *à* = 'by'

s'avancer pas à pas	*to move forward step by step*
partir un à un	*to leave one by one*
travailler à la lumière d'une bougie	*to work by the light of a candle*
fabriqué à la main	*made by hand*
reconnaître quelqu'un à sa voix	*to recognize somebody by his/her voice*

13.2.6 *à* used where English typically uses compound nouns

une tasse à thé	*a tea cup*
un livre à couverture de cuir	*a leather-bound book*
un moulin à vent, à café	*a windmill, coffee-mill*
un homme à cheveux gris, aux cheveux gris	*a grey-haired man*
un homme à barbe	*a bearded man*
une fille aux cheveux d'or	*a golden-haired girl*
un billet à 10 F	*a 10 franc ticket*
une pompe à main	*a hand pump*
un bateau à roue	*a paddle steamer*
une chambre à air	*an inner tube*

une omelette aux champignons	*a mushroom omelette*
une sauce au vin	*a wine sauce*
de la soupe à l'oignon	*onion soup*

13.2.7 *à* = no preposition in English

La falaise était à pic	*The cliff was steep*
Les volets étaient à demi fermés	*The shutters were half closed*
avoir mal à la tête	*to have a headache*
Rennes est à 348 kilomètres de Paris	*Rennes is 348 kilometres from Paris*
un restaurant à deux pas d'ici	*a restaurant a stone's throw from here*
Ils se sont arrêtés à mi-chemin	*They stopped halfway*
La voiture roulait à cent trente kilomètres à l'heure	*The car was travelling at 130 kilometres an hour*
à l'envers	*back to front*
rentrer à la maison	*to go home*

In the case of sports: *au, à la* is used:

> jouer au tennis, au football, au rugby, au billard, etc.
> *to play tennis, football, rugby, billiards, etc.*

But in the case of musical instruments: *du, de la* is used:

> jouer **du** piano, **du** violon, **de** la flûte, etc.
> *to play the piano, the violin, the flute, etc.*

13.2.8 *à* = other uses

monter/descendre à l'étage	*to go upstairs/to go downstairs*
C'est à vous de décider	*It's up to you to decide*
C'est gentil à vous de m'aider	*It's kind of you to help me*
C'est aimable à lui	*That's nice of him*
un oncle à lui (*also* un de ses oncles)	*an uncle of his*
un livre à moi (*also* un de mes livres)	*a book of mine*
boire à la bouteille, à la source	*to drink from the bottle, from the spring*
emprunter de l'argent à la banque	*to borrow money from the bank*
un repas à la française	*a meal in the French style*
des pâtes à l'italienne	*Italian style pasta*

13.3 *après/d'après*

après la fin du film	*after the end of the film*
après le repas	*after the meal*
après avoir acheté une glace	*after buying an ice-cream*
après être arrivé	*after arriving*
Il n'arrête pas de crier après tout le monde	*He shouts at everyone*
demander après quelqu'un	*to ask after somebody*
(both these uses of *après* are informal)	
d'après les journaux	*according to the newspapers*
d'après ce qu'on m'a dit	*from what I've been told*
D'après leur tête, ils ont perdu le match	*From the look on their faces, they lost the match*

D'après vous, lequel est le meilleur?	*In your view, which is the better?*
un tableau d'après Van Gogh	*a painting in the style of Van Gogh*

13.4 *auprès de*

Auprès de ces héros, nous sommes peu de chose (formal)
Compared with these heroes, we are as nothing

se plaindre auprès des autorités
to complain to the authorities

un ambassadeur auprès de la République française
an ambassador to France

13.5 *autour de*

autour de l'aéroport	*around the airport*
tourner autour de la question	*to go around the question*
Nous arriverons autour de huit heures	*We will arrive around eight*

13.6 *avant*

s'arrêter juste avant le tournant	*to stop just before the bend*
avant le mois de juin	*before June*
avant l'entracte	*before the interval*
avant l'aube	*before dawn*
avant le weekend	*before the weekend*
arriver avant qn	*to arrive ahead of sb*
faire passer qn avant les autres	*to let someone go first*

NB: 'ahead of' in the sense of 'outstripping' one's rivals is *en avant de*: *Il est en avant de ses contemporains* 'He is ahead of his contemporaries'.

13.7 *avec*

Il devait venir avec moi au garage	*He was to come with me to the garage*
une voiture avec des banquettes de cuir	*a car with leather seats*
elle est arrivée avec son père et sa mère	*She arrived with her father and mother*
s'entendre bien avec quelqu'un	*to get on well with somebody*
parler avec quelqu'un	*to speak with somebody*
remplir un verre avec de l'eau	*to fill a glass with water*
mouiller un ragoût avec du vin blanc	*to thin a stew with white wine*
Ce Calvados est fait avec nos propres pommes	*This Calvados is made with our own apples*

NB: In some of these examples it is also possible to use *de*: *remplir un verre d'eau, mouiller un ragoût de vin blanc*:

se raser avec un rasoir électrique	*to shave with an electric razor*
épousseter les meubles avec un plumeau	*to dust with a feather duster*
On s'est moqué d'eux, avec Alain	*Alain and I made fun of them*
On a fini l'article, avec Pierre (informal)	*Pierre and I have finished the article*
aller quelque part avec la voiture	*to go somewhere by car*

(For modes of transport also see 13.26.5.)

13.8 *bout: au bout de*

au bout de mon jardin	*at the bottom of my garden*
au bout de trois heures	*after three hours*

13.9 *cause: à cause de, pour cause de, pour raison de*

A cause de sa maladie, il n'a pas pu venir	*Because of his illness, he couldn't come*
Le restaurant est fermé pour cause de décès	*The restaurant is closed due to a bereavement*
Il a démissionné pour raison de santé	*He resigned for health reasons*

13.10 *chez*

Je suis chez moi samedi	*I am at home on Saturday*
Ils l'ont ramené chez eux	*They brought him back to their house*
Elle est venue chez nous en pleine nuit	*She came to our house in the middle of the night*
Est-il vrai que chez les Anglais on boit du thé avec chaque repas?	*Is it true that, among the English, tea is drunk with every meal?*
Tu coucheras chez nous	*You'll sleep at our house*
Chez Camus, le décor est très important	*In Camus, the setting is very important*

13.11 *contre*

Je n'ai rien contre lui	*I have nothing against him*
protéger ses plantes contre le froid	*to protect one's plants against the cold*
une table posée contre le mur	*a table placed against the wall*
agir contre qn	*to act against sb*
changer des francs contre des dollars	*to change francs for dollars*
livraison contre remboursement	*cash on delivery*

13.12 *côté: à côté de, du côté de*

La boucherie est à côté de la pharmacie	*The butcher's is next to the chemist's*
Elle s'est assise à côté de moi	*She sat down next to me*

A côté de ses œuvres précédentes, celle-ci est moins impressionnante
Compared with his earlier works, this one is less impressive

rouler du côté de Brive	*to travel in the direction of Brive*
arriver du côté de Brive	*to arrive from the direction of Brive; to be coming from Brive*
habiter du côté de Brive	*to live around Brive*

NB: *Du Côté de chez Swann* (the title of one of the volumes of Proust's *A La Recherche du temps perdu*) literally means 'around where Swann lives', and has been translated by Proust's English translator as *Swann's Way*.

13.13 *cours: au cours de*

au cours de la semaine	*during the week*
au cours de sa carrière	*in the course of his career*

13.14 *dans*

13.14.1 *dans* = 'in'

J'ai aperçu la ferme dans la vallée	*I saw the farm in the valley*
Elle était assise dans son fauteuil	*She was sitting in her armchair*
BUT s'asseoir sur une chaise, sur un banc, sur un siège	*to sit on a chair, on a bench, on a seat*
Il y avait de la pluie dans l'air	*There was rain in the air*

Nous l'avons croisé dans la rue, dans l'allée, dans l'avenue
We passed him in the street, in the alley, in the avenue

BUT **sur** la place, **sur** la route, **sur** le chemin, **sur** le boulevard, **sur** la chaussée, **sur** le trottoir
in the square, on the road, on the track, on the boulevard, in the road (as opposed to pavement), on the pavement

NB: When streets are named, there is usually no preposition in French for 'in': *Je l'ai rencontré rue de Rivoli* 'I met him in the rue de Rivoli', *Nous l'avons croisé boulevard Montparnasse* 'We passed him in the boulevard Montparnasse', *Il y avait un accident place du Châtelet* 'There was an accident in the place du Châtelet'.

Il est dans sa chambre	*He is in his room*
Elle habite dans une belle maison	*She lives in a fine house*
Je l'ai lu dans un journal, dans un livre	*I read it in a paper, in a book*
dans tous les sens	*in every direction*
dans les années trente	*in the thirties*
Il vit dans la misère	*He lives in poverty*
Cela l'a laissé dans le doute	*That left him in doubt*

dans with the meaning 'in' is used with French *départements*, English counties and American states:

dans le Calvados	dans le Yorkshire	dans le Massachusetts
dans la Marne	dans l'Essex	dans le Nevada
dans le Finistère	dans le Lancashire	dans l'Arizona
dans la Haute-Garonne		
dans l'Aveyron		
dans l'Isère		

dans is also used with the meaning 'in' with countries and towns modified by adjectives, quantifiers or other expressions:

dans toute la France	*in all France*
dans la Pologne ravagée	*in war-torn Poland*
dans le sud de l'Espagne	*in southern Spain*
dans le Mexique d'aujourd'hui	*in today's Mexico*
dans le vieux Paris	*in old Paris*

BUT *en France, en Italie, en Espagne, à Paris* etc. (See 13.26.1.)

13.14.2 *dans* = 'in(side)'

Le manteau est dans l'armoire	*The coat is in the wardrobe*
Mettez le couteau dans le tiroir	*Put the knife in the drawer*
un petit navire dans une bouteille	*a ship in a bottle*

Modes of transport

Nous sommes venus dans (*or* par) le bus, dans (*or* par) le train, dans un taxi, dans une ambulance
We came by bus, by train, by taxi, in an ambulance

dans is used when the 'containing' properties of the vehicle are given prominence e.g.:

Elle a perdu son porte-monnaie dans le bus
She lost her purse on the bus

Il est décédé dans l'ambulance
He died in the ambulance

BUT also

en auto, en voiture	*by car*
en vélo, à bicyclette	*by bike*
à cheval	*on horseback*
en navire	*by ship*
en avion	*by plane*
en hélicoptère	*by helicopter*
en ambulance	*by ambulance*
en taxi	*by taxi*

(See section 13.26.5.)

13.14.3 *dans* = '(in)to'

Elle est allée dans la cour	*She went into the yard*
emmener quelqu'un dans un restaurant	*to take somebody to a restaurant*

13.14.4 *dans* = 'in' (after a certain period of time has elapsed)

Je reviendrai dans une heure
I'll come back in an hour's time (i.e. after an hour has elapsed)

Il peut le faire dans quinze jours	*He can do it in a fortnight's time*
Je l'attends dans deux jours	*I expect him in two days*

Nous le ferons dans un instant
We'll do it in a moment (i.e. after a moment has elapsed)

This use of *dans* contrasts with *en* 'in' (within a certain period of time – see 13.26.3):

Je l'aurai lu en une heure	*I'll have read it (with)in an hour*
Il peut le faire en quinze jours	*He can do it (with)in a fortnight*
Ça se fait en un instant	*That's done in an instant*

13.14.5 *dans* = 'during'

Je le ferai dans la semaine	*I'll do it during the week*
Elle a écrit sa rédaction dans la journée	*She finished her essay during the day*
Il était tombé malade dans la nuit	*He became ill during the night*
Je l'avais vu dans la semaine	*I had seen him during the week*

13.14.6 *dans* = 'around', 'or so'

Nous avons gagné dans les mille francs	*We won around a thousand francs*
Ça pèse dans les 500 grammes	*That weighs around 500 grams*
Il avait dans les 26 ans (informal)	*He was around 26*

13.14.7 *dans* = 'among'

Il a disparu dans les sapins	*He disappeared among the firs*
J'ai cherché dans mes papiers	*I looked among my papers*

parmi is also possible with non-human objects: *Il a disparu parmi les sapins, J'ai cherché parmi mes papiers.* BUT in talking of people, 'among' can only be *parmi* or *entre*:

Il n'était pas parmi les spectateurs
He wasn't among the spectators

Elle se faufilait parmi les manifestants
She threaded her way among the demonstrators

Nous pourrons en discuter entre nous
We will be able to discuss it among ourselves

13.14.8 *dans* = 'on'

Nous l'avons rencontré dans l'escalier	*We met him on the stairs*
Il bricolait dans des fermes	*He did odd jobs on farms*

13.14.9 *dans* = 'from'

Elle a pris le portefeuille dans le tiroir
She took the wallet from the drawer

Il a pris son mouchoir dans sa poche
He took his handkerchief from his pocket

Nous avons découpé des photos dans un journal
We cut photos from a newspaper

Il boit son café dans un bol
He drinks his coffee from a bowl

J'ai copié cela dans un livre
I copied that from a book

BUT *sortir, retirer un portefeuille **du** tiroir.*

13.15 *de*

13.15.1 *de* = 'of'

une tasse de thé	*a cup of tea*
une boîte d'allumettes	*a box of matches*
un verre de vin	*a glass of wine*
un bol de café	*a bowl of coffee*

NB: There is a contrast between *une tasse de thé* 'a cup of tea' and *une tasse à thé* 'a tea-cup'. The first describes a cup which happens to have tea in it, the second describes a cup designed for drinking tea from. Tea cups can hold substances other than tea, so one can say *une tasse à thé de sucre* 'a tea-cup of sugar' (NOT **une tasse de thé de sucre*). Similarly *une boîte de lettres* 'a box of letters' contrasts with *une boîte aux lettres* 'a letter box', and *un verre de vin* 'a glass of wine' contrasts with *un verre à vin* 'a wine glass'. (See 13.2.6.)

une route pleine de virages	*a road full of bends*
J'entendais le bruit des campeurs	*I heard the noise of the campers*
le Tour de France	*the Tour de France*
le bombardement de Marseille en 1944	*the bombing of Marseilles in 1944*
la moitié des spectateurs	*half of the spectators*
la plupart de la population	*most of the population*
un tiers des concurrents	*a third of the competitors*
trois de mes amis	*three of my friends*
le plus grand joueur de tous	*the greatest player of all*
le plus intelligent de nous tous	*the most intelligent of all of us*

13.15.2 *de* = 'with'

une rue bordée de platanes	*a street lined with plane trees*
un mur couvert d'affiches	*a wall covered with posters*
un vestibule encombré de chaussures	*a hall cluttered with shoes*
un pichet rempli de cidre	*a pitcher filled with cider*

par is a less frequently used equivalent of *de* in these cases, with an indefinite article: *une rue bordée par des platanes, un mur couvert par des affiches*, etc.

rougir de honte	*to go red with shame*
tomber de fatigue	*to drop with tiredness*
trembler de peur	*to tremble with fear*
piétiner d'impatience	*to dance with impatience*
crier de colère	*to shout with anger*
sauter de joie	*to jump with joy*

13.15.3 *de* = 'in'

vêtu de noir	*dressed in black*
habillé d'un complet bleu	*dressed in a blue suit*

After a superlative ('best in . . .', 'biggest in . . .', etc.) or after *seul, dernier, premier, jamais*:

le bâtiment le plus haut du monde	*the tallest building in the world*
le train le plus rapide d'Europe	*the fastest train in Europe*
la seule fois de ma vie	*the only time in my life*
Jamais de ma vie je n'ai eu aussi peur	*Never in my life have I been so scared*
d'une certaine manière, façon	*in a certain manner, fashion*
trois dimanches de suite	*three Sundays in a row*
boire un whisky d'un trait	*to drink a whisky in one go*
Il est paralysé des jambes, court de jambes large d'épaules	*He is paralysed in the legs, short in the leg, broad in the shoulders*

13.15.4 *de* = 'from'

regarder quelqu'un d'en haut	*to watch somebody from above*
le train de Paris	*the train from (also for) Paris*
Elle venait de Marseille	*She came from Marseilles*
Il est sorti de derrière la maison	*He came out from behind the house*
regarder les choses d'un même œil	*to see things from the same perspective*

aller de Londres à Paris	*to go from London to Paris*
passer du rouge au vert	*to go from red to green*
citer quelque chose de mémoire	*to cite something from memory*
faire quelque chose de colère	*to do something from anger*

NB: *le train de Paris* is ambiguous between 'the train **from** Paris' and 'the train **for** Paris'; *le train en provenance de Paris* is unambiguously 'the train **from** Paris', and *le train à destination de Paris* is unambiguously 'the train **for** Paris'.

13.15.5 *de* = 'by'

Je le connais de vue, de réputation	*I know him by sight, by reputation*
un film de François Truffaut	*a film by François Truffaut*

de often corresponds to 'by' when a state is being described:

Il est connu de tous, détesté de certains, adoré de beaucoup
He is known by everyone, detested by some, adored by many

Il était accablé de fatigue, de sommeil, de douleur
He was overcome by tiredness, by sleep, worn down by pain

Le ciel est couvert de nuages
The sky is covered by cloud

When 'by' introduces an agent, and an event rather than a state is involved, *par* is usually used (as for example in passives: see Chapter 8.6):

Il a été effrayé par l'orage	*He was frightened by the storm*
Jean a été mordu par mon chien	*Jean was bitten by my dog*

But when a passive can be understood as a state, rather than an event, *de* may be used:

Quand il est arrivé au commissariat, il était accompagné de sa femme
When he arrived at the police station, his wife was with him

Les enfants ne sont autorisés que s'ils sont accompagnés d'un adulte
Children are not allowed in unless accompanied by an adult

13.15.6 *de* = 's (possessive)

la sœur de sa mère	*his mother's sister*
le vélo de mon oncle	*my uncle's bike*
la maison de mes parents	*my parents' house*
le nom de son chien	*his dog's name*

13.15.7 *de* = 'than' (*plus de, moins de*)

Elle gagne plus de 30 000 FF par mois	*She earns more than 30,000 francs a month*
Moins d'une dizaine de personnes assistaient au cours	*Fewer than ten people were at the lecture*
Cela est arrivé il y a plus de trente ans	*That happened more than thirty years ago*
Interdit aux moins de 15 ans	*No children under 15*

NB: *plus de, moins de* contrast with *plus que, moins que*. Whereas *plus de, moins de* are typically followed by a numeral, *plus que, moins que* introduce an implied clause:

Elle gagne plus de 30 000 FF	BUT	Elle gagne plus que sa sœur (ne gagne)
		She earns more than her sister (earns)

Il travaille moins de 2 heures par jour   *He works less than 2 hours a day*
Il travaille moins que son frère   *He works less than his brother (works)*
(ne travaille)

13.15.8 *de* = no preposition in English

Linking nouns to make them compound nouns

un vieux tronc d'acacia   *an old acacia trunk*
un homme d'affaires   *a businessman*
la boîte de vitesses   *the gear-box*
un vélo de course   *a racing bike*

Introducing parts of countries, states, towns, etc., in relation to the points of the compass

L'Afrique du Sud   *South Africa*
le Sud de l'Afrique   *southern Africa*
L'Italie du Sud   *southern Italy*
La France du Nord   *northern France*
les pays de l'ouest   *western countries*
La Gare du Nord
La Gare de l'Est

With many quantifiers

la plupart des gens   *most people (also 'most of the people')*
beaucoup de gens   *many people*
bien des gens   *many people*
la moitié des gens   *half the people (also 'half of the people')*

For more on these quantifiers see Chapter 6.9.

With the following adjectival construction used frequently in informal French

une journée de libre   *a free day*
encore un problème de réglé   *one more problem solved*
il y avait trois passants de blessés   *three passers-by were injured*

Linking indefinite or negative nouns and adjectives

quelqu'un d'important   *someone important*
personne d'intéressant   *nobody interesting*
rien d'autre   *nothing else*
quelque chose de drôle   *something funny*

After *ce que* ...

Ce qu'il y a de plus beau dans l'exposition, c'est le tableau de Constable
What's most beautiful in the exhibition is the painting by Constable

Ce qu'il y a de moins intéressant dans les livres que j'ai lus cet été, c'est ce roman d'aventures
What's least interesting among the books I read this summer is this adventure novel

Ce qu'ils produisent de bon, c'est le vin
What they produce that is good is wine

Measurements

un mur épais d'un mètre	*a wall one metre thick*
une rivière longue de 200 kilomètres	*a 200-kilometre long river*
une clôture haute de cinq mètres	*a five-metre high fence*
Elle est âgée de 15 ans	*She is 15*
Le train est en retard de 20 minutes	*The train is 20 minutes late*

(For measurements see also Chapter 6.5.1.)

13.15.9 de = other uses

Je ne me nourris que de pommes de terre	*I live on potatoes*
être de permanence	*to be on duty, on call*

On n'a plus revu Bernard de l'après-midi
We didn't see Bernard again for the rest of the afternoon

traiter quelqu'un de voleur	*to call somebody a thief*
Quoi de neuf?	*What's new?*
Quoi de plus éprouvant?	*What can be more harrowing?*

13.16 dehors: en dehors de

une randonnée en dehors de la ville
a hike outside the town

En dehors de ses cousins, elle ne connaît personne
Apart from her cousins, she knows no-one

13.17 delà: au-delà de

au-delà de la frontière	*beyond the frontier*

13.18 dépit: en dépit de

En dépit de mes conseils, elle s'est mariée	*In spite of my advice, she got married*

13.19 depuis

depuis longtemps	*for a long time*
depuis toujours	*from time immemorial*
Elle joue du piano depuis un très jeune âge	*She has been playing the piano since she was very young*
Je suis là depuis trois jours	*I have been here for three days*
Je ne l'ai pas vu depuis trois jours	*I haven't seen him for three days*

(For tenses with *depuis* see Chapter 10.4.4.)

depuis ... (jusqu'à) can be used as an alternative to *de ... à* when distance is being emphasized:

Il a marché depuis le port jusqu'au parc	*He walked right from the harbour to the park*
Elle a crié depuis le jardin	*She shouted from the garden*

Le bruit nous arrivait depuis la terrasse	*The noise reached us from the terrace*
depuis le haut jusqu'en bas	*from the top to the very bottom*
Je vous parle depuis Poitiers	*I'm speaking to you from Poitiers*
	(only on the radio and television)

13.20 *derrière*

une rue derrière la grande place	*a street behind the main square*
derrière chez lui	*behind his house*
Allez vous mettre par-derrière la cloison	*Go and stand behind the partition*
	(par-derrière implies movement)

NB: 'behind' in the sense of 'not keeping up with' is *en retard*: *Il est en retard par rapport aux autres enfants de sa classe* 'He is behind the other children in his class'.

13.21 *dès*

dès la nuit tombée, dès l'aube	*from nightfall, from dawn*
dès son arrivée	*as soon as he arrived*
Dès que je suis entré, j'ai compris que	*As soon as I came in,*
quelque chose ne tournait pas rond	*I knew that something was wrong*
dès maintenant	*from now on*
dès lors	*from then on*
dès l'enfance	*from childhood*

13.22 *dessous: au-dessous de/par-dessous*

Au-dessous de la salle à manger il y a une piscine
Below the dining room there is a swimming-pool

La température est tombée au-dessous de zéro
The temperature fell below zero

Il a rampé par-dessous la barrière
He crawled under the gate (par-dessous implies movement)

13.23 *dessus: au-dessus de/par-dessus*

J'ai regardé le ciel au-dessus du village	*I looked at the sky above the village*
Au-dessus de la porte d'entrée il y avait	*Above the entrance there was a sign*
un panneau	
porter un manteau par-dessus sa veste	*to wear a coat over one's jacket*
sauter par-dessus une barrière	*to jump over a gate*

13.24 *devant*

devant l'église	*in front of the church*
devant chez lui	*in front of his house*
mettre un pied devant l'autre	*to put one foot in front of the other*
Je l'ai laissé devant un chemin obscur	*I left him at the beginning of a dark track*

marcher devant qn
comparaître devant le tribunal

to walk in front of sb
to appear before the court

13.25 *durant*

durant la nuit, durant l'été

during the night, during the summer

NB: *durant* is an equivalent of *pendant*, but typically restricted to written French. Unlike *pendant*, it can follow the noun it modifies: *Elle s'est reposée la semaine durant* 'She rested throughout the week'.

13.26 *en*

13.26.1 *en* = 'in'

en, rather than *dans*, is used where there is no definite or indefinite article:

en plein air
en bonne santé
en terminale
une région riche en forêts
une thèse pauvre en idées
en cas d'urgence
avoir confiance en quelqu'un

in the open air
in good health
in the upper sixth year
a region rich in forests
a thesis poor in ideas
in an emergency
to have confidence in somebody

Il est sorti en tenue de soirée, en maillot de bain, en bras de chemise
He went out in evening dress, in his swimming costume, in shirt sleeves

Elle est en ville, en prison, en province
She is in town, in prison, out of town (i.e. 'in the provinces')

BUT where an article is used, *dans* is usual:

être transporté dans une prison lointaine   *to be taken to a distant prison*

Months

en janvier, en février, en mars, . . . en novembre, en décembre
in January, in February, in March, . . . in November, in December

Seasons

en automne, en été, en hiver . . . BUT **au** printemps
in autumn, in summer, in winter . . . in spring

Years

en 1992, en 1485, etc.
en l'an 1992, en l'an 1485, etc.   *in the year 1992, in the year 1485.*

BUT:

dans les années 90
au 20e siècle

in the 90s
in the 20th century

Languages

en allemand, en anglais, en français, en espagnol, en flamand, etc.
in German, in English, in French, in Spanish, in Flemish, etc.

en is used for 'in' or 'to' countries and continents of feminine gender:

en France	en Afrique
en Espagne	en Amérique
en Italie	en Europe
en Allemagne	en Australie
en Grèce	en Asie
en Turquie	en Chine

en is also used for 'in' or 'to' countries of masculine gender which begin with a vowel:

en Afghanistan
en Israël
en Iran

'in' or 'to' masculine countries not beginning with a vowel is usually *au* or *aux*:

au Japon	au Canada
au Portugal	au Danemark

NB: *aux Etats-Unis, aux USA*. See 13.2.3.

en is used for 'in' or 'to' French regions of feminine gender:

en Normandie
en Bretagne
en Provence
en Touraine

BUT *dans* is normally used with French regions of masculine gender:

dans le Berry
dans le Périgord
dans le Forez

dans is normal for 'in' or 'to' with French *départements*, British counties and American states. (See 13.14.1.)

en is used for 'in' or 'to' large islands:

en Sicile	en Crète
en Sardaigne	en Nouvelle-Zélande

See also 13.2.3.

13.26.2 *en* = 'in' used with articles in fixed expressions

regarder en l'air	*to look up*
des idées en l'air	*unrealistic ideas*
en la circonstance	*in the circumstances*
en l'occurrence	*as it turns out*
en l'espèce	*in this particular case*
en ce cas	*in this case*
en son for intérieur	*in his heart of hearts*

13.26.3 *en* = 'in' (within a certain period of time)

Il a fait des progrès en deux ans	*He has made progress in two years*
Je l'aurai lu en une heure	*I'll have read it in an hour*

Ça se fait en un instant	*It's done in a second*
le tour du monde en 80 jours	*around the world in 80 days*

This contrasts with *dans* = 'in' (after a certain period of time has elapsed):

Il peut le faire dans quinze jours	*He can do it in two weeks' time*
Je l'attends dans deux jours	*I expect him in two days*
Je le ferai dans un instant	*I'll do it in a minute*

13.26.4 *en* = 'made from'

une statue en bronze	*a bronze statue*
une robe en velours rouge	*a red velvet dress*
une montre en or	*a gold watch*
une robe en soie	*a silk dress*
un pont en ciment	*a concrete bridge*

13.26.5 *en* = modes of transport

The following are common in informal French:

voyager en taxi, en vélo	*to travel by taxi, by bike*
en bicyclette, en moto	*by bicycle, on a motorbike*
en avion, en car	*by plane, on a coach*
en train, en voiture	*by train, by car*
en ambulance	*in an ambulance*
en skis	*on skis*
en bateau	*by boat*

The expressions you are more likely to encounter in formal French are: *dans un taxi, à vélo, à bicyclette, dans l'avion, par avion, dans le car, dans le train, avec la voiture, dans une ambulance, par bateau.*

13.26.6 *en* = 'on'

en vacances, en congé	*on holiday, on leave*
en vente	*on sale*
en route	*on the way,*
en voyage	*on a trip*
en moyenne	*on average*
en feu	*on fire*

13.26.7 *en* = 'with'

une maison en briques	*a house built with bricks*
alimenter un restaurant en vin	*to supply a restaurant with wine*
ravitailler des terroristes en armes	*to supply terrorists with arms*

13.26.8 *en* = 'at'

en fin de semaine	*at the end of the week*
en haut de page	*at the top of the page*
en mer	*at sea*
en plein sommet	*right at the summit*
en même temps	*at the same time*
Les deux pays étaient en guerre	*The two countries were at war*
Sa vie est en jeu	*Her life is at stake*
être fort en langues, en maths	*to be good at languages, maths*
en vitesse (informal)	*at speed*

13.26.9 *en* = 'from'

aujourd'hui en huit	*a week from today*
lundi en quinze	*two weeks from Monday*

13.26.10 *en* = 'as'

parler en spécialiste	*to speak as an expert*
s'habiller en marin	*to dress as a sailor*
recevoir qc en cadeau	*to receive something as a present*
agir en lâche	*to act as a coward*
en signe de deuil	*as a sign of mourning*

13.26.11 *en* = 'into'

transformer la maison en hôtel	*to transform the house into a hotel*
changer une défaite en victoire	*to change a defeat into victory*
traduire un texte en allemand	*to translate a text into German*

13.26.12 *en* = no preposition

se mettre en colère	*to become angry*
une télévision en couleur	*a colour television*
un film en noir et blanc	*a black and white film*

13.27 *entre/d'entre*

la distance entre deux points	*the distance between two points*
une dispute entre eux	*a dispute between them*
J'ai le rapport entre les mains	*I have the report in my hands*
la frontière entre deux pays	*the border between two countries*
la plupart d'entre eux	*most of them*
beaucoup d'entre mes amis	*many of my friends*
une dizaine d'entre les serveurs	*ten or so of the waiters*
le moins beau d'entre nous	*the least handsome among us*
Lequel d'entre vous le fera?	*Which of you will do it?*
chacun d'entre eux OR chacun d'eux	*each of them*
personne d'entre les invités OR personne des invités	*no-one among the guests*
aucun d'entre les spectateurs OR aucun des spectateurs	*none of the spectators*

13.28 *envers*

ressentir de la haine envers qn	*to feel hatred towards sb*
être bien disposé envers qn	*to be well disposed towards sb*
ma gratitude envers votre oncle	*my gratitude to your uncle*

13.29 *excepté*

Excepté les grand-parents, tous étaient partis
Apart from the grandparents, everyone had left

NB: *hormis* 'with the exception of' is also possible, but rather formal.

13.30 *face: en face de*

Le parc est en face du bureau de poste   *The park is opposite the post office*

13.31 *faute de*

Faute d'argent, l'entreprise a fait faillite
Through lack of money, the company went bankrupt

J'accepterai le poste, faute de mieux
I'll accept the job, for want of anything better

13.32 *force: à force de*

A force de travail, il a réussi   *Through working, he succeeded*

13.33 *grâce à*

Grâce à ton aide, je pourrai l'acheter   *Thanks to your help, I will be able to buy it*

C'est grâce à toi que j'ai pu le faire   *It's thanks to you that I could do it*

NB: *grâce à* is always positive, so cannot be used to translate sentences like: 'Thanks to you we lost the contract'. Here *à cause de* is required: *A cause de toi nous avons perdu le contrat.*

13.34 *haut: du haut de*

sauter du haut de la falaise   *to jump from the cliff*

NB: 'from' tall objects like cliffs, towers, buildings is usually *du haut de*, rather than *de* alone.

13.35 *hors de*

hors de danger	*out of danger*
hors de saison	*out of season*
hors de lui	*beside himself with anger*
hors d'haleine	*out of breath*
sauter hors de son lit	*to jump out of one's bed*
une randonnée hors de la ville	*a hike outside the town*

13.36 *jusqu'à*

jusqu'à demain	*until tomorrow*
jusqu'au bout	*right to the end*
depuis Paris jusqu'à la Manche	*from Paris to the Channel*

NB: 'not ... until' is *pas ... avant*: *Je ne viendrai pas avant demain* 'I won't come until tomorrow'.

(For the conjunction *jusqu'à ce que* see Chapter 17.3.8.)

13.37 *lieu: au lieu de*

au lieu de son frère   *instead of his brother*

13.38 *long: le long de*

rouler le long du quai   *to travel along the river bank*
                                          (as in Paris or London)

Tout au long du boulevard il y avait des marchands forains
All along the boulevard there were market traders

13.39 *lors de*

lors de mon séjour en France   *at the time of my stay in France*

13.40 *malgré*

malgré son enthousiasme, ses défauts, le mauvais temps, sa promesse
in spite of his enthusiasm, his faults, the bad weather, his promise

13.41 *par*

13.41.1 *par* = 'through'

regarder par la fenêtre   *to look through the window*
passer par la forêt   *to go through the forest*
aspirer l'air par la bouche   *to breathe through the mouth*
Je l'ai eu par un boulanger de Tours   *I got it through a baker from Tours*

13.41.2 *par* = 'by', 'per'

Le village était coupé par la neige   *The village was cut off by the snow*
Par bonheur, il s'est évadé   *By good fortune, he escaped*
Il tenait son fils par la main   *He held his son by the hand*
prendre qn par surprise   *to catch sb by surprise*
travailler par groupes de quatre   *to work in groups of four*
heure par heure   *hour by hour*
Ils sortaient un par un   *They came out one by one*
La chambre coûte 100 F par personne   *The room is 100 francs per person*
par nuit   *per night*

L'Etranger, par Albert Camus, est l'un des romans français les plus étudiés
'The Outsider', by Albert Camus, is one of the most widely studied French novels

NB: *par* is used after a pause, *de* otherwise:

un roman d'Albert Camus   *a novel by Albert Camus*

When 'by' introduces an agent, *par* is usually used:

Il a été effrayé par l'orage   *He was frightened by the storm*
Jean a été mordu par mon chien   *Jean was bitten by my dog*

But when a passive can be understood as a state, rather than an event, *de* may
also be used:

Quand il est arrivé au commissariat, il était accompagné de sa femme
When he arrived at the police station, his wife was with him

(See also 13.15.5.)

13.41.3 *par* = 'on'

se rouler par terre	*to roll oneself on the ground*
se jeter par terre	*to throw oneself on the ground*
par une belle journée de printemps	*on a fine day in spring*

13.41.4 *par* = 'from', 'out of'

faire qc par crainte	*to do sth out of fear*
par orgueil, par respect de qn	*from pride, from respect for sb*
par amitié, par honte	*out of/from friendship, from shame*
par jalousie, par pudeur	*from jealousy, from modesty*
par ignorance	*out of/from ignorance*

13.41.5 *par* = 'in(to)'

par temps de pluie	*in wet weather*
sortir par beau temps	*to go out in fair weather*
par milliers	*in (their) thousands*
par ordre alphabétique	*in alphabetical order*
par endroits	*in places*
par écrit	*in writing*

13.42 *parmi*

parmi les spectateurs	*among the spectators*
parmi la foule	*among the crowd*

une rumeur courait parmi les gens de la ville
a rumour was spreading among the townspeople

parmi mes papiers	*among my papers*

(See also 13.14.7.)

13.43 *part: de la part de*

parler de la part des étudiants	*to speak on behalf of the students*
C'est de la part de qui?	*Who's calling? Who's it from?*

13.44 *partir: à partir de*

à partir de demain	*from tomorrow*

13.45 *passé*

Passé le pont, on s'est arrêté un instant	*Once passed the bridge, we stopped a minute*
Passé minuit il n'y a plus de taxis	*After midnight there are no more taxis*

13.46 *pendant*

pendant la guerre	*during the war*
Nous avons dansé pendant une éternité	*We danced for ages*
Je t'écrirai pendant la semaine	*I'll write to you during the week*

13.47 *pour*

Pour ma part, je suis heureux
For my part, I'm happy

Elle le faisait exprès pour attirer l'attention
She did it on purpose (in order) to attract attention

donner un cadeau à qn pour son anniversaire
to give a present to sb for his/her birthday

elle se prend pour une star
She considers herself to be a star

s'en aller pour de bon
to go away for good

passer pour intelligent
to be considered intelligent

être bon pour qn, dur pour qn, gentil pour qn, (in)juste pour qn, sévère pour qn
to be good to (or for) sb, hard on sb, kind to sb, (un)just to sb, severe on sb

NB: The verb *payer* 'to pay for' is not usually followed by *pour*:

payer la tournée	*to pay for a round (of drinks)*
On ne voulait pas que je paie ma place	*They didn't want me to pay for my seat*

Unless money is involved, or a person is being paid for:

payer 500 francs pour un micro-ondes	*to pay 500 francs for a micro-wave oven*
Je ne paie pas pour toi!	*I'm not paying for you!*

NB: Expressions like: 'for two days', 'for three weeks', 'for several years' are usually translated by the time expression alone (i.e. without *pour*) when they refer to events in the past:

Elle est restée deux jours	*She stayed for two days*
Il est resté trois semaines	*He stayed for three weeks*

When the time expression refers to a period in the future in relation to the time of speaking, *pour* is used:

Elle partira pour deux jours	*She'll be away for two days*
Il voulait s'absenter pour trois semaines	*He wanted to be away for three weeks*

When the events that take place during the time period are stressed, *pendant* is the usual form:

Il a été malade pendant la nuit	*He was ill during the night*
Elle va travailler pendant deux jours	*She is going to work for two days*

13.48 *près de*

Il s'est assis près de moi	*He sat down next to me*
Je l'ai aperçu près du pont	*I spied him near the bridge*

13.49 *quant à*

Quant à moi, je suis heureux
For my part, I'm happy

Quant à son roman, il est loin de l'avoir fini
As for his novel, he is a long way from finishing it

13.50 *sans*

sans moi	*without me*
sans sel	*without salt*
sans rien dire	*without saying anything*
sans me regarder	*without looking at me*

13.51 *sauf*

Sauf ma mère, toute la famille était là
With the exception of my mother, all the family was there

13.52 *selon*

selon l'opinion générale	*according to the common view*
selon la loi	*by law, under the law*

13.53 *sous*

sous la table	*under the table*
s'abriter sous un arbre	*to shelter under a tree*
nager sous l'eau	*to swim under the water*
sous l'ancien régime	*under the 'ancien régime'*
sous clef	*under lock and key*
sous les verrous	*under lock and key*
sous le règne de Louis XIV	*in the reign of Louis XIV*

sous la chaleur, sous la pluie, sous le soleil
in the heat, in the rain, in the sun

Sous prétexte de se renseigner pour les trains, elle a vite téléphoné à sa copine
On the pretext of finding out about trains, she quickly got on the phone to her friend

promettre sous serment	*to promise on oath*
interdire qc sous peine d'amende	*to prohibit sth on pain of a fine*
vendre qc sous conditions	*to sell sth on condition*
J'ai un annuaire sous la main	*I have a phone directory to hand*
passer l'affaire sous silence	*to keep quiet about the matter*
manifester sous les fenêtres de la mairie	*to demonstrate in front of the town hall*

13.54 *suite: par suite de*

par suite d'un accident   *following an accident*

13.55 *suivant*

suivant son habitude   *as was his custom*

13.56 *sur*

J'ai mis ma main sur son épaule	*I put my hand on his shoulder*
Il me regardait, appuyé sur les coudes	*He watched me, leaning on his elbows*
Elle était assise sur un vieux tronc d'arbre	*She was sitting on an old tree trunk*
sur le seuil	*on the threshold, on the doorstep*
Elle attendait sur les marches de la mairie	*She was waiting on the steps of the town hall*
lire qc sur une affiche	*to read sth on a poster*
Je l'ai vu sur la place	*I saw him in the square*
sur la route, sur le chemin	*on the road, on the track*
sur le boulevard, sur la chaussée	*on the boulevard, in the road*
sur le trottoir	*on the pavement*
Il a laissé la clef sur la porte	*He left the key in the door*
Les garçons étaient assis sur trois rangées de fauteuils	*The boys were sitting in three rows of seats*
marcher sur les pas de quelqu'un	*to follow in somebody's footsteps*
aller sur le terrain de football	*to go onto the football pitch*
sur la patinoire	*onto the ice-rink*
revenir sur ses pas	*to retrace one's steps*
un salon qui donne sur la rivière	*a sitting-room which overlooks the river*
Elle va sur ses vingt-six ans	*She is nearly 26*
deux sur trois	*two out of three*
Sur dix, trois étaient partis	*Of ten, three had left*
Sur mon salaire, il ne restait que 5 francs	*of my salary, only 5 francs remained*
Quatre chats sur cinq le préfèrent	*Four out of five cats prefer it*
Sur la fin, j'étais fatigué	*Towards the end, I was tired*

13.57 *travers: à travers/au travers de/en travers de*

Il me parla à travers la porte fermée
He talked to me through the closed door

L'arbre était tombé en travers de la route
The tree had fallen across the road

Ils y sont finalement arrivés au travers d'un champ labouré
They finally got there across a ploughed field

13.58 *vers*

se diriger vers la maison	*to head for the house*
vers le haut du col	*towards the top of the pass*
vers 10 heures	*around 10 o'clock*
vers la fin de mars	*towards the end of March*
Il avait vers 26 ans	*He was around 26 years old*

13.59 French translations for common English prepositions

Figures refer to the sections where the French prepositions are dealt with.

Across: *de l'autre côté de; en travers de; au-dessus de*
  across the room
  de l'autre côté de la pièce

The barricade had been erected across the street
La barricade avait été érigée en travers de la rue (13.57)

They will have to build a bridge across the motorway
Ils devront construire un pont au-dessus de l'autoroute (13.23)

After: *après; derrière*

after the meal	après le repas	(13.93)
after arriving	après être arrivé	
to ask after sb	demander après qn	
to come after sb (e.g. in a race)	arriver derrière qn	(13.20)
to clean up after sb	nettoyer derrière qn	

Among: *dans; parmi; entre; d'entre; chez*

to disappear among the firs	disparaître dans les sapins	(13.14.7)
to search among one's papers	chercher dans/parmi ses papiers	
among the spectators	parmi les spectateurs	(13.42)
among the crowd	parmi la foule	
among friends	entre amis	
several among you	plusieurs d'entre vous	(13.27)
among the English	chez les Anglais	(13.10)

Around (approximately): *dans; vers; environ, autour de*

He was around 26 years old	il avait vers 26 ans, il avait 26 ans environ	(13.58)
	Also: Il avait dans les 26 ans (informal), il avait autour de 26 ans	(13.14.6)
to win around 1,000 francs	gagner dans les 1,000 francs	

As: *en; en tant que; comme*

to speak as an expert	parler en spécialiste
to dress as a sailor	s'habiller en marin
to receive sth as a present	recevoir qc en cadeau
to act as the representative of	agir en tant que représentant de
to act as an intermediary	servir comme intermédiaire

At: *à; en; par; chez*

to slow down at every bend	ralentir à chaque virage	(13.2.1)
to be at school	être à l'école	
at the cinema, at church	au cinéma, à l'église	
at 3 o'clock	à 3 heures	
at the beginning, at the end	au début, à la fin	
one thing at a time	une chose à la fois	
at the same time	en même temps	(13.26.8)
at odd moments	par instant(s)	
at his house, at my house	chez lui, chez moi	(13.10)
at the weekend	en fin de semaine	(13.26.8)
at the top of the page	en haut de page	
at sea	en mer	
right at the summit	en plein sommet	
at war	en guerre	
at stake	en jeu	
at speed	en vitesse	
to be good at languages	être bon en langues	

By: *de; par; à; avant; selon*

to know sb by sight	connaître qn de vue	(13.15.5)
to be known by everyone	être connu de tous	
a film by François Truffaut	un film de François Truffaut	
to be accompanied by one's wife	être accompagné de sa femme	
to be frightened by the storm	être effrayé par l'orage	
to be bitten by a dog	être mordu par un chien	
to recognize sb by his/her voice	reconnaître qn à sa voix	(13.2.5)
to move forward step by step	s'avancer pas à pas	
to leave one by one	partir un à un (*or* un par un)	
to work by the light of a candle	travailler à la lumière d'une bougie	
to hold sb by the hand	tenir qn par la main	(13.41.2)
to work in groups	travailler par groupes	
hour by hour	heure par heure	
by night	par nuit	
cut off by the snow	coupé par la neige	
by the weekend	avant le weekend	(13.6)
by the rules	selon les règles	
by law	selon la loi	(13.52)

by taxi, by bicycle, by train, by plane, by car, by ambulance, by boat, by bus:

en taxi (*or* dans un taxi), en vélo (*or* à vélo)	(13.26.5)
en train (*or* dans le train), en avion (*or* par avion)	
en voiture (*or* avec la voiture), en ambulance (*or* dans une ambulance)	
en bateau (*or* par bateau), en bus (*or* dans le bus)	

During: *dans, pendant, durant, au cours de*

I'll do it during the week
Je le ferai dans (*or* pendant *or* au cours de) la semaine   (13.14.5)

From: *de; depuis; du haut de, à; dans; en; d'après; sur*

to watch sb from above	regarder qn d'en haut	(13.15.4)
to cite sth from memory	citer qc de mémoire	
from afar	de loin	
from close by	de près	
to go from London to Paris	aller de Londres à Paris	
He complained all the way	Il s'est plaint depuis Londres jusqu'à Paris	
from London to Paris		
to jump from the cliff	sauter du haut de la falaise	(13.34)
to borrow sth from sb	emprunter qc à qn	(13.2.8)
to drink from the bottle	boire à la bouteille	
to take a wallet from the drawer	prendre un portefeuille dans le tiroir	(13.14.9)
to cut photos from the newspaper	découper des photos dans le journal	
a week from today	aujourd'hui en huit	(13.26.9)
a fortnight from Monday	lundi en quinze	

to do sth from fear, from shame, from ignorance		
faire qc par (*or* de) crainte, par (*or* de) honte, par (*or* d')ignorance		(13.41.4)
from what I'm told	d'après ce qu'on me dit	(13.3)
from the look on his face	d'après son expression	
	d'après la tête qu'il faisait	
They selected five from ten	Ils en ont sélectionné cinq sur dix	

In: *de; à; en; dans; par; sur; sous; no preposition used in French*

dressed in black	vêtu, *or* habillé de noir	(13.15.3)
to go out in evening dress	sortir en tenue de soirée	(13.26.1)
in a swimming costume	en maillot de bain	
in shirt sleeves	en bras de chemise	
the first, last, only time in my life	la première, dernière, seule fois de ma vie	(13.15.3)
the fastest train in Europe	le train le plus rapide d'Europe	
three Sundays in a row	trois dimanches de suite	
paralysed in the arms, legs	paralysé des bras, des jambes	
broad in the shoulders, short in the legs	large d'épaules, court de jambes	
to live in Paris	vivre à Paris	(13.2.3)
in the shade	à l'ombre	
in the back, in one's hand, in paradise	à l'arrière, à la main, au paradis	
in the garden, in the cinema	au jardin, au cinéma	
in the restaurant, in school	au restaurant, à l'école	
in the village, in the park	au village, au parc	
BUT *in town*	en ville	(13.26.1)
in hell	en enfer	
in Japan, in Denmark, in the United States, in Malta, in Jersey	au Japon, au Danemark, aux Etats-Unis, à Malte, à Jersey	(13.2.3)
in France, in Spain	en France, en Espagne	(13.26.1)
in the evening, in the morning	au soir, au matin	(13.2.3)
in the 20th century	au 20e siècle	
in the interval	à l'entracte	
to glimpse sth in the valley	apercevoir qc dans la vallée	(13.14.1)
to meet sb in the rue de Rivoli, on the boulevard Montparnasse	rencontrer qn rue de Rivoli, boulevard Montparnasse	
to meet sb in Yorkshire, to meet sb in Nevada, in the Calvados region	rencontrer qn dans le Yorkshire, rencontrer qn dans le Nevada, dans le Calvados	
I'll come back after an hour	Je reviendrai dans une heure	(13.14.4)
I'm expecting him in two days	Je l'attends dans deux jours	

| *I'll have read it within an hour* | Je l'aurai lu en une heure | (13.26.3) |
| *He can do it in (under) two weeks* | Il peut le faire en quinze jours | |

in January, in February	en janvier, en février	(13.26.1)
in the autumn, in the summer,	en automne, en été, en hiver	
in the winter		

| *in the spring* | au printemps | |

| *in 1992, in the year 1992* | en 1992, en l'an 1992 | |
| *in the 50s* | dans les années 50 | |

| *in German, in Spanish* | en allemand, en espagnol | |

in wet weather	par temps de pluie	(13.41.5)
in their thousands	par milliers	
in alphabetical order	par ordre alphabétique	
in places	par endroits	

| *to see sb in the square* | voir qn sur la place | |
| *to be sitting in three rows of seats* | être assis sur trois rangées de fauteuils | |

| *in the reign of Louis XIV* | sous le règne de Louis XIV | (13.53) |

Into: *dans; en; à*

| *to go into the yard* | aller dans la cour | |

| *to turn the house into a hotel* | transformer la maison en hôtel | (13.26.11) |
| *to burst into tears* | éclater en larmes | |

| *to go into the office* | aller au bureau | (13.2.2) |
| *to get into bed* | se mettre au lit | |

Of: *de; à; sur; d'entre*

| *a cup of tea* | une tasse de thé | (13.15.1) |
| *half of the spectators* | la moitié des spectateurs | |

| *It's kind of you, nice of you* | C'est gentil à vous, aimable à vous | (13.2.8) |
| *one of my uncles* | un oncle à moi (un de mes oncles) | |

| *Of ten, three had left* | Sur dix, trois étaient partis | (13.56) |

| *most of them* | la plupart d'entre eux | (13.27) |
| *each of them* | chacun d'(entre) eux | |

On: *de; à; dans; en; par; sur; sous; no preposition*

| *I live just on potatoes* | Je ne me nourris que de pommes de terre | (13.15.9) |

| *to be on duty or on call* | être de permanence | |
| *to look on the bright side* | voir les choses du bon côté | |

on several occasions	à plusieurs reprises	(13.2.4)
on page 2	à la page 2	
on the television/on the radio	à la télévision/à la radio	
to knock on the door	frapper à la porte	
to be on the ground	être à terre	
on one's return	au retour	

on a bicycle, on foot, on horseback	à bicyclette, à pied, à cheval	
on military service	au service militaire	
to meet sb on the stairs	rencontrer qn dans l'escalier	(13.14.8)
to do odd jobs on farms	bricoler dans des fermes	
on fire	en feu	(13.26.6)
on holiday	en vacances	
on leave	en congé	
on sale	en vente	
on the way	en route	
on a trip	en voyage	
on average	en moyenne	
to throw things on the ground	jeter des choses par terre	(13.41.3)
on a fine spring day	par une belle journée de printemps	
to put one's hand on his shoulder	mettre la main sur son épaule	(13.56)
leaning on one's elbows	appuyé sur les coudes	
to sit on a chair, a bench, a seat	s'asseoir sur une chaise, un banc, un siège	
on the road, on the pavement	sur la route, sur le trottoir	
to promise on oath	promettre sous serment	(13.53)
to sell sth on condition	vendre qc sous conditions	
on Mondays	le lundi	
They're on me!	C'est ma tournée!	

Out of: *de; en dehors de; hors de; sur*

to pull a rabbit out of a hat	sortir un lapin d'un chapeau	(13.15.4)
Get out of here!	Sortez d'ici!	
out of the town	en dehors de la ville	(13.16)
out of the question	hors de question	
five out of ten	cinq sur dix	(13.56)

Than: *de; que*

She earns more than 30,000 francs a month	Elle gagne plus de 30 000 FF par mois	
She earns more than me/than I do	Elle gagne plus que moi	(13.15.7)
He works less than 2 hours a day	Il travaille moins de 2 heures par jour	

Through: *par; à travers; au travers de; par moyen de*

to look through the window	regarder par la fenêtre	(13.41.1)
to go through the forest	passer par la forêt	
to breathe through the mouth	aspirer l'air par la bouche	
to go through fields	passer à travers champs	(13.57)
to go through difficulties	passer au travers des problèmes	
through an advert	par moyen d'une annonce	

To: *à; en; dans; sous; jusqu'à; pour; avec*

to the north, to the south	au nord, au sud	(13.2.2)
to go to school, to the cinema, to the café	aller à l'école, au cinéma, au café	
to go up to one's room	monter à sa chambre	
to the right, to the left	à droite, à gauche	

to Japan, to Denmark	au Japon, au Danemark
to Malta, to Jersey	à Malte, à Jersey
to Paris, to London	à Paris, à Londres
to Sicily, to New Zealand	en Sicile, en Nouvelle-Zélande (13.26.1)
to France, to Spain	en France, en Espagne
to Europe, to Africa	en Europe, en Afrique
to Normandy, to Brittany	en Normandie, en Bretagne
to Essex, to Massachusetts	dans l'Essex, dans le Massachusetts
to have a phone directory to hand	avoir un annuaire sous la main (13.53)
to go up to 2,000 francs	aller jusqu'à 2,000 francs
a cheque to the value of ...	un chèque de la valeur de ...
to keep something to oneself	garder quelque chose pour soi
to be kind to sb	être gentil avec qn

Under: *sous; moins de; inférieur à; selon*

under the table, under the water	sous la table, sous l'eau (13.53)
under twenty francs	moins de vingt francs (13.15.7)
a price under a thousand francs	un prix inférieur à mille francs
under the law	selon la loi (13.52)

With: *de; à; avec*

a street lined with plane trees	une rue bordée de platanes (13.15.2)
to fill with water	remplir d'eau (*or* avec de l'eau)
to cover with posters	couvrir d'affiches (*or* avec des affiches)
to go red with shame	rougir de honte
to tremble with cold	trembler de froid
a man with a grey beard	un homme à la barbe grise (13.2.6)
to water the garden with a watering can	arroser le jardin avec un arrosoir (13.7)
to speak with sb	parler avec qn
to arrive with sb	arriver avec qn

14

Question formation

14.1 Introduction

There are two main types of question: yes/no questions, to which it is possible to answer simply 'yes' or 'no':

Aimez-vous la musique pop? Oui	*Do you like pop music? Yes*
Est-ce que tu as fait tes devoirs? Non	*Have you done your homework? No*

and information questions, to which it is impossible to answer simply 'yes' or 'no', but which require a piece of information in response:

Quand partira Jean? Demain	*When will Jean leave? Tomorrow*
Qui a-t-il rencontré? Jeanette	*Who did he meet? Jeanette*

Information questions involve the use of a question word or phrase like *qui, que, quand, comment, où, pourquoi, pour quelle raison, avec quel ami, de quoi*, and so on.

14.2 Yes/no questions

There are three ways in which yes/no questions can be asked in French. Each is characteristic of a particular style of French, ranging from the informal to the formal.

14.2.1 Yes/no questions formed with rising intonation

The simplest way to form a yes/no question in French is to add rising intonation to the final syllables of a declarative sentence:

Tu as quelque chose à dire?	*Do you have anything to say?*
Elle va rester ici?	*Is she going to stay here?*
Pierre est venu?	*Has Pierre come?*
Je peux mettre mes photos au mur?	*Can I put my photos on the wall?*

This kind of yes/no question is very common in informal spoken French, but less common in more formal spoken French and not normally used in written French (unless direct speech is being recorded, or an informal style is being imitated).

14.2.2 Yes/no questions formed with *est-ce que*

Yes/no questions may also be formed by placing the question formula *est-ce que* at the beginning of a declarative sentence:

Est-ce que tu as quelque chose à dire?	*Do you have anything to say?*
Est-ce qu'elle va rester ici?	*Is she going to stay here?*
Est-ce que Pierre est venu?	*Has Pierre come?*
Est-ce que je peux mettre mes photos au mur?	*Can I put my photos on the wall?*

Yes/no questions formed with *est-ce que* can be used in all styles of French, informal and formal, spoken and written.

14.2.3 Yes/no questions formed by inverting the verb and subject

Yes/no questions may be formed by inverting the subject and the verb which agrees with it. Such inversion takes two forms, depending on whether the subject is an unstressed pronoun or not.

Subject is an unstressed pronoun

If the subject is an unstressed pronoun, it changes places with the verb which agrees with it:

Es-tu content?	*Are you happy?*
Est-ce le facteur?	*Is it the postman?*
Avez-vous bien compris?	*Have you really understood?*
Peut-on se changer dans les vestiaires?	*Can you change in the changing rooms?*
Avaient-ils reçu de ses nouvelles?	*Had they had news of him?*
Avait-il pu réunir les actionnaires?	*Had he been able to assemble the shareholders?*

Such subject-verb inversion is possible with all verbs in French, whereas in English it is only possible with 'auxiliary' verbs like 'have', 'be', 'can', 'will', 'do', etc.:

Aime-t-il le Roquefort?	*Does he like Roquefort?*
Descend-elle en ville?	*Is she going down into town?*
Fumez-vous depuis longtemps?	*Have you smoked for long?*
Prennent-ils le train?	*Are they taking the train?*

Subject is not an unstressed pronoun

If the subject is anything other than an unstressed pronoun, i.e. a proper noun, noun phrase or stressed pronoun, then the subject is placed first, followed by the verb and an unstressed subject pronoun agreeing with the subject is inserted to the right of the verb:

Pierre est-il content?	*Is Pierre happy?*
Les joueurs peuvent-ils se changer dans les vestiaires?	*Can the players change in the changing rooms?*
Cela est-il vrai?	*Is that true?*
Personne ne veut-il m'accompagner?	*Doesn't anyone want to come with me?*
Les élèves avaient-ils reçu les résultats?	*Had the pupils received the results?*
Julie viendra-t-elle demain?	*Will Julie come tomorrow?*

NB: It is impossible to invert a subject which is not an unstressed pronoun with an agreeing verb:

NOT *Viendra Julie demain?
NOT *Est cela vrai?
NOT *Peuvent les joueurs se changer dans les vestiaires?
NOT *Est Pierre content?

Yes/no questions formed with inversion are typically used in more formal spoken and in written French.

14.2.4 Insertion of -*t*- between inverted verb and subject

When the inversion of subject and verb results in two vowels becoming adjacent, the consonant -*t*- is inserted between them:

A-**t**-il 17 ans?	*Is he 17?*
Aura-**t**-elle faim?	*Will she be hungry?*

This rule also applies where the verb ends in -*e*, even though in the spoken language the -*e* is not pronounced:

Epouse-**t**-il Marie?	*Is he marrying Marie?*
Dîne-**t**-elle au palais ce soir?	*Is she dining at the palace this evening?*

Where a verb already ends in a -*t* or a -*d* in the written language, it is pronounced as 't' in questions:

Est-elle contente?	*Is she happy?*
Boiven**t**-ils du cidre?	*Are they drinking cider?*
Vos amis son**t**-ils partis?	*Have your friends left?*
David ven**d**-il sa voiture?	*Is David selling his car?*
Le voyage te ren**d**-il malade?	*Is the journey making you feel ill?*

14.2.5 Inversion of the verb and *je* in yes/no questions

Inversion of the verb with first person *je* to form a yes/no question is characteristic of only the most formal French. Many speakers and writers these days would avoid it and use *est-ce que*. Furthermore, there are idiosyncratic restrictions on its use.

In the present tense, inversion between *je* and some very common verbs of one syllable is frequent:

Ai-je le droit? (avoir)	*Am I allowed to?*
Dois-je vous téléphoner? (devoir)	*Should I phone you?*
Puis-je vous déranger? (pouvoir)	*May I disturb you?*
Suis-je heureux? (être)	*Am I happy?*
Vais-je me laisser tromper? (aller)	*Am I going to let myself be deceived?*
Ne **dis-je** pas la vérité? (dire)	*Am I not telling the truth?*

but with most other verbs such inversion is impossible:

NOT *Mens-je?	*Am I lying?*
NOT *Prends-je le bus?	*Am I taking the bus?*

In future and conditional tenses, however, inversion with these same verbs is more acceptable (but again only in the most formal styles):

Mentirais-je?	*Would I lie?*
Prendrai-je le bus?	*Shall I take the bus?*

Some grammars suggest that where a verb ends in *-e* and it is inverted with *je*, the *-e* becomes *-é*:

> Demandé-je? *Am I asking?*

This, however, is extremely rare in modern French.

14.2.6 *n'est-ce pas*

n'est-ce pas? is the invariable French equivalent of English 'tag' question forms like 'doesn't he?', 'haven't you?', 'mustn't I?', etc.:

Il habite à Paris, **n'est-ce pas**?	*He lives in Paris, doesn't he?*
Vous avez vendu le terrain, **n'est-ce pas**?	*You've sold the land, haven't you?*
Je dois m'adresser au sous-directeur, **n'est-ce pas**?	*I must speak to the assistant director, mustn't I?*

14.2.7 Use of *jamais, rien, aucun, personne* in yes/no questions

In questions, *jamais*, *rien*, *aucun* and *personne* may mean 'ever', 'anything', 'any' and 'anyone':

Est-ce que vous avez **jamais** visité le Louvre?	*Have you ever been to the Louvre?*
A-t-il **rien** fait de meilleur?	*Has he done anything better?*
A-t-elle eu **aucune** réponse?	*Has she received any reply?*
Est-ce que vous avez vu **personne**?	*Have you seen anyone?*

NB: *qui que ce soit* 'anyone' is more used than *personne*:

> Est-ce qu'il confie à qui que ce soit ce qu'il fait?
> *Does he tell anyone what he is doing?*

14.2.8 *oui, si, non* and *merci* as responses to yes/no questions

non is the normal way of saying 'no' to yes/no questions, both affirmative and negative:

Tu viens?	- Non
Tu ne viens pas?	- Non

oui is used to say 'yes' to affirmative yes/no questions, but *si* is used to say 'yes' to negative questions:

Tu viens?	- Oui
Tu ne viens pas?	- Si

In each case the force of the response may be increased by adding *mais*, or *bien sûr que*:

Tu viens?	- Mais oui	- Mais non
	- Bien sûr que oui	- Bien sûr que non
Tu ne viens pas?	- Mais si	- Mais non
	- Bien sûr que si	- Bien sûr que non

merci 'thank you' used alone as a response to a yes/no question is normally treated as a response of 'No, thank you':

Voulez-vous du fromage?	- Merci
Would you like some cheese?	- *No, thank you*

To reply 'Yes, please' one can say *(Oui), je veux bien, S'il vous (te) plaît* or *Volontiers*:

Voulez-vous du fromage?	- Je veux bien
	- S'il vous plaît
	- Volontiers
Would you like some cheese?	- *Yes, please*

14.3 Information questions

There are four ways of asking information questions in French. Each is appropriate to a particular level of formality of style.

14.3.1 Information questions formed with rising intonation

The simplest way to form an information question is to replace an item in a declarative sentence by a question word or phrase, and add rising intonation to the final syllables of the sentence. (For question words and phrases see 14.6.) For example, taking a declarative sentence such as:

L'étudiant téléphonera à son député demain
The student will telephone his MP tomorrow

Information questions can be formed related to *demain, à son député* or *l'étudiant* simply by replacing the relevant words with a question word:

L'étudiant téléphonera à son député **quand**?
When will the student telephone his MP?

L'étudiant téléphonera **à qui** demain?
Who will the student telephone tomorrow?

Qui téléphonera à son député demain?
Who will telephone his MP tomorrow?

This kind of information question is very common in informal spoken French. The last example above involving *qui?* (where the subject is questioned) is also normal in formal styles (see 14.3.6). But the other types are less common in formal spoken and in written styles (unless direct speech is being reported, or an informal style is being imitated).

The full range of question words and phrases (see 14.6) may be used in this way, except *que?* 'what'. Instead, the stressed form of *que?* – *quoi?* – is used:

Vous avez vu **quoi**?	*What did you see?*
Elle a dit **quoi**?	*What did she say?*
Marcel a écrit **à qui**?	*Who did Marcel write to?*
Elle parle de **quoi**?	*What is she talking about?*
Tu recommanderais **quel film**?	*Which film would you recommend?*
Ils ont invité **combien de gens**?	*How many people did they invite?*
Vous l'avez vu **où**?	*Where did you see it?*
Bernard reviendra **quand**?	*When will Bernard come back?*

14.3.2 Information questions formed by 'fronting' a question word or phrase

Another common way of forming information questions in very informal spoken styles of French involves replacing an item in a declarative sentence by a question word or phrase, and then moving the question word or phrase to the front of the sentence, without making any other changes:

Qui vous avez vu?	*Who did you see?*
Qui c'est, celui là?	*Who's he?*
A qui Marcel a écrit?	*Who did Marcel write to?*
Quel film tu recommanderais?	*Which film would you recommend?*
Combien de gens ils ont invités?	*How many people did they invite?*
De quoi tu voulais me parler?	*What did you want to speak to me about?*
Où vous l'avez vu?	*Where did you see it?*
Pourquoi la police l'a arrêté?	*Why did the police arrest him?*

Nearly all question words can be used in this way except direct object *que?*, *quoi?* 'what?' Instead *qu'est-ce que?* is used (see 14.3.3):

Qu'est-ce qu'elle a dit?	*What did she say?*
Qu'est-ce que tu faisais dans ma chambre?	*What were you doing in my room?*

14.3.3 Information questions formed with *est-ce que?*

Information questions may be formed by 'fronting' a question word or phrase, as described in 14.3.2, and in addition inserting *est-ce que?* between the question word or phrase and the rest of the sentence. Questions of this type may be used in all styles of French, formal and informal. The full range of question words and phrases (see 14.6) may be used in this construction except *quoi?* 'what?' – the unstressed variant *que?* is required instead:

Qui est-ce que vous avez vu?	*Who did you see?*
Qu'est-ce qu'elle a dit?	*What did she say?*
Quel film est-ce que tu recommanderais?	*Which film would you recommend?*
A qui est-ce que Marcel a écrit?	*To whom did Marcel write?*
Combien de gens est-ce qu'ils ont invités?	*How many people did they invite?*
Où est-ce que vous l'avez vu?	*Where did you see it?*
Quand est-ce que Bernard reviendra?	*When will Bernard come back?*
Pourquoi est-ce que la police l'a arrêté?	*Why did the police arrest him?*

14.3.4 *qui est-ce qui?*, *qui est-ce que?*, *qu'est-ce qui?*, and *qu'est-ce que?*

qui est-ce qui? is used to form questions dealing with animate subjects:

Qui est-ce qui a pris mon crayon?	*Who took my pencil?*
Qui est-ce qui va avoir le prix?	*Who will get the prize?*

qu'est-ce qui? is used to form questions dealing with non-animate subjects:

Qu'est ce qui a abîmé mon pneu?	*What punctured my tyre?*
Qu'est-ce qui s'est passé?	*What happened?*
Qu'est-ce qui a effrayé le facteur?	*What frightened the postman?*
Qu'est-ce qui lui est arrivé, à Paul?	*What happened to Paul?*

qui est-ce que? is used to form questions dealing with animate direct objects:

Qui est-ce que vous avez vu?	*Who did you see?*
Qui est-ce qu'ils ont invité à la fête?	*Who did they invite to the party?*

qu'est-ce que? is used to form questions dealing with non-animate direct objects:

Qu'est-ce que vous avez dit?	*What did you say?*
Qu'est-ce que Marie va acheter?	*What is Marie going to buy?*
Qu'est-ce qu'elle a pris dans la grange?	*What did she take from the barn?*
Qu'est-ce que c'était, ce bruit, dehors?	*What was that noise, outside?*

Compare the following uses of *qu'est-ce?*, *qu'est-ce que?* and *qu'est-ce que c'est?*:

Qu'est-ce? (very formal)	*What is it?*
Qu'est-ce que c'est?	*What is it?*
Qu'est-ce que c'est que ça?	*What on earth is that?*
Qu'est-ce qu'une 'jonque'?	*What's a 'jonque'?*
Qu'est-ce que c'est qu'une 'jonque'?	*What on earth is a 'jonque'?*
Qu'est-ce que ça veut dire 'jonque'?	*What does 'jonque' mean?*

14.3.5 Information questions formed by the inversion of verb and subject

Information questions may be formed by 'fronting' a question word or phrase (as described in 14.3.2), and in addition inverting the subject and the verb which agrees with the subject. This kind of question is usually found in formal spoken and in written French. It takes two forms depending on whether the subject is an unstressed pronoun or not.

Subject is an unstressed pronoun

If the subject is an unstressed pronoun, it changes places with the verb which agrees with it:

Qui avez-**vous** vu?	*Who did you see?*
Qui est-**ce**?	*Who is it?*
A qui a-t-**elle** écrit?	*To whom did she write?*
Quel film recommanderais-**tu**?	*Which film would you recommend?*
Combien de personnes ont-**ils** invitées?	*How many people have they invited?*
Où l'avez-**vous** vu?	*Where did you see it?*
Quand reviendra-t-**il**?	*When will he come back?*
Pourquoi l'ont-**ils** arrêté?	*Why have they arrested him?*

(For inversion with *je* see 14.2.5.)

Subject is not an unstressed pronoun

If the subject is not an unstressed pronoun, i.e. if it is a proper noun, noun phrase or stressed pronoun, then the subject is placed first after the question word, followed by the verb and an unstressed subject pronoun agreeing with the subject is inserted to the right of the verb:

Qui **Robert** a-t-**il** rencontré?	*Who did Robert meet?*
A qui **Jean** donnera-t-**il** l'argent?	*To whom will Jean give the money?*
Quelle robe **Madame** préfère-t-**elle**?	*Which dress does madam prefer?*
Combien de romans **Camus** a-t-**il** écrits?	*How many novels did Camus write?*
Où **Marie** va-t-**elle** faire ses courses?	*Where is Marie going to do her shopping?*

Quand **le train** arrivera-t-**il** à Limoges?	*When will the train arrive at Limoges?*

Pourquoi **les examens** ont-**ils** toujours lieu en juin?
Why do the exams always take place in June?

(For insertion of *-t-* see 14.2.4.)

14.3.6 Exceptional behaviour of subject *qui?* and subject and object *que?* in information questions

When the subject is animate and questioned by *qui?* 'who', there is no inversion with the verb:

Qui parle?	*Who is speaking?*
Qui a tourné ce film?	*Who made this film?*

NOT *Qui parle-t-il?
NOT *Qui a-t-il tourné ce film?

que? 'what' can never be used directly as non-animate subject 'what', and nor can its stressed form *quoi?*. Instead, *qu'est-ce qui?* must be used:

Qu'est-ce qui brille dans le ciel?	*What's shining in the sky?*
Qu'est-ce qui a grignoté les gâteaux dans le placard?	*What has eaten the cakes in the cupboard?*
Qu'est-ce qui plaît à Pierre?	*What does Pierre like?*
Qu'est-ce qui a été donné à Marie?	*What was given to Marie?*

and

NOT *Que brille dans le ciel?
NOT *Qu'a gringoté les gâteaux?
NOT *Quoi plaît à Pierre?
NOT *Quoi a été donné à Marie?

When *que?* 'what' is a direct object, it may be used with verb and subject inversion, providing that the subject is a pronoun:

Que dit-**il**?	*What does he say?*
Que pense-t-**elle**?	*What does she think?*
Qu'ont-**ils** décidé?	*What have they decided?*

But it may not be used with inversion when the subject is a proper noun, noun phrase or stressed pronoun:

NOT *Que le docteur dit-il?	*What does the doctor say?*
NOT *Que Marie pense-t-elle?	*What does Marie think?*
NOT *Que le conseil municipal a-t-il décidé?	*What has the council decided?*

Instead, either *qu'est-ce que?* must be used:

Qu'est-ce que le docteur dit?	*What does the doctor say?*
Qu'est-ce que Marie pense?	*What does Marie think?*
Qu'est-ce que le conseil municipal a décidé?	*What has the council decided?*

Or a different kind of inversion must be used involving the subject and the whole verb group, but without the insertion of an unstressed pronoun:

Que dit le **docteur**?	*What does the doctor say?*
Que pense **Marie**?	*What does Marie think?*
Qu'a décidé **le conseil municipal**?	*What has the council decided?*
Que va faire **Marie**?	*What is Marie going to do?*
Qu'aurait dû déclarer **le ministre**?	*What should the minister have declared?*

This kind of inversion is known by linguists as 'stylistic inversion'.

14.3.7 'Stylistic inversion' in information questions

In formal spoken and in written French, as an alternative to subject-verb inversion of the kind: *Où Christine est-elle allée?* 'Where did Christine go?', it is also possible (with many question words and phrases) to invert the subject with the whole verb group, but without insertion of an unstressed pronoun:

> **Où** est allée **Christine**?

Notice that *Christine* and *est allée* have inverted, but without insertion of an agreeing unstressed pronoun. Stylistic inversion of this kind is possible with:

Object *que*?

Qu'avait dit le **docteur**?	*What had the doctor said?*
Qu'a décidé **le conseil municipal**?	*What has the council decided?*

Prepositional object *qui* (*à qui?, de qui?, avec qui?*, etc.)

A qui s'est adressé **Jacques**?	*To whom did Jacques go and speak?*
De qui aura parlé **le professeur**?	*Who will the professor have spoken about?*

Prepositional object *quoi* (*à quoi?, de quoi?, avec quoi?*, etc.)

A quoi aurait dû penser **Marie**?	*What ought Marie to have thought about?*
De quoi dépend **la décision**?	*What does the decision depend on?*

Object and prepositional object *quel?, quand?, combien*?

quel

Quel plat a commandé **Pierre**?	*Which dish did Pierre order?*
A quelle heure partira **Thomas**?	*At what time will Thomas leave?*
Par quelle porte est sortie **la vedette**?	*Which door did the star come out of?*

quand

Quand est entré **François**?	*When did François come in?*
Depuis quand travaille **Pierre**?	*How long has Pierre been working?*

combien

Combien de kilos a perdu **Philippe**?	*How many kilos has Philippe lost?*
Combien de cidre produit **ce verger**?	*How much cider does this orchard produce?*

Stylistic inversion is not possible with *pourquoi*:

NOT *Pourquoi travaille Pierre?	*Why does Pierre work?*
NOT *Pourquoi est partie Marie?	*Why did Marie leave?*

Stylistic inversion is also quite restricted by the type of verb with which it can be used. It occurs fairly freely with intransitive verbs which do not have complements:

Depuis quand travaille **Pierre**?	*How long has Pierre been working?*

And when the questioned phrase is itself a direct object:

> **Quel vin** recommande **le patron**?   *Which wine does the patron*
> *recommend?*

But it is **not** acceptable when an intransitive verb has an adverbial complement:

> NOT *Depuis quand travaille Pierre dans la cuisine?
> *How long has Pierre been working in the kitchen?*

or with transitive verbs when the direct object is present:

> NOT *Depuis quand connaît Pierre Marie?   *How long has Pierre known Marie?*
> NOT *Où va manger Pierre des escargots?   *Where is Pierre going to eat snails?*
> NOT *A qui a donné Paul ce livre?   *To whom did Paul give this book?*

14.4 Order of object pronouns in questions involving inversion

The order of unstressed object pronouns is unaffected by the inversion of the subject and verb in questions:

> Elle **en** a parlé à Charley
> *She spoke of it to Charley*
>
> **En** a-t-elle parlé à Charley?
> *Did she speak of it to Charley?*

> Il **le lui** avait prêté
> *He lent it to her*
>
> **Le lui** avait-il prêté?
> *Did he lend it to her?*

> Jean **te le** dira
> *Jean will tell you so*
>
> Jean **te le** dira-t-il?
> *Will Jean tell you so?*

> Ils **me** l'ont donné
> *They gave it to me*
>
> Pourquoi **me** l'ont-ils donné?
> *Why did they give it to me?*

14.5 Order of negative particles in questions involving inversion

The position of negative particles is unaffected by the inversion of the subject and verb in questions:

> Tu **n'**as **jamais** fait cela
> *You have never done that*
>
> **N'**as-tu **jamais** fait cela?
> *Have you never done that?*

> Vous **n'**avez **pas** vu cet homme
> *You haven't seen this man*
>
> Qui **n'**avez-vous **pas** vu?
> *Who haven't you seen?*

> Ils **ne** leur écrivent **plus**
> *They don't write to them any more*
>
> Pourquoi **ne** leur écrivent-ils **plus**?
> *Why don't they write to them any more?*

14.6 Use of question words and phrases: *qui?, que?, quoi?, quel?, de qui?, avec combien de?* etc.

14.6.1 *qui?*

qui? typically translates English 'who?', 'whom?' whether subject, direct object or object of a preposition:

Subject

Qui a pris le tire-bouchon?	*Who took the corkscrew?*

Direct object

Qui Robert invite-t-il à dîner?	*Who is Robert inviting to dinner?*

Object of a preposition

A qui la journaliste a-t-elle posé la question?	*Who did the reporter put the question to?*
De qui parlez-vous?	*Who are you talking about?*
Contre qui avait-il joué?	*Who had he played against?*
Sur qui peut-on compter?	*Who can one count on?*

14.6.2 *que?, quoi?*

que?, quoi? typically translate English 'what?'. *Que?* is used to question direct objects which are moved to the front of the sentence:

Que dit-il?	*What does he say?*
Qu'est-il arrivé?	*What's happened?*
Que sont-ils devenus?	*What's become of them?*
Que boiront les invités?	*What will the guests drink?*

que? cannot be used to question subjects, rather *qu'est-ce qui?* is used (see 14.3.6):

Qu'est-ce qui lui est arrivé? *What happened to him?*	NOT *Que lui est arrivé?
Qu'est-ce qui a taché le mur? *What made that mess on the wall?*	NOT *Qu'a fait cela?

quoi? is used to question direct objects which are not moved to the front of the sentence. It is also used to form questions related to the objects of prepositions; in this use it can be moved to the front of the sentence:

Direct object

Elles cherchent **quoi**?	*What are they looking for?*
Ça ouvre **quoi**, ça?	*What does that thing open?*
Tu seras **quoi** dans un an?	*What will you be a year from now?*

Object of a preposition

A quoi pensent-elles?	*What are they thinking about?*
Avec quoi a-t-il coupé le pain?	*What did he cut the bread with?*
On peut miser **sur quoi**?	*What can one bank on?*
Contre quoi est-ce que les gens manifestent?	*What are people demonstrating against?*
De quoi elle a parlé si longtemps? *What did she speak about for such a long time?*	

que? and *quoi?* can both be used with infinitives to form questions. *Que?* is used at the front of main clauses:

Que faire?	*What is to be done?*
Que faire de ces valises?	*What shall we do with these suitcases?*
Que dire?	*What can I say?*

quoi? is used in subordinate clauses, and in main clauses where the question word is not fronted:

> Elle a demandé **quoi** faire de ses valises
> *She asked what she should do with her suitcases*

Je rentre tout de suite	- Faire **quoi**?
I'm going home immediately	*- To do what?*

NB: *Quoi de neuf?* 'What's new?'

14.6.3 *quel?, quelle?, quels?, quelles?*

quel?, quelle?, etc are used to form questions based on nouns and noun phrases: *quel livre?, quelle page?, quels manuscrits?, quelles jolies fleurs?* Notice that *quel?* agrees in gender and number with the noun. Question phrases involving *quel?* can be subjects, direct objects or objects of prepositions:

Subject

> **Quelle écrivaine** n'a pas rêvé d'être célèbre?
> *What writer hasn't dreamt of being famous?*

> **Quel bruit** a effrayé les oiseaux?
> *What noise frightened the birds?*

NB. When a *quel* phrase is a subject it is not possible to invert subject and verb or use *est-ce que?*:

> NOT *Quelle écrivaine n'a-t-elle pas rêvé d'être célèbre?
> NOT *Quelle écrivaine est-ce qu'elle n'a pas rêvé d'être célèbre?

Object

Quel film tu recommanderais?	*Which film would you recommend?*
Quel film est-ce que tu recommanderais?	*Which film would you recommend?*
Quel film recommanderais-tu?	*Which film would you recommend?*
Quelles fleurs Josette a-t-elle cueillies?	*Which flowers did Josette pick?*

Object of a preposition

A quelle heure part Pierre?	*What time does Pierre leave?*
De quelle ville est-ce que vous parlez?	*Which town are you talking about?*
Il était arrivé **dans quel train**?	*Which train did he arrive on?*

> **Sous quel arbre** vous avez planté les jonquilles?
> *Which tree did you plant the daffodils under?*

> **Par quelle route** les cyclistes sont-ils partis?
> *By which road did the cyclists leave?*

With the verb *être, quel?* is separated from the noun phrase with which it agrees:

Quels sont **les atouts** de votre équipe?	*What are the strengths of your team?*
Quels sont **vos favoris**?	*Which are your favourites?*
Quelle est **la région** que tu préfères?	*Which is the region you prefer?*

NB: *Quel est cet homme?* 'Who is this man?', *Quelle est cette femme?* 'Who is this woman?' are alternatives to *Qui est cet homme?, Qui est cette femme?*

14.6.4 *lequel?, laquelle?, lesquels?, lesquelles?*

lequel?, laquelle? ... etc. ask 'which' noun or noun phrase when there is a choice of more than one. The form used agrees in gender and number with the noun or noun phrase it questions, whether this is present in the same sentence, or is understood from the context:

Laquelle de **ces couleurs** préférez-vous?	*Which of these colours do you prefer?*
Laquelle préférez-vous?	*Which do you prefer?*
Lesquels des **élèves** avez-vous choisis pour l'équipe?	*Which of the pupils have you chosen for the team?*
Lesquels avez-vous choisis?	*Which have you chosen?*
Elle a enfin décidé **quelle robe** elle va acheter	*She has finally decided which dress she is going to buy*
Laquelle?	*Which one?*

When the phrase involving *lequel?* is the direct object, and sometimes when it is the subject of an intransitive verb, it is possible to separate *lequel?* from the noun phrase it modifies:

Laquelle préférez-vous de **ces couleurs**?	*Which of these colours do you prefer?*
Lequel chante le mieux de **ces deux solistes**?	*Which of these two soloists sings the best?*

NB: When a *lequel?* phrase is the subject of a sentence, it is not possible to use *est-ce que?* or to invert subject and verb:

NOT *Lequel des deux solistes est-ce qu'il chante le mieux?
NOT *Lequel des deux solistes chante-t-il le mieux?

14.6.5 *combien?*

combien? 'how much?', 'how many?' may be used on its own:

Combien est-ce que ça coûte?	*How much does that cost?*
Combien sont déjà arrivés?	*How many have already arrived?*

Or it may be used with a following prepositional phrase:

Combien de pain nous reste-t-il?	*How much bread do we have left?*
Combien de spectateurs assistaient au match?	*How many spectators were there at the match?*

combien (de)? can be used to question subjects, direct objects and objects of prepositions:

Subject

Combien d'invités sont déjà arrivés?	*How many guests have already arrived?*

Direct object

Combien d'enfants ont-ils?	*How many children do they have?*

Object of a preposition

Avec combien d'argent est-il parti à l'étranger?	*How much money did he go abroad with?*

When *combien?* is used alone and functions as a direct object, the pronoun *en* is required:

Combien **en** as-tu vu?	*How many did you see?*
Combien est-ce qu'ils **en** ont tués?	*How many did they kill?*

NB: When *combien?* is the subject of the sentence, it is not possible to use *est-ce que* or invert the subject and the verb:

NOT *Combien de joueurs est-ce qu'ils ont participé au concours?
NOT *Combien de joueurs ont-ils participé au concours?

Although *combien?* translates 'how much', 'how many', it cannot be used to translate English 'how + adjective/adverb' like 'how big?', 'how tall?', 'how often?', etc. (For these see 14.6.8.)

14.6.6 comment?

comment? usually translates English 'how?' when it is not followed by an adjective or adverb (i.e. not 'how big?', 'how often?', etc.):

Comment allez-vous?	*How are you?*
Comment va votre mère?	*How is your mother?*
Comment est-ce qu'elle va?	*How is she?*
Comment s'étaient-ils comportés?	*How had they behaved?*
Comment allez-vous réparer le moteur?	*How are you going to repair the engine?*
Comment cela se prononce-t-il?	*How is this pronounced?*

comment? also translates 'what?' with the verb *appeler*:

Comment tu t'appelles?	*What's your name?*
Comment appelez-vous ce monument? *or*	*What is this monument called?*
Comment ce monument s'appelle-t-il?	

14.6.7 où?, quand?, pourquoi?

où? and *quand?* translate English 'where?' and 'when?' respectively, and are used in the same range of information question constructions as the other question words:

Où vous habitez?	*Where do you live?*
Où habitez-vous?	*Where do you live?*
Où est-ce que vous habitez?	*Where do you live?*
Où Pierre habite-t-il?	*Where does Pierre live?*
Quand vous partez?	*When are you leaving?*
Quand partez-vous?	*When are you leaving?*
Quand est-ce que vous partez?	*When are you leaving?*
Quand Pierre partira-t-il?	*When will Pierre leave?*

When the verb is *être*, 'stylistic inversion' of the subject is normal with *où?* and *quand?* (see 14.3.7):

Où est **le portefeuille**?	*Where's the wallet?*
Quand est **son anniversaire**?	*When's his birthday?*

pourquoi? 'why?' is used in the same way as the other two question words except that it cannot be used with stylistic inversion:

Pourquoi il a déménagé?	*Why has he moved?*
Pourquoi a-t-il déménagé?	*Why has he moved?*
Pourquoi est-ce qu'il a déménagé?	*Why has he moved?*
Pourquoi Pierre a-t-il déménagé?	*Why has Pierre moved?*

but NOT **Pourquoi a déménagé Pierre?*

14.6.8 Translating 'how big?', 'how fast?', 'how often?', etc.

Whereas English 'how?' can question adjectives and adverbs directly, in French there is no simple equivalent. For 'How big is the table?' you CANNOT say things like:

*Comment grande est la table?
*Combien grande est la table?

Instead, alternative expressions have to be found:

De quelle taille est la table?	*How big is the table?*
Avec quelle fréquence y allez-vous?	*How often do you go there?*
Est-ce souvent que vous y allez?	*How often do you go there?*
Dans quelle mesure en êtes-vous certain?	*How certain are you?*
Dans quelle mesure accepteriez-vous de faire cela?	*How happy would you be to do that?*

14.7 Indirect questions

Indirect questions are questions which are reported as having already been asked. They are introduced by verbs like *comprendre, demander, se demander, dire, expliquer, savoir*:

Qui est venu?	(direct question)
Elle a demandé **qui était venu**	(indirect question)
She asked who came	

Quel piège est-ce qu'on lui tend?	(direct question)
Il n'arrive pas à comprendre **quel piège on lui tend**	(indirect question)
He hasn't grasped what kind of trap they are setting for him	

Quand arrivera-t-il?	(direct question)
Dites-moi **quand il arrivera**	(indirect question)
Tell me when he will arrive	

14.7.1 Word order in indirect questions

There is no subject-verb inversion in indirect questions:

Où sont-ils?
Je ne sais pas **où ils sont**
I don't know where they are

NOT **Je ne sais pas où sont-ils*

Pourquoi Marie est-elle revenue?
Dites-moi **pourquoi Marie est revenue**
Tell me why Marie came back

NOT **Dites-moi pourquoi Marie est-elle revenue*

14.7.2 *si* in indirect questions

Direct yes/no questions are introduced by *si* 'if, whether' when they become indirect questions:

Est-ce que Julie viendra demain?
Je me demande **si Julie viendra demain**
I wonder if Julie will come tomorrow

A-t-il bien compris?
On ne sait jamais **s'il a bien compris**
One never knows whether he has understood properly

NB: This use of *si* should not be confused with *si* used to introduce hypothetical clauses like: *Si elle m'aimait, elle m'écrirait* 'If she loved me, she would write to me'. In hypothetical *si* clauses the verb cannot appear in future or conditional tenses (see Chapter 10.8). In indirect questions introduced by *si* it may do so.

14.7.3 *ce qui* and *ce que* in indirect questions

qu'est-ce qui? in a direct question becomes *ce qui* in an indirect question; *que?* or *qu'est-ce que?* becomes *ce que* in an indirect question:

Qu'est-ce qui a ravagé les champs des Dupont?
On ne sait pas **ce qui** a ravagé les champs des Dupont
They don't know what ruined the Duponts' fields

Qu'est-ce qui est arrivé?
Elle se demande **ce qui** est arrivé
She wonders what happened

Que dit-il?
Je ne comprends pas **ce qu'**il dit
I don't understand what he's saying

Qu'est-ce que Pierre fera?
Il a expliqué **ce que** Pierre ferait
He explained what Pierre would do

All other question words remain the same:

Elle lui demande **à qui** il écrivait	*She is asking him who he was writing to*
Je ne sais plus **de quoi** elle parlait	*I no longer know what she was talking about*
Je ne sais pas **laquelle** lui plaît le plus	*I don't know which he likes more*

14.7.4 Tense in indirect questions

The tense of a verb in a direct question may change if it becomes an indirect question (see Chapter 10.7). This depends on the tense of the verb which introduces the indirect question (i.e. the tense of *comprendre, demander, dire*, etc.). If the introducing verb is in the present, future or conditional, the tense of the verb in the indirect question remains the same as in the direct question:

Chante-t-il?	*Is he singing?*
Quand a-t-il chanté?	*When did he sing?*
Qui avait chanté?	*Who had sung?*

Elle ne sait pas s'il chante/quand il a chanté/qui avait chanté
She doesn't know if he sings/when he sang/who sang

When the introducing verb is in the past, however, the verb in the indirect question becomes imperfect or pluperfect if in the direct question it is in the present or past:

Elle ne savait pas s'il chantait/quand il avait chanté/qui avait chanté
She didn't know if he sang, when he had sung, who had sung

and it becomes conditional in the indirect question if it is in the future or conditional in the direct question:

Chantera-t-il?	*Will he sing?*
Qui chanterait?	*Who would sing?*
Elle ne savait pas s'il chanterait/ qui chanterait	*She didn't know if he would sing/ who would sing*

15

Relative clauses

15.1 Introduction

Clauses within a sentence which modify noun phrases or pronouns are known as 'relative clauses'. The noun phrases/pronouns in italics in the following examples are modified by relative clauses in bold:

> Il y avait *deux hommes* **qui sortaient une armoire à glace du camion**
> *Two men were getting a wardrobe out of the lorry*

> C'est *lui* **qui me l'a donné**
> *He is the one who gave it to me*

> La *clef* **qu'il a utilisée pour ouvrir la porte** est un vieux double
> *The key he used to open the door is an old spare*

> C'est *là* **qu'on creusera le trou**
> *There's where we will dig the hole*

> Elle a acheté *une vieille boutique* **dont il ne restait plus que les quatre murs**
> *She bought an old shop of which only the four walls remained*

> C'est *le moment* **où la locomotive se remet en marche**
> *It's the moment when the train starts off again*

> Il y a *plusieurs arbres* **sur lesquels on a cloué des pancartes**
> *There are several trees on which notices have been nailed*

Relative clauses are introduced by relative pronouns like *qui, que, dont, où, sur lesquels,* ... To choose the right relative pronoun you need to know the implied grammatical role played by the 'head' noun phrase/pronoun (those in italics above) in the relative clause.

In *La clef qu'il a utilisée pour ouvrir la porte est un vieux double* the noun phrase *la clef* is understood as the **object** of *utiliser* in the relative clause: *il a utilisé la clef pour ouvrir la porte*. This determines the choice of *que* as the linking relative pronoun. In *C'est lui qui me l'a donné* the pronoun *lui* is understood as the **subject** of *donner* in the relative clause: *il me l'a donné*. This determines the choice of *qui* as the linking relative pronoun.

Noun phrases/pronouns have a range of implied grammatical roles in the relative clause, each requiring a different form of relative pronoun:

Understood as subject

On l'entend ouvrir *la porte d'entrée* **qui se referme en claquant**
(la porte d'entrée se referme)
He can be heard opening the front door which closes behind him with a bang

Understood as direct object

Elle découpe *la tarte* **qu'elle a sortie du four**
(elle a sorti la tarte du four)
She is cutting up the pie which she got out of the oven

Understood as object of a preposition

La vedette **à qui j'ai écrit** ne m'a jamais répondu
(j'ai écrit à la vedette)
The star to whom I wrote has never replied to me

J'ai acheté *le texte* **auquel il a fait référence**
(il a fait référence au texte)
I bought the text he was referring to

Ils habitaient *un appartement* **derrière lequel il y avait un abattoir**
(il y avait un abattoir derrière l'appartement)
They lived in a flat behind which there was an abattoir

Voici *l'hôtel* **dans lequel il a passé les dernières années de sa vie**
(il a passé les dernières années de sa vie dans l'hôtel)
This is the hotel where he spent the last years of his life

15.2 Use of relative *qui*

qui is the relative pronoun used when the noun phrase or pronoun heading a relative clause is the implied subject of that relative clause, whether animate or inanimate:

Il y avait deux hommes **qui** sortaient une armoire à glace du camion
(deux hommes sortaient une armoire . . .)
Two men were getting a wardrobe out of the lorry

Quand on voit quelqu'un **qui** se noie il faut essayer de le sauver
(quelqu'un se noie)
When you see someone drowning you should try to save them

Je l'ai croisé dans l'escalier **qui** mène à la cave
(l'escalier mène à la cave)
I passed him on the stairs which lead to the cellar

C'est un ouvrage **qui** allie histoire, suspense et qualité
(l'ouvrage allie histoire, suspense et qualité)
It's a book which marries history, suspense and quality

NB: *voilà* and *voici* may also head subject relative clauses:

Voilà/voici qui complique les choses
That's something which complicates matters

15.2.1 *Je l'ai vu qui ...*

With perception verbs like *voir, regarder, entendre, apercevoir*, etc., a construction involving relative *qui* can translate an English present participle construction:

Je l'ai vu **qui** sortait
I saw him leaving

Elle l'a entendu **qui** chantait dans son bain
She heard him singing in his bath

15.2.2 Use of relative *qui* for *celui qui, celle qui, ceux qui, celles qui*

Sometimes relative *qui* may be used alone with the same meaning as *celui qui/que, celle qui/que, ceux qui/que, celles qui/que*. Such constructions are known as 'free' relative clauses (see also 15.9):

Tout est possible **à qui** sait ménager son effort
Everything is possible for he who knows how to harness his energies

J'ai invité **qui** vous savez
I invited you know who

15.3 Use of relative *que*

que is the relative pronoun used when the noun phrase or pronoun heading the relative clause is the implied direct **object** of the relative clause, whether animate or inanimate:

L'homme **qu'**on vient d'appeler Rossi se lève
(on appelle l'homme Rossi)
The man who has just been called Rossi gets up

Elle est née dans le village **qu'**on a détruit pour faire le barrage
(on a détruit le village)
She was born in the village which they destroyed to build the dam

Elle découpe la tarte **qu'**elle a sortie du four
(elle a sorti la tarte du four)
She is cutting up the pie which she got out of the oven

J'ai toujours souffert du nom **que** je porte
(je porte ce nom)
I have always suffered because of my name

C'est un poste **que** j'aurais aimé avoir
(j'aurais aimé avoir ce poste)
It's a job that I would have liked to have had

Unlike English, the relative pronoun in French may never be omitted:

NOT *C'est un poste j'aurais aimé
NOT *Elle est née dans le village on a détruit pour faire le barrage etc.

NB: The past participle agrees with feminine and plural noun phrases or pronouns which head object relative clauses, as in:

... **la tarte** qu'elle a sortie du four

This is because *la tarte* is an instance of a preceding direct object, and past participles agree with preceding direct objects (see Chapter 9.3.4).

15.4 Preposition plus *qui*

When the noun phrase or pronoun heading a relative clause is the implied object of a preposition in that relative clause, and is furthermore animate, the normal relative pronoun to use is *qui* (except when the preposition is *de* – see 15.6 below):

à	Le touriste **à qui** j'ai parlé vient du Québec (j'ai parlé au touriste) *The tourist I spoke to comes from Quebec*
en	C'est un commerçant **en qui** on peut avoir confiance (on peut avoir confiance en ce commerçant) *He's a shopkeeper in whom one can have confidence*
sur	L'intermédiaire **sur qui** on comptait s'est avéré malhonnête (on comptait sur l'intermédiaire) *The go-between we were counting on turned out to be dishonest*
par	Je recommanderais le garagiste **par qui** j'ai eu cette voiture (j'ai eu cette voiture par le garagiste) *I would recommend the garage I got this car from*
avec	Il n'a jamais revu le camarade **avec qui** il jouait quand ils étaient petits (il jouait avec ce camarade) *He has never again seen the friend he used to play with when they were little*
pour	Elle a invité son professeur, **pour qui** elle a beaucoup de respect, à dîner (elle a beaucoup de respect pour son professeur) *She has invited her teacher, for whom she has a great deal of respect, to dinner*
près de	Le jeune homme **près de qui** il est assis le reconnaît (il est assis près du jeune homme) *The young man next to whom he's sitting recognizes him*

NB: When objects of the prepositions *parmi* and *entre* are animate, the normal relative pronoun to use is *lesquels* or *lesquelles* (see 15.5), and not *qui*:

Un groupe d'universitaires **parmi lesquels** on compte des Américains
A group of academics amongst whom there are Americans

Des collègues **entre lesquelles** il n'y avait aucune rivalité
Colleagues between whom there was no rivalry

15.5 Use of *lequel* in relative clauses

When the noun phrase or pronoun heading a relative clause is the implied object of a preposition, and is inanimate, the normal relative pronoun to use is one of the forms of *lequel* (except in the case of *de*: see 15.6).

Lequel has the following forms:

	Singular	Plural
Masculine	lequel	lesquels
Feminine	laquelle	lesquelles

Furthermore, the *le-, la-* etc. components combine with a preceding *à* or *de* to form:

	Singular	Plural	Singular	Plural
Masculine	auquel	auxquels	duquel	desquels
Feminine	à laquelle	auxquelles	de laquelle	desquelles

à	Le texte **auquel** il a fait référence ...
	The text he referred to ...
	La conférence à **laquelle** je vais participer ...
	The conference in which I shall be taking part ...
dans	Cela illustre les contradictions **dans lesquelles** s'enferme la Grande-Bretagne
	That illustrates the contradictions within which Great Britain is locked
autour	Elle habite une maison **autour de laquelle** il y a une haie de lauriers
	She lives in a house around which there is a laurel hedge
durant	Des weekends interminables, **durant lesquels** je ne savais quoi faire
	Interminable weekends during which I didn't know what to do

NB: English 'The reason why ...' is translated in French by *La raison pour laquelle* ... and NOT **La raison pourquoi ....*

The prepositions *parmi* and *entre* are followed by *lesquels/lesquelles* whether the implied object is animate or inanimate:

Un groupe d'universitaires **parmi lesquels** on compte des Américains
A group of academics amongst whom there are Americans

Des collègues **entre lesquelles** il n'y avait aucune rivalité
Colleagues between whom there was no rivalry

Des papiers **parmi lesquels** j'ai trouvé notre arbre généalogique
Papers among which I found our family tree

Des haies **entre lesquelles** il avait planté des rosiers
Hedges between which he had planted rose bushes

15.5.1 Use of *lequel* as a subject and object relative pronoun

The use of *lequel* as a relative pronoun where the head of the relative clause is an implied subject or object is literary and extremely rare (it is also used in French legal texts). It is usually said that *lequel* is used in this way either to avoid ambiguity, or to avoid the repetition of *qui*:

Il allait se marier avec la sœur d'un collègue de travail, **laquelle** avait fait ses
études en Autriche
He was going to marry the sister of a colleague from work who had studied in Austria

laquelle is used here to make it clear that the person who had studied in Austria
is the *sœur*, rather than the *collègue* – *laquelle* can only refer to *sœur*, whereas
qui could refer to either *sœur* or *collègue*.

15.6 Use of *dont, de qui, duquel/de laquelle/desquels/desquelles*

15.6.1 *dont*

When the noun phrase or pronoun heading a relative clause is the implied
object of *de* in that relative clause, *dont* is the normal relative pronoun to use,
whether the object of the preposition is animate or inanimate:

Cela représente un effort **dont** je suis parfaitement capable
(je suis capable **de** l'effort)
That is an effort I am capable of

La maladie **dont** il est mort
(il est mort **de** cette maladie)
The illness from which he died

The *de* phrase which is turned into *dont* may itself be the complement of another
noun phrase:

Une collègue **dont** le frère est en Amérique du Sud
(**le frère de** ma collègue est en Amérique du Sud)
A colleague whose brother is in South America

Une maison **dont** les volets étaient fermés
(**les volets de** la maison étaient fermés)
A house whose shutters were closed

When the *de* phrase which turns into *dont* is the complement of an object, *dont*
is separated from the object, unlike in English:

Une collègue **dont** j'ai rencontré **le frère** pendant mes vacances
(j'ai rencontré **le frère de** cette collègue . . .)
A colleague whose brother I met on holiday

Une maison **dont** on avait fermé les volets
(on avait fermé **les volets de** cette maison)
A house whose shutters had been closed

NB: *dont* can be used to translate English 'including' and 'of which' in sentences like:

Il y a 30 moulins dans la région, **dont** 28 désaffectés
There are 30 mills in the region, including 28 out of commission

Trois personnes sont arrivées, **dont** Pierre
Three people arrived, including Pierre

Ils en ont acheté presque une centaine, **dont** plusieurs valaient très cher
They bought almost a hundred of them, some of which were worth a lot of money

J'en ai vu trois hier, **dont** une verte
I saw three of them yesterday, one of which was green

15.6.2 Cases where *dont* may not be used

Where a *de* phrase is itself the complement of a prepositional phrase – as in *il s'intéresse à la vie de cet écrivain* – *dont* may not be used. Nor may *dont* be used after a complex preposition which ends in *de* such as *à l'intérieur de, au bout de, auprès de, autour de, à côté de, en face de, en dehors de, au delà de, en dépit de, près de*. Instead either *de qui* (for animates) or *duquel,* etc. (for both animates and inanimates) must be used. Speakers have a strong preference for using *duquel* etc.:

un écrivain **à** la vie **duquel** (or, possibly, **de qui**) il s'intéresse
a writer in whose life he is interested

une voiture **sur** le capot **de laquelle** était assis un mannequin
a car on whose bonnet was sitting a model

Elle portait un blazer **dans** la poche **duquel** il y avait une lettre
She was wearing a blazer in whose pocket there was a letter

Nous avons dû vendre la maison **à l'intérieur de laquelle** se trouvaient nos plus belles moquettes
We had to sell the house in which were our most beautiful carpets

Le cheval blanc se trouve dans le champ **à côté duquel** nous avons pique-niqué
The white horse is in the field near which we had a picnic

NB: *duquel*, etc. agrees with the head of the relative clause in gender and number: *une voiture* sur le capot *de laquelle* (*de laquelle* agrees with *voiture* and not *capot*), *un blazer* dans la poche *duquel* (*duquel* agrees with *blazer* and not *poche*).

15.7 The use of *où* as a relative pronoun

15.7.1 To refer to place

où is used as a relative pronoun where the noun phrase or pronoun heading a relative clause is understood to be a place adverb in that relative clause:

La station balnéaire **où** j'ai passé mes vacances
(j'ai passé mes vacances **dans cette station balnéaire**)
The seaside resort where I spent my holidays

Un ponton **où** des bateaux sont amarrés
(des bateaux sont amarrés **au ponton**)
A pier to which boats are moored

Là **où** j'ai rangé ma voiture
(j'ai rangé ma voiture **là**)
The place where I've parked my car

Since many prepositional phrases describing a place also function as place adverbs (see Chapter 5.6.16) relative clauses involving *où* may be interchangeable with relative clauses involving a preposition plus a form of *lequel*:

La station balnéaire **dans laquelle** j'ai passé mes vacances
Un ponton **auquel** des bateaux sont amarrés

However, *où* is by far the more frequent in modern French.

où may itself be preceded by prepositions like *de, par*:

> Le pays **d'où** il vient
> *The country he comes from*

> La porte **par où** elle est entrée
> *The door she came through*

15.7.2 To refer to time

où is also used where the noun phrase or pronoun heading a relative clause is an implied time adverbial in that relative clause, and is definite. This use is usually translated in English by 'when':

> C'est le moment **où** la locomotive se remet en marche
> *It's the moment when the train restarts*

> A l'époque **où** elle était encore étudiante
> *At the time when she was still a student*

Similar expressions are:

le jour où ...	*the day when ...*
à l'heure où ...	*at the time (of day) when ...*
au temps où ...	*in the days when ...*
à la saison où ...	*during the season when ...*

This use of *où* with **definite** noun phrases contrasts with the case where the head noun phrase or pronoun is **indefinite**. Here *que* is used:

> Un jour **que** je sortais
> *One day when I was going out*

> Une fois **qu'**elle rendait visite à sa tante
> *Once when she was visiting her aunt*

In modern spoken French, *que* is often also used where the head is definite (rather than *où*):

> A l'heure **qu'**il est, on ne sait toujours pas s'il va se rétablir
> *At the time of speaking, we still don't know if he is going to recover*

NB: Although English uses 'when' in constructions like these, *quand* cannot be used in French:

> NOT *C'est le moment quand la locomotive se remet en marche
> NOT *Un jour quand je sortais

15.8 Use of relative *quoi*

quoi is found as a relative pronoun mainly in written French. Where the head of the relative clause is *rien, quelque chose, ce* or a clause, and is understood as the object of a preposition in the relative clause, *quoi* is used:

> Il n'y a **rien sur quoi** on puisse se baser
> (on ne peut se baser sur rien)
> *There is nothing on which one can rely*

C'est **quelque chose à quoi** on peut s'intéresser
(s'intéresser à quelque chose)
It's something you can get interested in

Ce à quoi tu fais référence
(tu fais référence à quelque chose)
The thing you are referring to

Finissez votre travail, **après quoi** on peut dîner
(on peut dîner après que vous avez fini votre travail)
Finish your work, after which we can have dinner

de quoi used as the subject of an infinitive means 'something':

On a ramené **de quoi** boire
We brought back something to drink

15.9 Free relative clauses and the use of ce *qui*, ce *que*, ce *dont*, ce *à quoi*, ce *sur quoi*, etc.

Ordinary relative clauses are headed by noun phrases or pronouns present in the main clause:

Elle a vu **les congressistes** (head) *qui assistaient à la réunion* (relative clause)
She saw the delegates who were present at the meeting

In 'free' relative clauses the head is non-specific:

Elle a vu **ceux qui** assistaient à la réunion
She saw who was present at the meeting

Ils avaient remarqué **celui que** Jo préférait
They had noticed who Jo preferred

When the non-specific head is understood to be human, *celui qui/que, celle qui/que*, etc., are the appropriate relative pronouns, as in the above examples. When the non-specific head is understood to be non-human, *ce qui* and *ce que* are used: *ce qui* where the non-specific head is understood as the subject of the relative clause; *ce que* where the non-specific head is understood as the object:

Subject

On a réparé **ce qui** était cassé
(quelque chose était cassé)
They repaired what was broken

Je ferai **ce qui** me plaira
(quelque chose me plaira)
I'll do what I please

Direct object

Je crois **ce qu'**il dit
(il dit quelque chose)
I believe what he says

On a vu **ce que** cela a produit
(cela a produit quelque chose)
We saw what that produced

Both *ce qui* and *ce que* may be preceded by *tout* 'all':

> Il s'est mis à détruire **tout ce qui** était à sa portée
> *He began to destroy everything that was within his reach*

> On a vu **tout ce que** cela a produit
> *We saw all that that produced*

NB: *ce* is obligatory in these cases: NOT *. . . tout qu' était à sa portée; NOT *...
tout que cela a produit.*

Where the non-specific head is non-human and is understood as the object of
a preposition in the relative clause, *ce* + preposition + *quoi* is used:

> Dis-moi **ce à quoi** tu penses
> *Tell me what you are thinking*

> Ne jette pas **ce sur quoi** j'écrivais
> *Don't throw out what I was writing on*

> Je vais te dire **ce en quoi** j'ai confiance
> *I'll tell you what I have confidence in*

When 'what' or 'which' are understood as the object of *de, ce dont* is used:

> Elle a envoyé **ce dont** on avait besoin
> *She sent what we needed*

15.9.1 Use of *ce qui, ce que, ce dont, ce à quoi*, etc., to refer to events
Compare the following:

> On a volé le magnétoscope **qui** était dans l'amphithéâtre
> *Someone has stolen the video recorder which was in the lecture hall*

> On a volé **ce qui** était dans l'amphithéâtre
> *Someone has stolen what was in the lecture hall*

> On a volé le magnétoscope, **ce qui** va interrompre les cours
> *Someone has stolen the video recorder, which will disrupt classes*

In the first sentence the relative clause *qui était dans l'amphithéâtre* modifies the
noun phrase *le magnétoscope*. In the second sentence there is a 'free relative'
where the head is non-specific. In the third sentence the relative clause modifies the whole preceding clause: *on a volé le magnétoscope*.

ce qui, ce que, ce dont, ce à quoi, etc. are used not only to introduce free relatives,
but also to introduce relative clauses which modify preceding clauses:

> Il a manqué le train, **ce qui** l'a mis en colère
> *He missed the train, which made him angry*
> (the missing of the train made him angry, not the train itself)

> On craint un durcissement dans l'attitude officielle, **ce qui** pourrait accroître les
> difficultés
> *A hardening of the official attitude is feared, which could increase the difficulties*

> Elle a réussi à le persuader, **ce que** je n'aurais jamais cru possible
> *She succeeded in persuading him, which I would never have thought possible*

NB: Where a relative clause modifies an event, *qui* and *que* alone cannot be used:

> NOT *Il a manqué le train, qui l'a mis en colère
> NOT *Elle a réussi à le persuader, que je n'aurais jamais cru possible

Where the verb is indirectly transitive and ends in *de*, two constructions may be possible: one using *ce dont* and one using *de ce que*. *ce dont* is used when the head word is present, *de ce que* is used when there is no head word. *ce dont* is normally rendered into English in these constructions by 'which'; *de ce que* is normally rendered by 'what' or 'that'. This concerns verbs such as: *féliciter qn de qc, excuser qn de qc, s'inquiéter de qc, s'irriter de qc, profiter de qc, souffrir de qc,* and adjectival constructions such as *être reconnaissant de qc, être stupéfait de qc*.

> Vous avez réalisé votre projet. Je vous félicite (de qc).
> *You have succeeded in your project. I congratulate you (on something)*
>
> Vous avez réalisé votre projet, **ce dont** je vous félicite
> *You have succeeded in your project, on which I congratulate you*
>
> Je vous félicite **de ce que** vous avez réalisé
> *I congratulate you on what you have achieved*
>
> Ils ont fait des bêtises. Ils devront s'excuser (de qc)
> *They did some silly things. They will have to apologize (for sth)*
>
> Ils ont fait des bêtises, **ce dont** ils devront s'excuser
> *They did some silly things, for which they will have to apologize*
>
> Ils devront s'excuser **de ce qu'**ils ont fait
> *They will have to apologize for what they did*
>
> Vous avez fait énormément de choses pour nous. Je suis très reconnaissant (de qc)
> *You have done a great deal for us. I am very grateful (for sth)*
>
> Vous avez fait énormément de choses pour nous, **ce dont** je suis très reconnaissant
> *You have done a great deal for us, for which I am very grateful*
>
> Je suis très reconnaissant **de ce que** vous avez fait pour nous
> *I am very grateful for what you have done for us*
>
> Vous êtes venu. Je suis stupéfait (de qc)
> *You came. I am astonished (about sth)*
>
> Vous êtes venu, **ce dont** je suis stupéfait
> *You came, which astonishes me*
>
> Je suis stupéfait **de ce que** vous soyez venu
> *I am astonished that you should have come*

15.10 Translating 'whoever', 'whatever', 'wherever', 'whenever', 'however'

'whoever'

'whoever', understood as the subject of a relative clause, is *quiconque*, and the verb in the relative clause is in the indicative:

> Ils accueillent **quiconque** arrive
> *They welcome whoever comes*

'whoever', understood as the direct object of a relative clause, is *qui que*, and the verb in the relative clause is in the subjunctive:

> **Qui que** vous **nommiez**, je lui mènerai la vie dure
> *Whoever you appoint, I'll make his life a misery*

NB: *quel que* may also mean 'whoever' when used with *être*:

> **Quel qu**'il **soit**, je l'accueillerai
> *Whoever he is, I'll let him in*

'whatever'

'whatever', understood as the subject of a relative clause, is *quoi qui*. When it is understood as the object it is *quoi que*. In both cases the verb in the relative clause is in the subjunctive:

> **Quoi qui puisse** arriver
> *Whatever may happen*

> **Quoi qu**'il **fasse**
> *Whatever he does*

NB: *quoi que*, meaning 'whatever', should be distinguished from the conjunction *quoique* 'although', which is written as a single word.

'whatever X' understood as the subject of a relative clause is translated as in the following examples:

> **Quel que** soit **le prix**, je l'achèterai
> *Whatever the price may be, I'll buy it*
>
> **Quelles que** soient **ses intentions**, méfie-toi
> *Whatever his intentions are, don't trust him*

Note that *quel* and *que* are separate words, and that *quel* agrees with the noun which is the subject of the relative clause.

'whatever X', 'whichever X' understood as the object of a relative clause is *quelque(s)*, and the verb in the relative clause is in the subjunctive:

> **Quelque livre** que vous **choisissiez**, vous bénéficierez d'un rabais
> (vous allez choisir un livre)
> *Whatever/whichever book you choose, we'll give you a discount*

> **Quelques efforts** que vous **fassiez**, on ne vous en accordera aucun crédit
> (vous allez faire des efforts)
> *Whatever efforts you make won't be recognized*

One way of distinguishing between the '*quelque* + noun' construction and the '*quel que* + *être* + noun' construction is to see if the verb in the relative clause can be omitted in English. If it can, use *quel que*, if it cannot use *quelque(s)*:

> Quel que soit le prix, je l'achèterai
> *Whatever the price (may be), I'll buy it*

| Quelque livre que vous choisissiez, vous bénéficierez d'un rabais | *Whatever book you *(choose), we will give you a discount* |

NB: *être* can never be omitted from the *quel que* constructions in French, even though 'be' can be omitted in English.

'wherever'

'wherever' is *où que*, with the verb in the relative clause in the subjunctive:

Où qu'il **aille**, nous le suivrons
Wherever he goes, we'll follow him

'whenever'

'whenever' is *toutes les fois que, à chaque fois que*, or simply *quand*, with the verb in the indicative:

Toutes les fois qu'elle **a** un moment de libre, elle révise son vocabulaire
Whenever she has a free moment she looks over her vocabulary

'however'

'however' + an adjective heading a relative clause can be translated in five ways:

quelque		
si		
aussi	+ adjective	+ verb in the subjunctive
pour		
tout	+ adjective	+ verb in the indicative

However demanding they may be, we still have to respect our customers' needs

Quelque (*invariable*) **exigeants** qu'ils **soient**, nous devons pourtant satisfaire nos clients

Si exigeants qu'ils **soient**, nous devons pourtant satisfaire nos clients

Aussi exigeants qu'ils **soient**, nous devons pourtant satisfaire nos clients

Pour exigeants qu'ils **soient**, nous devons pourtant satisfaire nos clients

Tout (*invariable*) **exigeants** qu'ils **sont**, nous devons pourtant satisfaire nos clients

NB: the verb and subject may be inverted after *si* and *aussi* as an alternative to the *que* construction, providing that the subject is a pronoun:

Si exigeants soient-ils, . . .
Aussi exigeants soient-ils, . . .

15.11 Indicative and subjunctive in relative clauses

The verb in relative clauses usually takes the indicative form, but there are some kinds of relative clause where the verb is in the subjunctive.

15.11.1 *qui que, quoi que, quel que,* etc.

qui que, quoi qui, quoi que, quel que, quelque, où que and *si/aussi/pour* are followed by a verb in the subjunctive (see 15.10 and also Chapter 11.1.12):

Qui que vous **nommiez**	*Whoever you appoint*
Quoi qui **puisse** arriver	*Whatever may happen*
Quoi qu'il **fasse**	*Whatever he does*
Quelque livre que vous **choisissiez**	*Whichever book you choose*
Quelle que **soit** la réponse	*Whatever the response*

Quelque		
Si	grand qu'il **soit**	*However big he is*
Aussi		
Pour		

NB: *quiconque* 'whoever' is followed by verbs in the indicative:

Quiconque **connaît** une langue étrangère aura le poste
Whoever can speak a foreign language will get the job

15.11.2 Relative clauses expressing hypothetical states of affairs

Relative clauses which modify indefinite noun phrases and express a hypothetical, rather than real, state of affairs, usually have a verb in the subjunctive (see Chapter 11.1.12):

Elle veut acheter **une maison** qui **ait** une piscine
She wants to buy a house which has a swimming pool

The subjunctive here suggests that she has no particular house in mind – her hypothetically ideal house would be one with a swimming pool. By contrast, a sentence like:

Elle veut acheter **une maison** qui **a** une piscine
She wants to buy a house which has a swimming pool

suggests that she knows of a particular house with a swimming pool which she would like to buy.

15.11.3 Relative clauses modifying *le premier, le dernier, le seul* and superlatives

Where a relative clause modifies noun phrases involving *le premier, le dernier, le seul* or a superlative, which can be interpreted as 'the first ever', 'the last one ever', 'the only one ever', etc., then the verb in the relative clause is in the subjunctive (see Chapter 11.1.8):

C'était **le premier film** qui **ait** traité de ce sujet
It was the first (ever) film that dealt with the topic

Le dernier roman qu'il **ait** écrit avant de mourir
The last (ever) novel he wrote before he died

Le seul portrait que j'**aie** vu d'elle
The only (ever) portrait I saw of her

La femme la plus riche que nous ayons photographiée
The richest (ever) woman whom we have photographed

Where the verb in the relative clause is in the indicative, however, the modified noun phrase is interpreted as just one of a set ('the first (of a set)', 'the last (of a set)', 'the biggest (of a set)', etc.):

C'est **le premier film** que j'**ai** vu, et le plus beau de toute ma vie
It's the first film (of the set of those I've seen) that I saw, and the finest one I've seen

C'est **le plus grand** qui **a** gagné le prix
It's the tallest of (the set of) them who won the prize

15.11.4 Relative clauses in *si* clauses, questions, after negation and in other subjunctive clauses

When relative clauses modify indefinite noun phrases or pronouns in *si* clauses or in questions, or modify noun phrases in negative clauses or clauses which themselves have subjunctive verbs, the verb in the relative clause is usually in the subjunctive:

S'il connaissait **un endroit** qui **convienne** il le dirait
If he knew of a place which would be suitable he would say so

Connaissez-vous un endroit qui **convienne**?
Do you know of a place which would be suitable?

Je ne connais **personne** qui **puisse** m'aider
I know no-one who can help me

Quelles que **soient les circonstances** qui **puissent** expliquer son erreur, je ne peux pas la lui pardonner
Whatever the circumstances which might explain his mistake, I can't forgive him

TABLE 15.A *Summary of major relative clause types*

Head of of clause	Function in clause	Pronoun	Example	See section
l'homme	subject (±animate)	qui	l'homme qui conduit	15.2
l'autobus	direct object (±animate)	que	l'autobus que je conduis	15.3
une maladie	object of *de* (±animate)	dont	une maladie dont il est mort	15.6.1
une maison	same	dont	une maison dont la porte est fermée	15.6.1
une maison	same	dont	une maison dont on ferme la porte	15.6.1
le touriste	object (+animate) of a preposition	à qui	le touriste à qui j'ai parlé	15.4
le texte	object (–animate) of a preposition	auquel	le texte auquel il fait référence	15.5
un écrivain	object (+animate) of a preposition in a prepositional phrase	à la vie duquel	un écrivain à la vie duquel il s'intéresse	15.6.2
un blazer	object (–animate) of a preposition in a prepositional phrase	dans la poche duquel	un blazer dans la poche duquel il y a une lettre	15.6.2
la ville	place adverb	où	la ville où je vis	15.7.1
le jour	time adverb (definite)	où	le jour où elle est partie	15.7.2
un jour	time adverb (indefinite)	que	un jour que je sortais	15.7.2
rien, ce, quelque chose, clause	object of a preposition	sur quoi	rien, ce, quelque chose sur quoi on peut compter	15.8
non-specific head	subject or object (+animate)	celui qui/que	j'ai vu celui qui est sorti	15.9
non-specific head	subject (–animate)	ce qui	je ferai ce qui me plaît	15.9
non-specific head	object (–animate)	ce que	je crois ce qu'elle dit	15.9
non-specific head	object of a preposition	ce preposition quoi	il se moque de ce en quoi j'ai confiance	15.9

16

Negation

16.1 Introduction

French sentences can be negated by using one of the following expressions:

ne ... aucun	*not any, none*
ne ... guère	*hardly*
ne ... jamais	*not ever, never*
ne ... ni ... ni	*neither ... nor*
ne ... nul	*not any, none*
ne ... pas	*not*
ne ... personne	*not anyone, no-one, nobody*
ne ... plus	*not any more, no longer*
ne ... que	*only*
ne ... rien	*not anything, nothing*

Although *ne ... guère* and *ne ... que* are not strictly negators – they are adverbs – they have similar distributional properties to the other negators, and so we include them in this chapter.

NB: the expression *ne ... point* 'not' is no longer used productively in modern French. It is used only in written French by writers who want to create an archaic or regional tone.

Individual words and phrases can be negated by placing the particles *pas, aucun, jamais, rien, personne* (without *ne*) in front of them. For example: *un après-midi pas comme les autres* 'an afternoon unlike others'; *jamais de ma vie* 'never in my life'; *rien d'intéressant* 'nothing interesting'; and so on.

16.2 Location of sentence negators

16.2.1 With verbs marked for tense

In all cases where sentences are negated, the element *ne* (if it is present: see 16.4) comes before the verb which is marked for tense in that sentence, and before any unstressed object pronouns which are in front of the verb:

Je **ne** dors pas chez moi ce soir	*I'm not sleeping at my place tonight*
Je **n**'ai pas dormi chez moi hier soir	*I didn't sleep at my place last night*
Je **ne** l'entendais pas	*I didn't hear him*
Il **ne** le lui a jamais envoyé	*He didn't ever send it to her*
Elle **n**'a rien voulu me raconter	*She didn't want to tell me anything*

The location of the second element – *pas, jamais, rien, personne,* etc. – varies, however. While all these negative particles immediately follow a main verb when no auxiliary is present:

Il ne me regardait **pas**	*He wasn't watching me*
La boîte ne contenait **que** des bonbons	*There were only sweets in the box*
Ça ne donne **aucun** plaisir	*That's not at all enjoyable*
Il ne mangeait **jamais** le soir	*He never used to eat in the evenings*

in compound tenses (i.e. when the auxiliary *avoir* or *être* is present), *guère, jamais, pas, plus, rien* immediately follow the auxiliary verb:

Il n'en a **pas** voulu	*He didn't want any of it*
Je n'ai **jamais** vu la mer	*I have never seen the sea*
Elle n'a **plus** voulu continuer	*She didn't want to continue*
Je ne l'ai **guère** connue	*I hardly knew her*
On ne m'a **rien** pris	*They didn't take anything from me*

By contrast, *personne* behaves just like an object, an indirect object or the object of a preposition:

Je n'ai vu **personne**	*I didn't see anyone*
Il n'a parlé à **personne**	*He didn't speak to anyone*
Elle n'est sortie avec **personne**	*She didn't go out with anyone*

and *aucun* precedes an object, an indirect object or the object of a preposition:

Ils n'ont vendu **aucun** tableau	*They didn't sell a single picture*
Je ne le vendrais à **aucun** prix	*I wouldn't sell it at any price*
Il n'a confiance en **aucun** autre que lui-même	*He doesn't trust anyone else but himself*

NB: *nul* is only used in formal French. (See 16.8.)

The location of *que* and *ni* varies depending on the intended meaning:

Il ne se permet un whisky **qu**'après avoir fini son travail
He only allows himself a whisky after he has finished his work

Il ne se permet **qu**'un whisky après avoir fini son travail
He only allows himself one whisky after he has finished his work

Elle ne m'a **ni** vu **ni** entendu
She neither saw me nor heard me

Elle n'a vu **ni** lui **ni** sa femme
She saw neither him nor his wife

Je n'ai écrit de lettre **ni** à sa mère **ni** à son notaire
I wrote a letter neither to her mother nor to her solicitor

NB: *Je ne fais que, tu ne fais que, il ne fait que,* etc. mean 'I do nothing but, you do nothing but, he does nothing but' etc.: *Il ne fait que mentir/travailler/se plaindre,* etc. 'He does nothing but lie/work/complain', etc.

16.2.2 With infinitives
Where the verb in a negated sentence is an infinitive, *ne* and *guère, jamais, pas, plus, rien* normally both precede the infinitive:

J'ai dormi au bureau, de manière à **ne pas** perdre de temps
I slept at the office so as not to waste any time

J'étais le seul à **ne jamais** boire d'alcool
I was the only one never to drink

Il pense **ne plus** croire en Dieu
He thinks he doesn't believe in God any more

Elle donnait l'impression de **ne guère** s'intéresser à mes activités
She gave the impression of hardly being interested in my activities

Il a envie de **ne rien** faire de la journée
He feels like doing nothing all day

Both elements of the negation also usually precede an infinitive auxiliary verb (*avoir* or *être*):

J'étais certain de **ne pas** avoir laissé de linge à sécher sur le radiateur
I was certain I hadn't left any underwear drying on the radiator

J'espère **ne rien** avoir oublié
I hope I haven't forgotten anything

For some speakers, however, the second element of the negation in these cases can optionally follow the auxiliary, without any change in the meaning:

J'étais certain de **n'**avoir **pas** laissé de linge …
J'espère **n'**avoir **rien** oublié

In the case of *ne … aucun, ne … nul, ne … personne*, the second component follows the verbal elements:

Je voudrais **ne** voir **personne**
I would like to see no-one

Elle me reprochait de **n'**avoir écrit à **personne**
She blamed me for not having written to anyone

Ils ont déclaré **n'**avoir eu **aucune** intention de le faire
They declared that they had no intention of doing it

Il s'étonnait de **n'**avoir ressenti **nul** désir de le faire
He was surprised not to have felt any desire to do it

que and *ni … ni* also follow the verb in infinitives, but their location varies depending on the intended meaning:

Je voudrais **ne** voir **que** Jean deux ou trois fois par semaine
I would like to see only Jean two or three times a week

Je voudrais **ne** voir Jean **que** deux ou trois fois par semaine
I would like to see Jean only two or three times a week

Elle espère **ne** rencontrer **ni** lui **ni** sa sœur
She hopes to meet neither him nor his sister

Elle espère **ne** rencontrer son voisin **ni** au marché **ni** au café
She hopes to meet her neighbour neither at the market nor in the café

NB: Verbs in clauses dependent on negated clauses take the subjunctive:

Ce n'est pas que je **sois** particulièrement timide
It's not that I'm particularly shy

Je ne connais personne qui **mette** autant d'acharnement à réussir
I don't know anyone (else) who puts so much energy into succeeding

(See Chapter 11.1.8.)

16.3 Order of negators in multiple negation

Two or more of *jamais, pas, personne, plus, rien*, and so on, may be combined quite acceptably in French to produce a multiple negation. The normal ordering of these elements is as indicated in the following tables:

ne ...	pas	past participle or infinitive	que

Il **n'**y a **pas que** des héros dans l'armée   *There aren't only heroes in the army*
Il **n'**a **pas** écrit **que** des contes de fées   *He didn't only write fairy stories*

ne ...	jamais guère	plus	rien	past participle or infinitive	personne	que

On **ne** le verra **jamais plus**   *We'll never see him again*
On **n'**en verra **jamais rien**   *We'll never see anything of it*
On **n'**en verra **plus rien**   *We won't see anything more of it*
On **n'**en verra **jamais plus** rien   *We won't see anything more of it ever again*

Elle **n'**a **jamais plus** écrit   *She never wrote again*
Elle **n'**a **jamais rien** écrit   *She never wrote anything*
Elle **n'**a **plus rien** écrit   *She wrote nothing again*
Elle **n'**a **jamais plus** rien écrit   *She never wrote anything again*

Elle **n'**a **jamais plus rien** écrit   *She never wrote anything again*
qu'une brochure de publicité   *except an advertizing brochure*

Ça **n'**impressionnera **jamais personne**   *That will never impress anyone*
Ça **n'**impressionnera **plus personne**   *That won't impress anyone any more*
Ça **n'**impressionnera **jamais plus personne**   *That will never impress anyone again*

Il **n'**a **jamais** critiqué **personne**   *He never criticized anyone*
Il **n'**a **plus** critiqué **personne**   *He didn't criticize anyone again*
Il **n'**a **jamais** plus critiqué **personne**   *He didn't ever criticize anyone again*

Elle **n'**a **guère plus** écrit après son deuil   *She hardly ever wrote again after her bereavement*

NB: Plus jamais! *Never again!*

16.4 Omission of *ne* in sentence negation

It is very common in modern spoken French for speakers to omit the *ne* of *ne ... pas*, and to a lesser extent the *ne* of other negative expressions, except in the most formal of styles:

C'est pas vrai	*It's not true*
J'ai pas eu le temps de le faire	*I didn't have time to do it*
Je sais pas	*I don't know*
Elle l'avait pas lu	*She hadn't read it*

16.5 Order of negative elements in questions and imperatives

The location and ordering of negative elements in questions and imperatives are the same as in declaratives:

Tu ne dors pas chez toi ce soir	
Ne dors-tu pas chez toi ce soir?	*Aren't you sleeping at your house tonight?*
Il n'a jamais vu la mer	
N'a-t-il jamais vu la mer?	*Hasn't he ever seen the sea?*
On ne lui avait rien appris	
Ne lui avait-on rien appris?	*Had they taught him nothing?*
Elle n'avait vu personne	
N'avait-elle vu personne?	*Had she seen no-one?*
Taquine-le!	
Ne le taquine pas!	*Don't tease him!*
Fais ça!	
Ne fais jamais ça!	*Never do that!*
Touchez quelque chose!	
Ne touchez rien!	*Don't touch anything!*
Présentez-lui quelqu'un!	
Ne lui présentez personne!	*Don't introduce anyone to him!*

(For the ordering of pronouns in affirmative and negative imperatives see Chapter 3.2.31.)

16.6 ne . . . pas

16.6.1 Negating sentences

ne . . . pas translates English 'not' (for the omission of *ne* see 16.4):

Ce n'est pas vrai	*It's not true*
Je ne me rappelle pas les circonstances	*I don't remember the circumstances*
Je n'ai pas eu le temps de comprendre	*I didn't have time to understand*
Ça fait/Voilà longtemps qu'on ne s'est pas vu	*It's been a long time since we saw each other*

NB: *ne . . . point* 'not' is an archaic form which is still found in some regional varieties of French as an equivalent of *ne . . . pas*. Some writers use it to give a regional or archaic flavour to their writing.

After *ne ... pas*, any indefinite article (i.e. one of *un(e), du, de la, des*) preceding a direct object becomes *de*:

Elle a écrit **une** lettre	Elle n'a pas écrit **de** lettre
She wrote a letter	*She didn't write a letter*
On lui a fait **du** mal	On ne lui a pas fait **de** mal
They did him harm	*They didn't do him any harm*
Il cultive **les** fraises	Il ne cultive pas **de** fraises
He grows strawberries	*He doesn't grow strawberries*

Where *un(e)* appears before a direct object after *ne ... pas* it means 'not one', (rather than 'not a'):

On n'entendait pas **un** bruit   *We couldn't hear a single noise*
dehors   *outside*

(See Chapter 2.5.)

pas un(e) followed by a noun can function as the subject of a negative sentence. Note the presence of *ne:*

Pas un brin d'herbe **ne** bougeait dans la prairie
Not a blade of grass stirred on the plain

Where *du, de la, des* appear before a direct object after *ne ... pas*, they are instances of *de* + definite article (and not indefinite articles):

Elle n'a pas parlé **du** mal qu'on lui a fait
*She didn't speak of **the** harm they did him*
(versus: *On ne lui a pas fait de mal* 'They didn't do him any harm)

Il ne s'occupe pas **des** fraises à présent
*He isn't busy with **the** strawberries at the moment*
(versus *Il ne cultive pas de fraises cette année* 'He's not growing strawberries this year')

(See Chapter 2.5.)

When adverbs are located sentence-internally in sentences negated by *ne ... pas*, they usually appear immediately before *pas*:

Il ne savait **visiblement pas** que faire de son grand corps
You could see that he didn't know what to do with his big frame

Je ne l'entendais **même pas**
I didn't even hear him

Je ne l'ai **toujours pas** compris
I still don't understand him

NB: *davantage* 'more' used in conjunction with *ne ... pas* has a similar meaning to *ne ... plus*:

J'ai fait un effort pour **ne pas** dépenser **davantage**
I made an effort not to spend any more

16.6.2 Omission of *pas*

In written French the *pas* of *ne ... pas* may be omitted with a small number of verbs.

With *cesser de* + infinitive

Elle **ne** cessait de répéter que c'était de sa faute
She went on repeating that it was her fault

With *savoir* followed by a question word like *quoi, comment*

Je **ne** sais comment ils se débrouillent
I don't know how they manage

Il y avait un je **ne** sais quoi de douceur dans l'air
There was a hint of mildness in the air

NB: *ne* + *savoir* in the conditional means 'wouldn't know how to', 'couldn't':
On ne saurait trop vous remercier 'We wouldn't know how to thank you', *Il ne saurait vous expliquer pourquoi* 'He couldn't explain why to you'.

With *oser* + infinitive

Il **n'**osa refuser de le faire
He didn't dare refuse to do it

Elle **n'**osa demander un second cognac
She dared not ask for a second brandy

With *pouvoir* + infinitive

Elle **ne** pouvait se l'expliquer
She couldn't explain it to herself

Je **ne** puis accepter cette décision
I can't accept this decision

pas is sometimes also omitted after interrogative *qui, que, quel*, after hypothetical *si*, after some sentence initial adverbs, and in the expressions *n'importe qui, n'importe quoi*:

Qui **ne** serait ému dans ces circonstances?	*Who wouldn't be moved in these circumstances?*
Que **ne** donnerait-il pour une bière?	*What wouldn't he give for a beer?*
Quel homme **n'**en serait fier?	*What man wouldn't be proud of it?*
C'est Pierre, si je **ne** me trompe	*It's Pierre, unless I'm mistaken*
N'importe qui pourrait le faire	*Anyone could do it*
J'inventerai **n'**importe quoi pour faire plus vrai	*I'll make up anything to make it sound more realistic*

16.6.3 Negating words and phrases

pas alone is used to negate words or phrases which do not contain verbs.

Nouns

Je ne garde rien d'elle. Même **pas** une mèche de cheveux
I keep nothing of hers. Not even a lock of hair

Il lui posa une question. **Pas** de réponse
He asked her a question. No reply

> Je le ferai. **Pas** de problème
> *I'll do it. No problem*

Adjectives

> Les autres la considéraient comme une fille **pas** bavarde
> *The others considered her to be a quiet girl*

> Il avait une intonation chantante **pas** déplaisante
> *He spoke in a singsong voice, not unpleasant*

Adverbs

> J'habite **pas** loin de la mer
> *I live not far from the sea*

> C'était un bel après-midi. Un après-midi **pas** tout à fait comme les autres
> *It was a fine afternoon. An afternoon not entirely like the others*

Conjunctions

> Il me regardait; **pas** comme un frère, plutôt comme un juge
> *He watched me; not as a brother, more as a judge*

16.6.4 Use of *non* and *non pas* to negate words and phrases

non can be an equivalent for *pas* for negating adjectives, adverbs and conjunctions in formal French (although *pas* is more often used even in formal styles):

un supplément **non** compris	*something extra which is not included*
habiter **non** loin de la mer	*to live not far from the sea*
non comme un frère	*not as a brother*

NB: *non* or *pas* are equally likely in formal French in expressions like: *Prêt ou non, je pars/Prêt ou pas, je pars*, 'Ready or not, I'm leaving'. But if the negated item is repeated, *pas* is more usual: *Prêt ou pas prêt, je pars*.

non is often used when it is combined with *mais* in the expression *non X . . . mais (aussi)*:

> Je l'ai fait **non (pas)** pour arranger quelqu'un d'autre **mais** pour ma propre convenance
> *I did it not to suit someone else, but to suit myself*

> Elle aimerait visiter **non seulement** le château **mais aussi** le parc
> *She would like to visit not only the chateau but also the park*

> On entendait **non plus** la mer, **mais** le chuchotement du vent dans les arbres
> *One no longer heard the sea, but the rustling in the trees*

non or *non pas* may negate an infinitive which is contrasted with an affirmative infinitive:

> Il faut travailler pour vivre, et **non (pas)** vivre pour travailler
> *One has to work to live and not live to work*

non (pas) que is a conjunction which introduces subordinate clauses in which the verb is in the subjunctive:

> Il a parlé de Besançon; non (pas) qu'il **veuille** y aller
> *He spoke about Besançon; not that he wants to go there*

(See also Chapter 17.3.8.)

non, pas and *non pas* are interchangeable in formal French when a contrast is drawn between a positive and negative statement:

Il est Gallois et	non pas non pas	} Anglais

16.7 *ne ... que*

ne ... que translates English 'only' (for the omission of *ne* see 16.4):

Ce **n'**est **qu'**après qu'il l'a remarqué
He only noticed it afterwards

Je **ne** le vois **qu'**une fois par semaine
I only see him once a week

Il **n'**y avait **qu'**une explication
There was only one explanation

Les autres **n'**étaient là **que** pour lui fournir ce dont il avait besoin
The others were only there to provide him with what he needed

In combination with other negators like *pas, jamais, plus, personne, ne ... que* can take on various meanings:

Il **n'**y a **pas que** des héros dans l'armée
There aren't just heroes in the army

Elle **n'**avait **jamais** parlé à un agent de police **que** pour demander un renseignement
She had never spoken to a policeman except to ask for directions

Il **ne** me reste **plus que** trois traites à payer
I've only got three more instalments to pay

16.8 *ne ... aucun(e), ne ... nul(le)*

ne ... aucun(e), ne ... nul(le) translate English 'no', 'none' (for the omission of *ne* see 16.4):

Il **n'**a eu **aucune (nulle)** hésitation à proposer son aide
He had no hesitation in offering to help

Except for the expression *ne ... nulle part* 'nowhere', *ne ... nulle* is very formal. *ne ... aucun(e)* is found in both written and spoken French, but tends to be replaced by *pas* in informal spoken French:

Il **n'**a **pas** eu d'hésitation à proposer son aide

Only *aucun(e)* and not *nul(le)* may be followed by a prepositional complement:

Je **ne** connais **aucune** de ses amies	*I know none of her friends*
Je **n'**en connais **aucune**	*I don't know any of them*
(NOT *Je ne connais nulle de ses amies/Je n'en connais nulle)	

Both *aucun(e)* and *null(e)* are rare in the plural. Instead one would use *pas de* or *sans*:

Il **n'**a **pas d'**amis/Il est **sans** amis   *He has no friends*

aucun(e) can negate direct objects, indirect objects, objects of prepositions and subjects:

Ça **n'**avait **aucun** sens   *That made no sense*
Il **n'**a parlé à **aucun** des trois   *He didn't speak to any of the three*

Aucune voiture américaine **n'**était signalée   *No American car had been reported*
en cavale

Aucun de nous **n'**est entré là-bas   *None of us entered there*
Aucun n'est entré   *None went in*

aucun(e) may be used alone as a response to a question:

Combien reste-t-il d'oranges sanguines? **Aucune**
How many blood oranges are left? None

The adverbs *aucunement, nullement* are formal equivalents of the expression common in spoken French: *pas du tout* 'not at all':

Elle **n'**en est **aucunement/nullement/pas du tout** fière
She is not at all proud of it

NB: *nul(le)* is also an adjective with the meaning 'zero', 'nil'. In this use it is found in all styles of French:

Les risques sont **nuls**   *The risks are nil*
Nuls points   *No points*
Elle est **nulle** en orthographe   *She is useless at spelling*
Match **nul**   *A draw*

Nul is also used in formal, legal texts, etc.:

Nul n'est censé ignorer la loi
Ignorance of the law is no excuse

16.9 *ne ... jamais*

ne ... jamais translates English 'not ever', 'never' (for the omission of *ne* see 16.4):

Il **ne** mangeait **jamais** le soir   *He never ate in the evenings*
Je **n'**ai **jamais** vu la mer   *I have never seen the sea*

Like English 'never', *jamais* may sometimes be located at the beginning of the sentence, but without the subject-verb inversion of English:

Jamais je **n'**ai vu autant d'algues
Never have I seen so much seaweed

Jamais plus elle **ne** serait tout à fait elle-même
Never again would she be quite herself

After *ne ... jamais* any indefinite article (i.e. one of *un(e), du, de la, des*) preceding a direct object becomes *de*:

J'ai **de la** monnaie   Je n'ai jamais **de** monnaie
I have change   *I never have change*

Elle porte **un** casque   Elle ne porte jamais de casque
She wears a helmet   *She never wears a helmet*

(See Chapter 2.5.)

jamais can be used without *ne* with the meaning 'never':

C'est maintenant ou **jamais**   *It's now or never*
Es-tu allé à Rennes? **Jamais**   *Have you been to Rennes? Never*

In formal French it can also be interpreted as 'ever' in questions, hypothetical sentences or comparisons:

As-tu **jamais** envisagé le suicide?
Have you ever thought of suicide?

Si une malle s'était **jamais** trouvée dans le grenier, elle n'y était plus
If there had ever been a trunk in the attic, it was no longer there

Elle chante mieux que **jamais**
She is singing better than ever

When adverbs are located sentence-internally in sentences negated by *ne ... jamais*, they usually appear immediately before *jamais*:

Je n'ai **d'ailleurs** jamais parlé à personne
What's more, I've never spoken to anyone

Je ne la vois **pratiquement** jamais
I hardly ever see her

16.10 *ne ... plus*

ne ... plus translates English 'no longer', 'not any more' (for the omission of *ne* see 16.4):

Elle **ne** savait **plus** pourquoi elle était sur cette route
She no longer knew why she was on this road

Soudain, je **n'**en peux **plus**
Suddenly I can't take any more

Elle **n'a plus** travaillé après la naissance de sa fille
She didn't work again after the birth of her daughter

NB: *ne ... pas plus* is NOT the French for 'not any more'. *ne ... pas plus* means 'not more than'. Compare:

Elle **ne** semblait **pas** avoir **plus** de vingt ans
She didn't appear to be more than 20

Elle **ne** semblait **plus** avoir vingt ans
She didn't seem to be 20 any more

After *ne ... plus*, any indefinite article (i.e. one of *un(e), du, de la, des*) preceding a direct object becomes *de*:

J'ai **un** crayon   Je n'ai plus **de** crayon
I have a pencil   *I don't have a pencil any more*

Elle vend **du** lait	Elle ne vend plus **de** lait
She sells milk	*She doesn't sell milk any more*

When adverbs are located sentence-internally in sentences negated by *ne ... plus*, they usually appear immediately before *plus*:

Je ne me rappelle **même** plus ce qu'il racontait
I don't even remember what he was saying

plus de + noun can mean 'no more':

plus de pain, merci	*no more bread, thanks*
plus de place!	*no (more) room*
Je me suis retournée: plus de valise	*I turned round: my suitcase had disappeared*

non plus is typically used in conjunction with one of the other negators to translate English 'either', 'neither' or 'nor':

Il ne mangeait jamais le soir, **ni** sa femme **non plus**
He never ate in the evenings, and neither did his wife

Ce **n'**est **pas non plus** que je sois particulièrement timide
It's not that I'm particularly shy either

Il **ne** pouvait **pas non plus** reporter son rendez-vous avec ce client-là
Nor could he postpone his meeting with that particular customer

Il **n'**avait **jamais non plus** levé la main sur qui que ce soit
Neither had he ever raised his hand to anyone

Elle fouilla dans la boîte à gants. **Rien non plus**
She rummaged in the glove compartment. Nothing there either

Pour son fils **non plus**, ça **n'**allait **pas** fort
Things weren't going well for his son either

16.11 *ne ... guère*

ne ... guère translates English 'hardly', and is an equivalent of the adverb *à peine*, which is used without a preceding *ne*:

On **ne** parlait **guère**
On parlait **à peine**
We hardly spoke

Cette histoire **n'**avait **guère** semblé croyable
Cette histoire avait **à peine** semblé croyable
This story had hardly seemed credible

After *ne ... guère* any indefinite article (i.e. one of *un(e), du, de la, des*) preceding a direct object becomes *de*:

Il y a **des** visiteurs	Il n'y a guère **de** visiteurs
There are visitors	*There are hardly any visitors*

NB: *à peine* cannot be followed by a plural noun phrase: NOT **il y a à peine des visiteurs*.

guère may stand alone as a response to a question:

Combien en avez-vous acheté?   **Guère** (à peine quelques-uns)
How many did you buy?   *Hardly any*

16.12 *ne . . . rien*

ne . . . rien translates English 'nothing', 'not anything' (for the omission of *ne* see 16.4). *rien* itself may be a direct object, the object of a preposition, or the subject of the sentence. When it is a direct object it is located immediately after the verb marked for tense:

On **ne** m'a **rien** pris   *Nothing was taken from me*
Je **ne** sais **rien** prévoir   *I am incapable of planning anything*

When it is the object of a preposition it is located in the normal position for prepositional phrases:

Cela **n'**a abouti à **rien**
That led to nothing

Je **n'**avais besoin de **rien**
I needed nothing

Je **ne** serais retourné chez moi pour **rien** au monde
I wouldn't have gone back for anything

When it is a subject it appears in subject position:

Rien ne lui faisait mal
Nothing did him any harm

Rien ne différenciait ce jour des autres
Nothing distinguished that day from the others

Rien ne m'avait échappé
Nothing had escaped me

NB: *Je n'en sais rien* means 'I haven't a clue'.

Expressions like 'nothing interesting', 'nothing else' are rendered in French by *rien* + de + adjective:

Il n'y a là **rien d'important**   *It's nothing important*

When *rien* + de + adjective functions as a direct object with a verb in a compound tense, *rien* follows the verb marked for tense:

Il ne dit **rien d'intéressant**   *He doesn't say anything interesting*
Je n'ai **rien** trouvé **d'intéressant**   *I found nothing interesting*
Il ne m'a **rien** dit **de surprenant**   *He said nothing surprising to me*

However, when the *rien* + de + adjective functions as anything other than a direct object, it is not split in this way:

Je n'ai pensé à **rien d'intéressant** à faire   *I didn't think of anything interesting to do*

Rien d'autre n'est arrivé   *Nothing else happened*

NB: the adjective remains invariably masculine in these constructions.

When adverbs are located sentence-internally in sentences negated by *ne ... rien*, and where *rien* is the direct object, they usually appear immediately in front of *rien*:

> Il n'y aura **probablement** rien pour moi à la maison
> *There would probably be nothing for me at home*

rien can stand alone (without *ne*) with the meaning 'nothing':

Qu'est-ce que vous voyez? **Rien**	*What do you see? Nothing*
C'est mieux que **rien**	*It's better than nothing*
C'est un **rien**	*It's nothing*

In formal French it can also be interpreted as 'anything' in questions or hypothetical sentences:

Avez-vous **rien** d'intéressant à lire?	*Have you anything interesting to read?*
Elle est partie avant que j'aie **rien** dit	*She left before I said anything*

16.13 *ne ... personne*

ne ... personne translates English 'no-one', 'not anybody' (for omission of *ne* see 16.4). Like *rien*, *personne* can function as a direct object, the object of a preposition or the subject of the sentence. Unlike *rien*, when it is a direct object it appears in the normal position for direct objects:

> Elle **ne** rencontre **personne** en dehors du bureau
> *She doesn't meet anyone outside the office*

> Je **n'**ai vu **personne**
> *I saw no-one*

> Ça, vous **ne** pourrez le faire croire à **personne**
> *As far as that goes, you won't be able to make anyone believe it*

> Ils **ne** l'ont fait avec **personne**
> *They didn't do it with anyone*

> **Personne n'**était en vacances, sauf moi
> *Nobody was on holiday except me*

personne may take an adjective complement preceded by *de*:

> Je n'ai vu personne **de** louche
> *I saw nobody suspicious*

> Personne **d'**étranger ne s'était présenté au bureau
> *Nobody foreign had come to the office*

NB: the adjective is invariably masculine in these constructions.

personne can stand alone (without *ne*) with the meaning 'no-one', 'nobody':

Qui a frappé?	**Personne**
Who knocked?	*Nobody*

In formal French it can also be interpreted as 'anyone' in questions, hypothetical sentences or comparisons:

As-tu rencontré **personne**?
Did you meet anyone?

Je le sais mieux que **personne**
I know it better than anyone

16.14 *ne ... ni ... ni*

ne ... ni ... ni translates English 'neither ... nor'. The *ni ... ni* elements can range over subjects:

Ni le cafetier **ni** sa femme **n'**étaient au courant
Neither the café owner nor his wife knew about it

over direct objects:

Elle **n'**a apporté **ni** bloc-notes **ni** stylo
She brought neither note pad nor pen

over prepositional phrases:

Il **n'**avait posé de question **ni** à son père **ni** à sa mère
He had asked neither his mother nor his father a question

Elle **n'**a répondu **ni** d'un mot **ni** d'un signe
She replied neither verbally nor with a gesture

over participles and adjectives:

Je **n'**ai **ni** vu **ni** entendu la querelle
I neither saw nor heard the argument

Elle **n'**est **ni** heureuse **ni** malheureuse
She is neither happy nor unhappy

Where two verbs marked for tense are involved, the phrase *ne ... ni ne ...* is used:

Je **ne** comprends **ni n'**accepte un tel comportement
I neither understand nor accept such behaviour

Where, in English, a negation is followed by 'or', or 'nor', or 'and', *ni* is used in French:

Ils **ne** voulaient accepter **ni** chèque, **ni** carte, **ni** liquide
They wouldn't take a cheque, a credit card or cash

Il **ne** mangeait jamais le soir, **ni** sa femme
He never ate in the evenings, nor did his wife

Rien **ni** personne **n'**était encore trahi
Nothing and no-one had yet been betrayed

ni is similarly used with the meaning 'or' or 'nor' after *sans*:

Le voyage aurait été impossible **sans** carte **ni** boussole
The journey would have been impossible without a map or a compass

Je fais ce qu'elle faisait mais **sans** son talent, **ni** sa chance
I do what she did but without her talent or her good luck

16.15 *sans* used with other negators

Negators like *aucun(e), jamais, plus, rien, personne* take on the meanings 'any', 'ever', 'again', 'anything', 'anyone' when used in conjunction with *sans*:

sans aucune hésitation	*without any hesitation*
sans jamais reculer	*without ever retreating*
sans plus se mettre en colère	*without getting angry again*
sans rien dire	*without saying anything*
sans déranger personne	*without disturbing anyone*

16.16 *ne* used alone

There are a number of contexts in which *ne* can be used alone. All of them are found in only the most formal of written styles. In less formal styles the *ne* is simply absent:

In fixed expressions (found only in formal styles)

à Dieu **ne** plaise!	*God forbid!*
Il **n'**a eu garde de se montrer	*He carefully refrained from showing his face*

In clauses dependent on comparatives

Il se porte moins bien que je **(ne)** pensais
His health is less good than I thought

Il est tout autre qu'on **(ne)** croit
He is quite different from what one imagines

La vie est plus chère qu'elle **(n')**était il y a un an
The cost of living is higher than it was a year ago

In clauses dependent on verbs which express fear, like *craindre, avoir peur que, redouter que, appréhender que*

Je crains qu'il **(ne)** vienne
I'm afraid that he will come

NB: when the verb of fearing is itself negated, *ne* is possible in the dependent clause only if the main clause is a question: *Je ne crains pas qu'il vienne* 'I'm not afraid that he'll come'; *Ne craignez-vous pas qu'il (ne) vienne?* 'Aren't you afraid that he will come?'

In clauses dependent on verbs which express some kind of prevention, like *empêcher que, éviter que, prendre garde que*

Mets-lui un bonnet pour éviter qu'il **(ne)** prenne froid
Put his bonnet on to stop him catching cold

After the conjunctions *à moins que, avant que, sans que*

Sans qu'ils **(ne)** sachent
Without them knowing

In clauses dependent on some verbs expressing doubt or denial which are themselves negated or questioned, like *douter que, ignorer que, nier que*

Je ne doute pas qu'il **(ne)** soit intelligent
I don't doubt that he's intelligent

Personne n'ignore qu'elle **(n')**ait été la cause de ses malheurs
Nobody is unaware that she has been the cause of her own misfortunes

Niera-t-on qu'il **(n')**ait commis une faute?
Will it be denied that he has made a mistake?

In clauses dependent on the expressions *il s'en faut que, peu s'en faut que*

Il s'en faut de beaucoup qu'il **(n')**ait réussi
He is far from having succeeded

17

Conjunctions and other linking constructions

17.1 Introduction

All languages have devices for linking words, phrases and clauses into more complex structures. This chapter deals with the linking function of **conjunctions, past participles, present participles and gerunds**.

17.2 Coordinating conjunctions

TABLE 17.A

Conjunction	Translation	Comments
et	*and*	Where coordinating conjunctions link two clauses, the verb in the second clause is always in the indicative, e.g. *il y avait des bals,* **mais** *on ne* **pouvait** *pas danser* 'There were dances, but we weren't able to dance'.
et . . . et	*both . . . and*	
mais	*but*	
ou	*or*	
ou . . . ou soit . . . soit	*either . . . or*	
puis	*then*	means '(first) X then Y'
car	*for (because)*	mainly used in written French
or	*now*	a logical connector (mainly used in written and formal spoken French) – see 17.2.1

Coordinating conjunctions link words, phrases or clauses into more complex structures:

> Le concours est ouvert aux garçons **et** aux filles
> *The competition is open to boys and girls*

> J'inviterai **et** lui **et** sa sœur
> *I'll invite both him and his sister*

Il y avait des bals, **mais** on ne pouvait pas danser
There were dances, but we weren't able to dance

Laisse-moi tranquille **ou** je te reprends ton argent de poche
Give me some peace or I'll take your pocket money back

Il arrivera **soit** demain **soit** après-demain
He will arrive either tomorrow, or the day after

J'ai allumé une cigarette, **puis** je suis descendu à l'étage du dessous
I lit a cigarette, then went down to the floor below

Je ne comprenais pas sa question, **car** cela ne correspondait guère à sa personnalité
I did not understand his question, for it was hardly in keeping with his character

Or, il se trouve que le connaissais déjà
Now, it so happened that I already knew him

Coordinating conjunctions differ from subordinating conjunctions (see 17.3) in that they, and the word, phrase or clause they introduce, cannot be placed at the front of the sentence, whereas subordinating conjunctions usually can. Compare *car* 'for' (a coordinating conjunction) with *parce que* 'because' (a subordinating conjunction close in meaning):

Il est heureux, **car** il est riche   NOT   *****Car** il est riche, il est heureux
He is happy, for he is rich   *For he is rich, he is happy*

Il est heureux, **parce qu**'il est riche
He is happy because he is rich

Parce qu'il est riche, il est heureux
Because he is rich, he is happy

Coordinating conjunctions never introduce clauses in which the verb is in the subjunctive, whereas a number of subordinating conjunctions do (see 17.3.8).

17.2.1 *or*

or 'now' is a conjunction which marks the next step in a narrative or a logical argument:

Or, Jean était déjà marié lorsqu'il a rencontré Suzanne
Now, Jean was already married when he met Suzanne

Tous les hommes sont mortels; **or**, le Roi est un homme; donc le Roi est mortel
All men are mortal; (now,) the King is a man; therefore the King is mortal

'now' in English can function as a coordinating conjunction (as above), a subordinating conjunction of time, and a time adverb. The subordinating conjunction of time function is fulfilled in French by *maintenant que* (see 17.3.1). The time adverb function is translated in French by *maintenant* (or *alors* if 'now' refers to an event in the past):

Jean est **maintenant** marié
Jean is now married

Jean était **alors** marié
Jean was now (= then) married

17.3 Subordinating conjunctions

Subordinating conjunctions introduce an item (usually a clause) which is dependent on another clause (for the use of subordinating conjunctions with infinitives see 17.6):

> Il est heureux, **parce qu**'il est riche
> *He is happy because he is rich*

> Je continue à dire 'chez nous', **bien que** la maison ne nous appartienne plus
> *I continue to say 'at our house', although the house no longer belongs to us*

> **Comme** il n'arrête pas de se plaindre, je l'évite le plus possible
> *As he does nothing but complain, I avoid him as much as possible*

Some introduce clauses in which the verb is in the indicative (as *parce que* and *comme* above). Others introduce verbs in the subjunctive (like *bien que*).

17.3.1 Subordinating conjunctions of time followed by the indicative

TABLE 17.B

Conjunction	Translation	Comments
après que	*after*	*après que* may sometimes be heard followed by a verb in the subjunctive, by analogy with *avant que* (see 17.3.8)
aussitôt que dès que sitôt que dès lors que	*as soon as*	
aussi longtemps que	*as long as*	Substitute another adverb for *longtemps* to create similar conjunctions: *aussi vite que*, *aussi peu que*
chaque fois que toutes les fois que	*every time*	
depuis que	*since*	Understood as 'from the time when'
maintenant que	*now*	
pendant que	*while, as*	Understood as 'during the time when'
quand lorsque	*when*	
tant que	*while, as*	Understood as 'the whole time while'
une fois que	*once*	

Après que sa femme **est** morte, il a déménagé
After his wife died, he moved house

Sitôt que je **serai** rentré, je te téléphonerai
As soon as I get home, I will phone you

On jouera aussi longtemps que tu **veux**
We'll play as long as you wish

Toutes les fois que nous lui **téléphonons**, elle est sortie
Every time we phone her, she's out

Depuis qu'il **est** chez nous, il est de plus en plus épanoui
Since he has been at our house, he seems more and more fulfilled

Maintenant que je **suis** installé, je peux me mettre au travail
Now I have settled in, I can start work

On a eu le temps de prendre un café pendant que les autres **se préparaient**
We had time for a coffee while the others were getting ready

Elle était déjà malade quand je l'**ai** connue
She was already ill when I first knew her

Tant qu'on n'**aurait** pas touché les dividendes de la paix, rien ne sera acquis
For as long as we haven't tasted the fruits of peace, nothing will have been achieved
(For the use of *aurait touché* in this context, see 17.3.2.)

Une fois qu'il **a eu** fait ses valises, il est descendu au bar boire une bière
Once he had packed his bags, he went down to the bar for a beer

17.3.2 Future and conditional tenses in clauses introduced by *quand, lorsque, aussitôt que, dès que, sitôt que, dès lors que, tant que, après que*

When subordinate clauses introduced by *quand, lorsque, aussitôt que, dès que, sitôt que, dès lors que, tant que* or *après que* are linked to main clauses in which the verb is in a future or conditional tense, the verb in the *quand, lorsque,* etc. clause is also in the future or conditional. This is different from English where the verb in a 'when', 'as soon as', etc. clause is usually in the present or past:

Est-ce que tu me **téléphoneras** quand il **arrivera**?
*Will you telephone me when he **arrives**?*

Dès qu'elle **reviendra**, j'**allumerai** le feu
*As soon as she **comes** back, I will light the fire*

Si on partait à midi, il **ferait** encore jour quand on **arriverait**
*If we left at midday, it would still be daylight when we **arrived***

Where the event in the *quand, lorsque,* etc. clause would be translated by the perfect or pluperfect tense in English, French has the compound future or compound conditional:

Il **arrivera** quand je **serai parti**
*He will arrive when I **have left***

S'il ne prenait pas l'avion avant mardi, il **arriverait** après que je **serais parti**
*If he didn't catch the plane until Tuesday, he would arrive after I **had left***

> Je **remplirai** le formulaire, aussitôt que je l'**aurai reçu**
> *I will fill in the form as soon as I **have received** it*

> J'**aurais rempli** le formulaire aussitôt que je l'**aurais reçu**
> *I would have filled in the form as soon as I **had received** it*

More generally, when an event described in a *quand, lorsque*, etc. clause has not yet taken place, the verb is in a future or conditional tense:

> Dès qu'il **aura** dit 'oui', faites-le signer
> *As soon as he says 'yes', get him to sign*

17.3.3 Double compound past and compound pluperfect tenses in clauses introduced by *quand, lorsque, aussitôt que, dès que, sitôt que, dès lors que, tant que, après que*

When clauses introduced by *quand, lorsque*, etc. describe an event which takes place prior to an event described by a past-tense verb in the main clause, French can use the double compound past or the compound pluperfect in the *quand, lorsque*, etc. clause (although it is not obligatory to do so – see Chapter 10.5.3):

> avoir eu + past participle
> avoir été + past participle

> Aussitôt que j'**ai eu fini** le livre, j'ai commencé à rédiger le rapport
> *As soon as I finished the book I began to draft the report*
> (My reading of the book took place prior to my writing the report)

> Quand elle **a été revenue**, il lui a présenté ses excuses
> *When she came back, he offered her his apologies*

When the verb in the main clause is in the compound past tense, the verb in the *quand, lorsque*, etc. clause is in the double compound past tense (as in the above examples); when the verb in the main clause is in the pluperfect, the verb in the *quand, lorsque*, etc. clause is in the compound pluperfect:

> Aussitôt que j'**avais eu fini** le livre, j'avais commencé à rédiger le rapport
> *As soon as I had finished the book I began to draft the report*

Alternatively, one can simply use the ordinary compound past and pluperfect tenses in the *quand, lorsque*, etc. clause: *Aussitôt que j'avais fini le livre, j'ai commencé ... , Quand elle est revenue, il lui a présenté ...*

NB: The double compound past can also be used in main clauses when adverbs expressing urgency or speed accompany a past event:

> J'**ai eu vite fini** le livre
> *I quickly finished the book*

> Il **a eu bientôt fait** de lui dire ce qu'il pensait d'elle
> *He had soon told her what he thought of her*

The use of the double compound tense emphasizes the idea that the event is over and done with.

In formal styles of written French where the dominant tense is the simple past (see Chapter 10.5.2), a form of the verb called the 'past anterior' is used in the contexts described above. The past anterior consists of the simple past forms of *avoir* or *être* and the past participle:

> Aussitôt que j'**eus fini** le livre, je commençai à rédiger le rapport
> *As soon as I had finished the book I began to draft the report*

> Après qu'elle **fut sortie**, il emballa son cadeau d'anniversaire
> *After she went out he wrapped her birthday present*

> J'**eus vite fini** le livre
> *I had quickly finished the book*

17.3.4 Tenses with *depuis que, voilà/voici . . . que, il y a . . . que*

When *depuis que* 'since', 'for' introduces a clause describing an event whose consequences are ongoing at the time it is being reported, the tense of the verb in that clause differs systematically from English as follows:

> English perfect: French present
> English pluperfect: French imperfect

> Depuis que nous **vivons** ensemble, je la vois travailler tard le soir
> *Ever since we **have been living** together, I have seen her working late into the evening*
> (We are still living together at the time I am reporting that she works late into the evening)

> Depuis que nous **vivions** ensemble, je la voyais travailler tard le soir
> *Ever since we **had been living** together, I saw her working late into the evening*
> (We were still living together at the time I was reporting that she worked late into the evening)

But when *depuis que* introduces a clause describing an event which has been completed by the time it is reported, without ongoing consequences, the tenses are the same as in English:

> Depuis qu'il **a fini** ses études, je le vois beaucoup plus
> *Since he **has finished** his studies, I see a lot more of him*
> (His studies are over at the time I am reporting seeing a lot more of him)

> Depuis qu'il **avait fini** ses études, je le voyais beaucoup plus
> *Since he **had finished** his studies, I saw a lot more of him*
> (His studies were over at the time I was reporting that I was seeing a lot more of him)

voilà/voici . . . que and *il y a . . . que* which also mean 'since', 'for' when used with time expressions – *voilà plusieurs années que . . .* 'it's been several years since . . .', *il y a/avait un mois que . . .* 'it has/had been a month since ...' – behave just like *depuis que*. When the clause introduced by these expressions describes an event whose consequences are ongoing at the time it is being reported, either the present tense or the imperfect tense is used in French where English uses, respectively, the perfect and the pluperfect:

> Voilà/voici plusieurs années qu'elle **travaille** tard le soir
> *For several years now she **has been working** late into the evening*

> Il y avait un mois que je la **connaissais**
> *I **had known** her for a month/It was a month since I **had known** her*

But when the clause describes an event which has been completed at the time it is reported, the compound past tense or the pluperfect is used:

> Voilà/voici deux ans qu'elle **a arrêté** de fumer
> *It's been two years since she stopped smoking*

> Il y avait un mois qu'il **avait disparu**
> *It was a month since he had disappeared*

For tenses with *depuis* as a preposition see Chapter 10.4.4.

17.3.5 Non-time subordinating conjunctions normally followed by the indicative

TABLE 17.C

Conjunction	Translation	Comments
ainsi de même que	*just as*	
(au fur et) à mesure que à proportion que	*as*	With the meaning: 'all the while'
attendu que vu que étant donné que dès lors que	*seeing that, given that, since*	*dès lors que* also has a time meaning: *Dès lors qu'elle a su la vérité, elle a cessé de lui faire confiance* 'As soon as she knew the truth, she lost confidence in him'
(pour) autant que	*as far as*	Is sometimes followed by the subjunctive to express uncertainty
plutôt que	*rather than, more than*	*ne* can be optionally inserted in front of the subordinate verb

> Je regardais la lune **de même qu'**elle devait la regarder
> *I looked at the moon just as she must have been looking at it*

> **A mesure qu'**il parlait, il s'animait
> *As he spoke he became more animated*

> **Vu qu'**il est déjà midi, je propose qu'on reprenne après le déjeuner
> *Seeing that it is already midday, I propose that we restart after lunch*

> Je délègue **autant que** je peux
> *I delegate as much as I can*

> **Pour autant que** je **sache**, ils sont partis lundi
> *As far as I know, they left on Monday*
> (My knowledge is uncertain, and so a subjunctive is used)

> Il sommeille **plutôt qu'**il **ne** dort
> *He is dozing rather than sleeping*

TABLE 17.C *(continued)*

Conjunction	Translation	Comments
comme	*as, like*	Also has a time meaning: *Il arrivait comme midi sonnait* 'He arrived as midday was chiming
comme si	*as if*	
puisque	*since*	Not to be confused with *depuis que* – see 17.4.1
excepté que sinon que outre que sauf que	*except that*	
parce que	*because*	

Comme il n'arrête pas de se plaindre, je l'évite le plus possible
As he does nothing but complain, I avoid him as much as possible

On a eu un été **comme** on n'en a jamais vu
We had a summer like we have never seen before

Elle a baissé la tête **comme si** elle avait honte
She lowered her head as if she had was ashamed of something

Elle parle français **puisque** sa mère est Française
She speaks French since her mother is a Frenchwoman

Elle n'avait rien à dire, **sinon qu**'elle avait faim
She had nothing to say except that she was hungry

Il est resté ici **parce qu**'il n'avait pas l'argent du billet
He stayed here because he didn't have the money for a ticket

TABLE 17.C *(continued)*

Conjunction	Translation	Comments
selon que suivant que	*depending on whether*	
si même si quand même	*if, even if*	For tenses with *si* see 17.3.6
tandis que alors que	*while, whereas*	*alors que* also has a time meaning: *Alors qu'il se promenait dans le parc, il a rencontré un vieil ami* 'While he was walking in the park, he met an old friend'

Je prends le bus ou j'y vais en vélo, **selon qu**'il pleut ou qu'il fait beau
I take the bus or go on my bike, depending on whether it is raining or is fine

Si on le branche là-dessus, on peut tenir jusqu'à demain matin
If you get him going on that subject, we'll be here until tomorrow morning

Même s'il était arrivé, je n'aurais pas pu lui parler
Even if he had arrived, I couldn't have spoken to him

Quand même il m'aurait dit le contraire, ça n'aurait rien changé
Even if he had said the exact opposite, it wouldn't have changed anything

Il est blond, **alors que** nous deux, nous sommes bruns
He is blond, while the two of us are dark-haired

17.3.6 *si* and the tense to use in *si* clauses

There are two *si*'s in French which function like conjunctions. One introduces indirect questions, and can always be translated by 'whether' :

Etait-elle venue?   Je ne savais pas **si** elle était venue
Had she come?   *I didn't know if/whether she had come*

(Indirect questions are introduced by verbs like *comprendre, demander, se demander, dire, expliquer, savoir* – see Chapter 14.7). In this usage the verb in the *si* clause can appear in all the tenses, including future and conditional tenses:

Je ne sais pas **si** elle **viendra**
I don't know if/whether she will come

On se demande **si** elle l'achèterait
We wonder if/whether she would buy it

The other *si* introduces hypothetical clauses:

Je n'aurais pas écrit **si** j'avais pu la joindre par téléphone
I wouldn't have written if I had been able to reach her by phone

Here *si* cannot be translated by 'whether', and describes what might have happened but didn't.

The verb in hypothetical *si* clauses can never appear in future or conditional tenses. Typical sequences of tenses are illustrated in Table 17.D:

TABLE 17.D *Sequence of tenses in* si *clauses*

Main clause		si clause	
Present, future, conditional		**Present, imperfect**	
Je le fais	*I do it*	si je peux	*if I can*
Je le ferai	*I'll do it*	si je peux	*if I am able*
Je le ferais	*I would do it*	si je pouvais	*if I was able*
Imperfect, compound conditional		**Imperfect pluperfect**	
Je le faisais	*I used to do it*	si je pouvais	*if I was able*
Je l'aurais fait	*I would have done it*	si je pouvais	*if I was able*
		si j'avais pu	*if I had been able*

17.3.7 Alternatives to (même) si in written French for constructing hypothetical clauses

One alternative to hypothetical *si* clauses in very formal written French is a verb in the conditional tense or in the past subjunctive tense inverted with the subject:

> **Devrait-il** en mourir, il n'y consentirait jamais
> **Dût-il** en mourir, il n'y consentirait jamais

Both mean: *'Even if he were to die as a result, he would never consent to doing it'.*

Another is to use *quand (même)* followed by a verb in the conditional:

> Quand (même) il me le **jurerait** sur l'honneur, je ne le croirais pas
> *(Even) if he were to swear to me on his honour that it was so, I wouldn't believe him*

or a conditional clause followed by *que*:

> Il me le **jurerait sur l'honneur que** je ne le croirais pas
> (Same meaning as the sentence above)

17.3.8 Subordinating conjunctions normally followed by the subjunctive

TABLE 17.E *Time conjunctions*

Conjunction	Translation	Comments
avant que	*before*	*ne* can be optionally inserted in front of the subordinate verb
en attendant que	*waiting for*	
jusqu'à ce que	*until*	

Avant que personne (n')ait pu lui demander d'explication, il a dit 'C'est moi le coupable'
Before anyone could ask him to explain himself, he said 'I am the guilty one'

En attendant que le beau temps revienne, on passait les soirées à lire au coin du feu
Waiting for the fine weather to return, we spent the evenings reading by the fireside

Attendez pour prendre la photo **jusqu'à ce que** le soleil soit plus bas dans le ciel
Wait to take the photo until the sun is lower in the sky

NB: 'not until', where it means 'not before', is translated by *pas avant que*:
Je ne partirai **pas avant que** vous (ne) me payiez
I won't leave until you pay me

TABLE 17.F *Non-time conjunctions*

Conjunction	Translation	Comments
bien que quoique encore que malgré que	*although*	*encore que* is found only in formal written French *malgré que* is found in informal spoken French
afin que pour que	*in order that, so that*	

Je continue à dire 'chez moi', **bien que** la maison ne nous appartienne plus
I continue to say 'at our house' although the house no longer belongs to us'

Il promenait la poussette le long du lac, **pour que** le bébé prenne l'air
He was pushing the push-chair along beside the lake for the baby to get some fresh air

Qu'est-ce qu'elle t'a dit **pour que** tu sois si malheureux?
What did she say to you to make you so unhappy?

TABLE 17.F *(continued)*

Conjunction	Translation	Comments
de façon que de manière que de sorte que si bien que	*so that*	Followed by the indicative these describe something which has happened Followed by the subjunctive they express a wish that something might happen
tel que	*such as*	*tel* in *tel que* agrees with the noun it refers to

Elle riait **de telle façon qu**'on **remarquait** ses jolies dents blanches
She laughed so that her beautiful white teeth could be seen
(Her teeth were seen, so the verb introduced by *de telle façon que* is in the indicative)

Elle parlait **de façon que** tout le monde la **comprenne**
She spoke so that everyone might understand her
(Her wish was that everyone might understand her)

Telle que vous l'**avez** décrite, la statue sera trop grande pour la galerie du rez-de-chaussée
Such as you have described it, the statue will be too big for the ground floor gallery

Et s'il avait créé un scandale **tel que** vous **ayez** été obligé de céder, vous auriez perdu beaucoup d'argent
And if he had created such a scandal that you had been obliged to give in, you would have lost a lot of money

TABLE 17.F *(continued)*

Conjunction	Translation	Comments
(soit/ou) que ... (soit/ou) que	whether . . . or	
à moins que	*unless*	*ne* can be optionally inserted in front of the subordinate verb – it is most likely in formal French
pour peu que si peu que	*however little*	
pourvu que à condition que	*providing that*	Conditional and future are possible in informal spoken French

Qu'elle ait perdu l'argent **ou qu'**elle l'ait dépensé, la caisse est vide
Whether she lost the money or whether she spent it, the coffers are empty

A moins qu'elle ne vende la maison de son vivant, en principe c'est nous qui héritons
Unless she sells the house in her lifetime, in principle we will inherit

Pour peu qu'on habite dans une zone où la réception est bonne, on peut capter une cinquantaine de chaînes
You just have to live in an area where the reception is good and you can pick up fifty TV stations

Pourvu que tout le monde soit d'accord, je commence tout de suite
Providing that everyone agrees, I'll start straight away

A supposer que la réponse soit favorable, qu'est-ce que vous allez faire?
Supposing that the reply is positive, what will you do?

Je lui ai demandé de modifier le manuscrit; **non que** je sois déçu, mais je voudrais qu'il y ait plus de dialogue
I asked her to change the manuscript; it's not that I am disappointed, but I would like there to be more dialogue

Elle aurait bien pu quitter le village **sans que** je m'en aperçoive
She could easily have left the village without me noticing

Elle s'enfermait ainsi **de crainte qu'**on (ne) vienne la surprendre
She shut herself away like that for fear that someone would come and surprise her

TABLE 17.F *(continued)*

Conjunction	Translation	Comments
à supposer que supposé que en supposant que en admettant que	*supposing that*	
non que ce n'est pas que	*not that*	
sans que	*without*	*ne* can be optionally inserted in front of the subordinate verb in formal French
de peur que de crainte que	*for fear that*	*ne* can be optionally inserted in front of the subordinate verb in formal French

17.4 Conjunctions sometimes confused by English speakers

Some conjunctions have several functions which only partially overlap between English and French.

17.4.1 'since'

(a) meaning 'from the time when' = *depuis que*

> **Depuis qu**'elle habite la même rue que moi, on ne se voit presque plus
> *Since she has lived in the same street as me, we hardly see each other any more*

(b) meaning 'given that' = *puisque, comme, vu que, étant donné que*

> **Puisqu**'elle a de l'expérience dans la matière, je pense qu'il serait bon de la consulter
> *Since she has experience in this area, I think it would be a good idea to consult her*

> **Comme** mes frères l'énervent, elle les évite le plus possible
> *Since my brothers annoy her, she avoids them as much as possible*

17.4.2 'while'

(a) meaning 'during the time that' = *pendant que*

> J'ai téléphoné à ma mère **pendant** qu'il préparait du thé
> *I telephoned my mother while he made some tea*

(b) meaning 'for as long as' = *tant que*

> **Tant qu**'elle faisait tout ce qu'il voulait, son frère était satisfait
> *While she did everything he wanted, her brother was satisfied*

(c) meaning 'whereas' = *alors que, tandis que*

> Il est blond **alors que** nous deux, nous sommes bruns
> *He is blond while the two of us are brown-haired*

> Elle s'occupe du bébé **tandis que**, moi, je fais tout le travail
> *She looks after the baby while I do all the work*

NB: *alors que* can sometimes mean 'while' in the sense of 'during the time that': *Alors qu'il se promenait dans le parc, il a rencontré un vieil ami* 'While he was walking in the park, he met an old friend'.

17.4.3 'as'

(a) meaning 'all the while' = *à mesure que*

> **A mesure qu**'il parlait, une idée se formait dans mon esprit
> *As he spoke, an idea formed in my mind*

(b) meaning 'at the same time as' = *comme*

> Il arrivait **comme** midi sonnait
> *He arrived as midday was striking*

(c) meaning 'in the manner of' = *comme*

> Les footballeurs s'embrassaient **comme** ils l'avaient vu faire à la télévision
> *The footballers kissed each other as they had seen it done on the television*

17.4.4 'when'

(a) meaning 'at the time when' = *quand, lorsque*

> **Quand** sa femme est morte, il a déménagé
> *When his wife died, he moved house*

(b) meaning 'whereas' = *alors que, tandis que*

> Je me demandais pourquoi il venait chez nous, **alors qu**'il habitait de l'autre côté de la frontière
> *I wondered why he was coming our way when he lived on the other side of the border*

17.5 Repeated subordinating conjunctions

When clauses introduced by subordinating conjunctions are themselves linked together, *que* replaces the first conjunction (and is obligatory in French, while the repeated conjunction in English is often omitted):

> **Quand** je suis pressé et **que** je sors la voiture du garage, elle cale
> *When I'm in a hurry and (when) I get the car out of the garage, it stalls*

The form of the verb in the clause introduced by *que* is in most cases the same as that of the verb in the first clause (indicative or subjunctive):

> **Même quand** j'étais gosse, et **que** je vivais à la campagne, je ne jouais pas dehors
> *Even when I was a child, and (when) I lived in the country, I didn't play outside*

> **Bien qu**'il plaisante et **qu**'il feigne l'indifférence, en réalité il est très touché
> *Although he is joking and pretending it doesn't matter, in fact he is really moved*

However, when *si* is repeated by *que*, the verb in the clause introduced by *que* is in the subjunctive:

> **S**'il fait beau demain, et **que** nous **ayons** le temps, nous pourrions aller à la plage
> *If it is fine tomorrow, and (if) we have time, we could go to the beach*

(See also Chapter 11.1.10.)

17.6 Subordinating conjunctions used with infinitive clauses

A number of the conjunctions which introduce clauses with finite verbs can also be used without *que* to link infinitive clauses to a main clause as shown in Table 17.G.

TABLE 17.G *Subordinating conjunctions without* que

Followed by *de*	
afin de (finir le premier) avant de (monter à l'étage) de crainte de/de peur de (déranger les voisins) à condition de (faire des bénéfices) à moins d'(avoir une augmentation)	*in order to (finish first)* *before (going upstairs)* *for fear of (disturbing the neighbours)* *subject to (making a profit)* *unless (I/you/we etc. get a pay rise)*
Followed by *à*	
(aller) jusqu'à (déclarer le contraire) de manière à/de façon à/de sorte à (assurer la victoire)	*(to go) as far as (stating the opposite)* *so as to (be certain of victory)*
Not followed by another preposition	
pour (finir le premier) sans (faire du bruit)	*in order to (finish first)* *without (making a noise)*

> Je m'étais arrêté **afin de/pour** vérifier le niveau de l'huile
> *I had stopped to check the oil level*

> **Avant de** payer j'ai passé l'addition au peigne fin
> *Before paying I scrutinized the bill*

> Il ne peut pas rencontrer quelqu'un **sans** lui parler de ses problèmes sentimentaux
> *He can't say hallo to someone without talking about his emotional problems*

NB: *plutôt que* 'rather than', 'more than' exceptionally keeps the *que*, but also adds *de* when it introduces an infinitive: *Plutôt que de chercher partout, on devrait commencer par les tiroirs du bureau* 'Rather than searching everywhere, we should start with the desk drawers'.

Where the subject of a main clause is the same as the subject of a subordinate clause linked to it, it is more natural in French to use an infinitive than a finite clause:

> Il a sorti le paquet de café **avant d'**allumer le chauffe-eau
> *He took out his packet of coffee before he switched on the water-heater*
> (*il* is the subject both of *a sorti* and *allumer*)

rather than: *Il a sorti le paquet de café avant qu'il (n')ait allumé le chauffe-eau.*

> Je n'irai pas **à moins d'**être certain d'avoir une place
> *I won't go unless I'm certain of getting a seat*
> (*je* is the subject both of *irai* and *être certain*)

rather than: *Je n'irai pas à moins que je (ne) sois certain d'avoir une place.*

A number of other conjunctions which are not capable of introducing finite clauses in modern French can introduce infinitive clauses:

> faute d'(avoir assez d'argent)
> *through lack of (having enough money)*

> à force de (s'entraîner)
> *by dint of (training)*

> au lieu de (dormir)
> *instead of (sleeping)*

> loin de (chercher à vous tromper)
> *far from (seeking to cheat you)*

> près de (renoncer)
> *close to (giving up)*

> quant à (proposer de vous accompagner)
> *as for (proposing to go with you)*

17.7 *après avoir/être* + past participle linking an infinitive clause to a main clause

A frequently used construction translating English 'having V-ed', 'after V-ing' is *après* + the infinitive form of *avoir* or *être* and a past participle:

> **Après avoir mangé** sa glace à la fraise, elle s'est essuyé la bouche sur sa manche
> *Having bought/after buying her strawberry ice-cream, she wiped her mouth on her sleeve*

> **Après avoir expliqué** à ses hôtes comment arriver au centre ville, elle s'est retirée dans sa chambre
> *After having explained to her guests how to get into the centre of town, she retired to her bedroom*

> **Après être allé** consulter son médecin, elle a constaté qu'elle avait moins mal
> *Having gone/after going to see her doctor, she found that it didn't hurt so much*

17.8 Past participle phrases used as linkers

The past participles of verbs which are conjugated with *être* in compound tenses (see Chapter 8.2.2) can be used without *après* to link subordinate clauses to main clauses, where English usually uses 'having V-ed':

> **Arrivé** à la gare, il a acheté un journal
> *Having arrived at the station he bought a paper*

> **Couché** de bonne heure, j'ai lu
> *Having gone to bed early I read*

> **Partie** pour de bon, elle n'a plus l'intention de revenir
> *Having left for good, she no longer intends to return*

The past participles of verbs referring to bodily posture are used where English uses 'V-ing': *assis* 'sitting', *appuyé* 'leaning', *agenouillé* 'kneeling', *couché* 'lying', etc.:

Je suis resté debout toute la séance, **appuyé** contre le mur
I remained standing throughout the showing, leaning against the wall

Assis sur un banc, on a parlé longtemps
Sitting there on a bench, we talked for a long time

17.9 Present participles and gerunds

This section concerns French verb forms ending in -*ant*. They are formed from
the stem of the first person plural (*nous*) of the present tense by deleting -ons
and replacing it with -*ant*: *donnons/donnant, finissons/finissant, dormons/dormant.*
They can also have a compound form composed of the -*ant* form of the auxiliary and the past participle of the verb: *ayant donné, ayant fini, ayant dormi, étant
devenu.*

-*ant* forms have three main roles: they can function as **adjectives**, in which case
they agree with the noun to which they refer, they can function as **present participles**, in which case they do not agree with any noun, and they can function as **gerunds** with the added form *en (en donnant, en finissant, en dormant).*

17.9.1 -*ant* forms as adjectives

Like all adjectives, -*ant* forms can occur close to a noun or be linked to it by a
verb like *être, devenir, paraître* (see Chapter 4.1.1). In both cases they agree with
the noun.

une histoire passionnante	*a fascinating story*
Cette histoire est passionnante	*this story is fascinating*
une eau de toilette séduisante	*a seductive perfume*
Cette eau de toilette est séduisante	*this perfume is seductive*
une femme plaisante	*an agreeable woman*
Cette femme est plaisante	*this woman is agreeable*
une chaise roulante	*a wheelchair*
une ferme avoisinante	*a neighbouring farm*
une injustice criante	*a flagrant injustice*

17.9.2 -*ant* forms as present participles

-*ant* forms can be used to form subordinate clauses. When they do so, they are
called present participles. Used in this way, they are invariable (i.e. they do not
agree with any noun):

Les circonstances **aidant**, ils ont terminé le projet à la date prévue
Given the favourable conditions, they finished the project on the agreed date

Voyant arriver sa sœur, elle s'est éloignée
Seeing her sister arrive, she left

Sachant qu'ils allaient perdre, ils ont néanmoins fait de leur mieux
Knowing they were going to lose, they nonetheless did their best

Il était heureux d'y aller, **reconnaissant** ce qu'il devait à son ancien collège
He was pleased to go there recognizing what he owed to his old school

Attirant un public international, l'exposition a atteint un million de visiteurs
Attracting an international audience, the exhibition reached a million visitors

Cette grange, **avoisinant** les bâtiments principaux, pourrait être transformée en
maison d'habitation

This barn, adjoining the main buildings, could be converted into living accommodation

Les contes de Roald Dahl, **passionnant** les enfants de toutes les nations, ont été traduites en plusieurs langues
The stories of Roald Dahl, fascinating the children of every nation, have been translated into several languages

Roulant à soixante-dix à l'heure, le conducteur n'a pas pu éviter un piéton
Driving at seventy kilometres an hour, the driver was unable to avoid a pedestrian

In some cases, where the present participle follows a noun, it may be difficult to decide whether it is an adjective or a present participle. In the following examples, the *-ant* forms are all present participles, and hence invariable:

un éditorial **ridiculisant** le gouvernement
an editorial poking fun at the government

une voiture **roulant** lentement est moins dangereuse
a car driving slowly is less dangerous

des manifestants **hurlant** des slogans passaient sous ses fenêtres
demonstrators shouting slogans passed below his windows

la belle au bois **dormant**
Sleeping Beauty

Je les ai surpris dans la clairière, **dormant** profondément
I came across them in the clearing, fast asleep

You can usually tell if an *-ant* form is an adjective (and hence must agree with a noun) if you can replace it by an ordinary adjective and still have a grammatical phrase. Compare:

un éditorial passionnant	*a fascinating editorial*
un éditorial ennuyeux	*a boring editorial (OK – adjective)*
une chaise roulante	*a wheelchair*
une chaise haute	*a highchair (OK – adjective)*
un éditorial ridiculisant le gouvernement	**un éditorial ennuyeux le gouvernement (not OK – present participle)*
une voiture roulant lentement	**une voiture haute lentement (not OK – present participle)*
des manifestants hurlant des slogans	**des manifestants délicats des slogans (not OK – present participle)*

The decision depends on whether the action described by the *-ant* form is seen mainly as a state (=adjective) or as an action (=verb).

NB: As with a number of other tenses, French marks tense sequences more precisely than English (see Chapter 10). Where English has a simple *-ing* form, French may require a compound present participle:

Etant partis à l'aube, nous sommes arrivés avant la nuit
Having left at dawn, we arrived before nightfall

Ayant ramassé ses vêtements en hâte, il sauta par la fenêtre
Having picked up his clothes in a hurry, he jumped out of the window

Ayant repéré un gendarme plus loin dans la rue, elle a pris la fuite
Spotting a policeman further up the street, she ran away

17.9.3 Set expressions with invariable present participles

argent comptant	*in cash*
Ils veulent être payés en argent comptant	*They want to be paid in cash*
ne pas avoir un sou vaillant	*not to have a red cent*
J'admets que je n'ai pas un sou vaillant	*I admit I am totally broke*
ce disant	*in so saying*
Ce disant il a fait un geste maladroit et a renversé un verre	*In so saying he made a clumsy gesture and knocked over a glass*
chemin faisant	*on the way*
Chemin faisant on a chanté des chansons	*We sang songs on the way*
donnant donnant	*a fair exchange, swop*
Nous sommes d'accord si c'est donnant donnant	*We agree as long as it's a fair exchange*
strictement parlant	*strictly speaking*
Strictement parlant je ne devrais pas vous le répéter	*Strictly speaking I should not say this to you*
tambour battant	*in an energetic manner*
La droite a mené la campagne tambour battant d'un bout à l'autre	*The right led a thoroughly energetic campaign from the beginning to the end*

17.9.4 -ant forms used as gerunds with en

Where present participles are preceded by *en* they are known as 'gerunds'. By using *en*, a speaker or a writer may be emphasizing the fact that the event described in the main clause and the event described in the gerundive clause take place simultaneously. This is often translated into English by 'while' or 'as':

En attendant Philippe, je me suis installé au café d'en face
While waiting for Philippe, I took up position in the café opposite

Je l'avais vue dans la semaine, **en rentrant** de l'école
I had seen her during the week, as I came back from school

Il est passé **en faisant** un appel de phares
He passed by, as he did so flashing his lights

Comment est-ce que tu arrives à tant bavarder **en conduisant**?
How do you manage to talk so much when you are driving?

Alternatively, the use of *en* with a gerund may emphasize a link of cause and effect between the gerundive clause and the main clause; this is translated by 'in' or 'by' in English:

En déclarant que vous étiez sur place vous vous êtes incriminé
In admitting that you were there you have incriminated yourself

En gérant une boutique comme si c'était un supermarché, on s'expose à l'échec
In managing a small shop as if it were a supermarket, you are running the risk of failure

Marianne a indiqué qu'elle ne voulait plus sortir avec lui **en refusant** son invitation
Marianne showed that she no longer wanted to go out with him by refusing his invitation

En augmentant le prix de vente vous risquez de voir chuter le nombre d'acheteurs
By increasing the retail price you run the risk of reducing the number of buyers

On a décoré la pièce **en mettant** des fleurs partout
We fixed up the room by putting flowers everywhere

When a gerund is preceded by *tout en*, it suggests that the event described in the gerundive clause is going on all the while the event described in the main clause takes place:

Tout en me parlant, elle nettoyait les vitres
All the while she was speaking, she wiped the windows

Tout en discutant de la pluie et du beau temps, il regardait discrètement dans le rétroviseur
Whilst chatting about this and that, he was keeping a discreet eye on the rear-view mirror

Les deux sœurs se sont quittées **tout en sachant** qu'elles avaient peu de chances de se revoir
The two sisters took leave of one another knowing that there was little possibility of them seeing each other again

When present participles are used without *en*, they can refer to any of the participants in the main clause: subject, direct object, object of a preposition:

Je l'avais vue dans la semaine, **rentrant** de l'école
*I had seen her during the week as **I** (or **she**) came back from school*

When *en* is present, however, the gerund can only refer to the subject of the main clause:

Je l'avais vue dans la semaine, **en rentrant** de l'école
*I had seen her during the week as **I** (NOT *she) came back from school*

NB: Gerunds may also be formed from compound present participles. These are frequently translated into English by a simple *-ing* form:

En ayant refusé de poursuivre des études supérieures, elle s'est privée de bien des possibilités
By refusing to undertake higher education, she cut herself off from a number of possibilities

En ayant contesté nos méthodes, il s'est exclu de notre groupe
By questioning our methods, he has excluded himself from our group

Appendix

Capital letters, lower-case letters and representing speech in written French

We note here briefly some of the differences between written English and written French in the conventions relating to the use of capital and lower-case letters, and in representing direct speech.

Small letters for days of the week, months, seasons

English uses capital letters, French uses lower-case letters:

> Il arrive lundi (**m**ardi, **m**ercredi, ...)
> *He arrives on Monday (Tuesday, Wednesday, ...)*

> Nous partirons en janvier (en **f**évrier, en **m**ars, ...)
> *We shall leave in January (February, March, ...)*

English can optionally use capital or lower-case letters with seasons, French always uses lower-case letters:

> Elle travaille dix-huit heures par jour en été (au **p**rintemps, ...)
> *She works eighteen hours a day in Summer (in Spring, ...)*

Small letters for streets, roads, avenues, etc.

English uses capitals, French uses lower-case letters:

> 11, **p**lace de la République
> *11 Russell Square*

> Je l'ai vue **r**ue de Rivoli
> *I saw her in Regent Street*

Small letters for titles

English uses capitals, French uses lower-case letters:

> Le **p**rofesseur Bouvier
> *Professor Bouvier*

> Le **d**octeur Picot
> *Doctor Picot*

Small letters for adjectives indicating origin, but capital letters for nouns

English always uses capital letters to introduce adjectives and nouns describing the origin or religious affiliation of a person or entity. French uses lower-case letters to introduce adjectives describing origin, lower-case letters to introduce adjectives and nouns describing religious affiliation, but capital letters to introduce nouns describing origin:

un touriste français (adj) *a French tourist*	un Français de ma connaissance (noun) *a Frenchman I know*
un livre américain (adj) *an American book*	un Américain célèbre (noun) *a famous American*
un prêtre catholique (adj) *a Catholic priest*	un catholique célèbre (noun) *a famous Catholic*

Small letters for languages

English always uses capital letters to introduce adjectives and nouns describing languages, French always uses lower-case letters:

la langue française (adj)
the French language

Elle parle bien le français (noun)
She speaks French well

Capitals and lower-case letters in citing book titles

Although there are different conventions for the use of capitals and lower-case letters in citing book titles, one common convention in French is to capitalize every word up to and including the first noun:

L'Etranger
L'Art de vivre
Le Grand Meaulnes
Les Petits Enfants du siècle

In English common conventions are to capitalize the first letter of every word, or to capitalize the first word and the 'content' words (and not the function words), or to treat the title like an ordinary sentence:

The Decline And Fall Of The Roman Empire
The Decline and Fall of the Roman Empire
The decline and fall of the Roman empire

Representing direct speech

Direct speech can be opened and closed by *guillemets*. Unlike English, where speech marks enclose only the speech itself, in French guillemets enclose dialogues, and are only closed when the whole dialogue is at an end:

«Et voilà, dit le père, filant sur la route. En voilà encore une de tirée.
- Eh, oui», répliqua la mère.
(From Christiane Rochefort, *Les Petits Enfants du siècle*)

'Well,' said our father, belting along the road. 'That's another one [holiday] over with.'
'Yes,' our mother replied.

Alternatively, speech can be introduced by dashes (*'tirets'*) in both languages:

- Etes-vous prêt?
- Pas encore.

- *Are you ready?*
- *Not yet.*

Verbs reporting who said what are always inverted with the subject in French:

«C'est plus fort en goût», **précise Vincent**
«C'est plus fort en goût», **précise-t-il**
'It has a stronger taste,' Vincent adds/he adds

«Le moulin, clef de l'économie», **annonce un panneau**
'Mills are the key to economic success,' a sign announces

«Ce n'est pas vrai», **répondirent les autres tranquillement**
'It's not true,' the others replied calmly

Bibliography

Cited works and main works consulted in the preparation of the text.

Astington, E. 1980: *French structures: a manual for advanced students*. London: Collins.

Batchelor, R. and Offord, M. 1982: *A guide to contemporary French usage*. Cambridge: Cambridge University Press.

Bonnard, H. 1983: *Code du français courant*. Paris: Magnard.

Byrne, L. and Churchill, E., revised by G. Price, 1991, 3rd edition: *A comprehensive French grammar*. Oxford: Blackwell.

Désirat, C. and Hordé, T. 1976: *La Langue française au 20e siècle*. Paris: Bordas.

Engel, D. 1990: *Tense and text: a study of French past tenses*. London: Routledge.

Grevisse, M. 1957, 26th edition: *Précis de grammaire française*. Gembloux: Duculot.

Grevisse, M. 1993, 13th edition revised by A. Goose: *Le Bon Usage*. Paris: Duculot.

Japrisot, S. 1966: *La Dame dans l'auto avec des lunettes et un fusil*. Paris: Editions Denoël.

Japrisot, S. 1977: *L'Eté meurtrier*. Paris: Editions Denoël.

Jones, M. 1996: *Foundations of French syntax*. Cambridge: Cambridge University Press.

Judge, A. and Healey, F. 1983: *A reference grammar of modern French*. London: Edward Arnold.

Kayne, R. 1975: *French syntax: the transformational cycle*. Cambridge, Mass: MIT Press.

Mailhac, J.-P. 1992: *Traduction anglais-français et information numérique*. University of Salford: Working Papers in Language and Learning.

Mauger, G. 1968: *Grammaire pratique du français d'aujourd'hui*. Paris: Hachette.

Ollivier, J. 1993, 2nd edition: *Grammaire française*. Laval: Editions Etudes Vivantes.

Réquédat, F. 1980: *Constructions verbales avec l'infinitif*. Paris: Hachette.

Secrétan, D. 1970: *La Pratique du français: cours supérieur 1*. Manchester: Manchester University Press.

Wagner, R. and Pinchon, J. 1962: *Grammaire de français classique et moderne*. Paris: Hachette.

Waugh, L. 1977: *Semantic analysis of word order*. Leiden: E. J. Brill.

Index

References are made to sections.